GENDER MEETS GENRE IN POSTWAR CINEMAS

GENDER MEETS GENRE IN POSTWAR CINEMAS

EDITED BY CHRISTINE GLEDHILL

UNIVERSITY OF ILLINOIS PRESS

URBANA, CHICAGO, AND SPRINGFIELD

Frontispiece: Divine in *Pink Flamingos* (dir. Waters, 1972)

Library of Congress Cataloging-in-Publication Data
Gender meets genre in postwar cinemas / edited by Christine Gledhill.
p.   cm.
Includes bibliographical references and index.
ISBN 978-0-252-03661-3 (cloth)
ISBN 978-0-252-07831-6 (pbk.)
ISBN 978-0-252-09366-1 (ebook)
1. Sex role in motion pictures. 2. Motion pictures and women.
3. Feminism and motion pictures. 4 Film genres. 5. Women in
motion pictures. 6. Men in motion pictures. I. Gledhill, Christine.
PN1995.9.S47G46   2012
791.43'6522—dc23   2011046230

For my Genre and Gender Class, New York University, 2005, where this anthology began

CONTENTS

PART FOUR. GENRE AND GENDER TRANSNATIONAL

PART FIVE. GENERIC "TRANS-INGS":
BETWEEN GENRES, GENDERS, AND SEXUALITIES

ACKNOWLEDGMENTS

Taylor and Francis Books UK for permission to reproduce a shortened version of Pam Cook, "No Fixed Address: The Women's Picture for *Outrage* to *Blue Steel*," in her *Screening the Past: Memory and Nostalgia in Cinema* (London: Routledge, 2005), 146–64.

Palgrave Macmillan for permission to reproduce a shortened version of Chris Straayer, "*Femme Fatale* or Lesbian Femme: *Bound* in Sexual *Différance*," in E. Ann Kaplan (ed.), *Women in Film Noir,* rev. ed. (London: BFI, 1998), 151–63.

GENDER MEETS GENRE IN POSTWAR CINEMAS

INTRODUCTION

CHRISTINE GLEDHILL

Genre and gender representation, two key areas of Film Studies, have generated challenging theories and debate. However, bar some notable exceptions (Williams 2000; Clover 1992), these concepts rarely intersect. Studies of gender representation and sexed spectatorship largely subsume genre into narrative and visual organization. Studies of genre too often assume gender as a relatively unproblematic component of specific generic worlds. This anthology of largely commissioned critical essays asks what happens if genre and gender are run through each other. Does thinking about the constructedness and performativity of gender and sexual identity enable us to approach the production of film genres and the cultural-textual work of generic convention differently? Might reconceptions of genre as "genericity" (Collins 1993)—subject to shifting processes of industrial generation and public circulation—impact on approaches to representation and the politics of film culture? Put simply, this volume asks: How does gender get into genre, and what does genre do with it?

While Western film studies has theorized genre largely in terms of Hollywood, media globalization and postcolonial thinking raise questions about the transmigration of genres between national cultures and the intersections of gender with race, nationality, and class. Such intersections challenge the limitation of genre theory to Hollywood and of gender as a totalizing identity. Not only are the boundaries between Hollywood's genres highly permeable, but, their figures and tropes spinning off to form a transnational generic storehouse, they attract elements from production centers elsewhere. In the process, differently expressive gender signs commingle and transmute. Thus some essays in this collection, exploring the traffic between national cultures and cinemas, put Western concepts of genre and gender into dialogues "beyond" Hollywood.

This anthology's writers respond to its invitation from different perspectives and with different answers. At the same time, since its focus is the imaginary territory opened up by filmmaking, conceptual problems are explored through exemplary films. The aim is not definitive interpretation but to open up questions about the complex interaction of aesthetics, cultural meanings, and affect in mass-mediated cinematic fictions. For too long, represented gender has been taken as a means of ideologically assessing films. The challenge, then, is to open a perspective from the side of genre: to explore the aesthetic and imaginative power of gender as a tool of genre, and to explore what genre returns to the cultural sphere.

Genre and gender—deriving from similar etymological roots referring to "kinds" or "types"—have been identified in terms of discrete bodies of conventions, governed by rules of inclusion and exclusion. However, the industry's uses of genre, merging with postmodernist mixing of protagonists, actions, and settings from different genres, exploit the permeability of generic boundaries, refocusing critical attention on genre as cross-media, cross-cultural *process* rather than end product. Similarly, while poststructuralism deconstructs the unified self, and gender, ethnic, and sexual identities have become increasingly available as commercial style-choices, gender, decoupled from sex, is reconceived as mutable, diverse, transsexual. Thus both genre and gender theories abandon their focus on discrete identities. No longer conceived as bounded representations, their relationship may be refigured not in terms of social reflection, ideological misrepresentation, or subject positioning but as cinematic affect and discursive circulation between society and story, public and imaginary worlds. Such circulation focuses the genrification of gender, thus enabling us to think about the productivity of gender in genre in terms of aesthetic appeals and symbolic imaginings. This is not to do away with the referential dimension or the textual work of producing positions of reading or viewing, but to recognize their relativity in relation to the heterogeneous processes involved in textuality and the production, circulation, and reception of films.

PART ONE: REFIGURING GENRE AND GENDER

Discussion begins by revisiting the history of feminist approaches to the generic, reorienting key concepts and introducing new ones. Given an association of generic repetition with reinforcement of stereotypes, and of Hollywood with a male-dominated industry, two issues became central for feminist criticism: how Hollywood addressed women—especially through the baggy, cross-generic category of the woman's film—and how women filmmakers might intervene. This raised the question of gendered authorship and aesthetics, linked by the search for subversion.

If genre was the enemy for early feminist criticism, film theory's discovery of melodrama opened new territory that in its use of familial relationships and high emotion seemed ripe for feminist appropriation as a site for the woman's contesting point of view. However, Jane Gaines, examining a two-minute melodrama by feminist film heroine, Alice Guy Blaché, demonstrates its several entry points for—mutually exclusive—readings. Crucially, such readings depend on familiar generically gendered possibilities. Thus against feminism's assertion of difference, rethinking gender as generic foregrounds the role of repetition and its dynamic of expectation. It is here, Gaines argues, that the woman filmmaker can work. Her "ingenuity" lies in responding to the "genius" of genre's play with expectation, working out of the past to stage permutations for future imaginings. Perhaps the true irony on which Blaché's film turns is the impossible choice between mother and fiancée posed not only for the hero but for female spectators—a type of binary thinking elucidated in the film's generic play and which feminism now challenges.

It was, perhaps, feminism's starting point in gender inequality that underpinned feminist film criticism's elision of the generative power of semiotic systems with representation, locking women into a segregated gender space defined by "women's culture." Revisiting her own contribution to the establishment of the woman's film as a critical focus, Pam Cook draws on poststructural conceptions of the mutability of gendered and sexualized identities to question cinematic identification with one's gendered like, an assumption underpinning categorization of genres by gender. Speculating that we go to the cinema to *lose* rather than confirm identities, Cook opens a conceptual space for male masochism and female violence, thus challenging a dominant binary in feminist thinking.

In questioning the gendering of genres, Pam Cook notes shared structures and affects between the western and women's picture, normally posed in antithetical terms. Arguably, such similarities can be traced to their common foundation in melodrama conceived as a mode underpinning Hollywood's genre system (L. Williams 1998, 2001; Gledhill 1987, 2000). However, melodrama has itself been subject to a gendered turf-war between presumed male action and female pathos-laden genres (Neale 1993, Altman 1999). Revisiting this binary, E. Deidre Pribram's study of *Crash* (2004) opens emotion to cross-generic and cross-gender analysis. Examining the generative role of anger as source of narrative development in the law-and-order genres, Pribram suggests how genres come to be historically gendered and racialized along an acculturated emotion-action axis that supports white, male power. In this respect, Pribram suggests that contemporary melodrama has shifted from its nineteenth-century equation of morality with the "feel-good"—culturally feminizing—empathy of pathos to an emphasis on hitherto male-associated retributive action and violence, driven by anger and oriented to guilt. We might speculate on the necessity of anger to the structures of feeling that sustained twentieth-century freedom struggles, including antiracist, feminist, and gay, lesbian, and transgender campaigns. However, later essays suggest, the violence that fuels and results from anger and the purging of guilt is now increasingly distributed across fictional genders.

Luke Collins's debate with constructions of Kathryn Bigelow as feminist auteur brings art theory's concern with "surface" to analysis of her quintessential action movie, *Point Break* (1991). Like Gaines, reinvesting value in repetition, and arguing against the search for "depth," Collins suggests that *Point Break*, rather than exhibiting an authorial agenda of homoerotic disruption, "fills out" the homosocial bonding already vested in the action movie. In this perspective, if "genius" lies in genre, Bigelow's full-on "repetition" stages the aesthetics and affects of an acculturated masculinity to cross-gender view and mixed pleasures.

All four pieces represent shifts in conceptualizing the genre-gender duo. Rather than one side represented in the conventions of the other—whether reconfirmed or subverted—genre offers a "constellation" of cultural, aesthetic, and ideological materials, containing, as Jane Gaines and Pam Cook suggest, a more inclusive range of possibilities than allowed by ideologically driven "readings." Not only can we speculate that audiences respond beyond, as well as within, gender, but a new sense of what the generic brings with it is opened up, which involves recognition not of authorial depth but of its grounding in cultural history and practice. Thus the generic—the basis, argues Mikhail Bakhtin, of all human communication— involves maneuvers with the past for work in the present: "all our utterances [are] filled with other's words, varying degrees of otherness and our-own-ness" (1986b, 89). Thus film genres, as larger fictive constellations of the generic, already contain possibilities that it takes the questions of succeeding generations to perceive, put into play, and perhaps refigure, not only by "going-against," but in Gaines's terms, "going with," or, as Collins from a different perspective suggests, "filling out."

PART TWO: POSTFEMINISM AND GENERIC REINVENTIONS

These new ways of conceptualizing genre and its relation to gender provide the context for parts 2 and 3, which repose in different ways questions about the registration of feminism in a mode of generic production now conceived as a condition of—resource for—creative imagining, cultural engagement, and political remaking. This work unfolds in the era, following the demise of Hollywood's studio system and the intensification of globalized, digitized cross-media circulation, that is noted for intersecting, sometimes dissolving, generic and gendered—as well as ethnic and national—boundaries associated with postmodernity, postfeminism, and postcolonial practices.

While the early phase of feminist film culture invested in a counter-cinema that in opposing was effectively tied to a mirror reversal of Hollywood's practices, the incorporation of feminist campaigns into equality legislation, the demise of film collectives, and a growing concern to impact on the mainstream rather than politically aware minorities combined to shift attention to "popular" cinemas, stimulating "independent" filmmakers to seek crossover access to wider audiences. At the same time, the "director-auteur," earlier established and then challenged in film studies, has been refocused institutionally as the figure recognizable to the funding sources, festivals, and mainstream distribution outlets through which independent films circulate. In these changed conditions, then, how does a "postfeminist" generation of filmmakers use the genericity of filmic storytelling to engage purposefully not only women's lives and the discourses of sexism, homophobia, and racism filtered through the generic, but postmodernist awareness of the "social constructedness of everything" (Gaines, 19) and of everything's mediation through or as image?

All the filmmakers discussed in part 2 work to the side of Hollywood, either in European art cinema/television, the American independent sector, or in international coproduction. They all set out to tell women's stories: of class and racial oppression and sibling love or of tensions between sexuality and motherhood (Kaplan); of making it in male-dominated fields or resisting placement in traditionally female spheres (Tasker); of historical women positioned precariously between private and public domains (Matin); and finally, of the aging woman, autobiographically recording the body's decay (Fischer). While these stories bear witness to the difference that social gendering makes, they all, in different ways, draw on tropes and motifs of Hollywood genres or twentieth-century popular culture. Markedly different, then, from earlier feminist criticism, is the acknowledgment here of the generic formations that occupy the field of the imaginable. Even realist endeavors pass through the relay of rites-of-passage and coming-of-age narratives (Tasker).

Central to Ann Kaplan's opening chapter is the productive energy of criticism itself. Reclaiming as a founding tradition for women filmmakers Rick Altman's account of feminism's "invention" of the woman's film, Kaplan shows how the strategies and tropes it identifies enter the contemporary field of boundary-crossing and genre-mixing practices to draw from conventions associated with presumed "male" genres. Rather than undoing genre, the films explored in part 2 activate the generative force of Hollywood's genres in the service of women's stories. Horror and film noir (Kaplan), boxing film and teen picture (Tasker), costume drama (Matin), and Hollywood's antithesis, the autobiographical documentary (Fischer), provide female protagonists aesthetic access to the violence and anger released in previously assumed male genres (Kaplan, Tasker), or renew validation of presumed feminine modes of being: interiority, material being, and contemplation (Matin, Fischer).

If Kaplan argues the "invented" woman's film as a retrieval of women's cultural perspectives, Samiha Matin sees in the costume drama's crossing between present and past configurations of femininity—between the excessive publicness of the postfeminist world and the confining intimacy of an earlier private sphere—a drama of epistemological loss and recovery: the staging of a "once and future feminine" (100). Here, echoing Kaplan's analysis of Meckler's *Sister My Sister* (1994), femininity is understood less as a gendered identity than a cultural repository for alternative modes of being, of subjective experience of time, and material existence absent from both the political agendas of second-wave feminism and the economic agendas of consumer capitalism.

This move to retrieve what is culturally embedded in generic femininity concludes part 2 in Lucy Fischer's study of Agnès Varda's *The Gleaners and I* (2000), an elision of documentary with autobiography that connects—through Varda's own working life, spanning feminist and postfeminist generations—to women's early film practice. Here, noting Varda's extension of the significance of "gleaning" for food to a woman's practice of collecting, Fischer delineates an encounter between a sensibility culturally defined as feminine with the feminized throwaway culture of mass consumerism. Authorship figures, then, as a form of creative recycling or bricolage.

In different ways these essays explore the generic as it dialogizes past and future, functioning not only as a constraining interpellation but as a dynamic site of fantasizing and remaking. Genres, then, not only constitute an imaginary horizon within which protagonists' life stories are made, but contribute to remaking a feminist imaginary. In particular, the impossible binaries confronted by second-wave feminism—now made visible in Alice Guy-Blaché's 1906 melodrama—give way: *female fatale* and mother, female sexuality and maternity, can be imagined in triumphal alignment; staking a claim in the masculine world of contact sports or on intellectual life need no longer proscribe romance or fashion. And if the violence now appropriated by women filmmakers lends a dystopic dimension to the feminist imaginary, recovery of intimate femininity, earlier rejected in its association with patriarchal domesticity, challenges the gendered division between subjectivity and publicness, returning sensuous experience and affectivity to conceptions of the public sphere.

PART THREE: GENDER AESTHETICS IN "MALE" GENRES

Given the feminist lead in gender studies, it may not surprise that "gender" for many means "women." But if gender is a performance in answer to a discursive call, not all calls require we function in gender. Too long, feminist criticism has assumed that "men" in movies and as audiences function like—men. But if we understand gender as generic, and "woman" as a symbolic as well as referential figure, and if we dissolve gender-to-gender identification, then exploration of the aesthetic effects, affective appeals, and significations of genrified masculinity becomes possible. And if women filmmakers access in genre imaginative resources long thought the province of a male imaginary, it is now time to explore what acculturated femininity and feminism opens up in and around masculinity. We need to understand the affective and symbolic appeals that hold genrified gender figurations in place as centers of dramatic production and aesthetic affect for different audiences, however identified. To dislocate the aesthetic and signifying dimensions of gender from social reference is to better understand its work in the inter-subjective space of cinematic fiction and cultural imagining.

Part 3 explores what feminism has released to imagining cultural masculinity in interaction with femininity and feminism itself. Its focus is those genres presumed to be male oriented—respectively the police procedural (Segal), the war film (Thomas), and the horror film (Model)—now operating in a social field adjusting to gender equality legislation, feminist criticism, and the postmodernist, postfeminist erosion of gender and genre boundaries. In this context the films discussed here realign in different ways the aesthetic and perceptual values of masculinity—especially its place in the opposition, action-emotion.

In Adam Segal's analysis, *Heat* (1995) makes a self-conscious call on gender as the source both of drama and spectator address in its deployment of feminist discourses within the traditionally male world of the crime film, suggesting in the film's ambivalent conclusion a masculinity poised between feminist problem and frisson of generic recognition for women and men. Against such specific calls on gender identity, Deborah Thomas moves beyond gender identification, to explore the reverberating impact of the Vietnamese female rape victim in *Casualties of War* (1989) that invites us, she agues, irrespective of gender, into more diffusely feeling territory. The film, Thomas argues, moves beyond melodrama's universalizing symbol of female victimhood. Haptic amplification of the close-up on the woman's face and insistence on her individuality through restoration of her name while diminishing the hero's attempt to bring justice, readjusts the conventional gender dynamics of the war film, converting melodramatic pathos—reassuring us of our own humanity—to discomfiture and shame. Echoing a shift in emotional registers noted by Deidre Pribram—towards guilt rather than pity—Thomas's move beyond gendered identification shifts the site of involvement away from characters into the dynamics of mise-en-scène and narrative tone.

Filmic protagonists, however, and especially film stars, may insist on their gender. This insistence is the focus of Katie Model's chapter. Applying the Freudian concept of the "uncanny" to Jack Nicholson's performance in Kubrick's horror film, *The Shining* (1980), Model suggests how genre and star performance generate horror in the aporias of cultural gender. Here, rather than the ambivalence of the fantastic premised on difference, Model emphasizes the uncanniness of hyperbole grounded in repetition. Thus *The Shining* draws out from Jack Nicholson's self-parodying performance a hyperbolic rendition of masculinity: a doubling that makes the gender norm itself a source of a horror, doubled again through haptic star-audience contact.

In this perspective, genres and stars as generic beings—both premised on our return to their neuralgic centers—embody shifting structures of feeling and perception on which cultural gendering turns. Challenges from emerging social discourses and movements for change, while providing new sources of dramatic conflict and updated codes of recognition, also stimulate repetitions that engage long-standing cultural, aesthetic, and psychical investments. Thus generic activity reveals what is at stake in the processes of gender transformation.

PART FOUR: GENRE AND GENDER TRANSNATIONAL

Cinema from the first, as a phenomenon of modernity arriving almost simultaneously in metropolitan centers around the world, created a space of transnational imagining, through which different indigenous practices meet and meld to produce distinctive cinematic forms. If Hollywood plays a dominant role in the global media field, this has been reflected in the orientation of Western film studies. But just as conceptions of genre and gender categories loosen, so cinema history and theory is decentralizing. Thus, where part 2 examines engagement with Hollywood's genres by American independent and European cinemas, the essays here consider how concepts of genre and its use of gender play out beyond the West—in India (Bhaskar), the People's Republic of China, and Hong Kong (Xiangyang, Rodriguez Ortega). Temporal and geographic circulation produces not only exchanges and amalgamations but translations and rearticulations requiring nuanced historical and critical understanding. A comparative film study, then, examines not only the relation between Western and—here—Asian cinemas, but puts their respective concepts of genre and gender into dialogue. In Bakhtin's words: "We raise new questions for a foreign culture, ones that it did not raise itself; we seek answers to our own questions in it; and the foreign culture responds to us by revealing to us its new aspects and new semantic depths" (1986a, 7).

If across Hollywood genres the aesthetics of gender have served a foundational melodramatic mode turning on the action-pathos axis, the dynamics of this opposition shift where traveling cinematic forms intersect with traditional cultural practices, anti-colonial nationalisms, and different gender imaginaries. Questions of emotion and aesthetic affect receive new answers from the cinematic histories emerging beyond the West.

Opening part 4, Ira Bhaskar's analysis of three Bombay melodramas of the 1940s and 1950s argues a revised account of melodrama in the context of the first decade of the postcolonial moment. If the anti-colonial imperative of building a new nation casts the woman as preserver of cultural heritage, this trapped male and female protagonists alike between the contrary demands of patriarchal tradition and modernization. Thus, central to Indian cinema's focus on the dilemmas of lovers separated by feudal divisions of class and caste is the generation of emotion as site of subjectivity and individuation, neither, Bhaskar argues, defined by gender. Rather the pains of emergent individuality for both male and female protagonists are realized through shared traditions of song, poetry, and music. Contrary to Peter Brooks's (1984) influential account of Western melodrama as a secular response to loss of the Sacred, these still-living traditions, translated into cinema, not only externalize and amplify the interior dilemmas of blocked desire, they reaffirm through an emotionalized mise-en-scène and soundtrack the ambient presence of a Sacred not lost. Thus Bhaskar finds in Indian practices an enlargement of cinematic aesthetics that in embracing musical and poetic expressivity uses gendered protagonists as conduits to states of inter-subjectivity. At the same time, for these films the combination of social impossibility and sacred desire leads to a tragic rendering of pathos rather than the uplift of innocence recovered, argued by Linda Williams of American melodrama (2001) or the modern purging of anger and shame found by Pribram and Thomas.

Nationalisms—as distinct from historically and regionally located cultures—operate in different ways with unforeseen impacts. Xiangyang Chen, examining the hybrid origins of Hong Kong's Huangmei opera film, shows how the Chinese Communist Party's demand for a cinema showcasing the national cultural past paradoxically facilitated the cross-border circulation of an indigenous, vernacular operatic tradition—featuring feisty rural women, female voice-over chanting, and frequent cross-dressing—into the modernizing idioms of Hong Kong's film industry. Under colonial suppression of local nationalist objectives, the resulting hybridized genre, Xiangyang argues, carried a vital female imaginary in nostalgic Chinese wrappings. Here, in contrast to Indian cinema's culture of emotion, female performativity contests Chinese conventions of restraint, opening up imaginary female power. This is supported, Xiangyang's analysis shows, by the impact of the female voice on point-of-view shooting, spatial organization, and narrative structure, foregrounding, against Western feminism's focus on the male gaze, a female counter-gaze within a patriarchal drama of conflicting desires.

Hong Kong's geopolitical position makes it a site of transaction between China and Hollywood, as it absorbs and recirculates generic motifs through the transnational medium of the action film. In Vicente Rodriguez Ortega's analysis of shifts in John Woo's oeuvre as he moves from Hong Kong to Hollywood, melodrama's action-pathos dynamic is critical as gender becomes infused by sexuality. For, he argues, if in Woo's Hong Kong movies the Confucian value of brotherhood—realized in time-extended close-ups and intimate looks—produces the bonding of former male antagonists against tradition-defying gang lords, the potentially homoerotic charge underpinning Woo's cult in the West is, in Hollywood's studios, submitted to cultural rerouting. The male duo gives way to polar opposition and a centralized hero, who is himself realigned in relation to the family, becomes again the primary site for American melodrama's recovery of lost innocence.

To put questions about gender to the genres of a "foreign culture" returns not only different meanings of gender but a generic deployment towards different effects and affects, not all focused on gender itself. If the aesthetics of the gendered body stage scenarios of desire, these reach in different directions, towards erotic sublimity, female empowerment or bonded brotherhood. Sexuality, then, is neither tied to the protagonist's body—witness the power of music and song and visceral cinematic effect to outrun the performers—nor to gender. Transnational circulation, however, highlights questions of cultural translation not only between national cultures but within local discursive circuits, when imagining through or confronted by others' cinematized stories leads to appropriation, new perception, or inventive misreading.

PART FIVE: GENERIC "TRANS-INGS":
BETWEEN GENRES, GENDERS, AND SEXUALITIES

The rerouting of homoerotic affect evident in the circulation of Woo's action movies from Hong Kong to America speaks to a dissociation of sexuality from gender becoming increasingly public as widely circulating gay, lesbian, and transgender discourses impact on legislation, the fluidity of identity becomes visible as personal style, and generic tropes escape from generic worlds into the culture at large. If gender is a response to discursive calls and film genres are sources of such calls, the freeing and cross-gendering of sexualized gestures from the specific generic worlds that once contained them permits new figurations of sexuality, the focus of part 5.

Exploring the connections between John Waters's gender-transgressing "underground" films and his later genre-bending mainstream productions, Derek Kane-Meddock proposes a type of genrified authorship grounded in resisting all categorization, not by elimination but by hyperbolic rendition of and confounded relationships between gender and genre signs. As the site of gendered sexuality, the heterosexual family, Kane-Meddock shows, is the fall-guy of Waters's trash-gender aesthetics and genre aberrations, now unseated as source of lost innocence for American culture.

If the parodic transgressions of John Waters are focused on producing a counterforce to cultural gendering and Hollywood's genrification of gender, Chris Straayer, analyzing neo-noir *Bound* (1996), shows how the splitting of sex from gender liberates generic conventions in the service of protagonists who, enacting a lesbian romance in film noir, avail themselves of generic formulas to double-cross the villains. Analyzing the creative capacity of noir gender "to turn cartwheels on both male and female characters within a system of sexual difference" (224), Straayer shows how *Bound*—self-consciously playing on the debated identities of butch, femme, and feminine—generates different-sex erotics through same-gender protagonists. Through such playful manipulations, the film, she suggests, opens up flexible reimaginings of sex and gender across the spectrum of gay and straight as alternatives to rigidifying heterosexual and homosexual binaries.

Finally, Steven Cohan's analysis of the reception of *Brokeback Mountain* (2005)—a film that in exploring a gay relationship references the iconography of the western—suggests how its challenge to the gendered opposition between action and emotion stimulated debates linking sexuality to genre, both threatening heterosexual binarism and opening it up to view. Examining the vociferous contentions carried in the popular tag, "Gay Cowboy Movie," Cohan shows how the "event" of *Brokeback Mountain* brings cultural gender, generic verisimilitude, and sexual politics into direct collision, as arguments turn on whether the film is a western or not, whether its protagonists are men or not, and whether its appeal to straight female audiences makes it a universal love story rather than a tale of homoerotic desire blocked by homophobia. Thus, Cohan shows, the cultural significance of genre exceeds any individual film. Rather the film's touch on an acculturated psychosexual nerve, combining with the generic as site of symbolic meaning-making, suggests the aesthetic and cultural work of *Brokeback Mountain* in engaging the western's myth of masculinity in order to refuse the gendering of either sexuality or emotional expressiveness.

This anthology invites us to look at the work of gender beyond representation—to understand how the aesthetics of the gendered body contribute to the shaping, affectivity, and dramatic potential of protagonists in different genres. Conversely, the genrification of gendered bodies circulates back to the culture icons and signs that contribute to shifting social imaginaries. For a major move made by this book's explorations of what happens when gender is spun through genre is recognition of the generic—its powerful dynamic of repetition and expectation—as the ground of all our imaginings and thinkings, offering both the resistances of past meanings and potential for remakings and resignifications. But equally, genericity's capacity for flexible recombination across not only generic but gender boundaries enables dissolution of bonds tying gender to subjectivity, enlarging cinematic experience beyond the confines of identification. Once gender-to-gender identification is let go, cross-gender investments in cinema dissolve the division between genres by gender. In the process the action-emotion binary on which this division depends disappears and with it the tie of sexuality to gender. This does not mean that films do not absorb and make dramas out of contemporary discourses and topical debates—to which gender, sexual, racial, and class categories are more often than not central. As some of these essays show, films often make deliberate gendered calls as genrified genders slip out of kilter with shifting contemporary practices. Audiences and critics may contest such calls and filmmakers intervene with new generic combinations and deployments of gendered protagonists. But that is not all that genrified genders do in films. Across these essays is a concern not only with genericity but with genre's use of the aesthetics of gender to reach into other dimensions of emotion and subjectivity as experiences open to anyone who cares to respond. This recognition is illumined both by moves in postfeminist film criticism to recover femininity as cultural and imaginative resource and by encounters between different practices and nuances of gendered and generic aesthetics in cinemas beyond the West. Thus cinema returns as a space of imagining and response beyond reading for meaning, a space fueled by the inventions of genre and the new dimensions such transformations open up of subjectivity and aesthetic apprehension, of feeling and inter-subjective engagement between filmmakers and audiences, our own and others' cultures. It is to this arena of subjectivity and affect that gender's travels through genre now invites us to turn.

PART ONE

REFIGURING GENRE AND GENDER

CHAPTER 1

THE GENIUS OF GENRE AND THE INGENUITY OF WOMEN

JANE M. GAINES

Every reference to the cinema director as author carries the weight of several centuries of literary and art historical criticism. This very weight makes it difficult to argue against authorship in motion-picture industry history. Nevertheless, it is my contention that authorship has been taken up too uncritically. One cannot hope to completely discredit the authorial approach, but the critical ascendance of the author has been successfully challenged in a number of ways, for example, for its eclipse of the audience's contributions to meaning. In this essay, however, I begin by picking up a thread from my earlier argument about the work of silent cinema director-producer, Alice Guy Blaché, namely that auteur criticism gives short shrift not only to the audience but to other texts as sources of meaning. Here "other texts" references genre, the repetition with difference of popular forms. The author, I maintained, blocked the most important insights of the critically convulsive 1970s, most significantly, the poststructuralist assertion that we are constituted through language (Gaines 2002, 98). As Stephen Heath put it, "the author is constituted *at the expense of language*" (1973, 88; my emphasis).

Approaches to cinema-as-language and to genre converged and later diverged in the 1970s. Film genre theory was one of the first critical heirs of the more systematic approach to culture promised by semiotics and structuralism. Initially, the rule-governed operation of the linguistic sign system was analogized with the iconic sign system and refined into genre theory's understanding of rules or conventions in the relatively stable western and gangster genres. Cinema-as-language shared with genre criticism an understanding of cultural conventionality: culture as a readable system. However, with the stress on "representation" as ideological symptom, cinema-as-language became ascendant and genre was subsumed. Here Heath's reference to the tension between "author" and "language" recalls Raymond Williams's three-tiered understanding of consciousness:

To be a writer in English is to be already socially specified . . . at one level to an emphasis on socially inherited forms, in the generic sense; at another level to an emphasis on socially inherited and still active notions and conventions; at a final level to an emphasis on a continuing process in which not only the forms but the contents of consciousness are socially produced. (Williams 1977, 193)

Here Williams challenges the individual creator as himself the source of cultural forms produced by his singular consciousness. Thus individual autonomy, so esteemed in notions of "the author," is negated.

It is this co-implication of authorship and genre that I want to revisit. Hence my title, which questions the location of genius, wants to force an earlier issue for feminists into the foreground. To be specific, when a woman director is said to "author" a melodrama, does she "transcend" the form in the way that the male auteur was said to have "transcended" industrially produced genre? One might assume that feminist film theory, new in the 1970s, would have taken up this question. Although feminist film theory was immediately interested in director Dorothy Arzner, her work was not considered in exactly auteurist terms, for feminist interest in film theory barely overlapped with early 1970s auteurism, anticipating, rather, later poststructuralist approaches. It is, then, a poststructuralist auteurism we find in Claire Johnston's well known analysis of the ending of Arzner's *Dance, Girl, Dance* (1940): "Towards the end of the film Arzner brings about her tour de force, cracking open the entire fabric of the film and exposing the workings of ideology in the construction of the stereotype of woman" (1973, 29). In 1973, this move was an exciting possibility for a nascent feminist film criticism. However, it was not a totally new approach but rather a variation on post-1968 French theoretical developments, echoing Jean-Louis Comolli and Jean Narbonis' 1971 theorization of the "category E" film, that exemplary popular work that was able to turn itself inside out so that it critiqued its own ideological scheme (see Klinger 1986). In retrospect, one wonders if the methodology of ideological critique, originally developed for popular genre films, was not in this moment gradually and imperceptibly moved into auteur criticism, where it remains today. We will return to the easy analogy between the author and the text that made such a move possible.

We find another indication of the proximity of authorship to genre in the way the discovery of Arzner was formulated. If Johnston attributes critique to Arzner, its object is the construction of "stereotype," a conceptualization straight from 1970s genre criticism. Furthermore, auteurism's consideration of an entire oeuvre is paralleled by genre's grouping of films, both the legacy of structuralism. Thus the approach to Arzner is both poststructuralist (uncovering ideological operations) and structuralist (uncovering authorial patterns).[1] Finally, it is important to recall that the new British feminist film theory did *not* then develop the auteur approach one might have expected following Johnston's attention to Arzner, but rather, pursuing richer developments in the broader field, concentrated on the function of women in film noir. Here, genre questions raised through ideological analysis of the femme fatale in the dark 1940s gangster film would meet an emerging feminist concern with women and representation. In E. Ann Kaplan's foundational 1978 collection two different directions for feminist film theory were rehearsed, together raising the question of sexual representation as a function of genre. However, what became the burning issue for feminist film theory—women, body, ideology, or representation-as-language—would soon eclipse the consideration of film genre-as-language.[2]

To my knowledge, no feminist lamented the emphasis on representation at the expense of genre, perhaps because representation engulfed the parameters of genre theory at the time: conventions of narrative, iconography, and stereotypage. However, feminist literary criticism was quick to notice that film theory's challenge to authorship coincided with the discovery of female writers, a move that effectively withdrew the possibility of individual critical acclaim before it could be conferred (Felski 2003, 58). This was less of a problem for feminist film theory since no large-scale claim had been staked for female auteur directors, although this is not to say that Dorothy Arzner, along with others such as Ida Lupino (Kuhn 1995) and Germaine Dulac (Flitterman-Lewis 1996) were not important theoretical points of departure.[3]

As I have argued before, however, every nomination of an auteur risks slipping back into prestructuralist discourse of the individual artist (Gaines 2002, 89). In this discourse, the elevation of the auteur director above the popular genre he uses invites the attribution of "genius." However, there was no established filmic discourse of either director or genius artist in the first decades of the new motion picture industry. Historically, the concerted move to treat mainstream motion picture directors as artists began with *Cahiers du Cinéma* in the 1950s, when unlikely studio director Howard Hawks was noticed by the French (Rivette 1953). Perhaps recent exposure of the relative arbitrariness of Hawks's elevation to the status of "genius" justifies a healthy skepticism about auteurism (Wollen 2002, 12). One objects to the elitism that attributes "genius" to one cultural worker to the exclusion of another. However, we would not abandon feminism's commitment to championing women innovators as a vehicle of historical restitution. While checking any tendency to look for "great women" on the analogy with "great men" in history, we do want to proclaim the genius of women found in unlikely places. Here, then, I officially proclaim the genius of women in general, exemplified by the particular genius of Alice Guy Blaché, whose achievements in silent-era motion picture production are unparalleled.[4]

Still, if we claim Alice Guy Blaché as auteur, we should acknowledge its antithesis—the conventional form she used as the locus of genius. Rather than commending the genius of the artist, we praise the ingenuity of the narrative and iconographic structure, a structure itself incorporating the director and her audience. So the alignment of "women" with "genius" in my title takes the term away from the Romantic notion of the individual by reaffirming the interchangeability

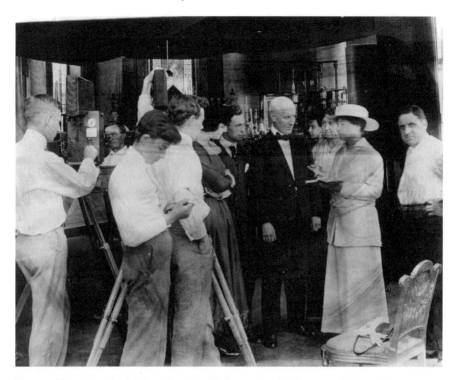

Fig. 1.1 Alice Guy Blaché directing *My Madonna* (1915). Courtesy: Ft. Lee Library, Ft. Lee, New Jersey.

of the critical categories "women" and "genre." And yes, this means reasserting "women" as generic, which, after all, has been one of the great achievements of second-wave feminist theory. This allows us to pose the codification of emotional knowledge in genre as both receptacle for and testimony to a remarkable facility—no natural gift but rather a highly developed social expertise in the ways and means of feeling. Recent critical developments have established "emotional knowledge" as anything but a contradiction in terms, as seen, for instance, in Deidre Pribram's study of *Crash* (2004) in this volume. From this historical vantage we look back to the genre theory of the 1970s with its important emphasis on formula but not yet accommodating the special problems of either emotion or visceral response. Now, most importantly, we are on the other side of foundational work on what have been termed the basic "body genres": horror, pornography, and melodrama (Dyer 2007, 178–80; L. Williams 1991). And yet, the study of these bodily genres appears to have gone around rather than through genre theory.

The question of what I am calling emotional expertise is, of course, automatically gendered and simultaneously genred (Berlant 2008). But the current critical alignment of melodrama as the emotional genre with women is not a natural arrangement. Melodrama was not always associated with women, but was rather a historical development, identified by David Grimsted in the nineteenth-century move that established feeling as source of moral value (1968, 11). Following Grimsted, Christine Gledhill argues the melodramatization of *both* male and female-gendered genres—the western and the woman's film, for instance (1987, 34, 13)—and action films are now commonly understood as male melodramas (Mercer and Shingler 2004, 98–105). But just as the gendering of genres seems settled, another question arises, that of melodrama as an ur-genre, now seen as a trans-generic mode. So I would incorporate into the malleability of melodrama, the corollary ingenuity of genre.

Much is at stake in melodrama theory following Linda Williams's assertion that melodrama is mainstream cinema's "dominant form," a direct challenge to classical narrative/realism as its founding, world-dominating form (2001, 23). In this vein Gledhill had earlier asked what it means for feminism to claim the critical capacity of melodrama when the rhetoric of melos now appears to be everywhere in classical narrative/realist films, the very films thought to be so uncritical and complicit (1987, 13). More recently she has conceived melodrama as a virtual "genre-producing machine," a machine that "generates" further genres (Gledhill 2000, 227, 229). Pair this with Richard Dyer's recent work on pastiche (2007), and we have a marked shift in genre theory. Dyer, awarding perhaps more to the spectator than any genre theory to date, understands our own historical selves as sources of genre knowledge as when viewing the pastiche of an earlier genre film we are able to feel as we once did all over again. In our recognition of the *noir* in *neo noir*, for instance, we acknowledge genre as having "generative powers," powers the film uses "to create a certain kind of world and feeling" (Dyer 2007, 176). Memories of genres past are returns to familiar "structures of feeling"; the pastiche is where our past and our present are put in relief (180). Crucial to this generative "historicity of emotions," and basic to my argument here, is that earlier critical moment when the social constructedness of everything was a new insight. Against individualization of feeling, Dyer argues that the history of feeling is not about the feelings we alone feel, but rather about shared feeling, or "living within the limits of cultural construction of thought and feeling" (180). Embracing these limits, Dyer helps us imagine a theory of genre in which viewers, you and me, are part of the same "structures of feeling," part of an orchestration of historical feelings felt historically.[5]

It seems, however, limits can be good or bad. In the cultural construction of everything, the limit endorses the socially shared aspect, but genre theory, since the 1970s, took another view. Limits were understood as negative restrictions on artists whose expression was constrained by set conventions. Again, here is where auteur met genre—when the auteur was expected to "transcend" the formal dictates of the industrial genre. Soon, in the move from structuralism to poststructuralism, authorial rule-breaking acceded to the political possibilities of "violation," "transgression," and "subversion" of the form. So, in the last two decades, we have seen a shift from genre as "containing" the possibilities of production and interpretation (Neale 1980, 53, 55), to genre as expansively generative, productive of more works. This supports the view of melodrama as larger than any one genre, as a modality generating many genres (Gledhill 2000). Here genre-as-limitation is reversed to genre as wonderfully and remarkably flexible ("protean") and highly productive ("machine-like") (L. Williams 2001, 12; Gledhill, 2000, 227).

Strangely, on this question of formal constraint, few asked how genres were policed. Genre, by definition, implies operative aesthetic laws and the possibility of their violation. But in his recent discussion of literary as well as popular film genres, John Frow asserts that the law of genre is effectively unenforceable. Genre law is, he says, "undermined by [its] lack of hold" over the individual works it appears to be regulating (Frow 2006, 26).[6] The concept of limits-as-culture becomes the productive principle (as in Dyer) when we consider that, hold or no hold, genre works are as fascinatingly predictable as they are unpredictable, paradoxically, by virtue of their inevitable repetition in some innovative form of the form. So where Frow responds to Jacques Derrida's generic "limits" with genre's "lack of hold," I would respond to Frow with Deleuze's intriguing claim that repetition is "in every respect" a "transgression" because by virtue of its return and replay function, it "puts the law into question," inviting our skepticism (Deleuze 1994, 5). Rather than thinking of the rule-boundedness of genre, we are encouraged by this formulation to think of genre as rule-breaking. With transgression, especially after queer theory, increasingly seen as politically productive, we can thus understand genre rules as meant-to-be-broken and genre pleasures as shared historical refeeling, only enhanced by anticipation of echo and imitation. Here lies the very genius of genre to which my title refers.

A generous theory of popular film genres is now needed, not only accepting imitation but expecting the ingenuities of cultural recombination. With this goal, then, what should we retain from the history of genre theory? Two aspects are crucial: repetition and expectation. Genre "expectations," seen early by Andrew Tudor (1973, 143), and in Steve Neale's recent retheorization (2000, 158), preserve the audience as well as historical moments of reception. But perhaps more important, allowing us to explain the popularity of "low" film genres over "high" literary genres, is the inevitable return of genre works and their unlimited updatability. Robert Warshow early observed that "form can keep its freshness through endless repetitions" arising from film's double mass character—both popular and reproducible (1974, 151). Finally, repetition is found in the genre history advocated by Altman (1999) and Neale (2000), and now developed by Dyer (2007). Combining these two principles, repetition and expectation, I see genre as produced and received expectations of "going with-against": for instance, the wonderfully paradoxical way repetition is understood by means, not of sameness but by the very differences or changes it expects.[7] But while my concern is to theorize the ingenuity of genre, in the 1970s a less generous paradigm organized our thought, to which I return in order to question how the author became analogized with the text.

According to Peter Hutchings (1995), the first model of 1970s genre criticism, Tom Ryall's artist/film/audience triangle (1975), was effectively uneven-sided, the audience remaining a mere placeholder. Since then, we have witnessed one position understood in terms of the other, and even an undecidability that defers or refers one to the other. But, in an attempt to resolve the source-of-meaning question, we have also seen analogy, most dramatically between film and author. For instance, looking back at the 1970s, Laura Mulvey recalls how structuralism's "discovery" of the auteur in the text paralleled the later psychoanalytic "discovery" of the "unspoken" in the film (Mulvey 1990, 69). Similarly, authorship was approximated to genre. Following celebration of Douglas Sirk as subversive director of melodrama scripts, Christine Gledhill noted that auteurism effectively brought melodrama as genre into critical existence (1987, 7). However, this implied less the sharper definition of the American family melodrama than a conceptual "slippage" between Sirk as "author" and "melodrama itself." Slippage—that incremental, imperceptible slide of one position into another—rested on the capacity of Sirk's elaborate cinematic style to "subvert" the ideological project of the genre. The family melodrama, after the slip, minus the cynical German émigré director, itself worked to undermine the American dream from inside its own household, where the dream had become a nightmare. Without our noticing, Gledhill says, the "subversion" attributed to Sirk, the Brechtian auteur, became "attached" to melodrama as genre (1987, 7).[8]

It is remarkable in retrospect that this slip did not seem a contradictory move. Seventies apparatus theory, challenging the primacy of the singular subject, was at odds with the agency of the singular subject that auteur theory advanced. Furthermore, the theoretical developments that underwrote melodrama theory, from gendered subject positioning to the ideological critique of capitalist patriarchy, did not accommodate empirical persons as either innovative artists or spectators. The constitution of the subject through language disallowed self-expression or artistic intervention. Colin MacCabe refers to the accommodation of auteur theory with poststructuralist Marxism and psychoanalysis as the "one massive contradiction" in film theory (2003, 40–41).

Since the auteur remained viable in the 1970s and was revitalized in the critical work on melodramas directed by Douglas Sirk and Vincente Minnelli, the concept was available for use in the new feminist work on melodrama in the 1980s (Nowell-Smith 1987; Mulvey 1987). Yet the confusion between the textual critique performed by the auteur and the so-called auto-critique performed by the film itself remained. In this regard, we could say that the slippage Gledhill notes (from subversive auteur to subversive genre) had been rehearsed in reverse in Claire Johnston's attribution of the subversive "cracking open the entire fabric of the film" to Dorothy Arzner as auteur director (1973, 29). Feminist film theory never sorted out this confusion, and the tension between the 1950s auteur as opposed to the 1950s family melodrama has remained unproblematized, with the notable exception of Barbara Klinger's work (1994) on the production context of Douglas Sirk's films. Still, it is the in-theory availability of the auteur as explanation for subversion that concerns feminist theory, and to pursue this I return to E. Ann Kaplan's important 1987 essay on the maternal melodrama between 1910 and 1940. Here she rehearses the major feminist uses of the concept of "subversion" in the development of melodrama theory, as well as the companion critical concept of "resistance" as it became associated with genre as a measure *of* and ultimately *for* feminist politics. In her discussion of the literary tradition of nineteenth-century American "domestic feminism," aligned with Harriet Beecher Stowe's *Uncle Tom's Cabin* (1852), Kaplan intimates that the woman director (had there been at least one in cinema's first decades), *would have* taken this tradition further. What happened instead, she says, was that the "more heroic" aspects of mothering in women's maternal sacrifice melodrama (e.g., *East Lynne,* 1863) were taken over and returned to male-centered ends, notably by D. W. Griffith in films such as *His Mothering Heart* (1913) (118, 125).

Significantly, Kaplan leaves room for the hypothesis that women as scenario writers and directors working from 1910 to 1940 *might have* produced films to compare with literary fiction such as Olive Higgins Prouty's novel, *Stella Dallas* (1923). Drawn from this context, Kaplan argues, mothering itself could be "subversive" in the relatively "subversive" genre of the woman's film (1987, 133). "However," she concludes, "it is significant that there is in film no set of texts written and directed by women to parallel women's fiction. The woman's film was directed mainly by men (women may have written the script)" (125). The assumption that there were no women does not, of course, mean that had there been, they would have continued in the same tradition of women's literary fiction. Yet it is difficult not to take Kaplan's statement as a lament ("If only there had been more women").

However, films directed by men, especially those amenable to Sirkian reading, can, according to Kaplan, produce feminist "subversion," sometimes, as in the case of Griffith, explained by an address to the female spectator (1987, 125). The possibility of gendered reading arises from the separation of male and female spheres, along with the feminist assumption, crucial in the 1980s, that women's experience counts for something.[9] Using *The Blot* (1921), directed by Lois Weber, Kaplan deploys close reading to feminist ends, focusing, for example, on close-up shots of the suitor's chair caught in the holes of the carpet and a scene in which the caring mother, Mrs. Griggs, distraught over her family's destitution, steals a neighbor's cooked chicken. Such attention to domestic detail becomes, in the tradition of authorial reading, the signature of director Lois Weber, "reveal[ing] the female director's special sensitivity to the domestic sphere that could only come from inside knowledge" (126).

Possibly the female auteur director was never as fully developed as was the female writer in literary theory or the female painter in art historical discourse because at the time there were so few texts on which to work. Nevertheless, feminist film theory developed along other lines in the 1970s (Butler 2008). Today it intersects with feminist film historiography, which, appearing in response to archival discoveries unforeseen earlier, finds women's crucial contribution to silent motion picture production undisputable. We now know that a significant number of U.S. short and feature films *were* written, produced, and directed by women, particularly in the silent era (Gaines 2004; Mahar 2006). The question now is whether to continue investigation into the legacy of women's fiction, together with that of Sirkian textual progressivism, in order to identify the subversive female auteur director of film melodrama.[10] In this regard Kaplan argues that in nineteenth-century woman's fiction the moral superiority of the mother is "subversive" in its reversal of the male as moral arbiter (1987, 118). However, applied to motion pictures this contention is complicated by Kaplan's more positive evaluation of the woman's film as against the maternal melodrama. This she considers too dependent upon the male oedipal drama, and therefore ensconced in patriarchal ideology. Sooner or later, however this distinction begins to crack. Can, for instance, the mother be subversive by virtue of her virtue if she also privileges her son? Besides reviving the tradition of morally central (and therefore subversive) mothering, Kaplan also argues that refusing traditional mothering is subversive, basing her case for understanding the film, *Stella Dallas* (1937) as *not* a maternal melodrama on Stella's "resistance" to this role (133).

To summarize the possibilities for subversion: the moral centrality of the mother is subversive (insofar as she is the measure of moral value); "heroic" aspects of mothering are subversive if characters reject traditional expectations; and the director, by virtue of her position as a woman, subverts gender values while also accruing the "resistance" of the character to mothering's requirements.

These positions represent different critical moves—the one based on the subordinate as an *alternative* to the dominant and the other on *refusal* of dominant expectations. The question remains how subversion can be both the mother returned and the refusal of mothering. Feminist theory, it would seem, gets to have its theoretical cake and eat it too. Subversion *is* both the mother returned and the refusal of mothering. But most remarkably, in offering the same but differently, again and again, the critical function of the auteur director here appears not unlike the function of genre. We are now in the position to argue that the interchangeability of genre and authorship allows us to see the real genius in the workings of genre.

THE NEW LOVE AND THE OLD (SOLAX, 1912)

To test the genius of genre over that of authorship, I turn to a recently rediscov-
ered two-minute short film, *The New Love and the Old* (1912). This film is not
only attributed to Alice Guy Blaché as director but as president of its production
company, Solax. In its bare two minutes the film privileges the mother-son as opposed to the mother-daughter relationship, a privileging that Kaplan (1987) says
defines the maternal melodrama genre (117, 126). It also features a love triangle,
but a triangle with a narrative twist.

In the briefest screen time, *The New Love and the Old* sets up the generic narrative expectation of conflict between the mother and her future daughter-in-law.
In the first frames, we see a close-up insert photograph of the mother alternated
with the photograph of the younger woman, her potential replacement. The son
is introduced in long shot as he kisses his mother's photograph. In the subsequent
scene, he brings a haughty, fashionably dressed young woman to his mother's tea
table. The diminutive white-haired mother appropriately fusses over the table lin-
ens and the tea service, but when the young woman is seated, the mother spills tea
on her guest's voluminous skirt. The young woman stands, enraged. The mother
attempts to ameliorate but her apology is refused. The young woman's angry
response places the young man between the two women, needing to choose one
over the other. He hesitates, then turns away from the insulted young woman.
As the "new love" exits the frame he embraces "the old," his little mother.

One might argue that there is too little conflict in these minutes to produce
the overload of emotionality that requires conversion to melos; there is little
"discharge" or semiotic run-off to convert to other signs.[11] But that is the point.
The New Love and the Old is historically early and highly condensed—all the better to study the evolution of the maternal melodrama genre and the mode that
generates it, to think what is meant by expectation, repetition, convention, and,
possibly, feminist subversion. Consider here one of the narrative conventions
identified by feminist melodrama theory, associated with potential subversion—
what might be called the "open up and shut down" narrative structure. Kaplan
argues that characters who find independence from men or who work outside
the home inhabit an opening narrative space understood as, in her words, the
"attempt of the films to subvert" the oedipal drama (1987, 126). By the end of
this drama, the "transgressing Mother" is made subordinate once again to the
Father. Or, the text opens up and screams out against conventional marriage in
the middle only to shut down at the end, confirming the patriarchal plan. Thus
we could argue, following Kaplan, that *The New Love and the Old* is generically
undecided in the middle but resolving at narrative closure into maternal melodrama. But does the ending give us the mother's traditional sacrifice for her son
or, since he refuses to marry, does he sacrifice for her? Is the "momma's boy" by
definition subversive or not?

It would seem there are endless ways Kaplan's model can find subversion in this short film. The values associated with middle-class motherhood—self-sacrifice, self-effacement, deferential politeness, and fastidiousness—are rewarded and consequently elevated to *the* moral standard. And, again, the mere rescue of the mother from the subordinate position at the cultural margin and her elevated placement at the center of the fictional world is a subversive reversal. But recall the film's narrative twist. The opening set-up raises expectation that the future daughter-in-law will successfully pass the test of social class, by impressing and not offending the mother. This is reversed when the young woman, refusing to be amenable, behaves rudely toward the mother, consequently losing her future husband. One could argue that this narrative reversal subverts the expectation of heterosexual coupling through marriage. If so, subversion is achieved by returning the son to his mother. We might, then, see reuniting son and mother and reinstating the maternal oedipal *not* as reactionary, insofar as this rejects the heterosexual union. Putting two conventional options for women into conflict—wife as opposed to motherhood—*The New Love and the Old* generates both a reactionary and a subversive maternal narrative: two bad options from the point of view of feminism. For the son's choice of either wife or mother would make no difference given the generic, effectively ideological expectation that a 1912 film will shut down options for women, whether wives or mothers. Perhaps claiming subversion is so problematic because we read contemporary Western feminism back into the situation of women in earlier historical moments, not to mention the difficulties of our claim that the domestic world of women is *both* the realm of bourgeois ideology (to be subverted) and itself the subversive defense against dominant male culture.

My interest in elaborating the perhaps infinite possibilities for subversion in a two-minute film has, however, a different goal. The theory of melodramatic subversion, developed for the cynical subversion-seeking auteur Sirk, prepared genres for other auteurs to slot into. In her choice of subject matter, her woman's point of view on marriage and the family, and her presumed interest in domestic detail, Lois Weber becomes an ideal subverter of the melodrama text and its generic variations. She, in Kaplan's terms, has "inside knowledge" of the very bourgeois world feminists expect her to subvert. Similarly we expect to place Alice Guy Blaché, director and producer of *The New Love and the Old,* exactly where we had placed Douglas Sirk. How do we do this? We begin to attribute "artistic" choices to Guy Blaché, choices at the level of gesture and device—perhaps the insert photograph—and even the dramatic use of props such as the table cloth. In thus finding the "hand" of the auteur in aspects of the image on the silent screen, we begin to personalize the aesthetics of cinema. We perhaps note the superfluity of the tea spilled, a minor disaster turned into a textual "outburst"; we find an aesthetic turned against the play of bourgeois manners. We begin to say things like "Guy Blaché's placement of the tea service," her "woman's understanding of the trauma of the ruined dress," and her "interest in motherhood," even "her" long-shot positioning of the camera and "decision to cut" to the mother and son alone in the frame at the end. But there is a world of difference between arguing that male director Sirk has mastered the mise-en-scène of the domestic interior all the better to subvert the ideology of the familial and arguing that a woman director has mastered this world because, historically, it has been her domain by virtue of her gender. If we say that a woman director's genius lies in the "woman's genius" of knowing the infinitesimal details of domesticity and seeing how to manipulate this world of brocade curtains, tea services, and familial claustrophobia, have we not given her a back-handed compliment?

Recall, however, that 1950s melodrama theory was based on a slippage between Sirk the auteur and melodrama form—in his case, the family melodrama—as it evolved critically. To return to my point of departure, let me ask again if we do not assert the author at the expense of generic language. Should we credit the maternal melodrama genre with the alternation of wife and motherhood, the emphasis on domestic detail (the throbbing object), and the tendency to revert to the patriarchal resolution confirming the mother-son oedipal relation? Or, conversely, should we credit the female auteur with the dramatic alternation, the melodramatization of the detail, and the narrative resolution that achieves closure? The ease with which the 1950s family melodrama genre assumed the subversive powers of the critical German auteur perhaps indicates the theoretical reversibility of two terms—"author" and "genre." Raymond Williams once posed the constitution of the author through the forms he or she "spoke" as a reversible relation. The older literary question, "What did this author do to this form?" became, "What did this form do to the author?" (1977, 192). This responds to the critical move against bourgeois individualism and its assumption that persons can and do make choices outside the social that continually forms them (194). Did feminism lose this socially constructed author in the reaction against the psychoanalytic gendered spectator, or is this author so taken for granted that the construct has effectively evaporated (see Mulvey 1975)? As an antidote to this forgetting, I suggest—against genre as cramping authorial style—that we start with the social over the individual and conceive innovation as anticipated and "contained within" the generic, that is, in the sense of already there, already-in-form.

We need to ask if what we have called "subversion" in the maternal melodrama genre is not the effect of paradoxical changes effected through repetition of so many historically conditioned motherings. In 1912 alone, numerous short films were produced in the United States with "mother" in the title. If "subversion" is basically the operative necessity of known form, its success is the result of its permutation. Consider how many times the structure of maternal self-sacrifice returned the son to the mother after threatened separation, beginning with all the versions of Mrs. Henry Wood's novel *East Lynne* (see Barefoot 2001), which would become the many versions of *Madame X* (1920, 1929, 1937, 1965). The genius of genre lies in the enormity of its repertoire, its vast cultural storage, its knowledge of both itself and the socioemotional raw material of the cultures that sustain it. What do we gain by attributing the genius to genre and not to the auteur? While the former contains the latter, the latter only contains the former insofar as the auteur coincides with a genre. Here is Dyer's move from "autonomous" thought and feeling "out of the innermost imperatives of the self" to the sociality of "genre's generative powers" (2007, 179, 176). Genre's powers are capacious; they can, in Dyer's words "create a certain kind of world and feeling" (176). In the silent era, then, let us say, the deep worlds of feeling are the wells of women's genius, elaborated and given play as the ingenuity of genre, and melodrama's genres are, in turn, reinvested in and through the emotional ingenuity of women, whether actress, audience member, auteur-director, or author-writer, all experts in the ways and means of feeling (see Berlant 2008, 4). Genre is generated by films produced, expected, remembered, and returned as genre generates more, reiterates more popular genre films.

Finally, the generosity of film genre is its assumption that all know and feel—no privileged auteur knows or feels more than an audience member or any of the other creative personnel on the motion picture production set. This acknowledges the repertory actors in the Solax stock company as well as the innovation of this company within the history of the very studio system that would develop into the industry. Thomas Schatz in *The Genius of the System* (1988) saw in Guy Blaché's remarkable studio the cradle of the genre system's ingenuity, in story structures that delivered expectations and pleasurable returns to known forms. As Janet Staiger has established, the industry's approach to popular moving picture production evolved into an exquisite balance between product standardization and differentiation (1985, 96–112). The director and the actors step into the genre which, like a ready-made, takes over and generates the work we have historically designated as "theirs." If genre is the locus of genius, however, is not "theirs" more properly "ours"?

EPILOGUE

Our feminist theory, also like a popular genre, comes with critical expectations about the device of the expectation. In this critical tradition, the writer is expected to challenge the reader's expectations of what he or she will say next. I must challenge your expectations, for instance, about the problem of "subversion." And here is a productive going with-against—to return to, repeat, and to reference the uses of the concept of "subversion" in feminist melodrama theory while making a change in it. Having said that *The New Love and the Old* will contain a narrative twist, I have set up an expectation in the reader of this essay that the twist will be explained. In the tradition within which I write and you read, however, the critic's burden is not only to explicate the twist in the film narrative, but to add to that twist another—ideally, a feminist theoretical turnabout. If there is a feminist twist, it is that genre teaches us that the criticism that made "gender" also makes genres.[12] And if Rick Altman (1999, 72–7) is right in attributing to feminists the creation of the woman's film (and I think he is), then even, and especially, feminist criticism has made genres. In the genre-making sense, feminist criticism belongs neither exactly or exclusively to authors. Feminist criticism is us.

Notes

1. See Andrew (1993, 77—79) on Wollen's structuralist approach to the auteur (1972).

2. See Butler on the history of feminist film theory (2008).

3. See Mayne, "Female Authorship Considered" (in Mayne 1990), for a critical overview. See Gaines (2002 and 2004) for recent feminist work on women directors and discussion of feminism and authorship.

4. McMahan (2002) records Guy Blaché's remarkably productive career at Gaumont, 1895–1907, as head of production and later as president of Solax, her own company, 1910–1914. She "controlled" art direction, script writing, and editing, in addition to directing the majority of titles (xxvii).

5. Dyer (2007) returns to a forgotten aspect of Williams's concept that allows for continuous change. "Structure of feeling" is distinguished from both "ideology" and "world-view," designating where and how meanings are "actively lived and felt" (R. Williams 1977, 132).

6. Frow responds to Derrida (1980, 224) on how norms become "interdictions": "do" and "do not." Moretti (1989) argues that "with modernity, it has become harder to fix genres," his reason being that "social mobility" has made the "realm of cultural forms" more hazy. At this juncture, every new step implies a "weakening of genres, or a proliferation of subgenres" (160).

7. Deleuze (1994) describes the paradox of repetition: "One can speak of it only by virtue of the change or difference it introduces" (70).

8. For example, Mulvey (1987).

9. This notion was roundly critiqued. See de Lauretis (1986), who argues that what is at stake is the "relation of experience to discourse" (5).

10. See Ann Kaplan's own development of her analysis in this volume.

11. Elsaesser (1987, 55) says that the "melos" given to "drama" is translated into aspects of mise-en-scène, while Nowell-Smith (1987, 73) argues melodrama's ability to "siphon off" into such signs "undischarged" emotion that can't be "accommodated" by ostensibly realist devices.

12. See Gayle Rubin's 1975 formulation of the sex/gender system, when "gender" became the operative feminist term productively substituting for the problematic term "sex."

CHAPTER 2

NO FIXED ADDRESS:

THE WOMEN'S PICTURE FROM *OUTRAGE* TO *BLUE STEEL*

PAM COOK

The women's picture has played a major role in the development of feminist film criticism, partly in response to a certain tendency in 1970s feminist film theory to prioritize the "male spectator," and partly as a strategic move to reassess a critically devalued and neglected genre. This debate, which has centered on questions of female spectatorial pleasure and address, has produced some remarkable textual analyses and trenchant critiques of the ways in which classical Hollywood cinema both represents and positions women, opening up issues such as narrative structure, masochism, and consumerism. Despite the revisionist impulse motivating much of this work, it has tended to locate itself within a more general critique, inherited from 1970s film theory, which perceives classical Hollywood as inherently bourgeois and patriarchal, and therefore inimical to feminist interests. My own article, "Melodrama and the Women's Picture," while attempting to account for the genre's popular appeal, betrayed a deep suspicion of the whole idea of the women's picture.

> One question insists: why does the women's picture exist? There is no such thing as "the men's picture," specifically addressed to men; there is only "cinema," and the "women's picture," a sub-group or category specially for women, excluding men; a separate, private space designed for more than half the population, relegating them to the margins of cinema proper. The existence of the women's picture both recognizes the importance of women, and marginalizes them. By constructing this different space for women (Haskell's "wet, wasted afternoons"), it performs a vital function in society's ordering of sexual difference. (1983, 17)

There is more than a hint of conspiracy theory in this formulation, which implies that the category of the women's picture exists in order to dupe female spectators into believing that they are important, while subtly marginalizing and disempowering them. This is an intellectual position that echoes through much feminist writing on the Hollywood women's picture. More recent work in the area of audience response has suggested that through identification with stars and emulation of their image, female spectators may feel empowered and act out that feeling in their everyday lives.[1] Although I still consider that feminist discussion of the women's picture has been enormously productive, I no longer believe that popular texts necessarily operate to marginalize and disempower female spectators. However, nor do I think that a simple reversal of that position, which looks at the women's picture in terms of the way it offers pleasures of female empowerment, gets us closer to understanding the complexities of audience engagement with popular films.

My concern here will be to trace, selectively, shifts in discussion of the women's picture by feminist writers, in order to ask some preliminary questions about genre and gendered address. At the same time, I shall explore the differences and continuities between a specific manifestation of the classical woman's film and some postclassical developments, with the aim of assessing what has changed in Hollywood cinema since the 1950s with respect to women filmmakers and audiences. First, a couple of caveats. Since the relationship of the woman's film to classical Hollywood cinema is uneasy, it is somewhat misleading to refer to "the classical women's picture."[2] Moreover, if the transition to what is known as "postclassical" or "new" Hollywood can be seen as spanning the period between the 1948 Paramount decrees and the completion of divorcement at the end of the 1950s, then the "classical" status of films produced in the late 1940s, and the designation of 1950s Hollywood cinemas as "postclassical," are clearly problematic.

While recognizing the difficulties inherent in the terms "classical" and "post-classical," particularly when used to impose definitive formal or temporal boundaries, I employ them here to indicate a process of transformation of the Hollywood industry and its products rather than a strict demarcation between two distinct phases of production. The Hollywood film industry, like any other, is always in the process of transition; indeed it has been argued that since the classical studio system has been reorganized rather than dismantled, new Hollywood and its products are not that different from the old (Bordwell and Staiger 1985). Nevertheless, changes following the Second World War—such as the reorganization of the studio system, the relaxation of censorship, the expansion of low-budget independent production, the trend towards high-concept blockbusters, and the growth of new production and exhibition sites such as drive-in cinemas, theme parks, television, video and DVD—have initiated a profound shift in the way cinema is produced and consumed (Collins 1993). One of the characteristics that clearly differentiates postclassical from classical cinema is the move towards greater visibility of sex and violence, and it is this development that partly concerns me here.

The dissolution of boundaries—between different modes of production such as television, video, and cinema and between different generic forms—has also been identified as a distinctive postclassical characteristic (Corrigan 1991). The permeability of boundaries is central to my discussion of genre and gendered address. Approaches to classical generic categories have traditionally assumed a gender-specific address. Thus the woman's film is perceived in terms of a primary address to female spectators, an assumption supported by reference to textual strategies such as narrative and mise-en-scène, to extra-textual discourses such as promotional material and fan magazines, and to historical evidence of industry policy. Though it is sometimes accepted that women's pictures are also addressed to male spectators, these are perceived as secondary audiences and have received little or no critical attention. Most other genres—even those such as musicals and musical comedies that do not appear to be clearly gender specific—are discussed in terms of their address to the ubiquitous male spectator. The western, the gang-ster movie, or the horror film, which appear to feature central male protagonists and secondary female characters, are perceived as "masculine" genres.

With the exception of feminist work on melodrama and the woman's film, film studies has overwhelmingly privileged male spectatorship, and has thereby contributed to the consensus that cinema is primarily addressed, and belongs, to men. Yet while teaching a course on John Ford and the western, I was struck by the similarity of many classical western narratives, with their emphasis on circularity, digression, and delay, to the structure of classical women's pictures. The choices facing the western hero, between love and duty, family life, and a wanderer's existence are not that different from those encountered by women's picture heroines. In several of Ford's classical westerns, the expressive use of music and mise-en-scène to heighten emotional affect can only be described as melodramatic—indeed, I would suggest that a comparative analysis of *My Darling Clementine* (1944) and *Written on the Wind* (1957) would produce interesting results in terms of generic cross-fertilization. In his study of *Stagecoach* (1939), Edward Buscombe (1993) examines the way that the film was marketed using Claire Trevor's costume and hairstyle, one of the strategies employed in promot-ing women's pictures.

The idea that genres are mixed is not new, nor am I the first to suggest that we cannot make easy assumptions about genre and gendered address. Broadly speaking, a tension can be discerned between approaches that identify a single, gender-specific mode of address, and those that posit multiple address, whether in terms of gender duality, or by spreading the net more widely to include groups defined by class, race and ethnicity, age, and sexual preference. Since it is the increased visibility of sexual violence in the postclassical period that has inspired a number of critiques, feminist and otherwise, I shall look at a tendency in the woman's film that concerns itself with sexual violence. This route will take me from the 1940s Gothic-influenced paranoid woman's film analyzed by Mary Ann Doane (1987), via its transformation in 1950s family melodrama, 1970s and 1980s low-budget rape-revenge, and 1990s sci-fi blockbusters.

In her introductory chapter to *The Desire to Desire*, Doane outlines the ways in which psychoanalytic film theory's account of the cinematic apparatus has over-whelmingly privileged male subjectivity (1987). One of her reasons for choosing the 1940s cycle of woman's films was to open up questions of female subjectivity in one of the few genres to put a feminine sensibility at the center. In contrast to the voyeurism and fetishism associated with the male spectator, Doane sees femininity in cinema defined in terms of masochism, paranoia, and hysteria. She examines a number of women's pictures—such as *Rebecca* (1940) and *Secret Beyond the Door* (1948)—for the ways in which they narrativize masochistic and/ or paranoid scenarios in which the heroines' assumption of active investigative and heterosexually desiring roles is turned around on them to reveal and confirm their destiny as victims.

Doane claims that it is through such scenarios of victimization and suffering that the 1940s woman's film addresses a specifically female spectator. She is careful to assert that audience address and spectator positioning are not the same thing:

> Women spectators oscillate or alternate between masculine and feminine posi-tions . . . and men are capable of this alternation as well. This is simply to empha-size once again that feminine and masculine positions are not fully coincident with actual men and women. (1987, 8)

She goes on to qualify this statement:

> Nevertheless, men and women enter the movie theater as social subjects who have been compelled to align themselves in some way with respect to one of the reigning binary oppositions (that of sexual difference) which order the social field. Men will be more likely to occupy the positions delineated as masculine, women those specified as feminine. (8)

It is the slippage between the first and the second proposition that interests me. It would have been as easy, and as convincing, to reverse the second assertion: social subjects who have been compelled to align themselves with binary op-positions of sexual difference are likely to occupy other, opposing positions in the movie theater. But what is significant is that there is no evidence to support either proposition. While the oscillations or multiple identifications offered by fictional texts may be defended, in theory, by recourse to psychoanalysis, there is no way, beyond the anecdotal, of knowing what happens when real spectators enter the cinema.

In her overview of theories of spectatorship, Judith Mayne (1993) takes issue with the way many film theorists have over-simplified identification in the cin-ema, in that they assume that identification takes place between spectators and characters, and that spectators identify with those characters that correspond most directly with their own identity. She sees this assumption as contravening the psychoanalytical theories on which much of this work was based, which question the very idea of stable identities. Mayne discerns a shift in notions of identification that has taken place with the emergence of reception studies, which takes spectators rather than the cinematic institution as the point of departure. This shift has opened up a gap between what is perceived as the homogenizing impulse of the institution and the potentially multiple, conflicting responses to it, and a space between address and reception. Thus the implied spectator positions offered by popular Hollywood texts are not necessarily inhabited by real audience members, who may experience such films in ways that go against the ideological grain. Later in her discussion, Mayne develops one of the implications of the idea of the gap between texts and spectators:

> Film theory has been so bound by the heterosexual symmetry that supposedly governs Hollywood cinema that it has ignored the possibility, for instance, that one of the distinct pleasures of the cinema may well be a "safe zone" in which homosexual as well as heterosexual desires can be fantasized and acted out. I am not speaking here of an innate capacity to "read against the grain," but rather of the way in which desire and pleasure in the cinema may well function to problematize the categories of heterosexual versus homosexual. (97)

One could take this suggestion further by arguing that, contrary to the claims made by much film theory that "the cinematic institution" works to endorse and sustain dominant ideology, popular cinema problematizes all social categories—of class, race and ethnicity, national identity, gender sexuality, age, and so forth. The invitation to the cinema is based on the promise that spectators may experience the thrill of reinventing themselves rather than simply having their social identities or positions bolstered.

Despite the loosening of the bonds between spectators and cinematic texts in revisionist film theory, the implications of this "gap" or "safety zone" idea have not generally been embraced, presumably because it challenges a number of film theory's underlying assumptions. For example, by positing that popular cinema is more ideologically open, and processes of identification more fluid than has previously been imagined, it suggests that opportunities for resistance are more available than the opposition between "dominant cinema" and "counter cinema" allows. Moreover, the proposition accepted by so much feminist film theory, that Hollywood cinema works to exclude, marginalize, and victimize women, whether as fictional characters, filmmakers, or spectators, is radically questioned by the idea that all spectators may redefine themselves in relation to the dominant social categories, not only in the darkened space of the cinema, but outside it too.

To return to Doane's account of the 1940s women's pictures, while I do not deny the masochistic pleasures offered by the woman's film, the assumption that these pleasures are gender specific is too limited. Doane's negative notion of female masochism, defined in terms of passive suffering, ignores the extent to which many of the films she discusses have as their back stories dramas of male

masochism. Titles such as *Rebecca, Secret Beyond the Door, Jane Eyre* (1943), and
Now, Voyager (1942) feature damaged male characters who in the past have been
punished and/or abused by dominant, powerful women who continue to exert a
hold over them. In these films, the hero is not the only sexual aggressor, and he
is also a victim. Thus, in the course of the women's picture narrative, the heroine
confronts not only her own victimization but also that of the hero (and sometimes that of subsidiary characters). In the Gothic-influenced films in particular,
female pathology is matched and often outdone by male psychosis in a kind of
overlapping of male and female desire.

There are two significant points here: first, these multiple masochistic scenarios
bear a striking resemblance to those identified by Carol J. Clover in *Men, Women,
and Chainsaws* (1992) as being at work in the modern American horror film,
where psychologically damaged and sexually impaired men turn their aggression
against female characters. There are, however, two major differences—the 1940s
heroines do not usually turn the tables on their aggressors in the same way as
their 1970s counterparts (indeed, they often end up in an uneasy and haunted
couple relationship with them), and the sexual violence is implied in the 1940s
cycle rather than graphically depicted. Second, the multiplication of masochistic
scenarios in the 1940s woman's film implies a dual address to male and female
spectators. This suggests that we should look again at the widely accepted notion
that the woman's film is primarily addressed to female spectators. For example,
a notable feature of the 1940s films discussed by Doane is their deferral of grati-
fication. The possibilities of happiness and fulfillment offered by heterosexual
romance and marriage are constantly postponed by the failure of both male and
female characters to resolve their oedipal problems. The much vaunted textual
openness of the melodramatic narrative can partly be put down to this playing out
of scenarios of postponement and deferral. This problematizing of heterosexual
romance and deferral of consummation is not confined to melodrama and the
women's picture, and the pleasures offered by such narratives are presumably
available to all spectators.

The cracks appearing in the surface of film theory herald a changing perception of popular cinema and its ideological operations towards a more historical
sense of the relationship of women to cinema that reveals their role as more significant and central than has so far been argued. Barbara Klinger's work on the
studio promotion of 1950s family melodramas such as *Written on the Wind* offers
historical evidence of address to audiences defined in gender terms. In a chapter
titled "Selling Melodrama" in her book on Douglas Sirk (1994), Klinger takes issue
with the idea put forward by 1970s film theorists that the melodramas directed
by Sirk, Minnelli, and Ray articulated a subversive critique of 1950s repressive,
consumerist America, particularly through their visual style. Instead, she argues,
the visual excess characteristic of these "sophisticated" melodramas participated
in and was sustained by ideological discourses of sexuality and affluence prevalent

at the time. Examining the promotion, reception, and other discourses surrounding the movies, Klinger demonstrates that the liberalization of discourses around sexuality in the postwar period privileged heterosexuality at the expense of others, such as homosexuality and African American sexuality, that were demarcated as deviant. The increase in explicit representations of sexual display were, she argues, often focused on the nude or scantily clad female body. Magazines such as *Playboy*, launched in 1953, were devoted to a philosophy of extramarital male sexual freedom, while exposé journals such as *Confidential*, directed at women readers, luridly revealed the private lives of celebrities in articles devoted to such questions as Robert Wagner's problems in the bedroom (Klinger 1994, 54).

The promotion of adult melodrama during this period mobilized both discourses—that of female sexual display directed at presumably heterosexual men and that of sexual scandal directed at women. Klinger also identifies a discourse of sexual violence against women in the promotional campaigns, associated with a double language that exploited the films' adult, sensational content as well as their serious, realistic approach. At the same time, advertising foregrounded spectacular mise-en-scène devoted to displays of affluence in order to appeal to the upwardly mobile aspirations of audiences, thus introducing a class address. Since women were key figures in the shift to a postwar consumer economy, these discourses, according to Klinger, were primarily addressed to them. Thus sexual display was not only a source of erotic fascination, it was intimately linked to acquisitiveness. The images of sexual and material excess in 1950s melodramas were, in Klinger's account, embroiled in current strategies of capitalism and patriarchy, and there is reason to suppose that audiences would enter the cinema expecting to enjoy them in voyeuristic and consumerist terms.

Klinger's analysis of the promotional discourses employed by Universal suggests that both generic identity and audience address must be considered historically rather than via the attribution of transcendental, unchanging formal characteristics. It also questions authorial intention. However, Klinger is not concerned with displacing authorial interpretation only to replace it with another institutional one:

> Examples of social readings like those geared towards voyeurism and consumption are particularly important to consider in relation to assessments of the film/ideology relationship. They do not necessarily produce a unified text with a coherent ideology, but suggest that institutional and social forces can act to produce a heterogeneous text offering a variety of viewing pleasures—grounded in various kinds of social ideologies—to its audience. (1994, 68)

Klinger's contextual approach suggests that the potential shifts of identity offered by multiple modes of address are consonant with marketing strategies that tie spectators in to prevailing ideologies of consumerism, sexuality, and class rather than loosen ideological and social bonds. But in the absence of historical evidence of audience response, the question of what actually happened to spectators in the cinema remains obscure. Nevertheless, her investigation does make it clear that although the 1950s melodramas, like the 1940s woman's films, were addressed to women, they were certainly not just addressed to women, nor were women the primary audience addressed in all cases.

Klinger's emphasis on the conflicting discourses in play during the 1950s, and her identification of multiple modes of address in and around the adult melodramas, provides the context for *Outrage* (1950), a story of the traumatic rape of a young woman by a psychologically damaged war veteran, directed and co-scripted by Ida Lupino for her independent company The Filmakers. In the space it gives to the perspectives of different characters, it is a good example of multiple, conflicting textual address. Indeed, the multiplicity tends to obliterate the predicament of the rape victim, which has proved difficult for some present-day viewers expecting a recognizable feminist agenda. Its emphasis on sexual violence and its relentless victimization scenario, in which almost everyone is perceived as damaged in some way, recall the 1940s Gothic paranoid cycle, while its comparatively explicit depiction of the causes and consequences of rape looks forward to later adult melodramas. *Outrage* is also partly a rape-revenge story, though the revenge element is somewhat obscured by the narrative drive to pathologize the rape victim. However, in the twenty or so years separating Lupino's rape movie from its 1970s sisters, quite a lot happened. Arguably, it is in postclassical horror and associated cycles such as slasher films and rape-revenge that sensationalized displays of sexual violence reach their apotheosis, a factor that has provoked critiques from several directions. Many of these antagonistic responses, feminist and otherwise, have focused on the visibility of sexual violence, claiming that such spectacularization is both morally offensive and socially undesirable, insofar as it panders to sadistic, voyeuristic male fantasies. In her chapter on rape-revenge in *Men, Women, and Chainsaws*, Clover challenges this received wisdom, arguing that the focus of such films on the perspective of the female victim-turned-avenger may actually place viewers in a masochistic position—doubly so, in that they are invited to identify not only with the rape victim, but also with her male victims as she goes about killing, maiming, and castrating those who have harmed her. Clover detects a shift from the male-centered rape films of the early 1970s such as *Straw Dogs* (1971) and *Frenzy* (1972), in which spectators are encouraged to collude with the rapist's sadism, to female-centered rape-revenge films such as *I Spit on Your Grave* (1977) and *Ms .45* (1980), where the female rape victim's perspective and her quest for bloody revenge in kind move center stage:

> Ironically, it may be the feminist account of rape in the last two decades that has both authorized a film like *I Spit on Your Grave* and has shaped its politics. The redefinition of rape as an offense on a par with murder, together with the well-publicized testimonials on the part of terrified and angry victims, must be centrally responsible for lodging rape as a crime deserving of the level of punishment on which revenge narratives are predicated. (1992, 153)

A similar argument is made by Linda Williams in *Hard Core* (1991) about changes in the depiction of rape in pornography in the early 1980s. Williams claims that due to a number of factors, including the heightened acceptance of the feminist critique of male sexual violence, enjoyment-of-rape scenarios became increasingly unacceptable to an industry trying to expand its viewership (153). Clover, on the other hand, seems to regard the rape-revenge cycle as an appropriation of, rather than engagement with, feminist politics. Despite the gender implications of her arguments about feminist influence and the female victim heroes and final girl survivors, and her problematization of male spectatorial pleasure, she adheres to the commonly held opinion that viewers of low-budget horror are predominantly young men and considers that the films are addressed to them, though she offers little hard evidence in support of her claim. In her brief discussion of horror audiences at the beginning of her book, she glosses over the question of privatized video viewing and the lack of reliable statistics for the composition of horror film audiences in favor of the accepted notion of the younger male as "majority viewer" (1992, 6–7). Yet, as with the woman's film, the masochistic scenarios she identifies are surely not so gender specific in their address as her argument suggests. Nor should the greater visibility of young men as horror viewers lead us to assume that they are always the genre's primary audiences.

Evidence that audiences for horror are not confined to men is offered by Linda Williams in a 1994 article about the exhibition context of *Psycho* (1960). The article includes frame stills from a cinema managers' training film that show a line of ticket holders waiting outside the DeMille Theater in New York for a matinee screening. They are all women, mostly middle-aged. Other photographs taken with infrared cameras during a screening at the Plaza in London show male and female audience members reacting to what they see and hear. Williams interprets these images as performative responses to the unresolved gender disturbances at the heart of *Psycho*, suggesting that some gender destabilization took place in the cinema audience as well as on screen. From the photographs it appears that some women were adopting contained, stoical ways of looking associated with masculinity, while some men reacted with anxious gestures closer to the histrionic performances of fear associated with femininity. Taken at the time of viewing, these photographs are perhaps the most convincing evidence so far of the potential fluidity of gender identification among the cinema audience, and of cinema experience as offering a "safe zone" for the enjoyment of such adventures in masquerade.

Williams links the gender performance in the film (Norman Bates's masquerade as his mother) to what takes place in the movie theater, arguing that the exaggerated poses adopted by audience members suggest "a pleasurable and self-conscious performance" (1994, 17) . Such arguments imply that this destabilization of gender and other social categories in the cinema is more common than we are prepared to admit. Nor, I would suggest, can the performative response be limited to what takes place in the movie theater itself, since people may adopt disguises outside the cinema too. I have discussed elsewhere (1993) a particular example of gender masquerade in the critical reception of Scorsese's *Cape Fear* (1991), in which some male writers reacted to the film's disturbing gender reversals by adopting the mantle of femininity. This has implications for studies of audience response that rely on the evidence of people recalling their experiences.

While we should be wary of identifying a single film as a historical benchmark, *Psycho*, like *Outrage* ten years before, seems to stand at a frontier of cinema history. In the shower sequence, Hitchcock created, through editing and sound, an illusion of graphic sexual violence. In fact, the audience had seen very little. Even so, a border had been crossed. Nudity and graphic sex and violence became more visible. This situation intensified with the move of low-budget exploitation into the mainstream as the major studios began to penetrate new markets in the 1970s and 1980s, and with the expanded availability of video. The graphic representation of rape and sexual assault against women in exploitation genres has been vociferously contested by those concerned that such scenarios perpetuate misogynist attitudes and encourage men to perform real acts of sexual abuse. As we have seen, such critiques have had a powerful effect on what is considered permissible to show.[3]

In their wake, the representation of rape and the viewing of such representations have become associated with the act of rape itself. Those who enjoy watching sexual violence on screen, particularly in its "low" manifestations, are highly suspect. If they are men, they are potential rapists, if they are women, they are potential rape victims. The revisionist work by feminist critics such as Clover on low-budget horror and Williams on pornography has demonstrated that the situation is more complex. The gender reversals characteristic of these "low" genres allow for the empowerment of female victims and the disempowerment of male aggressors. It is important to note that this fluid situation is not necessarily in the interests of feminism. For example, *Disclosure* (1994), in which a happily married businessman, played by Michael Douglas, is "raped" by his female boss (Demi Moore), reverses the pattern of female victim/male aggressor in what can only be construed as a highly anxious response to the power of women in the workplace. However, it should also be pointed out that the film highlights with startling clarity the fact that its motivating fantasy of sexual submission and dominance is not gender specific.

In light of the above discussion, the assumption that genres employ a single gender address can no longer be taken for granted. Nor can the potentially fluid situation of multiple address and plural identifications at work in popular cinema be associated simply with postclassical Hollywood. By the same token, the idea that certain genres are, or ever have been, more "suitable" for women as either viewers or as filmmakers has come under pressure. This is Kathryn Bigelow, quoted in Jim Hillier's book *The New Hollywood* (1993):

Conventionally, hardware pictures, action oriented, have been male dominated, and more emotional material has been women's domain. That's breaking down. This notion that there's a women's aesthetic, a woman's eye, is really debilitating. It ghettoizes women. The fact that so many women are working as directors now . . . across the spectrum, from comedy to horror to action . . . is incredibly positive. . . . You're asking the [Hollywood] community to reprogram their thinking. (127)

Bigelow perhaps overestimates the numbers of women directors who have moved into contemporary Hollywood, and it is well known that those who have made that difficult transition rarely make the "A" list. Without diminishing the real problems faced by women working in Hollywood, the historical contribution of women to cinema across the board has increasingly been recognized. This has involved a shift in perception—away from counting the relatively small numbers of female directors towards a more historical and contextual analysis of different points of entry into the industry by women in what is, after all, a collaborative medium. The influence of female audiences, and the considerable impact of different feminisms across the full range of production have begun to be addressed (Lant 2007).

Bigelow herself is a high-profile example of a crossover phenomenon—a woman director who works with traditionally male action genres, who collaborates with male filmmakers, and whose work cannot easily be assimilated in gender terms. Her films *Near Dark* (1987) and *Blue Steel* (1990), both generic hybrids, confront head-on difficult questions of violence and sexuality, while the bigger-budget *Point Break* (1991) and *Strange Days* (1995) handle the technical problems of blockbuster action filmmaking with masterly style and verve. In 2010, she became the first woman to win the Academy Award for best director with *The Hurt Locker* (2008), a compelling depiction of male heroism and violence set in the Iraq War. Like Ida Lupino almost fifty years earlier, Bigelow is a writer and producer as well as director, and interesting comparisons could be drawn between their production contexts and their work, particularly between Lupino's rape film *Outrage* and Bigelow's cop movie *Blue Steel,* which includes a rape-revenge scenario. The comparison suggests that the conjunction of post-1970s feminism and the presence of women filmmakers at all levels of the industry with the greater visibility of graphic sex and violence, deplored by many, has had some beneficial effects for women, in that it has allowed feminism to move into a wider arena. Women filmmakers can, it seems, now use sexually explicit and violent material to confront issues of representation before much larger audiences.

It also appears that the concerns of the paranoid woman's film have moved from the localized, domestic arena they occupied in the 1940s on to the global stage in the 1980s and 1990s. For example, in the *Alien* series a paranoid woman saves the world, while in *Terminator 2: Judgment Day* (1993) a paranoid woman changes the course of history. Thus the question I raised in my 1983 article, echoed in Kathryn Bigelow's comments above, about the ghettoizing effect of a woman's film defined in terms of an exclusive address to female spectators, has come full circle, answered, at least partially, by the increased gender fluidity and genre hybridity characteristic of the new Hollywood. However, I do not think we can make any assumptions about "progress," in feminist terms at least, based on a classical/postclassical divide.

If it is true that there are greater numbers of women working in contemporary Hollywood, the impact of the presence of women as producers, directors, writers, designers, actors, and critics remains unclear. How, for feminist purposes, do we weigh up the value of Jonathan Demme's feminist-influenced *The Silence of the Lambs* (1990) against Kathryn Bigelow's *Strange Days?* Is it the case, perhaps, that female audiences have at times exerted greater control over Hollywood production than those working inside the industry? As I have already suggested, only a historical investigation of the contribution of women to all aspects of cinema can assess the significance or otherwise of their contribution at specific conjunctures.[4] Such an investigation will produce a more complex map of the role of women in Hollywood cinema than models defined by exclusion and marginalization. This implies the need for a shift in the agendas and methodologies adopted by historians. These are just as much subject to social and cultural forces as the objects chosen for study, while the conclusions drawn from historical inquiry and evidence depend on what is being looked for.

Notes

This is an edited version of Pam Cook's earlier article, published in *Screening the Past* (London: Routledge, 2005). It was originally delivered as a paper at a conference on post-classical Hollywood at the University of Kent in 1995.

1. See, for example, Jackie Stacey's study of the interaction of female audiences with star figures (1994).

2. In *The Desire to Desire: The Woman's Film of the 1940s* (1987) Mary Ann Doane identifies an ironic approach to classical Hollywood narrative conventions as a characteristic of women's pictures.

3. See Catherine MacKinnon and Andrea Dworkin's radical feminist critique of pornography, cited by Linda Williams in *Hard Core* (17–18).

4. This work is now underway—see, for example, Lizzie Francke (1994), Jackie Stacey (1994), Miriam Hansen (1991) on Rudolph Valentino and female audiences, Antonia Lant (2007), and the University of Illinois Press Women and Film History series. See also the international Women Film Pioneers Project, based at Columbia University, Women and Film History International, and Women's Film and Television History Network–UK/Ireland.

CHAPTER 3

CIRCULATING EMOTION:

RACE, GENDER, AND GENRE IN *CRASH*

E. DEIDRE PRIBRAM

"I wake up like this every morning. I am angry
all the time . . . and I don't know why."
—Jean, *Crash*

Crash (Paul Haggis, 2005) follows a range of diverse but intersecting characters
who, in their entirety, are meant to represent a social landscape: modern American
urban existence. Through an ensemble cast and a multi-story structure, the film
depicts a circuitous society in which one part affects other parts that, in turn,
affect all parts.

The film is structured by means of three entangled, sometimes complementary,
sometimes competing, cultural discourses. The first discourse is race. In a deeply
troubling way, race is most overtly what the film is "about." In the world of the
film, virtually every character is at some point explicitly racist. Additionally, in
certain subplots, racial discourse is inextricably intertwined with gender.

The second discourse is law and order. Again, the majority of characters take
up a role in this discursive range. Some are the designated upholders of law and
order: District Attorney Rick Cabot (Brendan Fraser); uniformed police officer
John Ryan (Matt Dillon); police detective Graham Waters (Don Cheadle). Other
characters are either criminals like Anthony (Ludacris) and Peter (Larenz Tate),
or victims of crime like Jean Cabot (Sandra Bullock) and Daniel (Michael Peña).
Over the course of the film many come to occupy more than one position in the
law and order spectrum. The effect is a kaleidoscope of police officers, detectives,
criminals, crime victims, police officers who become criminals, criminals who
become the victims of crime, and so on.

The third discourse is anger. Although specifically voiced by Jean Cabot, her words, "I wake up like this every morning. I am angry all the time . . . and I don't know why," represent a moment of insight into the motivations of many of the people in this social landscape. The film's representation of anger is varying and nuanced, taking the form of outrage, frustration, distrust, or fear, provoked by different causes, and acted upon in different ways. Yet, it is a common denominator that further binds together the individuals who make up this metaphorical microcosm of contemporary society.

In this chapter, I take up the complex, multi-discursive world depicted in *Crash* in order to explore the place—or absence—of emotion in genre studies. Looking specifically at the moments of collision between characters in which the issues of race and gender are inseparable, I consider how anger specifically, and perhaps emotion in general, can be understood to ignite and fuel complex social relations. Such an analysis tells us about the ways emotions as cultural phenomena are understood or, equally, overlooked in media and other social representations.

EMOTION AND GENRE STUDIES

For the most part, and surprisingly, emotions have not been incorporated as a fundamental element in the analysis of genres. Rarely discussed in detail, emotion is often noted. For instance, Corrigan and White note that "horror films are about fear—physical fear, psychological fear, sexual fear, even social fear" (2004, 309). Similarly, from Bordwell and Thompson: "Thrillers obviously aim to thrill us—that is, to startle, shock, and scare" (2004, 113), and "some genres are defined by the distinctive emotional effect they aim for: amusement in comedy, tension in suspense films" (109). Despite this widespread identification of emotional values across genres, and the "obviously" emotional component of specific genres, little systematic study has been undertaken on the place and function of emotion as an integral component of "genreness," or on the role particular emotions might play in the development of specific genres.

There are exceptions to this, for example, in the study of melodrama. Even so, emotion in melodrama too often has been considered in terms of its usually problematic "excess." Steve Neale, citing Daniel Gerould, describes the dominant tendency of melodrama as involving "the subordination of all other elements 'to one overriding aesthetic goal: the calling forth of "pure," "vivid" emotions'" (1995, 179). While seeming to celebrate the presence of emotion in melodrama, this view constructs it as dominant to the detriment of all else.

In contrast, Linda Williams (1998) argues that characterizing melodrama as emotionally excessive obscures the pivotal and complex role of emotion in melodramatic forms and in American popular culture in general.

We are diverted, therefore, from the significance of melodrama if we pay too much attention to what has been condemned as its excessive emotionality and

theatricality. . . . They are the means to something more important: the achievement of a felt good, the merger . . . of morality and feeling. (55)

The achievement of a "felt good" is the recognition of a commonly held notion
of morality through the narrative establishment of guilt and innocence. In popular
cinema, we are led to feel the pathos of "protagonists beset by forces more powerful than they and who are perceived as victims" (42), and we come to believe that
"virtue and truth can be achieved in private individuals and individual heroic
acts" (74). In Williams's argument, the narrative *mode* of melodrama, featuring
the dialectic of emotion and physical action, enables us to recognize and deeply
identify with victimization, innocence, and redemptive acts of justice. Emotion
is, therefore, an integral part of most popular film genres that seek to determine
or reinforce principles of morality and justice. However, she argues, due to the
critical association of particular melodramatic genres, like the woman's film and
the family melodrama, with excessive sentimentality and female audiences, melodrama itself is often perceived as the antithesis of supposedly non-emotional
masculine genres, such as the western or the gangster film (50).

As a result, in many popular genres, particularly those understood as masculine, the relationship of emotional action to physical action has been overlooked.
The separating out of emotionality and physicality in film studies, each to be
positioned as the antithesis of the other—present only where the other is not—
leads to a misreading of much popular American cinema. The significance of the
coupling of emotional and bodily action is that it enables the impulse for justice
to be represented. Williams suggests it is time to return to an understanding of
"moving pictures" in both senses of the term: as movement in action and as the
ability to move us emotionally (47). Following Williams, I consider the role of
anger in *Crash* and, in particular, how it relates to the film's central concern with
the impulse for justice in the context of the injustices of racism.

JUSTICE GENRES

Through its multi-storied structure, *Crash* evokes a range of police, detective,
criminal, and legal genres. It appears less concerned with fulfilling the expectations tied to a single genre than in accessing the discourses of law and order
within which all these genres are embedded, seeking in particular the factors that
produce obstacles to the impulse for justice. The film's multiple generic citations
cohere because they share a common foundation in the processes or failures of
juridically established right and wrong, innocence and guilt.

In the justice genres—the representational forms that reinforce and sometimes
call into question widely held conceptualizations of justice—the emotion of anger
plays a pivotal role. Sometimes it is the criminal who is motivated by anger, turning to transgressive behavior in response to perceived offenses, whether personal
or social, committed against him or her. If not motivated by comprehensible,

"reasonable" anger, the criminal wrongdoer is often deranged—"mad" in both senses of the term. Anger, mixed with sorrow and grief, is a common emotion felt by the victims of crime, or by the victims' surrogates, their family and friends, who seek justice on behalf of themselves or their loved ones, normally manifested as desire for the detection, arrest, and prosecution of the offender—a juridical reckoning for their personal loss.

Police officials, detectives (public or private), and legal personnel are often motivated by anger: moral indignation at the transgressions committed by the offending party; sympathy for the victims that becomes displaced as outrage at the perpetrators. Anger, then, often motivates behavior leading to the capture of the wrongdoer and the reinstatement of an equilibrium of law and order. In turn, physical action is the typical form in which representatives of law and order offer comfort and consolation to crime victims and their surrogates.

Given *Crash*'s preoccupation with injustices around race, it draws on genres that closely link justice and anger. The film portrays the way people interact with one another in contemporary American urban society as analogous to a car accident. Sometimes the crash is a rear-end collision, sometimes head-on, but rarely are people depicted as interacting with others through tenderness, sympathy, concern, curiosity, affection, and so on. The "feeling angry all the time" identified by Jean produces encounter-as-collision: the only form of human contact available in this depicted world. So Anthony, the car thief, rails against the social injustices of racial discrimination. Jean, the victim of a carjacking, is angry at having been made to feel afraid. Graham, both detective and victim, seeks his brother's murderer both as law enforcer and avenger of his family's loss.

Although originating within generic foundations of crime and punishment, anger in the film is not limited to the specific purpose of pursuing wrongdoers and reinstating an equilibrium of justice. In the first place, no equilibrium of justice seems attainable in *Crash*'s social landscape of encounter-as-collision. Second, anger in the film is elevated into a force that propels social relations, most notably racism. The fact that anger is not solely a property of the individual, either a personal flaw that leads to criminal acts or a personal strength that enables law enforcement officials to do their jobs, is precisely what renders *Crash*'s depiction of anger notable. Instead, anger in *Crash* is a climate of the times, dispersed and shared across the social landscape, connecting otherwise estranged individuals, and helping to form a community of sorts, "in anger." Emotion as represented in *Crash* functions as a cultural, not a personal, property.

RACE/GENDER

In order to explore how the film envisions anger as propelling social relations, I focus on a specific series of events in which the issues of race and gender are complexly interwoven and inseparable. This race/gender sequence involves insurance representative Shaniqua Johnson (Loretta Devine), police officer John Ryan, and married couple Christine (Thandie Newton) and Cameron Thayer (Terence Howard). Like the ensemble metaphor underpinning the film in which one part affects all parts, their stories function as a relay of action, moving from one to the other to form a circuit, motivated by anger, exercised through racial and gendered identity, which then escalates with stunning consequences.

We are first introduced to Shaniqua Johnson, an African American administrator for a medical insurance company, and John Ryan, a white, uniformed Los Angeles police officer, during a phone conversation intercut between them. Ryan calls Johnson's office after-hours to complain that his father is in a great deal of pain and can't sleep. Johnson is unhelpful, insisting that because his father's urinary tract infection does not constitute an emergency, she can't help outside daytime office hours. In subsequent scenes, we learn that his father's pain is due to misdiagnosis by his insurance-company-assigned doctor. Ryan's anger, therefore, resonates as understandable. A frustrated Ryan asks for her name.

Johnson: Shaniqua Johnson.
Ryan: Shaniqua. Big fucking surprise that is.

Johnson abruptly hangs up on him, both characters exiting the phone conversation in states of anger.

Singling out Johnson's recognizably African American first name, Ryan's angry reaction is to suggest that the problem (whether her unwillingness to help or her insurance company's incompetence) is attributable to the fact that Johnson is black. Conflict over a medical issue has shifted to a racial confrontation, leaving both parties angrier than when they began. Ryan's anger is partly motivated by his frustration in failing to help his father but also by his powerlessness in the situation. Ryan is a man used to exerting power over others, a cop accustomed to being listened to, as his later behavior makes clear.

The fact that Johnson is both African American and a woman is not incidental. Ryan's inability to compel Johnson to do as he wishes challenges his sense of authority as a police officer, as a white person, and as a man. Thus his next act attempts to reinstate his shaken sense of masculinity as much as it is intended to reestablish his racial and professional authority. Hanging up the phone, Ryan returns to his police car and waiting partner, Tommy Hanson (Ryan Phillippe), and pulls over a black SUV driven by an African American man.

Ryan has stopped an affluent African American married couple, Christine and Cameron Thayer. In retribution for his experience with Johnson, he proceeds to harass them with the skill and efficiency of practiced methods. Unlike his recent phone demeanor, he never raises his voice, staying calm and superficially polite the entire time that he provokes, threatens, and humiliates them. His composure, in this instance, seems to return with his control over the situation, control that he lost when dealing with Johnson.

Christine and Cameron are initially polite and accommodating; indeed, they find amusement in the situation because Christine was in the process of giving her husband oral sex when they were pulled over. However, as the harassment escalates, Christine becomes vocally angry. For his part, Cameron attempts to placate Ryan by being as compliant and nonconfrontational as possible.

Failing to render Christine docile, and on the pretext of performing a body search to check for concealed weapons, Ryan proceeds to sexually assault her. Returning from a party, Christine is wearing a cocktail dress that conceals very little, negating the necessity for such a search but making Ryan's hands all the more intrusive. The assault begins with a wide shot of all four characters present—two civilians, two officers—as Ryan runs his hands along Christine's breasts under her dress. It continues in close-up on rotating shots of each of the four faces, intercut with tight shots of Ryan's hands as they violate various parts of Christine's body. Crouching down behind her, Ryan fondles Christine's buttocks, runs his hands slowly down her legs, caresses each ankle, then brings his hands back up between her legs and reaches into her crotch. In a close-up on her face, we see Christine flinch and gasp at the moment of penetration.

However, the assault is not visualized primarily through shots of Ryan's hands on Christine's body. Instead, the scene plays as a relay of close-ups on the faces of the four people present. Though thirty-two tight shots comprise the scene, only three of these directly show Ryan's hands. The remaining twenty-nine close-ups focus on the characters' facial expressions as they watch, perform, or endure the assault: a total of ten shots on Cameron, eight on Ryan, seven on Christine, and four on Hanson. The focal point of the scene is on the characters' emotional responses, rather than on the physical occurrence of the sexual assault.

During the entire time Ryan is violating Christine's body, he is—calmly, "politely"—looking at and talking to Cameron. The content of Ryan's remarks focus on threatening Cameron and his wife with arrest for reckless endangerment and lewd conduct. Finally, his hand penetrating Christine's vagina, Ryan asks Cameron, "What do you think we should do, sir?" In the moment of final defeat, Cameron apologizes to him: "Look we're sorry and we would appreciate it if you would just let us go with a warning. Please." Only at this moment, when Ryan has completely subdued and humiliated Christine and, the text suggests, emasculated Cameron, thereby supposedly regaining his own masculine status, does Ryan step back from Christine and let the couple go.

The encounter between policeman John Ryan and Christine and Cameron Thayer is established as egregiously racist. Ryan's behavior towards the couple generates one of the most disturbing sequences in the film, especially horrific because his actions are so purposeful—intentionally racist, intentionally humiliating—and deriving from the motive of misplaced vengeance. However, while the narrative purpose of the Ryan-Thayer confrontation is a deliberate critique of the debilitating effects of racism, what the encounter represents about gender relations is not exposed in a similar manner. In its construction as a relay of close-ups between characters, the scene works dominantly as an interaction between Ryan and Cameron. Christine's body and person serve as the surface upon which this showdown between the men takes place, explaining why the greatest number of close-ups and screen time belong to Cameron, followed by Ryan. In one sense, Christine has become a witness to the events happening to her, akin to Hanson who, through his own series of close-ups, registers his angry disgust at Ryan's racist abuse of power.

The main event occurs between the two principal male characters, one white, one black. Christine's body is separated from the integrity of her person—displayed as discrete, tight fragments under the control of Ryan's hands—primarily to make a point about male power and authority between races. Ryan is able to humiliate Cameron because, if Cameron doesn't possess Christine's body outright, as her husband his identity is inscribed upon it. Ryan controls Christine's body through touch, but as the direction of his gaze and words make clear, Cameron is the person he is challenging. In the confrontation between Ryan and Cameron, the stakes are played out over race *and* masculinity.

As part of the relay of emotion, in which the circuit progresses from person to person, the encounter with Ryan also incites conflict between Christine and Cameron. In a bitter argument once they arrive home, Christine explicitly ties the confrontation with Ryan to the issue of masculinity, taking up and articulating the basis of Ryan's unspoken challenge to and defeat of Cameron: "What I need is a husband who will not just stand there while I'm being molested" and "[do] you have any idea how that felt? To have that pig's hands all over me. And you just stood there. And then you apologized to him."

Christine and Cameron's disagreement brings up issues concerning race, in their case what it means to "be black," as professionals and upper-middle-class African Americans. But the accusations based on gender, on what Christine has the right to expect from her husband, are as pointed and hurtful. Like Ryan, Christine attacks Cameron on the grounds of his virility, or lack of it. In the process, by taking up the argument in Ryan's terms, her character reaffirms her "feminine" identity as principally the body or ground upon which masculine relations are determined.

Simultaneously, Christine and Cameron dispute different approaches to social relations, particularly the appropriateness or inappropriateness of anger when dealing with conflict. Christine's strategy is to fight back rather than acquiesce. The fact that Cameron has apologized (and apparently not the sexual assault itself) is what most upsets Christine, and what she believes humiliates Cameron as a man and as an African American. When Cameron walks out of their bedroom in anger, Christine has the last words of the scene: "That's good. A little anger. It's a bit late but it's nice to see."

In contrast, Cameron conceals anger, conciliates, in the hope of defusing the situation. Acting out anger or suppressing it are generally stereotyped as, respectively, masculine and feminine modes of behavior. In this instance, however, it is Christine who takes up the stereotypically "masculine" position while Cameron is aligned with the conventionally "feminine" stance. Christine's character finds fault with her husband on the grounds of his apparent failure to exhibit "authentic" masculinity, rather than calling Ryan's structuration of race *and* gender to account. Similarly, Cameron's alignment with a more acquiescent "feminine" position makes his encounter with Ryan all the more humiliating. This leads to a later, highly confrontational scene completely at odds with his earlier demeanor, when he attempts "suicide-by-cop," taunting several police officers with provocations to shoot him. His death or injury is prevented only by the intervention of coincidentally present Officer Hanson.

In narrative terms, though, Cameron saves himself. As Hanson works to defuse the situation, Cameron refuses to acquiesce this time. He defies Hanson's instructions to put his hands on his head, sit on the curb, or engage in any other action that Cameron believes is demeaning. Through his newfound anger Cameron establishes a renewed equilibrium of masculinity for himself. A significant aspect of the representation of anger in *Crash*, confirming a commonly held social perspective, is that anger is most appropriately male, indeed, an essential property of masculinity. Cameron's humiliation and dignity have become the principal issues, leaving Christine's arguably more humiliating experience of sexual assault to fall by the wayside. The degradation of the sexual assault is primarily Cameron's, and only secondarily, Christine's.

Through the complex dealings among this subset of characters, we begin to understand how *Crash* depicts anger as a force shaping social relations. Anger functions like a relay, traveling from one person to the next, altering its manifestations and effects in the process, but constructing an ongoing social circuit.

CIRCULATING EMOTION

Recently, cultural theorists have begun to explore the organization and functions of emotions as social events. Sara Ahmed, for instance, argues that the pertinent question is what emotions do and how they circulate, rather than what they "are" (2004, 4). Under the dominance of psychology, most models have posited emotions as interiority, as the effects of individual self-expression, in which the question, "How do I feel?" is understood as the most penetrating means of locating and analyzing the meaning of emotions (8). In contrast, other scholars have begun to argue "that emotions should not be regarded as psychological states, but as social and cultural practices" (9).

In Ahmed's analysis, emotions occur through the movement or circulation of subjects, objects, or concepts that have become "saturated with affect, as sites of personal and social tension" (11). *Crash* takes up the issue of race precisely in terms of its extensive and tangled saturation of affect. In the film's world, anger is not simply an individual flaw or failing, or a motivator to jump-start law enforcement action. It is, in Raymond Williams's terms, a "structure of feeling," a culturally widespread complex of emotion by which social relations are negotiated and exchanged (2009). Emotional experience, then, is a pivotal means by which the individual and the cultural are seamlessly interwoven and simultaneously produced. I would add that because social relations never occur beyond or outside of social differences, structures of feeling are also a means by which power circulates, establishing and reestablishing its discrepancies.

In order to determine what the film has to say about anger as a structure of feeling that shapes contemporary social relations, we need to turn to the inverse, the matched action, of the sexual assault scene: the fiery car crash in which Ryan rescues Christine.

NARRATIVE PAIRINGS: EMOTIONAL AND PHYSICAL ACTION

The most prolonged, elaborate physical action sequence of the film, the rescue scene, requires the heightened intensity of bodily action to offset the emotional and moral depths to which Ryan has descended in his encounter with the Thayers, thereby functioning as dramatic compensation for Ryan's sexual violation of Christine. In this sequence, Christine finds herself in a life-threatening car accident and Ryan, her recent aggressor, manages, at great personal risk, to free her in the nick of time, dragging her to safety seconds before the car bursts into flames.

Three aspects of the rescue sequence are particularly pertinent in a consideration of the relationship between emotional and physical action. First, the rescue sequence transforms the emotional tension between Christine and Ryan into the corporeal tension of the last-minute escape. Ryan behaves in a generically familiar way as a male officer in a police drama, performing as a "man of action" rather than confronting his own shame or regret. This suggests that one of the roles of physical activity is to offset the necessity for emotional action and accountability. In this sense, bodily endeavor may be used as a defense against recognizing feelings. Physicality in place of emotional encounter dispels the necessity of acknowledging difficult feelings, allowing for some kind of resolution to the problem, although an indirect one.

The second aspect is that in rescuing Christine, the film suggests that Ryan has redeemed his previous racist and sexist violent behavior. In other words, the transformation of emotional conflict into physical action enables a particular ritualized redemptive process to occur. Once Ryan extricates Christine from the car, he walks her to an awaiting ambulance as Christine leans her head against his chest, crying. When the emergency medical specialists lead Christine away, we watch an out-of-breath Ryan as he continues to look after her—looking after her visually now, as he looked after her physically moments earlier. The scene cuts to a close-up of Christine as she reciprocates Ryan's look. Then, in arguably the most manipulative shot of the scene, the camera returns to Ryan down on one knee, in his police uniform, a fire truck and smoke filling the background behind him. This is *Crash*'s "9/11 shot," an image reminiscent of the first responders at the scene when the World Trade Center towers collapsed. This iconic reference appears intended to engage audience empathy for Ryan and admiration for what he has done in rescuing Christine.

The lingering exchange of looks between Christine and Ryan conjures up the familiar exchange of gazes between parted lovers in romance genres. In the mutual relay of gazes, we are meant to understand that something has transpired between the two, something of an intimate nature. If, however, the final exchange of looks suggests that Ryan, through the exchange of physical exertion for emotional engagement, has redeemed himself, there is no immediate correlation between the act of redemption and the earlier transgression for which he must morally account. That is, his physical exploit does not directly address the nature of the earlier conflict between the two. As a result, how redemption through physical activity occurs remains unclear. We might assume that Christine looks back at Ryan in gratitude for saving her life. Perhaps we are meant to interpret Christine's return gaze as her reciprocating action, the act of forgiveness.

Ryan's motivations and emotions, and therefore his current moral status in the narrative, remain murkier. Does his physical effort negate the necessity for articulated or performed emotional exchange because, in saving Christine, he has canceled out his previous debt? Has he effectively apologized, his extraordinary efforts to rescue Christine the acknowledgment of his errors? Does he go to such extremes in the rescue attempt, placing his own life in jeopardy, because he feels guilt? Remorse? Shame? In light of the 9/11 shot, are we meant to understand that the job makes him heroic despite his other flaws because in the final analysis he follows the dictum to serve and protect? Or does his previous conduct endanger his professional competence because, in losing Christine's trust, he nearly fails to save her? All of these are credible interpretations, leaving indeterminate how, precisely, physical display reinstates moral equilibrium.

The third aspect of the rescue sequence significant to a consideration of the relationship between emotional and physical action is that Christine's character is not afforded a similar enlightening, compensating, or clarifying feat. The car crash rescue scene is most centrally about Ryan and his redemption that, like his most egregious transgression, occurs upon the ground of Christine's body. She is "the rescued one," serving the role of victim, to be dragged back to life through the literal and figurative wreckage that surrounds her. Since Christine has not erred as Ryan has, she does not require the same degree of redemption. However, narrative physical action functions not only to redeem individual moral failings but also to right social and personal imbalances. Bodily acts also operate as a way of dealing with emotional events, providing the means to survive such events, as in the case of Christine's husband, Cameron.

Cameron's racial and masculine identities are recouped by the physical act of standing up to the second set of police officers he encounters, affording him the opportunity to reclaim his identity as an African American and as a man. In the process, Cameron also reclaims his emotional and psychological equilibrium by regaining his dignity and, therefore, his will to live. No similar action sequence is offered Christine. She is always *acted upon*. Both Cameron's and Christine's lives are physically threatened; his in the suicidal confrontation with the police, hers by the car crash. Both their lives are also threatened in metaphorical terms, by the loss of a sense of self. However, Cameron finds his own way back. Christine, on the other hand, is "rescued"—and by the very character who jeopardized her well-being in the first place. She is the ground or site for others' realizations: for Ryan by assaulting her body and then rescuing it; for Cameron in losing his own identity as a result of what occurs upon her body, but then acting to retrieve his self-respect.

That some characters are provided with the possibility for self-redemptive physical acts, while others are not, suggests that action itself is culturally gendered. Privileging action as the rightful realm of certain characters maintains an interconnectedness between masculinity, generic anger, and physical action. Although susceptibility to emotions in general is socially coded as feminine, anger, a highly potent emotion for concepts such as justice, is more likely in the law and order genres to be coded as masculine.

The narrative interconnectedness of masculinity, anger, and action allows the justice genres to utilize anger as their propelling emotion while continuing to be perceived as a masculine genre. Further, the transformation of emotional into physical action enables the narratively vital presence of emotion to be concealed, resulting in the false perception of action-based films, such as the justice genres, as non-emotional forms of storytelling. As Linda Williams argues, this has led to the historic tendency in film studies to establish an erroneous dichotomy between genres—*either* emotion *or* action—instead of tracing the crucial relationship *between* emotional and physical action in popular film.

POWER AND SATURATION

Anger is depicted in *Crash* not as a property of the individual—as barometer of a personal psyche—but as a structure of feeling that propels social relations. This distinction is exemplified by the degree of and access to anger allowed specific characters, as defined by social differentials and unequal power relations. Power is a critical element in the cultural exchange of emotions. As Ahmed's work suggests, the saturation of words and actions with cultural affect is pivotal to the mechanisms by which emotion circulates, generating social relations that *affect* others.

In the argument between Christine and Cameron in the aftermath of Ryan's assault, Christine's claim that Cameron's behavior indicates a lack of self-respect is based on a complex network of racial relations in which individual and racial pride are linked to angry defiance in the face of socially enforced racial inequities. The non-expression of anger in this context is a sign, then, of surrender to or compliance with racial injustices. The attack on Cameron's self-esteem succeeds as a result of a mutually understood context of social insult and debasement in the operation of race relations.

Functioning in a similar manner is Ryan's remarkably concise response to Shaniqua Johnson when she tells him her name: "Shaniqua. Big fucking surprise that is." This can only be understood—by Ryan, Johnson, and the audience— as a deliberate racial insult on the basis of knowledge of African American names and, more importantly, historical and contemporary racist assumptions in the United States that question African Americans' competencies. We cannot understand or participate in cultural configurations of social power without a complex network of knowledge about one's own and others' social standings in the context of a prevailing set of social relations and constructed identities. It is this knowledge that enables our words and behaviors to be saturated with affect.

Anger, as an experience or expression, cannot be understood if removed from its anchoring social relations and practices, hence the different consequences of expressing anger for Christine, Cameron, and Ryan. Christine is portrayed as losing her dignity and notion of self-worth by expressing her anger to Ryan, while Cameron manages to preserve something—their safety?—by relinquishing his anger and performing obsequiousness. Further, the expression or non-expression of anger does not determine whether the exertion of power through anger is successful. Its demonstration is effective between Christine and Cameron—she manages to wound him—but ineffective between Christine and Ryan, while the greatest exertion of power in this particular subplot occurs when Ryan's anger is not overtly exhibited.

The ineffectiveness of Christine's rage at Ryan has much to do with the gendered identities of women characters. The association of women with disproportionate emotionality, as in the "excessive" emotion of melodrama, allows the perception of women's deployments of anger as uncontrolled and uncontrollable—fits of passion. Conversely, a cultural association between masculinity and controlled rage—a cold, "reasoned," anger—helps account for the biting effectivity of Ryan's calm, "polite" assault.

The majority of characters in *Crash* have clear psychological reasons for their anger. However, the film doesn't delve deeply into their individual psychological states, nor does it question the validity of their psychological motivations. Instead, it takes individual psychological manifestations—the reality that in this world everyone is angry, and mostly for good reason—as a starting point from which to narrativize the effects of anger as they are exerted and circulated in the social context of the film.

CONCLUSION

As a final note, I would like to return to Linda Williams's idea of "a felt good," a commonly shared morality recognized through the establishment of narrative guilt and innocence. In this argument, one of the benefits of the melodramatic mode is that it enables audiences to identify with representations of innocence and redemptive acts of justice as a reaction against the guilts of victimization, injustice, and immorality.

Speaking of the specific case of theatrical melodrama, Christine Gledhill notes that throughout the nineteenth century it functioned effectively as a central cultural paradigm (1987, 19). Melodrama's qualities of sentimentalism and spectacle and its moral dilemmas based on binary antagonisms of good and evil could articulate the values and conflicts of the age. Yet, its widespread critical acceptability in the nineteenth century declined fairly abruptly early in the twentieth century, no longer making sense of the world in as compelling a manner.

Instead of melodrama's "felt good," the prevalence of the law and order genres, in their stories based on justice, anger, and failed or limited redemption, indicate something akin to a "felt guilt," in the juridical sense, a shared culpability that represents a more resonant contemporary cultural paradigm. While nineteenth-century melodrama emphasizes the recognition of innocence and moral virtue through pathos, contemporary justice genres privilege an ideological structuration that calls forth the identification of moral guilt by means of both justifiable and unjustifiable anger. In these terms, *Crash* points to an alternative cultural paradigm in which concepts of a harsher form of justice, impelled by anger, supersede an earlier moment dominated by the possibility of innocence and moral virtue.

In comparison to anger, pathos is a naïve but, simultaneously, more forgiving emotional paradigm. Moral virtue remains attainable through pathos. In contrast, justice, in its more contemporary conceptualization, is preoccupied with the establishment of a shared notion of guilt. As *Crash* indicts, all parties, in some way, share in the collective cultural guilt of racism.

CHAPTER 4

100% PURE ADRENALINE:

GENDER AND GENERIC SURFACE IN *POINT BREAK*

LUKE COLLINS

The platform for this chapter is the contention that we experience *Point Break* (1991) as generic surface. Despite critical efforts to construct the film as a creative play with masculinity or with the action genre, the film remains culturally and politically ambivalent. As is often noted, *Point Break* repeats the "vessel" of the action genre without rupture, spillage, or slippage. In this sense *Point Break* expresses an awareness of its cultural/commercial form by filling out the homosocial trope latent in the action genre's intense male relationships and fetishization of the male body. But, I argue, at no point does it seek to exceed, parody, ironize, or reflect upon its genre. The fullness that this produces is a flatness: a surface. This surface is not a negative construction but provides a way to address the network of relations between film, audience, and industry.

Surface becomes a challenge for theory and criticism that traditionally rely on paradigms of cultural depth. As a theoretical proposition, surface asks: How can we assess the importance of a work, whether in generic or gendered terms, if its aim is not to interrupt cultural or political discourse? If its object is not the penetration of this discourse but its repetition? I use such provocative terms intentionally to argue the gendering of value in cultural criticism *outwith* the director's biological sex. Academic criticism often reads *Point Break* within a political agenda—"female director makes action films as political statement"—or emphazises questions around masculinity and male specular desire. Meanwhile Kathryn Bigelow has remained reticent about the political and cultural resonance of her work. This emphasis on gender serves to give Bigelow an auteur's voice within the patriarchal cultural hierarchy but misunderstands the interest of *Point Break,* which, significantly, marked her movement from independent to industrial filmmaking.[1]

This misapplies a model of authorship that has been shown to be unsustainable in relation to industrial film production. While representation of gender in the film adheres to precedents within the genre, as an act of generic repetition *Point Break* has important *gendered* implications for cultural theory. This essay's exploration of generic gender as surface challenges gender distinctions and divisions that define a heterosexual action film as conformist and a homoerotic one as progressive. It proposes a reading of *Point Break* that attempts to avoid the binary trap of constructing the film (and by implication culture more broadly) as either subversive/progressive or conformist. I am using surface as a critical construct to intervene in how film theory has approached genre and gender.

GENDER AND GENERIC SURFACE

Surface is the sophisticated and seamless production of a series of recognizable signs made available for consumption by the audience. The audience actively chooses to give themselves over to the ride. These signs (this surface) are engaged as a performance or a production, not an essential reality. Culture is experienced in a context of repetitive social rituals that form a tight circle of engagement between producer and audience. The arena of this engagement (cinema, television, advertising) is negotiated and well understood by both producer and audience, allowing for novelty, or even self-reflection, within the *content* while leaving extant power relations intact.

It is easy to understand how this construction of surface relates to genre as a negotiated repetitious space. The action genre repeats sets of recognizable tropes negotiating a set of expectations in the viewer. We understand these parameters, we read them and they inform our choices well before the opening credits roll. Our enjoyment of a film can be defined in relation to how the film meets or deviates from these expectations. Sometimes we want deviation, challenge, and invention and sometimes our viewing pleasure is dependent on how much the film conforms to a set of parameters negotiated through marketing; or how much a film performs or repeats the tropes of its genre.

In approaching gender as surface, do the genders become culturally less differentiated? This question can be pursued through *Point Break,* where there is a convergence of gender representations. We read signs of masculinity and femininity across both male and female characters who physically are thrown into androgynous relief. We also clearly experience both heterosexual and homo*social* tension.

This gender equivalence might be read as critique of action cinema but I would argue instead that it responds to a changing understanding of demographics and taste. The argument that any inflection of a stereotyped image serves critical purpose ignores the commercial logic that uses a plethora of representations across popular cinema. In line with changing social and political forces, representation changes, in part, to access larger changing markets.

BIGELOW, *POINT BREAK,* AND GENDERED CULTURAL VALUE

The ways in which *Point Break* has been interpreted and used within the critical construction of Kathryn Bigelow highlights the continued gendering of cultural value. This points to underlying issues that need to be addressed in cultural theory beyond the evident gender gap in the cultural canon. The marked discrepancies in scholarly criticism of Bigelow (from avant-garde auteur to artistic bankruptcy) highlight the gap between what the films themselves tell us and how Bigelow's practice as a director is constructed within cultural politics. This discrepancy can be attributed to the critical supposition that in order for her work to be considered valuable it must be constructed in oppositional relation to the extant (sexist) cultural hierarchy.

The construction of Bigelow proposed across the essays in Sean Redmond and Deborah Jermyn's 2003 volume *The Cinema of Kathryn Bigelow: Hollywood Transgressor,* the only book dedicated to her work, and by Yvonne Tasker (1993 and 1999), who has written most consistently on Bigelow, suggests that she actively intervenes in cultural discourse through the production of films that disrupt, challenge, and subvert models of gender and generic relations: that she does this through "blends" and "bends": through unusual combinations and the fusing of opposites that directly critique the history of Hollywood cinema.

Redmond notes that in a call for papers for the volume, no submissions were received dealing with *Point Break.* Redmond takes up the challenge, seeking a place for the film within a reading of "Bigelow the auteur" by performing some theoretical gymnastics.

> I want to explore what I consider to be the stylistic and political depth(s) of this supposedly sugar coated action spectacle, and to find Bigelow's voice, her knowing and troubling cinematic gaze. . . . Bigelow I will contend, is an outsider on the inside, subverting the machine from within. (2003, 106–7)

Similarly Tasker (1999) argues:

> Bigelow never presents herself as making "art" despite Hollywood's limita-tions—her subversion of genre is derived not from dissatisfaction or contempt but rather demonstrates a genuine involvement with popular cinema. And this subversion is as often the result of stretching or combining genres as of up-ending them. (14)

While Tasker (rightly) proposes Bigelow's genuine engagement with popular cin-ema, she emphasizes Bigelow's subversion of that same popular cinema. Within her critical framework, it is only through this subversion that Bigelow's genuine engagement can be valued. For the important critique of an exclusive and sexist cultural history, it is unsurprising that critical effort is exerted to accede women into this extant model. However, this may not help us to clearly address the film.

In a review of *The Cinema of Kathryn Bigelow* for *Filmwaves* magazine (2003), Valentina Vitali further problematises this strategy:

> In the 1970s, feminist film theory and author-structuralism sought to understand not simply what makes an author. . . . As a pre-requisite to address that question was a questioning of film theory itself, not simply of the role of film theory in auteur construction. . . . None of the theories featuring in this monograph question existing theoretical parameters. On the contrary, various brands of theory are "marketed" in order to be recognised as legitimate candidates for institutionalization. (26)

When we return to Bigelow's films themselves, the gap between these critical constructions and both the films' narrative content and their conditions of production becomes apparent. Nowhere is this more evident than in *Point Break*.

THE VALUE OF REPETITION

What is the relationship between repetition and generic production? Genre is in fact a highly mobile category, and the bounds of generic purity cannot be clearly drawn within an industrial context that is constantly developing and shifting in terms of popular narrative. Generic production functions through the play of familiarity and difference, rather than fixing static criteria. The development of generic hybrids, along with other forms of intertextuality, adds, as Tasker suggests, a further complexity to our understanding of genre in contemporary Hollywood cinema (1993, 55). However, she later notes that the critical reception of *Point Break* "judged [it] to enact rather than subvert genre" (1999, 14), while Hannah Ransley argues that "the 1991 film *Point Break* is Bigelow's biggest commercial success to date, perhaps because it most successfully conforms to its action genre" (2002, 46–51). Taken together these analyses articulate the binary opposition in critical approaches to the film. Either genre is flexible (and thus repetition is not itself but creatively moderated in conditions of fluidity and difference) or, genre is fixed and repetition is flat, serving no critical interest; *Point Break* perfectly repeats the action genre. My question asks what implications does considering the film as repetition have for our understanding of popular forms? How does the repetition inherent in these films function and what implications does it have for genre and gender theory?

To say that *Point Break* repeats the action genre is not to say that there is an essential form from which all other action films derive or which they corrupt. Instead, there is a constellation of motifs that are used by the industry, by filmmakers, and by the audience to recognize and condition the experience of action cinema. Genres are not preexistent forms but are defined through relationships between texts (and importantly how they are used/consumed by the audience). This intertextuality isn't so much a question of bricolage, or of quotation (ironic or not), as of a shared space in which the negotiation of "what is and what isn't" takes place. The genre of action cinema is particularly nebulous because it describes an energetic state within the film rather than a narrative device. The action genre is marked by the presence of spectacular set pieces, physical violence, and, lately, the deployment of increasingly fast-paced editing. It is also marked by a variety of generic inflections, including war, detection, martial arts, science fiction, fantasy, and many other combinations. My argument that *Point Break* repeats its generic form is based on the film's production of spectacular and innovative action sequences that play an equally, if not more, important role as the narrative in the consumption of the film. In this regard I seek to define a point between criticism of the film that condemns it as mere repetition and appraisal that stakes all on its innovation and authorial intent. I am trying to articulate my own experience of the film, which remains attentive to the surface.

GENDER EQUIVALENCE

A reading of homoerotic frisson in *Point Break* has been used to argue that the film transgresses the action genre and "male norms" (Lane 2000; Grant 2004; Tasker 1993; Redmond 2003). "Homoeroticism is central to the male action movie, and while gay desire might be unspoken within dialogue, it is very much present within the frame" (Tasker 1993, 154). Much is made of the catalyst for Utah's recognition of the bank robbers' identities—the camera's tight focus on "a surfer's ass." Barry Keith Grant (2004) reads the final sky-diving sequence as sublimated gay sex.[2] Meanwhile, Bigelow laughingly dismissed a question posed in a London Film Festival interview that asked if the finale of the foot-chase sequence is a metaphor for ejaculation.[3]

I question readings that elide male bonding and competitive homosociality with homoeroticism and homosexual desire. Here the over-emphatic search for a gay undercurrent in an emphatically commercial film aims for critical and subversive credibility rather than a nuanced recognition of what is possible generically in the representation of masculinity on screen. The charged relationship between Johnny Utah (Keanu Reeves) and Bodhi (Patrick Swayze) fills out the intense homosociality of action cinema rather than subverting or ironizing the genre. Tasker and Grant use a homoerotic strain in *Point Break* to argue its subversion of a more explicitly heterosexual mainstream. But neither Swayze's much quoted clues to his performance—that he wanted to play the relationship as a love story (Errigo 1991, 70)—nor Christina Lane's reading (1998) of the film's intense "homosocial" relations exceed the generic conventions of action cinema, which has a history of depicting intense and varied male relationships through *Top Gun* (1986), *Platoon* (1986), *Lethal Weapon* (1987), *Fight Club* (1999), and *Apocalypse Now* (1979).

There is chemistry, tension, and without doubt a subtle seduction between Utah and Bodhi. But to equate love, flirtation, and desire with specific sexualities cannot help us explore so nuanced an image of masculinity as Swayze performs. Such a performance—and similarly Dafoe's more explicitly sexualized rendition in *Platoon*—suggests that assumptions about male representation and male cultural identity need complicating. There is no simple masculinity, "typical men," or male norms "out there" (or indeed within cinema) to be reflected or subverted in the films. Furthermore, foregrounding a reading of explicit homoeroticism does not account for the narrative's explicitly heterosexual context.

The implications of how the film balances an intense homosocial relationship within a heterosexual context can be explored in its surfing sequences. Utah has learned to surf under the tutelage of female surfer Tyler (Lori Petty) and is trying but failing to infiltrate the surfer culture. In a subsequent scene, Bodhi intervenes as Utah is attacked by the "Razorhead" gang. Bodhi subsequently introduces the spirituality inherent in "true" surfing, which is equated with Utah's refusal to back down in the face of aggression. Bodhi invites Utah to a party at his house. At the party, this quasi-mystical and adrenaline-fueled rhetoric continues. We learn of Bodhi's quest to surf the "fifty-year storm." When he opines, "If you want the ultimate, you've got to be willing to pay the ultimate price," Tyler leaves, stating, "There's too much testosterone here!" and invites Utah to follow with a trailing hand. We cut and see Utah has followed her to a small chamber celebrating Bodhi and his acolytes' pursuits; their pictures engaged in "extreme sports" adorn the walls. Even with the finely honed quip, "I hope you're not buying into this banzai bullshit like the rest of Bodhi's moonies," Tyler cannot deflate the heated atmosphere of the scene. Bodhi arrives and in a close shot-countershot (which excludes Tyler), he challenges Utah to come surfing with them at night. Despite his fear and inexperience, Utah gets his first proper wave as he and Bodhi descend the water together. His shouts of delight and ecstasy demonstrate that he finally feels "*it*."[4] Bodhi is right beside him on the wave sharing this pleasure. We cut to a later scene with Utah and Tyler alone as they consummate their flirtation in a very delicately handled love scene.

Before I draw out the implications of these relations, let me call up another moment in the film. In an earlier scene when Utah is finally able to stand up and ride his first small waves, Tyler holds up her arms and jokingly but affectionately says, "You are surfing!" It is only when Bodhi overrides Tyler's warning, "He's not ready for this," that we hear Utah beside himself screaming, "I'm fucking surfing!" This scene shows how, while Tyler (a woman) can teach the mechanics of surfing, she cannot grant Utah access to its transcendent qualities. Bodhi overrides Tyler's sexual advances with his challenge to Utah, and we are shown a lingering, brooding, and intense look passed between the two men. Bodhi's challenge is intense but the heterosexual context is so explicitly stated that the film demands that we read it as social. It is once Utah has met that challenge that he returns to Tyler and they consummate their heterosexual flirtation. It is important to note two things: that any homoerotic temptation offered by Bodhi is played out in heterosexual coitus, and that the character of Tyler is given no power to influence Utah. To further this examination of the film's intense homosociality framed within an explicitly stated heterosexuality we can look to the publicity material. These show images of Utah and Bodhi clasping hands alongside both men embracing women (see figs. 4.1 and 4.2).

The concurrent statement of this heterosexuality with Bodhi's seduction of Utah allows the homosocial tension to be consumed without any "threat" to the industry's assumption of the mainstream audience's heterosexuality. My contention is that these contradictory representations function as a set of signs consumed for their (delicious) tension within the "social safety net" of the characters' heterosexuality. Further, does not the argument that homosocial bonding is prevalent in the action film—and in popular culture and social relations generally—suggest that there is no such thing as purely hetero- or homosexuality? That human rela-

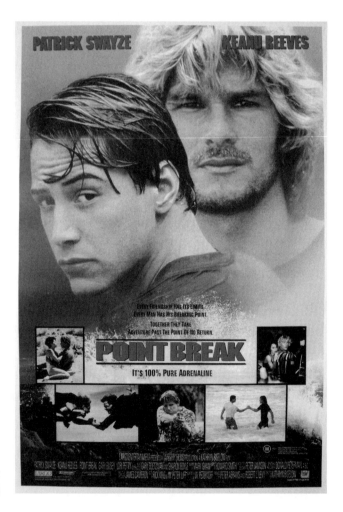

Fig. 4.1 Poster for
Point Break (1991)

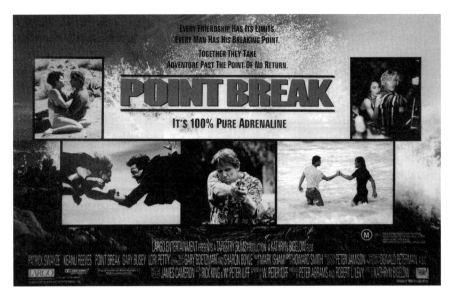

Fig. 4.2 Detail from *Point Break* poster

tions exist on a continuum and the emphasis can fall either way, but that filmic representations in particular—because of their comprehensive capture of surface detail—inscribe both unwittingly? These images offer an abstraction through which we negotiate images of ourselves, in complex relationships that are enacted as a series of performed and recognizable (shared) positions and references.

In a short essay on *Paris Is Burning*, Judith Butler (2002 [1998]) presents an interesting advance on her notions of gender performativity. She notes that when cultural critics apply the concepts of drag and/or gender performativity to expressions of "nonnormative" sexuality, then they lose any possibility of subversion. It is to reappropriate drag as part of the normative hegemonic heterosexual culture; there is nothing inherently subversive or destabilizing to gender performativity, which instead can be used to reaffirm the dominant order. In discussing *Tootsie* (1982), *Some Like It Hot* (1959), and *Victor, Victoria* (1982), Butler notes:

> Indeed, one might argue that such films are functional in providing a ritualistic release for a heterosexual economy that must constantly police its own boundaries against the invasion of queerness, and that this displaced production and resolution of homosexual panic actually fortifies the heterosexual regime in its self-perpetuating task. (452)

While the films Butler addresses are much more explicit in their play with drag, the central point clearly carries over to this discussion of *Point Break*: there is nothing inherently destabilizing in gender performativity or in the production of homosocial or even homoerotic tension where these are used to reassert the dominant order as in *Point Break*.

Where this film *can* be argued to develop action cinema is in the regendered balance between the film's central characters: just as strength is given to the women in the film, a sensitivity is allowed in the male leads. Indeed, I would suggest that gender is muted in *Point Break* through a balance that is rendered close to an equivalence.[5] Rather than offering a critique of gender construction, examination of the "surface" shows gender as a near balance between male and female. The bodies of the main protagonists are thrown into androgynous relief by the cartoonish excess of the "Razorhead" gang and their girlfriends. The body-builder physiques of the men and the hour-glass figures of the women cast a shade of androgyny on the slim figures of Utah/Reeves, Bodhi/Swayze, and the tomboy-ish Tyler/Petty. This is furthered by the angry histrionics of the FBI supervisor Ben Harp (John McGinley) and the physicality of Utah's partner Angelo Pappas (Gary Busey).

Such equivalences develop representations of gender in popular cinema by drawing on images of masculinity and femininity that were beginning to circulate much more widely in the early 1990s. Gender operates as surface, mutable and consumable rather than aggressively proscriptive. Desire is inscribed and performed across beautiful male and female bodies, offered to the hungry eyes of an audience construed as equivalently gendered consumers.

"100% PURE ADRENALINE"

I have sought to address the arguments that consider *Point Break* as subversive through its depictions of gender. While it is impossible to separate these concepts, I turn now to focus on the film's relation to genre. *Point Break* is structured around a series of spectacular action sequences that are linked by the relationship between Utah and Bodhi. In his discussion of "action-adventure" as Hollywood genre, Steve Neale sums up the tropes of the action genre as having "a propensity for spectacular physical action, a narrative structure involving fights, chases and explosions, and . . . an emphasis in performance on athletic feats and stunts" (2000, 52).

These sequences and the effect they create in the body of the viewer, are the principal site of engagement. The central tagline attached to the film and used across its publicity material is "100% Pure Adrenaline" (see fig. 4.2). This has been continued on the U.K. DVD edition, where the enclosed trailer is built around the phrase. And it also appears in the recent U.S. DVD and Blu-ray special edition release, which is called the "Pure Adrenaline Edition." While much has been made of the film's depiction of the relationship between Bodhi and Utah, the question of the action sequences (the sequences that stimulate the viewer) has not been considered. It is through these scenes that the film is marketed and these scenes are central to the pleasures it offers.

The cinematography and editing stimulate adrenaline and while the catalyst for the release of this hormone is vicarious, the audience's experience of it in the body is primary. It is offered up again and again by the weightless fluidity of the camera movement and precise, quick cuts. During the intensity of these sequences the narrative is suspended while both characters and audience are subsumed by the *affect* of the experience. Throughout the technical virtuosity of the celebrated foot-chase sequence, the narrative is poised to unfold once the chase has been completed. But during the six minutes of the chase the viewer has no room for reflection under the incessant momentum of the sequence. This is repeated in the first sky-diving sequence, which is book-ended by somber and tense scenes, but once the characters have jumped out of the airplane and are free falling through space the narrative is suspended to focus on the physical pleasure of the free-fall (represented in reactions of the characters but also repeated vicariously in the body of the viewer). Utah even comments once he lands, "I gotta be losing it"; that is, the intensity of these experiences is making him forget his agency within the narrative. During the fluid and inventive action sequences, the velocity of the moment takes over and the audience is left to enjoy the pleasures of these extreme spectacles: spectacles that are carefully crafted to stimulate the viewer.

It is the constant stimulation within an ambivalent and balanced narrative that creates an experience of the film as "surface" and highlights its repetition of the action genre. Surface here denotes the pleasure of experiencing (consuming) a known product. It is the pleasure of the return, the consistency and, at its extreme, the invariable. While Tasker rightly notes that we need a different critical framework (if all we see in popular cinema is the same thing repeated again and again), this argument attaches the logic of innovation wholesale to an industry whose very economics depend on the pleasures of repetition. This is to say nothing of the culture that has developed out of pastiche, quotation, and repetition in its baldest form. I am not only thinking of the plethora of remakes but also experiments such as Gus Van Sant's remake of *Psycho* (1998) shot for shot.

Genre is of course dependent on repetition and difference, with difference generally taken as the primary value. However, Tzvetan Todorov's construction of genre as repetitious can aid our understanding of repetitious popular forms rather than assisting their condemnation. According to Todorov,

> As a rule, the literary masterpiece does not enter any genre save its own; but the masterpiece of popular fiction is precisely the book which best fits its genre. Detective fiction has its norms; to "develop" them is also to disappoint them; to "improve upon" detective fiction is to write "literature," not detective fiction. (quoted in Tasker 1993, 55)

This much-quoted phrase doesn't dismiss "popular culture" in relation to "high culture." Rather it serves as a definition of a repetitious form in which we take pleasure, in part, *because* of its conformity and repetition. In this we need to develop new theoretical concepts that do not seek to elevate repetitious forms into the "high art" canon, but seek to redefine how we understand and value culture.

CAUGHT-UP-NESS, OR PROBLEMS OF AESTHETIC DISTANCE

In *The Cultural Logic of Late Capitalism* (1991) Fredric Jameson seeks to articulate the manifest break between modernism and postmoderism. This chapter is a compelling analysis of the distinct paradigms that underpin models of cultural value represented (for instance) in a comparison of Van Gogh with Warhol. The essay is particularly noted for Jameson's reading of the Bonaventure Hotel in Los Angeles.[6] Jameson concludes the essay by mapping out an analysis of a "full-blown postmodern building," offering a kind of practical guide to the experience of postmodernism. He notes the paradigm shift that postmodern cultural practice makes in its repetition of form rather than its disruption:

> These newer buildings are popular works . . . they no longer attempt, as did the masterworks and monuments of high modernism, to insert a different, a distinct, an elevated, a new Utopian language into the tawdry and commercial sign system of the surrounding city, but rather they seek to speak that very language, using its lexicon and syntax as that has been emblematically "learned" from Las Vegas. (39)

Postmodernism is (was), Jameson declares, suffused across every strand of culture and poses challenges to thought, theory, and politics. Jameson reads across architecture, literature, and art to insist that culture is telling us that we are in a significantly different aesthetic phase and therefore need to formulate new models of thought that respond to these conditions. The alternative is to misapply modes of criticism and assessments of cultural value based on nineteenth-century romanticism to the cultural objects of the late twentieth/early twenty-first century.

> The end of the bourgeois ego, or monad, no doubt brings with it the end of the psychopathologies of that ego—what I have been calling the waning of affect. But it means the end of much more—the end, for example, of style, the sense of the unique and the personal, the end of the distinctive individual brush stroke (as symbolized by the emergent primacy of mechanical reproduction). (15)

Jameson's implication is that we need new means to account for a culture produced by a fragmented rather than an alienated cultural identity. Jameson identifies this earlier pathology as theorizing culture through a model based on the expression of a unique (monad) subject. The model of the monadic alienated ego as the unique location of creative vision and direction has encountered many problems in film criticism. From its inception, film has been a collaborative medium which has developed to full industrial production where the single hand of an author is difficult to sustain.[7] Jameson insists that our contemporary cultural sphere

> also suggests that some of our most cherished and time-honored radical conceptions about the nature of cultural politics may thereby find themselves outmoded. However distinct those conceptions—which range from slogans of

negativity, opposition, and subversion to critique and reflexivity—may have been, they all shared a single, fundamentally spatial, presupposition, which may be resumed in the equally time-honored formula of "critical distance." No theory of cultural politics current on the Left today has been able to do without one notion or another of a certain minimal aesthetic distance, of the possibility of the positioning of a cultural act outside the massive being of capital, from which to assault this last. What the burden of our preceding demonstration suggests, however, is that distance in general (including "critical distance" in particular) has very precisely been abolished in the new space of postmodernism. We are submerged in its henceforth filled and suffused volumes to the point where our now postmodern bodies are bereft of spatial coordinates and practically (let alone theoretical) incapable of distanciation. (48–49)

Jameson develops this lack of aesthetic distance in the experience of postmodern culture through his reading of the Bonaventure Hotel, noting that the interior spaces emphasize movement and activity. From the constant rising and falling of the elevators (the architect John Portman appropriated Disney's phrase of "people movers") to the revolving restaurant. The use of hangings and banners make perceptual experience of the space a constantly active process as one tries to read the very volume of the lobby spaces. Jameson's implication that postmodernism also produces a different form of experience, of stimulation, of affect is entirely pertinent to this discussion.

This is not to say that the cultural products of the postmodern era are utterly devoid of feeling, but rather that such feelings—which it may be better and more accurate, following J. F. Lyotard, to call "intensities"—are now free-floating and impersonal and tend to be dominated by a peculiar kind of euphoria. (16)

This stimulation bears a fundamental relationship with the stimulation produced by a film like *Point Break*. The audience *feels* continually. We are bound up in the sensations of our body, and as Linda Williams formulates in her essay, "Film Bodies: Gender, Genre, and Excess" (2000):

What may especially mark these body genres as low is the perception that the body of the spectator is caught up in an almost involuntary mimicry of the emotion or sensation of the body on the screen. . . . What seems to bracket these particular genres from others is *an apparent lack of proper aesthetic distance,* a sense of over-involvement in sensation and emotion. We feel manipulated by these texts. (210, my emphasis)

The question of "aesthetic distance" for Williams and "critical distance" for Jameson is removed by the constant stimulation that the action genre offers: or the Bonaventure, or (by implication) postmodern culture. And particularly: industrial culture carefully crafted to stimulate the viewer. Action films like *Point Break* are a useful place to identify and start to consider this phase of culture.

CONCLUSION

The preceding section outlined the relationships between repetition, stimulation, aesthetic distance, and surface. In concluding, I will draw out their relations to and implications for genre and gender theory. The task we face is to develop a form of theory that can elegantly account for the network of relations through which we experience film within the context of late-capitalist cultural production. This must accommodate the conditions of the film's production and its marketing, and its implied construction of the audience, within a focused analysis of the film itself. This chapter has sought to sketch these relationships in addressing *Point Break,* but also to account for the discrepancies between my repeated returns to the film since my early teens and the film's construction in academic criticism. It is this discrepancy that first led me to articulate the notion of "surface."

Our experience of film now is influenced by the substantial history of film theory and criticism that has formulated a complex relationship between audience and industry. We understand how film stimulates and manipulates us and we return to film for these experiences. Even before seeing a film we have a multitude of fragments (marketing) through which to read it, understand how it has been positioned, and form our expectations of what our experience should be. The previews, interviews, posters, and trailers we see for a film tell us exactly how the film is being sold. These fragments draw on generic tropes to address the audience's taste and desire. Genre is thus used very intelligently in the marketing of the sensations and pleasures of a film. The stimulation offered by action films is something we return to again and again (whether across different films or by repeated viewings of particular films). We repeat and examine these effects in different ways both as the techniques of film production change and our experience grows with repeated viewings. The understanding of what that stimulus will be (in action, horror, porn, etc.) is clearly understood prior to seeing the film and is regulated through its marketing. This "call and response" is fundamentally different (I would suggest) from the aesthetic shock that creates critical distance. Rather it flattens the experience into cooperative consumption. It is aesthetic shock that academic criticism tries to recoup in order to accede Bigelow into a particular cultural canon. Part of my proposition then becomes a reformulation of our analysis of consumption as a mode of viewing.

Gender theory has also been used to accede Bigelow and *Point Break* to a club of auteurs, but as I have argued, this is misconceived. The bodies of the central protagonists express the gender equivalence, the lack of distanciation, the flatness that underpins the film. Jameson suggests that postmodern architecture does not seek to intervene in the architectural city space around it but instead to repeat and appropriate these surroundings. Thus our conception of gender and genre (and their interrelations) must be developed to consider questions of role, form, and performance in terms of their repeated effects: in terms of how they reframe our understanding of cultural production and cultural value. Genre and gender theories must be developed with attention to the flatness, seamlessness, and a lack of cultural distanciation rather than perpetuating critical cycles dedicated to the penetration and distinction of aesthetic and theoretical models. This is the challenge of surface.

Notes

1. Christina Lane notes that "Bigelow's *Point Break*, distributed by Twentieth Century Fox, is certainly more commercial than her previous three features. The film grossed $8,514,616 in its first week, appearing on 1,615 screens and ranking number eight at the box office" (1998, 73).

2. "For both men it is an experience in which the earth has moved. The sequence ends with them rolling on the ground, the parachute flapping gently to the ground in post-coital calm" (380).

3. *Guardian* Interview: Kathryn Bigelow, London Film Festival 1996. Held at BFI Library.

4. True abandon, or as Bodhi puts it earlier in the film: "That place where you lose yourself and you find yourself."

5. Which is, of course, entirely different to equality.

6. This hotel was used as the backdrop for the end of millennium party in Bigelow's film *Strange Days* (1995).

7. Even though the marketing and promotion of a film can often emphasize the actions of individuals as the principal authors of the work (director/lead actor).

PART TWO

POSTFEMINISM AND GENERIC REINVENTIONS

CHAPTER 5

TROUBLING GENRE/RECONSTRUCTING GENDER

E. ANN KAPLAN

In *Film/Genre*, Rick Altman notes the irony of "producers . . . actively destroying genres by creating new cycles," while film scholars "are regularly trying to fold the cyclical differences back into genre, thus authorizing continued use of a familiar, broad-based, sanctioned and therefore powerful term" (1999, 71). Meanwhile, Christine Gledhill notes postmodern practices of "picking and mixing" that enable "film-makers to take inspiration from critical as well as studio categories" (2000, 223). In a situation, then, when many Hollywood studios regularly collapse traditional genres into each other, and filmmakers do not confine their work within a specific genre, should we assume that genre is waning as a critical and production category? I hope to argue that this is far from the case. Genre and gender are still mentioned in trade journals like *Variety,* even if in terms often different from classical categories.[1] And as Gledhill has argued, with the waning of critical auteurism and "grand theories" of cinema, genre criticism became a mechanism for remapping Hollywood (223). "Genre analysis," Gledhill notes, "tells us not just about kinds of films, but about the cultural work of producing and knowing them" (222).

In this chapter, I am interested in the cultural work feminist critics performed in "inventing" the genre of the woman's film, and how genre impacts on feminist cinema practices in the current postmodern moment. I distinguish what critics do in furthering cultural and aesthetic knowledge through studying genre from what studios do in the interests of marketing, and from what filmmakers do influenced by both.

Early on, Hollywood saw the utility of genres for successful marketing of films. Genres are constructs rather than natural entities, and so, as critics discovered and despite Hollywood's marketing efforts, genre is a very unstable category. As Rick Altman argues, genre is a multivalent term multiply and variously valorized by diverse users (1999, 99). Once initiated, however, Hollywood continued the business of making genre films and marketing them accordingly, despite the fact that genre aspects of marketing always change.

But gender is also a construct—one that genres have helped to reinforce. Genres have traditionally been central to preserving female (and male) stereotypes in classical Hollywood cinema (e.g., virgin/whore or mother/mistress in family melodrama, the *femme fatale* in film noir), and therefore have attracted feminist scholars' attention regarding representation.[2] If genre in the traditional sense has ceased to occupy its determining position in Hollywood film production, that may result from challenges by the women's movements of the 1970s as well as by feminist scholars' research that opened up the stereotypes and necessitated more complex gender representation; there is now awareness of gender as a construct—as unsteady, easily destabilized, but equally more open to adventurous invention. Newly emerging stereotypes illustrate postmodern genre mixing (the killer woman, for example, may be found across a range of films and the figure is not being marketed in regard to genre), requiring us to distinguish critical understanding of film from studio concerns.

In what follows, I argue first that historically, genre was important in providing a useful pathway through which feminist film theorists could assert a critical position vis-à-vis dominant cinematic and critical strategies. That is, feminist critics used genre as a concept to invent a new genre—the women's picture or woman's film—thereby drawing attention to aspects of Hollywood melodrama that had been neglected by (largely male) critics. Secondly, through my examples—*Sister My Sister* (Nancy Meckler, 1994) and *Memsahib Rita* (Pratibha Parmar, 1994)—I show how some female directors have drawn on traditional Hollywood genres for feminist ends. That is, genre categories not only proved useful as critical referents through which to comment on positions women occupied in certain genres (such as the horror film or film noir featured in my case studies), but they inspired feminist directors to imagine aspects of their social and political worlds through a genre lens, combining aspects of Hollywood genres with the genre feminist critics "invented," namely the woman's film. Such uses turn genre to purposes very different from those of Hollywood. Both Meckler and Parmar use a cross-generic address: we could say that each converts her chosen traditional genre into something new, or that each adds cultural resonance and depth to her work by introducing into the woman's film aspects of traditional genres.

INVENTING THE WOMAN'S FILM

Academic feminist critics, then, freed from the business of marketing film, found it necessary to invent the genre of the woman's film (conceived as a subset of an already contested category, the melodrama) in order to address neglected aspects of classic films.[3] Molly Haskell first posited the genre of the woman's film in 1973, but feminist theorization came later. In 1987 in *The Desire to Desire: The Woman's Film of the 1940s,* Mary Ann Doane made the first in-depth study of the genre. While, as Rick Altman points out, Doane vacillates before claiming the woman's film as a genre, she finally arrives at a broad definition. "The 'woman's film' is not a 'pure' genre—a fact which may partially determine the male critic's derogatory dismissal of such films. It is crossed and informed by a number of other genres or types—melodrama, film noir, the gothic or horror film—and finds a point of unification ultimately in the fact of its address" (quoted in Altman 1999, 73).

In a recent entry on the "Woman's Picture" for the *Schirmer Encyclopedia of Film,* Annette Kuhn echoes Doane's definition, noting that it is a film that is "about, or made by, or consumed by, women" (2006, 367).[4] A more precise definition, she claims, references a subtype of the film melodrama whose "plot is organized around the perspective of a female character, and which addresses a female spectator through thematic concerns socially and culturally coded as 'feminine.'" These films, Kuhn says, were dubbed "women's weepies" to the derogation of the gender address to their audience. While scholars like Steve Neale (1993), examining the American *trade* press, argue that Hollywood never labeled melodramas addressing women's painful lot as "weepies," the many films with tear-inducing plots—recognized as such at the time and since by *journalists* and *film critics*—were part of Hollywood's A production cycles over the years. What differentiates the general run of Hollywood melodramas from the "woman's picture," Kuhn says, "lies in the fact that in the latter the story is told from the perspective of the central female character and sympathy for her eventual fate" (2007, 367). In 1987, joining the discussion, I argued that the feminist-invented "woman's film" genre is not only defined by certain thematic concerns and its address to a female audience but also by resistance to normative female roles, a refusal to be reconciled to patriarchal requirements.

In this essay, I propose to show that genre remains important in contemporary feminist filmmaking. Female directors not only self-consciously make "woman's films" (the "invented" genre) but also draw on traditional Hollywood genres (whether self-consciously or not) to enrich and layer their meanings. In so doing, they destabilize both gender stereotypes and genre categories, creating hybrid cinema and new figurations of the feminine.

While in *Motherhood and Representation* (1992) I showed that Hollywood could produce woman's films in the challenging sense, logically one would expect to find many more such films in the postmodern, feminist era made by independent directors outside Hollywood. But it is perhaps paradoxical that in developing their respective woman's films, both Meckler and Parmar, as independent filmmakers, draw on prominent Hollywood genres. In *Sister My Sister,* Nancy Meckler feminizes the horror genre by making a horror film without any male characters (although patriarchy is symbolically present) and by having women—who are neither evil nor remorseful—violently murder other women. In the process, Meckler uses a cross-generic address, combining the horror film and the woman's film, with elements of the family melodrama. In so doing, Meckler creates something new—but she relies on Hollywood conventions in order to achieve this. In the second case, *Memsahib Rita,* Pratibha Parmar draws on film noir to create an imaginary world referencing social concerns from a feminist perspective—their meanings opened up via the lens of the genre. She uses aspects of film noir with elements of the woman's film to create something original, hybrid, but that required the referent of classic genre for its force.

SISTER MY SISTER: TROUBLING GENRE, GENDER IN TROUBLE

Meckler (an American living in Britain) made her film in London's Pinewood Studios and also shot footage in Amiens, France. The film was produced with funding from BBC's Film Four and NFH Productions. Its category, then, is independent cinema, while its European rather than American context allows it to push the envelope in regard to sex and violence. The film's postclassical moment, when pressure from second-wave feminism opened up a space for feminist filmmakers, meant that Meckler could approach darker aspects of the female psyche in relatively more sympathetic ways than were generally possible in the classical Hollywood genre system.

Based on Wendy Kesselman's stage play, *My Sister in This House,* the film's action is mainly confined to events within the home, and it shares certain features with Hollywood's woman's film as defined by Doane and Kuhn. The film is made by a woman, it is organized around the perspective of female characters, and it addresses the female spectator through themes coded as "feminine." But it also shares features with my expanded definition of the "woman's film," namely in challenging genre stereotypes of the feminine, and in having heroines who transgress the male order and remain unrepentant if, in this case, officially "punished."

Through its source in Wendy Kesselman's play, *Sister, My Sister* draws on Jean Genet's 1946 drama, *The Maids.* Both Genet and Kesselman refer back to the dramatic historical case of the Papin Sisters. Christine and Léa Papin murdered their employer and her daughter in the small French town of Le Mans in 1932. Perhaps because Jacques Lacan gave the case immediate notoriety in his essay "Motifs du Crime Paranoiaque" printed in *Minotaure* (a special issue on the case, edited by André Derain and Man Ray), it came to the attention of Genet. Yet it was not until the 1990s that the case became of interest to filmmakers and analysts. The Papin Sisters were loosely the subject of Rafael Zelinsky's *Fun* (1994), while Peter Jackson's *Heavenly Creatures* (1994) dealt with a similar historical event in New Zealand. Claude Chabrol's 1995 thriller, *La Cérémonie,* also studies a case of two women who murder, but it lacks Meckler's feminist sympathy for the characters. Several studies of the Papin case appeared in French between 1984 and 2000.[5] Meckler's use of a female-gendered, cross-generic address to a genre normally conceived as male-oriented, namely the horror film, extends the critique of patriarchy achieved by the woman's film, and goes further in destabilizing gendered constructs through her representation of the sisters and unsettling of time as realized in normative bourgeois culture and classical Hollywood narrative.

Meckler's turning to the Papin case shows her willingness (along with other 1990s feminists) to challenge stereotypical notions of the feminine as gentle and passive. Interest in female violence and aggression may be a reaction to the utopianism of 1980s hopes for female solidarity, across race and class, as I note below. But the film is not a documentary, and in turning history into fiction, Meckler turned to generic conventions as a way to access and communicate insight not available to analytic discourse. The invention of the Hollywood woman's film as a critical (and indeed political strategy) in the 1970s and 1980s had the effect of enabling independent female directors to produce explicitly feminist woman's films, developing shared feminist conventions but utilizing (sometimes unconsciously) productive aspects of Hollywood genres. With the rapid expansion of Film Studies in colleges across the United States in these years, filmmaking students studied Hollywood cinema, and its varied imaginaries could be consciously drawn on when possibilities for women to direct films had opened up.

In *The Monstrous Feminine* (1993), Creed notes that the horror film traditionally has been made by men for male spectators. Yet, if horror films "define woman as monstrous in relation to her reproductive function to reinforce the phallocentric notion that female sexuality is abject," Creed shows nevertheless that "the notion of the monstrous-feminine challenges the view that femininity, by definition, constitutes passivity." Feminist critics tend to assume that only phallic masculinity is violent, that the "feminine imagination is . . . essentially non-violent, peaceful, unaggressive" (156). Women make horror films not because the female unconscious is fearless, without its monsters, Creed argues, "but because women still lack access to the means of production in a system which continues to be male-dominated in all key areas" (156). When women like Meckler *do* gain access, they are able to imagine the violent, aggressive woman such as we find in *Sister My Sister,* while showing her relatively sympathetically and in ways far from stereotypes of the female killer such as the classic *femme fatale.* It is women's attraction to violence, long unacknowledged, that Meckler dares to address through figures that are cathartic because imaginary.

But how is it that Meckler's heroines end up murdering their employer and her daughter? And that viewers are able (at least partially) to identify with these female murderers? Meckler achieves the almost impossible through her reformulation of the horror film and the family melodrama. This reworking is indicated in the shadowy black-and-white pre-credit sequence that seems to place viewers in the family melodrama. Two little girls are shown in shockingly deprived conditions, but the older sister, Christine, is lovingly tending the younger one, Léa, when a woman enters and takes the child away. The stony expression on Christine's face remains in the viewer's mind, its pain indicating the psychological trauma that will haunt her throughout the film. The credit sequence, now in color, offers graphic shocks as it takes us abruptly into the horror genre. The camera pans down deserted wooden stairs, to a second set of stairs, where the walls are dripping with blood; objects are strewn around, body parts visible, and two bloody mutilated figures, splayed on the floor, come into view.

If the viewer is prepared for something violent and catastrophic, we have no idea what or who is involved. A prolonged flashback builds gradually to the horrific event. Here the film's cross-generic address provides something new that is neither woman's film, nor horror film, but draws on elements of both. From the formidable bourgeois house to which the film now cuts, to the last section of the film, we share the perspectives of Christine and Léa and perceive their oppression. For, despite the absence of men, the house is organized along patriarchal lines, with women divided amongst themselves—at odds because Christine and Léa resist the dominant order.

The result of this cross-generic address is to destabilize normative concepts of femininity and the cinematic genre-d stereotypes that such concepts have long produced. Cumulatively, the sisters represent figures that do not fit any genre-gender category, revealing gender as a construct in that they belie normative female types. These are figures, then, made possible by Meckler's transgressing and reworking classical genre boundaries. However, in recalling the powerful women of gothic horror films—women like Mrs. Danvers in *Rebecca* (1940), Gladys Cooper in *Now, Voyager* (1942), or "mother" in *Psycho* (1960)—the figure of the sisters' employer, Mrs. Danzard, exposes genre: while patriarchy authorizes the exercise of power by men, Meckler highlights how female power is undercut because imagined as terrifying.[6] One source of such power—as we see in the pre-credit sequence—is the giving or withholding of maternal love. This conventionally produces sibling rivalry, but the sisters in Meckler's film try to establish something else—albeit they fail.

At the start of the film Christine, already a maid for Mrs. Danzard and her daughter, Isabelle, welcomes her sister Léa, whom Mrs. Danzard has agreed to employ for the same single wage. Like her female gothic filmic predecessors, Danzard uses the domestic space to exert her will. While Meckler shows time weighing heavily on the Danzards, who, in their conventional female roles, are largely confined to the main rooms of the house (bored, they sew, play cards, read, and look out on the street), the sisters engage creatively and (initially) lovingly in the attic to which they are relegated.

Through use of the staircase, Meckler's film destabilizes normative time associated with classical narration and bourgeois domesticity. The staircase not only refers to the hierarchy central to the traditional family but also, paradoxically, offers a liminal and ambivalent space between the mistress/employee levels that it divides. That is, the staircase at once symbolizes (and reminds viewers of) genre-d class and gender positions—familiar in family melodramas and gothic horror films—and is a space where, ironically, things happen that violate the dominant order classical genres reproduce. The staircase is where the sisters suddenly make love while cleaning the banisters; it is where they whisper their desire; it is also where, in finding dust later on, Mrs. Danzard senses something is wrong, and where the murders finally take place.

At first, the maids perform their duties perfectly and their employers are thrilled with them. Gradually, however, under pressure of their entrapment and their employers' increasing abuse, the sisters become disorderly, resistant, and dysfunctional. As in Chantal Ackerman's *Jeanne Dielman* (1976) (a film that is also about female resistance to patriarchy), small signs of the system breaking down begin to show in the sisters' behavior. Significantly, the dysfunction starts with sexual "disorder." Lesbianism is already a violation of the heterosexual codes that mainstream cinema traditionally insisted on (indeed, required) because it challenges the future-oriented reproductive order with children at its core; but female-female incest is an even more serious violation of traditional mores. Meckler's focus on sex between the sisters shifts the address in a feminist direction and disturbs the traditional form of the horror film. Here sex between sisters no longer figures as taboo, and Meckler's depiction of the relationship enables viewers to move with her narrative, to accept what we see.

Meckler does not belabor the psychology of the sisters, or show fully what brings them to incest, or to commit murder. The film disturbs precisely because it offers no clear explanations, because it challenges generic female-female conventions most visible in the gender stereotyping of popular culture and pornography, and finally because it portrays rarely shown female sibling incest. The sisters turn to each other because there is no one else; they are driven to exist differently. Alone in the world, they seek to repair their wounds by merging into one.

Through postmodernist genre mixing, Meckler's feminist context reveals itself, enabling such *explicit* and uncondemned incestuous desire to escape the sexual positions generally available in mainstream cinema. The sisters move beyond both cultural and generic stereotypes, reject their place prescribed by patriarchal relations, and dare to desire each other. In their attic space, time appears different, indeed it seems to stop altogether. Instead of hierarchy and progression, and instead of the deadness of the house below, in the attic scenes the sisters come alive, a different order is suggested. The soft hazy lighting and the general whiteness of the attic (contrasted with the heavy dark furniture below) add to the sense of the sisters creating their own lateral space. But such a different order cannot coexist with the linear time of the household. Once the sisters cross the established boundaries between the different temporal orders, the established system begins to crumble.

In its last section, and depiction of the murders, the film uses the conventions of the horror film to question those of the feminist-invented woman's film. In freeing the women from the stranglehold of the household, should such terrible violence be foresworn? Or, in postfeminist times, can the woman's film, as a generic form of imagining, legitimately utilize, indeed offer as liberatory, precisely such violence? For as Meckler builds up to the terrifying murders using horror conventions, so she expands the woman's film.

Meckler traces visually, step-by-step, signs of the domestic order being disrupted. The pace of the editing increases, and Christine's mood becomes uglier, more paranoid, brittle. The sequence of events is intercut with, and the deterioration of the sisters marked by, repeated shots of a leaking tap, the length between shots decreasing as things worsen. Rivalry and pain now take over the attic space—another signal that the different spatial-temporal order through which the sisters achieved a certain livability is breaking down. In a spectacular scene, Christine finally talks to Léa of her traumatic rejection by Sister Veronica in the convent—a memory viewers have already been privy to and that repeats the earlier rejection by her mother figured in the pre-credit sequence.

Ultimately, the sisters' private world, so precariously created outside patriarchal law, totally crumbles. Their daring to defy one prohibition (that of incest), leads to their defying their roles within the domestic order, and finally to defying the most basic law of all against the taking of life. In Kelly Oliver's words about the Papin sisters, they were denied essential access to the operations of meaning-making: they were not only "othered to a world of meaning not of their making," but confined there "as incapable of making meaning" (2004, 88). In the film, an explosion is the only way the sisters can channel their frustration. Murder comes about in a kind of blind rage at the impossibility of their attempt to create a world of caring, equality, and justice out of the patriarchal order of class boundaries and hatred, domination and oppression. The result is powerlessness, lack of agency, outside the confines of their attic. The murders are not premeditated; rather, Meckler presents them as the product of the breakdown of the same patriarchal system out of which traditional genres construct and reconcile their symbolic conflicts. By crossing the horror genre with the woman's film, Meckler exposes this system. The sisters' violence is horrendous, but in a sense, the maids murder people who were already dead—as Catherine Breillat remarked of the people in her film, *Fat Girl* (2001, also about sisters). In the closing sequence, Meckler highlights the power of the system revealed by the sisters' impossible position in the bourgeois household, a patriarchy now symbolized by the court of law. The sound of the gavel and the loud clink of the prison door suggest the traditional order regaining control, reestablishing the linear social realm the sisters dared to contest.

But there is no evidence within the film (or in the historical record) that Christine is remorseful. Meckler's representation thus challenges social and cinematic norms of female behavior. Hollywood genres work with normative emotional sets, but Meckler's characters do not adhere to these sets. Her sisters in their servant roles only play at fulfilling the passive feminine roles of melodramatized bourgeois ideology. Gradually resisting these positions, they embark on a different trajectory—one that the Danzards cannot tolerate partly because they unconsciously envy the sisters' escape from the entrapment in which they—the Danzards—are caught. The murders are stunningly horrific, and Meckler does not spare us the grisly details. And yet the viewer finds herself in no position to judge Christine and Léa. Meckler departs from the horror genre, for which the horror appears precisely as unjustified—perpetrated for evil gain, out of madness, psychosis, the action of a bad seed—by showing the murders as almost necessary.

It is to Meckler's credit that in addressing the conflicting conventions of the horror genre and the woman's film, she brings viewers to a position where judging the sisters seems inappropriate. Meckler exposes by genrifying through gothic horror the terrible constraints within which the sisters live, representing the system that confines them as tyrannical and oppressive. While female address is part of family melodrama, viewers are rarely invited to identify with murderous women. The horror genre gives Meckler's feminist point more power because we confront a violation of the genre's code (its equation of violence and men) and are forced to ponder feminine aggressivity and its causes.

PRATIBHA PARMAR'S *MEMSAHIB RITA:* FILM NOIR AS TRANSFORMING LENS FOR FEMINIST PRACTICE

Hollywood provides a context and shared language for Meckler and Parmar, although Parmar in *Memsahib Rita* uses genre differently. Parmar made *Memsahib Rita* in Britain, but she has worked within the American as well as the British independent and feminist film context. Her earlier films include a documentary on the late African American poet June Jordan, and another, *Warrior Marks,* on clitoridectomy, cowritten with Alice Walk for BBC's C4. However, in this short fictional film, Parmar, inspired by film noir, opens up a unique feminist imaginary about race and violence in 1990s London. The world of film noir enables Parmar to move beyond the paranoia and violence of racism to an imaginary feminist hope.

Like *Sister My Sister*'s use of the horror film, *Rita* offers an atypical female address to the male-oriented film noir. The heroine of *Rita*, Shanti, is the mixed-race daughter of a glamorous white woman, whose similarity in her slinky, sexy desirability to Rita Hayworth, famous for her *femme fatale* roles in film noir, wins her the name "Memsahib Rita." While the film is set in 1990s Britain and focuses on Shanti's experiences, flashbacks to colonial India (where Shanti's mother and father met) emerge through Parmar's use of two different visual strategies. The first involves Shanti's hallucinatory childhood memories—a classic result of trauma. Second is the device of an old home movie repeatedly screened by Shanti's father that features his wife—a sign of his continuing grief over her tragic suicide—and portrays Rita as she was in India, as a kind of *femme fatale* qua "memsahib," gorgeous and unattainable except by Shanti's father.

Parmar's reworking of film noir enables her to shift its conventional male address to suggest the complexity of feminine roles on screen. The normative

Hollywood mother role is impossible for the noir heroine, suggesting tension between family melodrama and film noir—a tension foregrounded through Parmar's turning to Hollywood's maternal melodrama to contest genre conventions, while making use of the feminist "invented" woman's film genre. Parmar's contrasting images of Rita—mimicking Rita Hayworth's *femme fatale* in *Gilda* while struggling to perform normative mothering in her cramped London flat—challenge both sets of images. In this way, Parmar inserts a specific female address into film noir while reshaping the genre's stereotype of the *femme fatale*.

The woman's film is also present in Shanti's role as the film's main protagonist. Shanti assumes the function of the detective (usually male in film noir), investigating her dead mother as she tries to understand her own as well as her father's unhappiness. As Shanti investigates her mother's past, we find that Rita is far from a fatal figure. She is, rather, a bored, unhappy, and frustrated housewife, trying to mother Shanti while abhorring babies and their constant demands. Rita's blossoming once more into a splendid *femme fatale* at the film's conclusion itself transforms noir stereotypes, for she comes forward blazing her gun not as betrayal of a male lover, but rather as a mother saving her daughter from racist violence.

Parmar uses black-and-white film stock for sequences dealing with Shanti's past, and color stock for sequences in contemporary London. But the foreboding and suspense of film noir penetrate throughout. The use of noir-style black-and-white film for the memories, reconstructions, and flashbacks, so important for conveying both the white mother's and the tiny daughter's traumas, also suggests the black/white binary that torments Parmar's characters. Noir overtones in past footage provide a way for Parmar to reference the film noir genre and its suppressed racial undertones. Parmar's use of the woman's film and its female address allows her to show that if racism rendered the mixed-race marriage a nightmare for both husband and wife, it also impacted on the mixed-race daughter. Rita, the white mother, falls apart once removed from her elevated, sexualized, but nonmaternal status in colonial India—a status we learn about not only through Shanti's father's old home movies but in photographs displayed in the house. Shanti begins to investigate her mother out of resentment of her father's constant grieving and his living passively in the past, peeking at her father's home movies and "interviewing" her aunt about her mother.

In explanation of Rita's assumption of the *femme fatale* stereotype, Shanti finds that she was unable to confront or to follow through on traditional gender roles. Indeed, her suicide, as reconstructed in Shanti's mind from scraps of information, appears to result partly from an inability to tolerate her daughter's dark form because of what it signified to her community. However, although unable to identify with or care for her mixed-race daughter, Rita is not defined as evil, as is the *femme fatale*.

Shanti's investigation reveals also her own struggle between two mother imagos—the narcissistic "fatal" white mother, and the warm, maternal Indian mother-substitute, Shanti's aunt, with whom Shanti and her father live. The references to Rita Hayworth, then, evoke not only the white, seductive *femme fatale*—as male fantasy—but also Western culture's imaginary split between sexuality and motherhood. As a sexual woman of that era, Rita cannot bear to be a mother.

If Rita's incipient narcissism recontextualizes the *femme fatale* stereotype within female desire, by definition film noir, in its marginalization of the family, excludes the mother. Parmar's combining mother and sexual woman in Rita exposes the limitations of gender dichotomies—virgin/whore, mother/mistress—prevalent in classic genres. Shanti's birth required quite other qualities and abilities than those offered by the *femme fatale,* including putting one's own needs and desires last, and summoning the opposite figure—the Angel of the House of maternal melodrama. Thus Parmar's film introduces into film noir social issues concerning racism and gender that through the generic compass of the woman's film explain Rita's suicide.

Parmar's turn to the woman's film suggests that things are no better for Shanti growing up in a home still controlled by the father, in a London that is still racially divided in the 1990s, but Parmar pushes against the stereotype of the depressed daughter of immigrants and gives her heroine the power that noir detective work provides. In a sense, Shanti is "shocked" into detection through her hallucinatory, traumatic flashbacks seen in the opening credits—images of exotic flowers and water. These images recur several times, triggered by something unexpected in Shanti's present. These memories, as in classic cases of trauma, are split off from Shanti's daily consciousness. They refer to her mother's suicide in Shanti's infancy, but the overwhelming shock of this loss dissociates the memories that return in hallucinations.

Film noir rarely, if ever, made race central, yet its paranoid world where darkness symbolized danger, its modality of foreboding and threat, seems, in Parmar's reference, to always have had race as subtext (see Lott 1997 and Flory 2008). Parmar's reworking of noir by her cross-generic address enables this subtext to emerge. So parallel to Shanti's investigation of her mother is her shock at the slurs she endures on the London streets, including a confrontation with white youths. Parmar links the world of the street to the world of the family—otherwise separated in film noir—by having one of the youths follow Shanti home. The threatening mood of film noir intensifies the viewer's fear that Shanti will be murdered or raped. The racist youth waits ominously outside the family shop, through whose windows he can easily be seen from inside. The cinematic structure explicitly shows the inevitable interconnections between domestic and public space. Only a slight vulnerable barrier (represented by the glass) separates the two realms.

Once Shanti's aunt and father have left for an Indian cultural meeting, Shanti seems to reenact her mother's suicide by drowning as she takes a bath. However, as she sinks into the water, she hears the noise of glass breaking. The white youth has returned and threatens to enter the shop. Shanti's vulnerability to racist danger seems inescapable. Parmar here, like Meckler, constructs a classic paranoid scene, familiar from the gothic melodrama, of a woman left home alone—her space threatened from without—only (again like Meckler) she does something else with it. In this case, Parmar reverses the generic scenario. For the "colored" home really is threatened by the white "outside." In this case we do not have the common unconscious displacement onto the racial Other of the white father's threat to his own home. Rather, Parmar shows the real threat of white society to the British-Indian home. The violence we expect from film noir increases the viewer's anxiety.

However, it is at this precise moment of physical threat to Shanti and her home that the feminist-invented woman's film offers a vision of a different kind of time and of a mother-daughter mode of relating that before seemed impossible. Down on the shop floor, hiding amongst the mannequins, Shanti seems to have no hope of escape; however, her two mother-imagos miraculously come to her aid. The mannequins, displaying the Indian gowns Shanti's aunt sells and who represent her aunt, seem to come alive. Their eyes open wide, watching out for Shanti and warning her of danger. Meanwhile, silently moving about amongst these Indian mannequin-mothers, Shanti's white mother emerges, at once stepping out of film noir and into a transformed noir scene. Her appearance is foreshadowed as in classic noir films by the loaded gun-point emerging between the folds of the mannequins' bright saris. The *femme fatale* as mother now combines her two—from Hollywood's perspective, incongruous—roles: Rita shoots the gun, the white youth falls, and Shanti is saved.

In very short space, through her cross-generic address, Parmar powerfully communicates complex issues concerning gender stereotypes, their inadequacy to lived experiences, the constructedness of gender in genre, and the power of genre for feminist ends. Parmar also introduces concerns familiar from the woman's film, referencing social concerns such as violence and racism alongside intra-family dynamics, and demonstrating that the two spheres of family and society are intricately linked. The film's generic "hybridity" is carried in its different kinds of material—photographs, home movies, black-and-white/color film stock, documentary locations, noir treatment of the city.

CONCLUSION

Genre, as we see, remains important in film practice by independent feminist directors. It is a placeholder from which to launch critiques of patriarchy, sexism, and racism. Feminist directors feminize genre through changing subject positions. They make female subjects central and active instead of peripheral, exotic, or mere victims, while rendering male figures as either absent or peripheral to the main focus of the narrative. In so doing, feminist directors inevitably turn to the invented genre of the "woman's film." Classic genres fuse with Hollywood's woman's film through gendering genre in the feminine—creating hybrid forms that in the end resist categorization. More explicitly, the feminist-invented woman's film on which Meckler and Parmar draw exposes the gender assumptions implicit in genres by the reversal of subject positions and refusal of traditionally genre-d female stereotypes. In the end neither gender nor genre remain solid constructs, but rather, through feminist practice, are revealed precisely as constructed. Both gender and genre are, as a result, destabilized.

Notes

1. On September 3, 2007, *Variety* labeled a new Sydney Lumet film a "tragedy," not a term it frequently uses. The new version of *3.10 to Yuma*, termed "a Western remake," was also called an "R-rated Oater." *Shoot 'em Up* was labeled an "actioner"; *Atonement,* a "romancer"; *Romance and Cigarettes,* "an Indie Musical Comedy"; and *Hatchet,* a horror film. "Bio-pic" is still a category used, but only one film, *Hunting Party,* was called a "drama" (not melodrama). The way gender is noted is interesting: *3.10 to Yuma* is "male-centric," and *Shoot 'em Up* is said to be aimed at "younger males." Sundance films are listed under "the specialty side."

2. It is notable that there are fewer sexualized male "types." The gigolo, philanderer, Don Juan occasionally appear. Otherwise, male characters figure in terms of roles such as adventurer, gangster, detective, scientist.

3. I agree with Steve Neale (1993) that in Hollywood cinema every film, broadly defined, is a melodrama. However, as part of "inventing" subsets of genres, feminist critics located the "maternal" melodrama, related to Thomas Elsaesser's "family melodrama" (Elsaesser 1987 [1973]; Kaplan 1983).

4. As terms referring to an "invented" genre, "woman's film" and "women's pictures" are sometimes used in mixed form as here: "woman's picture." However, the general practice is to use "women's pictures" as a term emphasizing the audience aimed at by the film industry and "woman's film" to highlight the textual properties of a genre.

5. See Dupré 1984; Houdyer 1996; Fortin 2000; Edwards and Edwards 2001.

6. Thanks to Christine Gledhill for suggesting the closeness of Danzard to Danvers and the female gothic horror reference. Here as elsewhere, I have gladly made use of Gledhill's comments in her close reading of my chapter.

CHAPTER 6

BODIES AND GENRES IN TRANSITION:

GIRLFIGHT AND *REAL WOMEN HAVE CURVES*

YVONNE TASKER

Genre cinema depends on an articulation of gendered types and a presentation of bodies defined by gender. The richness and pleasure of genre films has much to do with their iteration and occasional modification of these gendered types. But most genre fictions also assume a central male subject, requiring considerable effort to position female characters as meaningful protagonists. Bearing these limits and possibilities in mind, this essay explores how women filmmakers working within independent cinema have used genre to tell women's stories. Of course, independent cinema is a contested category; there are complex connections between independent production and major corporations at the level of marketing and distribution, such that independent is not so much a hard and fast category as a concept, one that marks out a space understood as defined by, yet to one side of, Hollywood. Nonetheless, it remains meaningful to view independent cinema as, in Kathleen Rowe Karlyn's words, "articulating a self-conscious, irreverent and funky countervoice to mainstream filmmaking." For Karlyn, this relational position has much to do with genre. She writes: "Typically it [independent film] has fed off Hollywood traditions and genres in order to rewrite them for the smaller and more particularised audiences it targets" (1998, 169). Karlyn's essay centers on Allison Anders's independent hit *Gas Food Lodging* (1992), a film that centers women's lives and concerns through a shrewd juxtaposition of genres and generations. This essay pursues Karlyn's suggestion, exploring further how independent women filmmakers use genre. Examining *Girlfight* (2000) and *Real Women Have Curves* (2002), I foreground strategies by which genres are deployed, combined, and remade in order to tell women's stories. These independent productions had initial festival success, secured wider distribution, and, particularly in the case of *Real Women,* achieved a measure of commercial success.[1] They work with very different generic and gender codes, although there is common ground in that both are rites-of-passage narratives enacted on and around the bodies of young Latina protagonists. The young women at the center of these two films are situated as out of place and as extraordinary; their attempts to light on a workable adult female identity are both unconventional and compelling.

The desire to tell women's stories has been formative for diverse traditions of feminist and feminist-informed filmmaking. Such filmmaking is often driven by a realist impulse, a perception that Hollywood/genre cinema trades in fantasized images of women that bear little correspondence to actual women's lives. In using genre to tell such stories, these films foreground contradictions between realist and generic codes, suggesting a number of questions. For instance, how far can a film shift the presentation of women's lives from those usually associated with a genre before it effectively becomes a parody? Can realist (rather than fantastic) feminist filmmaking itself be understood as generic, defined by its commitment to telling women's stories? How might such a genre relate to the "woman's film," that mode of Hollywood production defined as much by its intended audience as by content? In addressing these questions, I argue that genre has proved both productive and constraining for women filmmakers.

GIRLFIGHT: GENDER AND GENRES OF VIOLENCE

Girlfight centers on Diana Guzman's (Michelle Rodriguez) transformation from disaffected high school student to disciplined fighter through her covert training and amateur bouts as a boxer. Overviewing gender and contact sports in the United States, Sarah K. Fields cites Joyce Carol Oates's provocative summary of boxing as a gendered spectacle: "Raw aggression is thought to be the peculiar province of men, as nurturing is the peculiar province of women. (The female boxer violates this stereotype and cannot be taken seriously—she is parody, she is cartoon, she is monstrous)" (2005, 121). Oates's comments, made in 1987, provide a useful starting point, since here she pinpoints how intimately connected gendered stereotypes are to the narratives associated with violent sports. If we extrapolate her comments to the context of narrative cinema, the implication is clear: the female boxer cannot be center stage in a serious drama since her presence converts it into parody. This is the conundrum that Karyn Kusama faced in her avowed desire to formulate in *Girlfight* "a different kind of story . . . a new protagonist in an old form" (Baker 2000, 23). She achieves this in part through a strategy of combining genres, reformulating the conventions of the boxing movie.

Kusama suggests that "there will always be a shortage of physically powerful and emotionally complicated women on screen" (Baker, 26), a shortfall that she attempts to address through the coupling of sports, social realist drama, and a rites of passage narrative. Boxing narratives routinely foreground class, racial, and ethnic inequalities, with the individual's struggle to succeed in the sport either a brutal assertion of social boundaries or a sentimental rendition of those obstacles being overcome.[2] This narrative pattern has obvious resonance for the dramatization of gender—objections to women in the sport provide one more obstacle in Diana's struggle to succeed as a fighter. Indeed, Oates adds to her characterization of the female boxer as grotesque the observation: "Had she an ideology, she is likely to be a feminist" (1987, 73). As this rhetorical alignment of the unimaginable female boxer with feminism suggests, boxing enacts conventional (though far from straightforward) hierarchies of male and female, masculine and feminine. Women feature as supportive wives and girlfriends; spectators rather than athletes or competitors. The female boxer disrupts this system; the body she displays is athletic, muscular rather than conventionally feminine or eroticized spectacle. Kusama, speculating on the interest in her film, suggests, "Perhaps there is a growing public consciousness of women as physical beings beyond sexual objects, as physically powerful beings—it's now a reality that can't be denied" (Baker 2000, 26). That Kusama imagines Diana as a complex yet plausible figure relates both to her realist goals and her willingness to work with and extend the genre's more limited articulation of gender.

The female boxer can be recuperated into more conventional display, as with featherweight professional boxer Mia St. John's controversial November 1999 *Playboy* cover and nude spread; St. John defends her posing as a gesture of female strength and independence, insisting that "female athletes don't have to look like men" (76). The *Playboy* feature includes full page glamour shots in the ring, locker room, and shower; the shoot eroticizes the female athlete, posing St. John naked but for her boots, or wearing lingerie in the locker room. Against these erotic images suffused with boxing iconography, the spread features smaller inset boxes showing St. John fighting and training along with a commentary on the toughness of her workout. This visual separation seems if anything to confirm that the activities of training/fighting and posing really are quite distinct and differentially gendered despite being ostensibly performed by the same body. Diana's training and physical transformation is at the heart of *Girlfight;* her developing physical discipline brings strength, skill, and self-confidence, but at the same time it emphasizes her relative isolation and atypicality. The film must situate her transformation in a culture defined by, on one hand the anxieties associated with the potential masculinity (and indeed implicit feminism) of the female athlete, on the other the sort of erotic play on sexy female strength that *Playboy* enacts around the body of St. John.

Girlfight's opening sequence positions Diana as out of step with the hierarchies and rituals of high school. The first shot picks her out in the background, leaning against lockers as students pass back and forth, oblivious to her presence. Cut from midriff to head and shoulders, Diana seems impassive, her face unsmiling, eyes downcast. When Diana's eyes do open, an unblinking stare at the camera emphasizes her challenging intensity. These establishing scenes emphasize two key character traits: first, Diana's aggression, her tendency towards confrontation and violence as an outlet for her anger; second, her hostility towards conventional performances of femininity. These two traits are apparent in Diana's attack on fellow student Veronica, who evidently stands for a particular version of conforming high school femininity characterized by heightened sexuality, arrogance, and popularity. Diana's hostility towards Veronica mobilizes her intolerance towards sexual display and her implicit rejection of the rules of femininity. As she tells her father, Diana is no "girly girl." This position eschews the coming to femininity trope so common within the teen movie (or indeed the makeover scenario so prominent in the woman's film), articulating instead a feminist scenario of coming of age, one centered on the discovery of and delight in physical abilities. Later, following their most intense and violent confrontation in which she almost kills her father, Diana observes: "All these years you just looked right through me." Indeed, the film repeatedly contrasts Diana's relative invisibility with the way in which conventionally attractive/feminine girls and women are noticed on the street, at the gym, and in school. While in these terms Diana is a figure on the sidelines, the film itself centers on the spectacle of Diana's body and her transformation into an athlete. Rodriguez attracted considerable favorable comment in this debut role, with writers emphasizing the intensity of her performance and the eroticism of her character's gender ambiguity. *Time* magazine's Richard Corliss, for instance, described Rodriguez as "the young Brando womanized" (2000, online). *Girlfight* then maintains cinema's interest in the female body as a site of cross-generic erotic spectacle while emphasizing physical transformation and gender ambiguity. Thus while Diana's female masculinity, her embodiment of physical strength and aggression, is pointedly contrasted to the conventional model of femininity represented by Karina—girlfriend of young boxer Adrian (Santiago Douglas)—it is to Diana that Adrian is insistently drawn. The couple's uncertain reconciliation in the film's final scene, following Diana's defeat of Adrian in the ring, centers on a desire for respect as much as love, suggesting a partnership that, reworking the romance narrative, does not simply comply with gendered roles of male protector/female display. In male-dominated genres such as the boxing movie, the presence of female characters is overwhelmingly bound up with couple formation: that is their primary narrative function. *Girlfight* retains that convention while suggesting that Adrian too must change. The romance plot is thus bound into the boxing narrative rather than to one side of it.

Teen films concern themselves with the physical and emotional consequences of adolescence, as children become adults, assuming a social identity shaped by gender, social class, and ethnicity. These themes are routinely expressed through narratives that detail the incorporation or inclusion of misfit characters and the development of unlikely romantic partnerships across previously impermeable boundaries. Teen films are simultaneously—at times contradictorily—concerned with accepting the self and with the transformation of the body into a more conventionally desirable form. Themes of generational conflict, rituals such as prom night and initiation into romantic and/or sexual experience are also commonplace in the genre and are effectively played out in *Girlfight*. Diana's anger, violence, and distance from conventional femininity all mark her as physically unruly and emotionally rebellious; dissatisfied with the models of adult womanhood available to her, Diana defines her identity in the positive but decidedly masculine space of the gym. On her first visit to the gym she throws a punch at the sparring partner of brother Tiny (Ray Santiago), suggesting her impulsive violence while displaying her physical power. Here and in Diana's assault on Veronica, her aggression is triggered by the treatment of another, suggesting a protective rather than a generalized aggression. On one hand, this is in line with the conventional attribution of "caring" to women, yet on the other, these values are applied to an implicitly male sphere of action. *Girlfight* is a sports film, but it is also a coming-of-age narrative in which Diana learns to control but not repress her anger. These narrative trajectories support each other, and it is in the juxtaposition of teen film conventions with those of the boxing movie that the use of generic combinations to centralize a tough yet complex female protagonist is most apparent. In the process, female anger—an emotion that Western culture typically deems repellent and associates with feminism—is staged and maintained but not contained.

Mary Beltrán writes that with its emphasis on female dignity through physical achievement, "*Girlfight* challenges gender typing with respect to the physical and mental training and qualities we associate with heroism" (2004, 194). This physical strength becomes integral to the film's domestic drama, in which Diana confronts the indifference of her father, Sandro (Paul Calderon). The claustrophobia of the Guzmans' apartment underscores the economic limitations against which Diana struggles to develop an independent adult identity. Her hostile relationship to her father clearly articulates both gendered and generational conflict: he suggests she dress and behave in what he regards as more appropriately feminine fashion (just as he attempts to school Tiny in masculinity by paying for his training at the gym); in turn Diana attributes her mother's suicide to the physical abuse she experienced at his hands. Thus the film makes visual and thematic reference to the domestic environment as a site of gendered violence and surveillance, tropes common to social realist drama. At first Diana steals from her father to fund her training; subsequently she takes her brother Tiny's fees to fund her place at the gym since he has no interest in boxing, secretly occupying the position of a son and further emphasizing the constricting nature of familial gender norms. The domestic drama comes to a climax as Diana lays public claim to her status as boxer in defiance of her father's gendered expectations. As their argument turns to violence, Diana overpowers her father, her escalating aggression and rage staged intensely through tight camerawork.

The scene allows the expression of Diana's rage at her own treatment and that of her mother, yet Kusama does not celebrate violence as retributive here. The audience is not easily aligned with the film's protagonist as she kicks her father as he lies on the floor or chokes him almost to death; her brother offers a voice of reason, pleading with Diana to desist. Diana's reversal of domestic violence and the gendered hierarchies on which they are built—"You belong to me now" she gloats as she throttles Sandro—leads to her departure. Though brother Tiny sits in the audience for her final boxing match, from this point in the film Diana effectively rejects her home. The film's staging of a rites-of-passage narrative involves Diana's violent rejection of her father rather than a sentimental reconciliation with him. Contrast this to the recurrent staging of a father-daughter dynamic in teen films such as *10 Things I Hate About You* (1999). Yet the importance of such a connection with a paternal authority figure remains via Diana's trainer Hector (Jaime Tirelli), who welcomes her into his home and expresses immense pride in her achievements. The persisting importance of the paternal relationship suggests the parameters of socially conditioned imagining—an insistence that female strength should not preclude fantasies of either romantic intimacy or cross-generational acceptance between men and women. Yet we can contrast *Girlfight*'s articulation of this latter relationship with that seen in Clint Eastwood's award-winning drama, *Million Dollar Baby* (2004). Though the film tracks a female boxer, Maggie (Hilary Swank), it centers on Frank (Eastwood), the trainer who has been estranged from his biological daughter. Morgan Freeman's voiceover narration insistently foregrounds what Maggie's story means for Frank.

In *Girlfight* Diana's achievements are marked as starkly removed from school and home; in school her movement is restricted by classes in which she has no interest or in the tedium of detention, while at home she is pictured as frustrated in front of the TV and cramped in the confines of the apartment and the limited ambitions it represents. In contrast, her enthusiasm for boxing represents a submission to the very discipline she will not accept in school or at home. The gym not only provides Diana with a supportive male authority figure in Hector but introduces her to romance and adult sexuality through her encounter with Adrian. These two relationships underline the ways in which the film accepts male authority in conventional terms while also insisting on the need for men to change in order that women might reach their potential. Boxing also provides Diana with physical abilities that make her stand out from her peers further still, a difference evident in the comically played scenes detailing the school's presidential physical fitness exam. Diana's fitness is celebrated visually against her ineffective female classmates. Veronica's snide comment on hormones reinforces Diana's distance from gender norms and the extent to which her status as athlete connotes female masculinity.[3]

Although Kusama had begun work on the script some years earlier,[4] *Girlfight*'s release in 2000 fortuitously chimed with popular culture's most recent fascination with women and violence. On the back of the commercial successes of diverse films featuring women as martial artists such as *Charlie's Angels* and *Crouching Tiger, Hidden Dragon* (both 2000), the press delighted in reports suggesting young women's renewed interest in more aggressive—and thus "masculine" physical pursuits. Under the heading "Coming to a Gym Near You," *Newsweek* ran a piece that year on increased female interest in martial arts schools, speculating that such women were "inspired by a new breed of lip-gloss wearing warrior" (Ali 2000, 76). Such journalistic rhetoric and the cinematic imagery of female action it employs can be framed by the developing visibility of female athletes in 1990s U.S. popular culture. Contrast Oates's 1987 characterization of the female boxer as grotesque with Heywood and Dworkins's 2003 comment: "Female athletes were once oddities, goddesses, or monsters, exceptions to every social rule. Now the female athlete is an institution" (xvi).

If Hollywood's most visible figuring of the female boxer, *Million Dollar Baby,* suggests a different narrative of physical ruin, this is far from representative of commercial cinema's take on female violence. Crucially, both the commercially successful cinematic figure of the violent woman and the newly visible female athlete serve a postfeminist culture geared towards marketing images of female power. The cinema's violent women can be understood as a sign of the success of a postfeminist media culture in at least three ways. First, her performance and provisional acceptance in a masculine-coded arena renders her an embodiment of the success of feminism, without the need to ever explicitly articulate a feminist position. In the context of U.S. sports culture, as Fields (2005) demonstrates, a prominent position is accorded to equality legislation such as Title IX (enacted in 1972 and prohibiting gender exclusions in sports within educational settings), so that the increase in visibility of female athletes has been attributed to feminist campaigns that have thus effectively run their course.[5] Second, the violent woman is seen to react against or reject male figures who articulate a misogyny clearly presented as extreme or unacceptable (that is, distinct from everyday misogyny). She thus embodies feminism as concordant with mainstream or normative standards of gendered civility. Finally, as a sexually codified, conventionally attractive female, the active or violent woman of genre films continues to confirm the importance of appearance and, implicitly, consumption centered on appearance. These features underline the ambiguity of postfeminist culture for feminism since it revels in an imagery of female strength—and thus creates a visual repertoire upon which filmmakers may productively draw—while simultaneously perpetuating gender norms that are frequently quite at odds with women's actual lives. Of course genre films speak as much to our fantasies about gender as to the experience of living it, a contradiction that *Girlfight* effectively dramatizes. Indeed, as I'll argue below in relation to *Real Women Have Curves*, postfeminist culture is akin to genre cinema in its simultaneously productive and constraining character.

In this postfeminist context wherein female violence and toned athletic bodies are routinely commodified, Kusama's insistence on Diana's emotional complexity and the film's refusal of straightforward resolution seems particularly important as an instance of the recasting of genre. Thus Diana's father does not simply reform and accept her; her victory as an amateur is not for the grand stakes of

Hollywood boxing movies; no magical transformation or definitive knockout ensues—indeed, victory brings a sense of isolation and loss. Instead the film concludes in a freeze frame, with Diana having found a space for herself at the gym and with Adrian. Setting aside the more fantastic embodiments of female violence displayed in popular cinema, *Girlfight* manages to make use of the conventions of the boxing film, social-realist drama, and the teen film, centering a fighting female protagonist without becoming an instance of either generic or gender parody. It is a genre film that effectively pictures the unimaginable female fighter, while taking account of the complexities of women's actual lives and the gendered codes of body and behavior that govern them.

REAL WOMEN HAVE CURVES:
WOMEN'S WORK/WOMEN'S BODIES

Girlfight exploits the connection between gender and genre by positioning a young woman in the boxing movie, reworking sports movie conventions with domestic drama and the teen film. *Real Women Have Curves* suggests different practices and types of generic combination used by independent women filmmakers. Thus *Real Women Have Curves* inflects genres more familiarly associated with women. It is a comedy, a melodrama, and a coming-of-age narrative centered on the character of Ana (America Ferrera), whose developing sense of self brings her into conflict with her mother. Generational conflict is here plainly orchestrated out of the clash between traditional and more modern perspectives on gender and aspiration. Realism is once more central; the film's title points to a desire to evoke real women as against commodified images or media-generated idealizations of women. Such idealized female bodies are present in the film by proxy, evident in the glamorous, small-sized dresses that are assembled in Estela (Ingrid Oliu)'s factory before being sold in Bloomingdales for many times the amount received by the factory workers. In the film's avowedly feminist terms, "real women" are women who must work hard and whose bodies do not conform to the feminine norms posited by these empty dresses. The distance between Hollywood/celebrity bodies and actual women's bodies serves as a sign of other differences to do with working conditions and opportunities for advancement. These "real" women's curves also allude to Latina bodies set against white-defined standards of beauty (Beltrán 2002). While "real" is a synonym for "normal" or "average," Ana is also defined as distinct from the other women in the factory, her capability already evident in having secured a place at a high school in Beverly Hills and (with her teacher's help) a full scholarship to attend Columbia University. As a consequence of her status as both average and exceptional, *Real Women Have Curves* traces Ana's rites of passage in terms of both developing knowledge—of her body and sexuality, of the world of work—and her need to make a choice (should she leave her family to seek a college education?).

A major strand in feminist criticism has long understood narrative cinema as associated with the exclusion of women, defined in terms of a femininity that is persistently denigrated, coded as excessive, in need of control or mastery. Against this context *Real Women* stages a coming-of-age narrative in which its protagonist must come to terms with the limitations and responsibilities of the adult world. It draws on and centralizes not just genre but the pervasive cultural dynamics through which actual women might come to internalize the thin body as desirable. While *Girlfight* opposes the athletic female body to that emphasized as the feminine ideal, *Real Women* addresses a pervasive cultural opposition between bodies that are appropriately bounded and disciplined in terms of norms of feminine thinness and those that are undisciplined, overweight, and thus require "work." Here the film dialogues primarily with popular media rather than film, not least since Hollywood films aimed at female audiences rarely feature nonnormative bodies.

Ana and her mother Carmen (Lupa Ontiveros) argue about her body throughout the film, a dispute that opens up questions of what it means to be a woman and the rules governing an appropriate performance of femininity. According to Carmen, Ana must lose weight; her jibes and admonishments to that effect punctuate the film, being variously played for comic and emotive effect. Here the film touches on contemporary popular discourses that insist—in contradictory fashion—that women should know themselves and feel confident in their bodies, while also persistently monitoring and disciplining those bodies for signs of excess or physical nonconformity. The prurient tabloid policing of celebrity bodies—particularly female bodies—as either too fat (unattractive, unhealthy) or too thin (dangerous, unhealthy), requiring constant attention, exemplifies this contradictory insistence on a supposedly healthy, self-confident conformity.[6]

An oppressive figure who is played for one-dimensional comedy, Carmen's body too is scrutinized in the film, and marked as in transition. She is entering menopause, as her daughter is becoming a young woman, facing choices to do with sexuality and reproduction. The film scores comic points at Carmen's expense with her misguided reading of the onset of menopause as pregnancy, a "secret" that she confides only to the indifferent Ana. Above all Carmen wants Ana to lose weight in order to perform femininity more effectively, to make herself attractive to men, marry, and have children. In short, she wants Ana to follow in her own path and is both frustrated and uncomprehending at Ana's refusal to see herself in these terms. There are moments of connection between the two—as when Ana glimpses the scar left by her own birth—but ultimately the film cannot reconcile mother and daughter. Indeed, Carmen withholds the blessing that Ana's father and grandfather both bestow when she leaves for university, locking herself into her bedroom with her memories. Carmen's grief at her disappointment is accorded less significance and pathos than Ana's choices. Where mainstream films such as *Monster-in-Law* (2005) suggest reconciliation between generations of women, this is almost always centered on the rituals of romance and marriage.

Real Women certainly encompasses the familiar generic themes of romance (via Ana's developing relationship with classmate Jimmy), but this does not provide the film's narrative resolution.

Generational conflict between women is a prominent feature of the contemporary woman's film. A number of popular examples of the genre, such as *Something's Gotta Give* (2003) or *Monster-in-Law* associate the mother with a restrictive and isolating feminism in contrast to the younger women, who may emphasize freedom through sexuality or celebrate traditional conceptions of marriage and reproduction.[7] In contrast to this mainstream alignment of feminist views with an older generation, *Real Women* has Ana confronting questions as to her own sexuality, how to understand her body in relation to restrictive gender norms, and whether to pursue a college education. The maternal figure of Carmen remains outside, representing an identity that Ana comes into conflict with and must seemingly move beyond as she adopts an adult identity. Rather than accept her mother's understanding of sex as exclusive to the institution of marriage, for instance, Ana initiates a sexual encounter with Jimmy. We see her buying condoms in a local store, suggesting her ability to exercise control over her body. Such scenes suggest a feminist filmmaking that intersects with the more traditional themes of the woman's film, such as the suggestion of personal transformation via costume or the achievement of self-realization through romantic intimacy.

While Ana does not celebrate her physicality, neither does she engage in self-loathing: she expresses her desire to lose weight while reveling in her body's symbolic assertion of her right to take up space in the world. This ambivalence is nicely expressed in the scene in which Ana and the other women at her sister's factory strip to their underwear against the heat, comparing their "real" bodies and celebrating their physicality. The scene is played for both pathos (women's lives are inscribed on our bodies) and humor, a doubleness evident in Ana's ambiguous assertion, "Who cares what we look like when no one's watching us?" While Carmen routinely expresses her disgust at her daughter's body, the film makes clear that others value Ana's body; Jimmy pronounces her beautiful and Ana insists on keeping the lights on while they have sex, wanting to be seen even as she expresses her insecurity. Ana's sister Estela also expresses implicit approval of her body, designing a beautiful dress for her. Images of Ana holding this dress were widely used in promotional materials; in withholding of an image of Ana wearing it, the film's emphasis falls not on her makeover but on the connection between the sisters. *Real Women* more generally eschews the crudity of the makeover (a prominent feature of the teen film and of media culture more broadly), offering instead a transformation narrative in which Ana comes to terms with her body. This much is conventionally expressed in the final shots of Ana confidently emerging from the subway in New York. Here she is visibly wearing makeup and adopts the stance of an adult woman rather than a slouching teen. Indeed, as some observers have commented, she seems in this parting shot to be following her mother's advice with respect to posture, advice she mocks earlier in the film.

Chris Holmlund describes *Real Women Have Curves* as (largely) a feminist film, consciously differentiating it from postfeminist versions of the woman's film. For Holmlund, the film's emphasis on education and average (rather than media idealized) bodies is crucial in this designation, as is a recognition of women's work (2005, 119). Again it is the realist impulse that defines feminist film for Holmlund, although Ana's personal development through the course of the film is also generic. The tensions in the film are mediated narratively not only through generational conflict between women but in terms of work. Graduating high school, Ana quits her job as a waitress, reluctantly agreeing to work in sister Estela's factory. Ana immediately comes into conflict with her sister and the women who work there; these women's pride in their work is contrasted to Ana's dismissal of the factory as a sweatshop and her labor as dirty work. While she is not wrong about the exploitative conditions in which they labor, the film is at pains to reveal that, through the course of the film, Ana comes to respect her sister's efforts and to understand the harshness of the economy in which she operates. Indeed, she tells her father, "I never realized how hard she works." Estela's aspirations are glimpsed, too—her desire to start her own line and her skill evident in crafting a dress for Ana. In acknowledging the reality of work even as the film triumphantly follows Ana to New York and her new life as a student, *Real Women* simultaneously questions how much choice the majority of women actually have and celebrates Ana as an exceptional young woman who claims a space for herself in a new arena.

CONCLUSION: WOMEN FILMMAKERS
AND FEMINIST FILMMAKING

Independent feature film production has not been an unconditionally receptive home for women's work. By all accounts, women filmmakers face an uphill struggle to secure funding for such films. Yet these examples demonstrate the rich possibilities for feminist use of genre fictions that fictionalize women's gendered lives. They suggest the potential for telling women's stories by combining and remaking genres. It is no coincidence that both films explore girls becoming women, following female characters who grapple with the restrictive codes of femininity to which adult women are expected to conform. Both films decidedly reject the teen film's emphasis on the prom as a ritual of heterosexual conformity, without functioning as exercises in subversion or smart self-reflexivity; driven by the realist impulse so important to feminism, they represent a productive use of genre conventions to tell women's stories. Both films also distance themselves from a postfeminist media culture in which female choice is celebrated (as long as the right choices are made) without reference to the material conditions in which contemporary women live and work.

Notes

1. Christina Lane writes that *Girlfight,* financed through the Independent Film Channel and John Sayles, for whom she had previously worked, was sold to Sony for $3 million following its award of the Grand Jury Prize at the 2000 Sundance Film Festival (2005, 193). Chris Holmlund notes that the HBO-funded *Real Women Have Curves* won an Audience Award at Sundance and went on to make almost $6 million at the U.S. box office on a $3 million budget (2005, 120–21).

2. For a more detailed discussion of the boxing film (including *Girlfight*) in this context, see Aaron Baker (2003).

3. A wealth of scholarship explores gender and sport. For example, Krane et al. address the "paradox" facing "physically active women and girls" with respect to gender norms, suggesting that sportswomen effectively "live in two cultures" (2004, 315).

4. Aaron Baker reports that Kusama began writing the script in 1995 while working as an assistant to John Sayles, who subsequently helped the project secure funding (2000, 22).

5. Since boxing is a contact sport, however, it was explicitly excluded from Title IX. Nonetheless it was the courts that opened up amateur boxing for girls and women in 1993 (Fields 2005, 127).

6. The makeover, extensively addressed in feminist media scholarship as a trope of post-feminist culture, is particularly relevant here. For a recent analysis, see Angela McRobbie (2008).

7. Susan Bordo describes the current generation of young women as claiming a public space unavailable to their mothers, a space they negotiate through a self-effacing performance of "vulnerable femininity." "They apologize profusely for whatever they present of substance, physically or intellectually. And they desperately want to be thin" (1997, 138).

CHAPTER 7

PRIVATE FEMININITY, PUBLIC FEMININITY:

TACTICAL AESTHETICS IN THE COSTUME FILM

SAMIHA MATIN

As early as the 1930s, critics categorized the costume film as "feminine," because it focused on the emotional subject of love in contrast to historical bio-pics that were deemed "masculine" by tending to political topics (Robe 2009, 71). While the distinctions between types of historical films are neither absolute nor exclusive, costume films give primacy not just to romance but also to female protagonists while highlighting the visual drama of private life through costume and interiors. Though a prevalent genre in the 1930s and 1940s, costume films declined in the postwar years until the late 1980s and 1990s, when a new cycle emerged, buttressed by BBC period drama serials broadcast in America on public television.

The distinctiveness of the costume film lies in drawing together history and the private sphere to investigate femininity, a project that relies heavily upon the nineteenth-century organization of separate gendered spheres, making the feminine private and masculine public easily legible. The instant "women's world" that the separate spheres formation provides also comes with social protocols that inhibit sexual relations between men and women, thus creating conditions for romance and emotionality to flourish. Because the domestic novel contributed to naturalizing divisions of public and private and offered representations of the psychologically interiorized self, costume films characteristically draw on literary sources as channels for gender history. While the gendered spheres structure has receded, it produced images and concepts that continue to resonate for many men and women, since women still take primary responsibility for children and home management even though working outside the home.

Given that costume films have often been viewed through the lens of British heritage critiques that subordinate questions about gender, it is important to rethink these films through the rubric of genre, for this refocuses narrative and aesthetic elements as registering cultural changes, particularly shifting investments in femininity that feed back into social imaginaries. This approach examines femininity as an identity style influenced by broader experiences of private and public. As historical setting and romantic plots are elements shared with other genres, differentiating their deployment in the costume film can tell us about the resonance of the genre as well as about cultural demands on narratives of femininity.

Arguably, the contemporary costume film responds to a pervasive perception that social changes wrought by the rising profile of women's careers, digital media, and intensifying commercialization of femininity have increased publicness for women while the private grows less accessible. Losing some of its practical ground, femininity in the postfeminist era "goes public"—where its ties to privacy are simultaneously romanticized and reimagined. These films access privacy as a "structure of feeling," defined by Raymond Williams as "meanings and values as they are actively lived and felt" (1977, 132). Based in affective knowledge, these are unprocessed ways of understanding social vicissitudes. The costume film articulates privacy as a structure of feeling through dilemmas of feminine behavior, in order to realign the private sphere with autonomy or, conversely, to find meaning in publicness for women.

This chapter examines the contemporary costume film's unique interrelationship of femininity and privacy by focusing on how the historical constraints of privacy force the postfeminist heroine to make herself anew as a feminine subject. I use the two poles of privacy and publicness to organize relationships between gender, feeling, time, aesthetics, and identity, worked through and re-envisioned by costume films for present-day viewers. By these means, the values of privacy and publicness are recalibrated to accommodate a mutable femininity that uses aesthetics and feeling as creative methods of adaptation. The heroine's process of identity construction consists of tests, experiments, and play with self-presentation to find and utilize the sanctioned meanings and covert privileges afforded by femininity. In reassembling elements of gender and galvanizing their force to new ends, spaces for covert resistance and pressure-release emerge. This course is one of "tactical aesthetics," or the deployment of style to access power which makes use of gendered acts, expressions, dress, and etiquette to design new advantages.

To explore this concept, I analyze two films, *Elizabeth* (1997) and *Marie Antoinette* (2006), as divergent visions of femininity. Costume films often use the figure of the queen (*Elizabeth, Mrs. Brown* [1997], *Marie Antoinette, The Other Boleyn Girl* [2008], *The Duchess, The Young Victoria* [2009]) to position a woman at the juncture of public and private, thereby hooking into an opposition between duty and desire that while limiting also foregrounds women's choices. As I will show, in both films the heroines employ tactical aesthetics to make femininity into power for different ends. However, first I consider cultural and generic themes as they inform and structure the negotiations of femininity in the current cycle of costume films.

POSTFEMINISM, HISTORY, ENGLISHNESS

The costume film belongs to a postfeminist popular culture addressing female audiences through questions of femininity and power while invested in traditional forms of women's culture such as fashion, makeup, knitting, cooking, and etiquette—informed, often with hints of irony, by feminist gender politics. Regarding the costume film, I read postfeminist reclamation of femininity through popular culture as a bid to retain values and subjective experiences associated with a private sphere that allows femininity to retain a recognizable shape. Romance, emotional caretaking, therapeutic conversation (the "talking cure"), women's intuition, grooming, and dress are such practices of femininity that rely upon a sense of the private. The costume film presents the past as a conduit to these experiences, once given place and meaning by nineteenth-century protocols of the private sphere, that in postmodern culture are increasingly left to the individual to understand, define, and manage on their own: hence the popularity of self-help books, makeover television shows, and magazines that offer guidance from "cultural experts." In characterizing and reinforcing such experiences as feminizing, the costume film participates in the culture of management and expertise around femininity.

Postfeminist popular culture operates as an "intimate public," which Lauren Berlant (2008) identifies as

> a market domain where a set of problems associated with managing femininity is expressed and worked through incessantly. . . . In all cases, it [femininity] flourishes by circulating as an already felt need, a sense of emotional continuity among women who identify with the expectation that, as women, they will manage personal life and lubricate emotional worlds. (5)

Berlant's emphasis is on the resonance of femininity as a structure of emotional expectation and identity-making that imaginatively binds together women who may have nothing else in common.

For femininity to be something felt, it must be a condition, a form of experience recognized by its effects. In this light, we can see that women's fantasies of being a housewife, a bohemian, or stay-at-home mother, so exploited by the mainstream press, are not necessarily about dissatisfaction with feminism or female independence but rather a muddled way of expressing belief in and value for subjective forms of knowledge and emotionally rich relationships as vital to women's lives because they make gender feel real.

Costume films build upon postfeminist-era desires for a femininity-friendly world that merges feminist ideas with female experience by presenting heroines who are themselves seeking this balance.

Typically, the heroine expresses thoughts and values regarded as progressive for her period, underlining her idiosyncratic composition as both modern and historical, a combination that usually enables her greater happiness. Though speaking to the present, costume films deal in historical femininities using the past as a resource, delimitation, or an aesthetic, but rarely to recount facts. When women's history and the history of femininity are addressed, they become emotionalized into histories of experience. History enforces particular scenarios, locations, and protocols that give rise to distinctive emotional situations for the heroine in order to showcase her heightened sensitivity. Affectivity acts as a barometer of the heroine's true self, often against her will as with the blush, stammer, or faint, and such spontaneous revelation often marks a turning point. The past facilitates a more feeling life that the genre purports is also a richer life.

Through its attention to dialogue, self-reflection, and feeling, particularly falling in love, the costume film narrates process-oriented experiences and locates them in an aestheticized past. The heightened expressiveness of visual elements provided by period setting—particularly the repertory of costumes, interior decor, locations, and gestures—belong to a recognizable feminine iconography. Anachronisms and license with period details, argues Sue Harper (1994), reinforce the past as a feminized place infused with sensual feeling, luxury, pastoralism, and most of all romantic passion. The contemporary costume film participates in a broader history aesthetic that foregrounds other cultural forms such as fashion, interior decorating, and architecture that can all be combined synergistically in cinema. If history shows the expanded possibilities of femininity, the costume film expands the possibilities of history.

Through costume films, elements of historical femininities may re-enter the cultural imagination and inform new figurations of femininity, notably, at a time when most women's experiences of the private sphere and femininity do not correspond to representations of either limited conservative roles or feminist visions of full equality. Each generic cycle reconfigures its characterization of historical femininity. The contemporary costume film, in linking femininity and privacy, invokes themes such as female political power; gender construction; secrecy and information circulation; display, surveillance, and public effects; affectivity, creativity, and bohemian lifestyles.

Distinctions between different eras in costume dramas are often nominally acknowledged in the mise-en-scène only to be countered by a generalized gloss of Victoriana so that history becomes a haze of "pastness" and "olden times" when life incurred greater formality, women were relegated to the home, female sexuality was repressed, and women wore corsets and long skirts. The Victorian imaginary deploys styles and silhouettes recognizable from nineteenth-century photography and art that impart a sense of familiarity and stability to the fictional world. Victoriana, however, is also shorthand for Englishness, the romanticized idea of England that calls upon aesthetics, sensations, feelings, and the authority of tradition to justify particular practices of living (Ribiero 2002, 17). Always a retrospective and sentimental construct, its emblems of afternoon tea, the monarchy, the country house, the garden, the hunt, and politeness supply the genre's iconography.

More significantly, however, Englishness is a gateway to a classed ideal of femininity tied to the protocols of genteel society, a configuration that cannot be accessed through Americanness, which at its foundation disavows class privilege and embraces a rhetoric of ordinariness. By rejecting the current approach to the costume film through heritage critique and class politics, we see that class assumes more dynamic and productive functions than often supposed. The aristocracy, characterized by access to time, provides a form that interlaces the personal with the historical, and this structural combination undergirds the genre's dual effect: history becomes personalized, within reach, and the personal becomes timeless, gaining import. Imagined aristocratic ancestry endows the personal life of a woman with amplified significance that makes personal history also social history and lays claim to an ideal femininity as her inheritance.

The second and more nuanced effect requires us to recognize that Englishness and upper-class status are not end desires in the costume film but represent a relationship to time that was once built into genteel womanhood. This slow, yet grand form of time is crucial to the genre's valuation of femininity. As a route into the temporality of leisure and personal feeling, class is treated in the costume film as a lifestyle that showcases the benefits of privacy to femininity. In scenes of romantic excitement, intimate conversation, grooming, contemplation, and affect, the transcendence of time is an aesthetic component of the heroine's experience. Because processes of feeling cannot be measured, they are consigned to the personal life and it is these very experiences—romance, empathy, reverie, meditation, ecstasy—that find in the costume film presence, worth, and authority.

The genre also aids a psychic transversal in time for viewers who can project their modern sense of self into the past. In her study of the Gainsborough cycle of costume films, Pam Cook emphasizes the imaginative engagements found in the interplay between now, then, and what is to come, noting that these films "exorcise the past and rehearse the future . . . in order to look forward to a more egalitarian future in which the role of women will be crucial" (1996, 89). Similarly, in the contemporary costume film, history envisions the future as a place in which imagined historical femininities can be reconstructed, emancipated from the constraints of prior cultural meanings and contingencies, to become part of a superior feminine way that accumulates the best of past and present. The genre's vision of a feminine return that will improve the lot not just of women but society as a whole, a sort of "once and future feminine," is justified by a display of the sensitivity that femininity entails. The vision of a feminine return imagines the denigration and trivialization of values and pleasures deemed feminizing to be reversed as respect and commendation, thereby ameliorating many ills of a male-dominated society. This hopeful assertion of femininity as an all-in-one tool, a form of knowledge, and a resource for living is the contemporary costume film's fundamental proposition.

ELIZABETH: GENDER ACTS AND THE POWER OF STYLE

Propelling Shekhar Kapur's film *Elizabeth* is the question, what happens to femininity when a woman, defined by personal desires and spaces, enters the public sphere of politics? The film introduces Elizabeth (Cate Blanchett) entrenched in a private-sphere model of femininity, consumed by her romance with Lord Robert (Joseph Fiennes). However, throughout the film, romantic and sexual liaisons lead to mortal danger and the protection of intimate spaces prove illusory. Undressing after her coronation, we see Elizabeth through a window, her image distorted and stretched, establishing the malleable, unfocused character of her identity as queen and clearly linking it here to the space of the boudoir.

If the expansion of femininity to encompass agency and individuality is the underlying project of any costume-film heroine, its import for viewers is clarified in Robert Connell's argument that gender "is a becoming, a condition actively under construction. . . . Part of the mystery of gender is how a pattern that on the surface appears so stark and rigid, on close examination turns out so fluid, complex and uncertain" (2002, 4). Gender is a way of organizing bodies and their meanings in the social world, and *Elizabeth* narrates the process of making gender through phases of experimenting, testing, and refining. Elizabeth remakes femininity, shifting from a conventional model to one that accommodates and reinforces absolute power.

Initially, Elizabeth attempts mimicry of male power, lowering her vocal register when speaking before her war council, which to her advisors rings untrue. Her failure at impersonation leads her next to alternate between different models of female power—virgin, wife, mother, coquette, and *femme fatale*—in order to integrate femininity with her office. Speaking before parliament in a head-to-toe red velvet ensemble, a color and fabric associated with the courtesan or seductress, her words draw upon more modest figurations of femininity: "I ask you to pass this Act of Uniformity not for myself, but for my people, who are my only care." When accused by a bishop of forcing her own agenda, Elizabeth replies coyly, "How can I force you, Your Grace? I am a woman." The simultaneity of her claims to the maternal and coquetry show off the composite and paradoxical nature of gender as identity style. Yet, as a testing ground for control of outcomes, her flirtatiousness is subject to the compliance of others and so fails to meet the exigencies of leadership.

To elevate the status of its heroine, the film seeks to relocate femininity's source. To the advisors and courtiers anxious for Elizabeth to marry and beget an heir, she is a woman identified by her reproductive capacity. Like other postfeminist films about single women, *Elizabeth* invokes "time panic" for a life based on the biological clock, whereby fertility dictates social value (Tasker and Negra 2007, 10). The female body in *Elizabeth,* however, is continually denied as the register of femininity, most notably when the queen exposes her suitor, the Duc D'Anjou, as a secret cross-dresser and more subtly in appropriating the spiritual eminence of the Virgin Mary. Instead, in *Elizabeth,* femininity is carried in surfaces and gestures.

Over the course of the film, transformations in Elizabeth's manner and speech are buttressed by the evolution of Blanchett's costumes as the softened silhouettes, brighter palette, and Victorian-style bustle skirts give way to stiffer gowns, wide panniers, and ornately embellished brocades that formalize the queen's political ascension. The visual monumentality of dress adds gravitas to the character's image; however, her increasing hyper-stylization also encodes femininity with other symbolic and practical functions beyond mere spectacle. In the costume discourse, Elizabeth's aggrandized self-presentation is the substance of her feminine power: architectural garments exaggerate the female shape beyond human proportions, enlarging her presence while the erasure of her earthly body feigns the divine. Inhabiting these cathedral-like vestments, she transcends the female through the idealized feminine. Elizabeth's sartorial pageantry also arrests attention, distracting from her gender-transgressing behavior. The feminine ideal polices the boundaries of her social acceptability. The film's focus on formulas of presentation and dress comments on the limits of available tools of femininity even as they are taken up with new relevance.

Exalted femininity secures authority for Elizabeth but cannot grant her the exercise of power. This necessitates co-opting male acts of privilege and reinstitutionalizing them. Accordingly, Elizabeth's public confrontation before the court with her repentant lover, Robert Dudley—and implicitly with those who would marry her to the Duc D'Anjou—ends with her self-masculinizing declaration of absolute power: "I will have one Mistress here and no Master!" With these words reorganizing how others may respond to her, Elizabeth dictates a new gender regime for the state. Sarah Kozloff observes that, "Whenever speech is valued as an important act in the public sphere, it is seen as masculine . . . the reason that women are silenced and objectified is to deny them access to powerful speech" (2000, 11). It is through the command of monarchical language, already coded as masculine, that Elizabeth takes hold of the male prerogative to decide and reverses the traditional feminine script of receptivity and accommodation. Here, speech and power mutually define each other, catalyzed by publicness.

If we understand what we are by how others respond to us, then sociality is an identity-making process that works back from effects to verify the source. Public effects supply a means of "discovering" the self, conceiving identity as relational and improvisational (Margolis 2005). Monarchs access a unique form of subjectivity through their public effects; the very reach of these effects confers authority. Rather than sweeping away Elizabeth's intentions and desires, we can see queenhood as reconfiguring her sense of self from the outside in, via public effects.

Consequently, for Elizabeth, the public arena is transformed from an oppressive space of constant scrutiny to one where her actions as queen have public effects, and thus is her identity made and verified to herself. However, if monarchical subjectivity is bound up with public effects, this complicates the designs of private desire. Elizabeth resolves this tension along the axis of political ambition, redirecting her desire to service her power. In the synthesis of desire and self-actualization, gender acts shift from tactics of power to identity style. This culmination is staged in a shot of Elizabeth framed as a portrait with her long hair let down, scolding her advisor, Lord William: "The word *must* is not used to princes." Her self-identification as Tudor son positions Elizabeth as a psychic transvestite, exhibiting fluidity and ambivalence, yet crystallizing her compound of feminine appearance and masculine action. A gender-composite being uncontainable in one category, Elizabeth destabilizes binary gender and in its lacuna redefines possibilities. To borrow a description of the historical Queen, she comes to "possess the privilege of two bodies" (Garber 1992, 28).

Elizabeth presents an anomalous view of publicness and power for women, one that reorganizes gender, autonomy, and display to overturn the generic preoccupation with emotionality and romantic healing. Yet, even as the film challenges masculinist paradigms of power and takes up second-wave feminist views of the private sphere as a site of oppression, its vision of female empowerment is limited by traditional oppositions of romance versus power, which forces a heavy compromise. Similarly, in reconfirming the alignment, feminine/visual: masculine/verbal, *Elizabeth* is unable to fully reimagine the uses of femininity.

MARIE ANTOINETTE: SUBVERSIVE STYLE
AND THE IMAGINATIVE LIFE

In contrast to *Elizabeth,* femininity is presumed to be desirable in Sofia Coppola's film *Marie Antoinette,* which advances the genre's characteristic view of privacy as a generative condition for femininity. However, the film locates femininity and power within the arena of fashion, taking very seriously what is often considered most frivolous in women: the ardent pursuit of self-adornment. From the first scenes onward, Marie (Kirsten Dunst) is treated as a visual object irrevocably led into a strange world of display, her life presented through a contemporary fashion lens that retrospectively aligns eighteenth-century style with femininity.

Accordingly, like *Vogue* come to life, *Marie Antoinette* draws upon the fashion magazine for a visual lexicon of femininity that combines luxurious clothing, grand locations, and opulence with gestures of boredom, desire, and excess in order to explore the relationship between aesthetics and feminine identity. The relation of both to fashionability is exemplified by the figure of Marie Antoinette, who, historian Caroline Weber explains, "will always speak to designers because she is shorthand for French glamour, elegance, individualism and hyper-decoration" (quoted in Krum 2006, 18). Coppola's own influence on the current style elite is evident in her fashion resumé, which includes modeling, editing, designing, and directing various projects with *Vogue,* Chanel, Marc Jacobs, Louis Vuitton, and Christian Dior.[1] Her use of Versailles as a location authenticates not so much

French history as the icon Marie Antoinette, a woman redefining femininity for herself and, through her impact, for the modern woman of fashion as well.

As with many fashion images, the film takes the form of the *tableau vivant,* comprised of staged poses and compositions, vivifying key moments of a larger narrative already familiar to the audience. Freed by this format from the burdens of exposition, the visual assumes other functions such as metaphor, mood, and fantasy. The look of the fashion tableau is produced through a conflation of techniques: frequent use of a stationary camera; orchestrated compositions; choreographed movement; the juicy candy color palette of magazine graphics, particularly pinks; and Marie's striking poses framed by doorways, windows, and other architectural forms.

The power of dress to make an impression has long been recognized in social practices such as sumptuary law, official pageantry, and use of uniforms to enforce exclusivity and image control. The system of fashion, however, entails a more fluid relationship between attire and person, one in which aesthetic choices influence and transform personality. Fashion choices also invoke cultural meanings that may be sought or disavowed by the wearer. Women, then, implicitly understand through fashion that gender is constructed, nuanced, and mutable. The sensuality of clothes both elicits and expresses a bodily sense of femininity, and this somatic quality makes it feel authentic. In this relationship between body and dress, *Marie Antoinette* finds a compelling dynamic of resistance and power. Rather than denoting era or symbolizing character, the film's costumes and settings are used as thematic elements that, following Stella Bruzzi's argument, demand to be "looked at" for their explication of women's desires (1997, 36). In *Marie Antoinette,* beauty is never trivial and surfaces are only as superficial as language itself.

As the critical literature about the Queen shows, Marie Antoinette's iconicity rests in her capacity for interpretation in a multitude of ways and, so too, Coppola's film constructs her multiply.[2] The film imagines Marie's experiences and responses *as a woman,* a condition the character illuminates for viewers. The historical Marie Antoinette is of no real concern here; this film is not a bio-pic, it doesn't look past her iconicity, it justifies it. Through the queen, the film charts an alternative discourse on femininity and fashion, focusing on how experiencing the sensual provides a basis for feminine self-construction and agency.

Nowhere is this articulated more clearly than at Versailles. Here Marie's agency is constrained under the continuous public gaze of the court, but through fashion she temporarily harnesses some of that power for herself. Fashion is first a distraction from her boredom and comfort for the neglected wife, a point made clear when her anguished sobbing at being childless is immediately followed by the film's upbeat montage of indulgent shopping set to the Bow Wow Wow song, "Candy." Consolation, though, is the reward of the follower, whereas the trendsetter, driven by vision, garners public power by style. A master of tactical aesthetics, the fashion leader rules as much by the power of suggestion as by innovation.

When Marie leads a theater audience to break protocol and follow her in clapping for the performers, she demonstrates not only her wide influence but also agency in turning publicness to her own ends. Impending ostracism is deftly turned into adulation via seductive charisma. It is through her intuitive understanding of spectacle that Marie becomes premier style maker of France, gaining some of the attention she craves.[3] *Marie Antoinette* supports seduction as a clever mode of power for women but ultimately this subordinates the seducer more than the seduced, for as Marie's influence grows, her image comes to replace her self with dire consequences. Nevertheless, the film demonstrates the use of fashion as a mechanism for coping with publicness, as well as its limits: for exceeding Marie's visual persona is her feeling.

As much as fashion is a tool for making femininity, feeling is material for its construction. The affectivity and emotionality of the heroine constitute the generic verisimilitude of the costume film, expressed primarily through the close-up which, Julianne Pidduck notes, focuses "feeling, affect, and intensity" (2004, 17). Credible femininity is performed in a heroine's moments of everyday affect when the blush, the smile, and the tears held back give evidence of a genuineness that has been repressed by propriety. The frequency of close-ups in *Marie Antoinette*, overlaid with music, showing Marie's face when crying, dreaming, bored, or embarrassed turns her emotionality into a distinctively visual property, hence her unequalled refinement is demonstrated by her hyper-sensitivity. Afflicted by disappointment in love and lack of intimacy in friendship, family, and community, Marie's loneliness is repeatedly shown by her passivity and disconnectedness within lively social situations. In the logic of romance, not to be the beloved, not to be nurtured, are forms of injustice and deprivation. Berlant observes that, "Aloneness is one of the affective structures of being collectively, structurally unprivileged" (2008, ix). Breaking from this conception, *Marie Antoinette* presents aloneness as a condition necessary for feeling, distinct from loneliness. In states of humiliation and grief, aloneness provides relief from surveillance and the cessation of stimuli. The pain of not producing an heir builds to a climax for Marie when she reads of her sister-in-law's pregnancy and the close-up on her anguished face constitutes a filmic event (see fig. 7.1). Crying, she slides against the wall to the floor, the floral print of her dress echoing the wallpaper pattern, suggesting Marie's shifting status from the forefront of court life to decorative wallflower. Aloneness, however, also offers key moments of awareness, daydreaming, and reverie, and thus it constitutes a rare state of privacy rather than the result of abandonment. Three important notions linking affect and femininity are confirmed in *Marie Antoinette*: that a woman's feeling has value and significance of its own; that its display underwrites a therapeutic project, taking emotional expressivity as agency; and that the affective forms an aesthetic of heroine-hood. If femininity is a style of self-management and affectivity one of its key expressions, then privacy is its essential procedural condition.

Fig. 7.1 At Versailles: bad news in *Marie Antoinette* (2006)

Marie Antoinette represents the impact on identity of two time regimes: first, the sense of timeliness that orders Marie's life at Versailles and second, a sense of time flow in her experiences at the Petit Trianon, her country retreat, that fosters a new form of feminine subjectivity. Linearity, progress, and history are the traits of masculine empirical time, whereas repetition and ahistoricity mark femininity with what Julia Kristeva terms cyclical time and monumental time, which characterize events at the Petit Trianon. Throughout, the film omits historical information, narrational causality, and dialogue that would anchor scenes to linear time. Instead, it employs a series of vignettes and montages comprised of scenes of eating, entertaining, gossiping, dressing, and parading through the palace to create a timescape of routine and distraction, emphasizing the emptiness threatened by boredom at Versailles. At the Petit Trianon, however, extended scenes of intimate social interaction and creative pursuit emphasize duration and timelessness. Temporal processes of feminine construction such as grooming, dressing, and secret-sharing are prioritized throughout the film; however, it is in the country where feeling supersedes time as the ordering principle of Marie's life, infusing her activity with new purpose.

Scenes of leisure and play unfold in real time with ambient sound suggesting a life of Marie's own making: gliding by in a boat as her fingertips graze the water, picking strawberries, feeding a lamb with her young daughter, tasting fresh milk, and lounging in the grass with her lover, Count Fersen (Jamie Dornan). In these vignettes, the film asks us to consider how unrestrained time might reshape subjectivity by highlighting moments of daydreaming and sensual discovery as central to Marie's changing agency and self-construction. In *Marie Antoinette,* real life, rather than excluding fantasy, is incomplete without it, for the imagination

Fig. 7.2 Daydreaming on the water at the Petit Trianon: *Marie Antoinette* (2006)

enriches material living. Private space is integral to forging a complex and satis-fying construction of self, and it is only at the Petit Trianon that Marie achieves a true home that allows her to direct her relationships with her self, with others, and with art. *Marie Antoinette* asks us to attend to femininity as process rather than outcome, positing that in aesthetic experiences of self, Marie transcends product-oriented time and forges happiness.

Fashion invokes a rhetoric of personal style, embraced by *Marie Antoinette*, seemingly in tacit resistance to the double overdetermination of women's choices by patriarchy and feminism. In this manner, Marie's independent creativity in-tervenes in cultural authority. However, while the film sites political power in the aesthetic, this is directed not at social change but rather at resisting social limitation on the possibilities for self-discovery, agency, and meaning. In a world of artifice and prescribed roles, fashion is the means by which Marie's individual voice prevails over officialdom. So, rather than mask loneliness, dress provides the greatest intimacy with her self. At the Petit Trianon, Marie abandons the corset and luxury fabrics required of courtly dress for the more "natural" look of simple shifts in muslin and linen. This disruption of royal protocol and social order translates the politics of taste into the liberty of choice, keeping the film's focus on self-expression.

Style synthesizes different pieces of affective knowledge into an expressive statement of the self, linking processes of identity construction and aesthetic creation. If creative activity is the portal to self-possession, singing, amateur dramatics, gardening, and designing clothes move Marie from passivity to the active position of artist and producer. Marie's reconstruction of a village farm on the Petit Trianon's grounds brings her creative exploration together with daily living, combining reality and play in pastoral therapy. Linking aesthetic experience with nature, the film has Marie read Jean Jacques Rousseau to her friends, asking rhetorically, "What is the natural state?" This is not to recuperate essentialist claims for femininity but to show the natural world as a place where sensual experiences abound and a sense of self is recognized in relation to a sense of place (see fig. 7.3). This touches the capacity of the physical and metaphysical to make possible at the Petit Trianon what is impossible at Versailles: a whole life aesthetic, an existential philosophy that is lived in, thus delivering what analysis and thought alone cannot: *joie de vivre*. Coppola herself, explaining why *Marie Antoinette* had to be made in France, places sensual temporality within a French cultural aesthetic of daily living: "In America, we're all in such a rush. Here, they have lifestyle priorities. . . . Here, everyone takes their time" (*The Independent,* Oct. 15, 2006).[4] Without a qualitative approach to life, the film suggests, the self will eventually shatter like the fallen chandelier that closes the film.

HISTORY AND OTHER AESTHETICS

If artifacts and historical objects collapse past and present, their reproduction transfers authority from origin to style. In this sense, *Marie Antoinette* functions as conscious reproduction-as-style that turns past and present into acts of imagination and feeling. The reproduction stratagem has antecedents in two other films also set in the years surrounding the French Revolution, Stanley Kubrick's *Barry Lyndon* (1975) and Eric Rohmer's *The Lady and the Duke* (2001), both of which imagine the period through the conventions of fine art. The period itself is so familiarly imagined for us that history is already style. In this vein, *Marie*

Fig. 7.3 A sense of place at the Petit Trianon: *Marie Antoinette* (2006)

Antoinette uses portrait-style framing, tableau arrangements, and depth-of-field shots to mimic oil painting, fairy-tale illustration, and contemporary fashion images. The film's use of the history aesthetic, eliding past and present through anachronism and stylistic juxtaposition, finds an intensified expression in dress.

Contemporary trends in vintage and period-inspired clothing draw upon costume films not only for specific references but also for the character stories that lend desire and glamour to clothes. In this respect, *Marie Antoinette,* in its visual vocabulary of poses, settings, color palette, details of sleeve shape, skirt length, and corset lacing, draws on contemporary fashion sensibilities as much as historical sources. Casting Kirsten Dunst as Marie references her own standing as a fashion trendsetter in popular culture, calling for reading multiple personas into her performance, including that of fashion model. A publicity tie-in with *Vogue* featured Dunst costumed as Marie Antoinette on the cover of its September 2006 issue. Its editorial copy, headed "Teen Queen," was shot on location at Versailles and featured the actress wearing evening gowns by top couturiers, showing off what a modern-era Marie would wear. The issue also included an advertising spread for popular label, Juicy Couture, featuring a model in Marie's signature pouf hairstyle in pink and trays of pastries and gift boxes strewn about Louis XVI chairs, all in a popsicle-hued palette.[5] More than just clever publicity and tongue-in-cheek homage, the magazine illustrates the cross-platform fashion idiom of period dress through which a sense of the historical is *felt* as a presence. In the history aesthetic, period dress represents simultaneously identity, costume, and artifact; it facilitates entry, like a pass card, into imaginary scenarios not presupposed in the present everyday world, temporarily bestowing on them the status of the real.

The crossover influence between fashion and film extends beyond costume in Coppola's film. *Marie Antoinette* deploys its own tactical aesthetics, crafting a collaged fashion layout that fits together seemingly incongruous styles of performance, cast, period setting, and props to highlight the complex and highly worked visual surface of the film. Stylistic coherence is disrupted through performance: costume is altered by the actor's deportment and posture, dialogue gets revised by accent, cadence, and intonation, the authority of historical characters is undermined by casting, and relationships between characters are attenuated by lack of chemistry between actors. The motley cast of indie-film actor Jason Schwartzman, British parodist Steve Coogan, French horror film actress Asia Argento, *Saturday Night Live* comedian Molly Shannon, singer Marianne Faithful, and the coarsely carnal Rip Torn creates a pastiche of acting styles, accents, and personas that borders on camp, displacing the formal acting styles common in costume films. In particular, Kirsten Dunst's colloquial American speech refuses the usual collapse of actress and role that supports stardom. The film exposes the genre as reconstruction, thwarting the fantasy of immersion in historical period while facilitating other fantasies of personal time-travel and identity switching whereby modern girl Dunst *experiences* the historical like a theme park ride through Marie Antoinette's life. Commenting on the role, the actress explained, "I felt like I was Marie Antoinette's ghost, or her perfume, more so than actually her" (Schwartzman 2006, 170).

Using the construction of history, of cinema, and of the self as analogues for each other, *Marie Antoinette* takes the costume film far beyond its conventional template, privileging visual elements over the narrative. Recurring images of Marie looking out of her carriage window remind the viewer of images, looking, and watching as pleasures integral to femininity and to the genre. The film has reimagined femininity as an aesthetic where surfaces bear the burden of meaning, where identity is improvisational, where creativity is the key to agency, and privacy guards the self in order to assert the value of feeling, imagination, and love as human needs. It is this very vision that the costume film genre claims as the true meaning of life, the drama that turns all women into heroines.

Notes

1. Coppola's roles include: co-designer of the label Milk Fed, intern at Chanel, model on the cover of Italian *Vogue* (Dec. 1992), guest editor of French *Vogue* (Dec. 2004), appearing in advertising campaigns for Marc Jacobs and Louis Vuitton, and directing a television commercial for Christian Dior's Miss Dior Cherie fragrance, which debuted on November 10, 2008, during an episode of *Gossip Girl*.

2. See "Writings on the Body of a Queen," which explores diverse interpretations and uses of Marie Antoinette's public persona, particularly during her own time (Goodman 2003).

3. The historical Marie Antoinette appointed dressmaker Rose Bertin and hairdresser Leonard as her own Ministry of Fashion, and her ensembles sparked trends in women's dress throughout France. For discussion of the political meanings of her clothes, see Weber (2006).

4. Although aesthetic living is shown as more accessible through femininity, there is nothing to exclude men from taking up Marie's protobohemian lifestyle.

5. Coppola's commercial for Miss Dior Cherie fragrance features a model resembling Kirsten Dunst enjoying a sunny day in Paris filled with colorful macaroons and petit fours, bouquets of flowers, balloons, and perfume, once again in the same palette of bright pastel shades.

CHAPTER 8

GENERIC GLEANING:

AGNÈS VARDA, DOCUMENTARY, AND THE ART OF SALVAGE

LUCY FISCHER

In several of her films, Agnès Varda is concerned with the homeless. In *Vagabond* (*Sans toit ne loi*, 1985), for instance, she depicts a few weeks in the life of a young female vagrant as she wanders through the French countryside in winter—camping out, scavenging food, doing odd jobs, joining and leaving packs of drifters, and, ultimately, freezing to death in a ditch. While, clearly, Varda is far from homeless in this sense (having lived for decades in the same Paris apartment), she is, perhaps, somewhat "rootless" in her aesthetic and generic affiliations.

On the one hand, some Varda films, like *Happiness* (*Le Bonheur*, 1965), have been viewed as rather conventional dramas. On the other hand, critics like Sandy Flitterman-Lewis (1993 and 1996) and Judith Mayne (2002) have seen some of her narrative work as compatible with the avant-garde. *Cleo From 5 to 7* (*Cléo de 5 à 7*, 1961), for example, employs such inventive strategies as: the mixture of color and black and white, the division of the story into chapters, direct address to the camera, and dizzying mirror and reflection shots. Similarly, Vincent Canby (1969) once called *Lion's Love* (1969) a "cockeyed" "Pirandellian" "meta-Warhol movie," and Varda, herself, talks of wanting to make "strange films" (1996). Finally, Varda's opus has been uniquely balanced between fiction and documentary poles, with such texts as *Black Panthers* (1968), *Daguerréotypes* (1979), and *The World of Jacques Demy* (*L'univers de Jacques Demy*, 1995) veering toward the latter. Ultimately, Varda's aesthetic "itinerancy" is to be applauded, in that, like the female vagabond of her 1985 film, she boldly operates "without roof or rule" within the cinematic and generic terrains. Furthermore, her artistic "vagrancy" is inextricably tied to her passionate interest in the dispossessed and nomadic subject—be it of the animate or inanimate kind.

The film on which I will focus is one that strongly invokes this theme: *The Gleaners and I* (*Les glaneurs et la glaneuse*), made in 2000. By most traditional estimations (including its categorizations on the Internet Movie Data Base, Block-buster, and Netflix Web sites), the film is a documentary; and in keeping with this, it depicts non-acted, real-life events. But having called it this, I am immediately uneasy with the label—since Varda's film seems far more ingenious than the kind of text usually associated with the term. Varda herself feels the word has been "spoiled." As she notes: "You say . . . documentary and people say 'What a bore.' We should have a middle word" for it (Carter 2002, 3). As this essay will demonstrate, if not a middle *word*, Varda has fashioned a middle *form* for it.

A brief description of *The Gleaners* will help to surface reasons for the work's categorical fluidity—even as it is positioned within a documentary frame. The film depicts an extended "road trip" that Varda takes (through city and country) in order to encounter and film a variety of people who "glean" things—be their plunder the traditional rural harvest or urban garbage. In the first category, she films potato gleaners in Beuce, grape gleaners in La Folie, and oyster gleaners by the coast. In the second group, she follows (among others) some teenagers from Prades who live on the street, a man who has eaten only trash for the past ten to fifteen years, and a Parisian who haunts produce markets and bakery dumpsters, foraging his food exclusively from the "remains of the day." But Varda's target is not entirely those who must glean to subsist. Rather, she also investigates those who do so as an avocation, like Chef Loubet, who forages to find the freshest vegetables. As Varda's voice-over remarks, each of her scavengers has "various reasons for doing so; each experiences it differently."

To understand the inventiveness of *The Gleaners,* however, it is first necessary to comprehend how documentaries have been traditionally conceived. As we know, conventional definitions have tended, albeit naively, to deem such films objective and devoid of artifice—this, despite the fact that all of them are edited and many of them are scripted, utilize staged sequences, and/or take a particular point of view. In recent years, of course, such unsophisticated notions have been contested, but the aura of "objectivity" still hovers over the form. For examples, the Web-based Film Site Glossary states that a documentary is a "factual, narrative film with real people (not performers or actors)" that presents a "journalistic record of an event, person, or place." Its maker "should be an unobtrusive observer—like a fly-on-the-wall, capturing reality as it happens" (see http://www.filmsite.org/ filmterms7.html, accessed March 24, 2011). Beyond defining the form, critics have often divided it into a set of discrete subgenres, with differences established be-tween them. Bill Nichols, for instance breaks the genre down into six constituent types: poetic, expository, observational, participatory, reflexive, and performative (2001, 99 and 138). As we shall see, on almost every level, *The Gleaners* challenges objectivity and fuses together documentary's component forms.

Were Varda's film only a survey of the contemporary practice of agricultural gleaning, it would be a rather standard social documentary (like one we might see on the *Frontline* series on PBS). Even on this level, however, *The Gleaners* is more complex than most, since it combines two of Nichols's six approaches to the subject: the expository (which "objectively" presents information to the viewer as though from an omniscient eye) and the participatory (which places the filmmaker directly in her subjects' world). But *The Gleaners* simultaneously invokes other categories that Nichols lists. Beyond simply picturing Varda within the screen image, it utilizes her voice-over monologue to make the film a personal meditation on her life—the opposite of an objective text, and one that invokes the performative and the poetic. While, often, Varda's narration simply relates where she is traveling and why, at moments it becomes shockingly intimate. Early on, we view extreme close-up footage of her thinning, white-rooted, hair as she combs it, and of her wrinkled, liver-spotted hands. Accompanying these images, her voice elegiacally intones: "It's not old age, my enemy. It might even be old age, my friend; but still my hair and my hands keep telling me the end is near." Varda was a woman in her seventies when *The Gleaners* was made, and here and elsewhere she makes us painfully aware of her consciousness of mortality as well as the toll the years have taken on her body. Later (when she returns to her home from a trip to Japan), we see her hands again, accompanied by lyrical words that speak of "the horror of it" (by which we assume she means aging). As she continues: "I feel as though I am an animal—worse, an animal I don't know." Thus, in the midst of a social documentary about gleaning (one that focuses on factual, external events), we find introspective material about an aging woman's dismay at her corporeal state. Clearly, the film is, on one level, a self-portrait, and in the course of its unraveling, Varda underscores the point by briefly contemplating a similar study by Rembrandt, a canonical male artist.

In its focus on the female authorial self, *The Gleaners* joins the ranks of numerous innovative documentaries directed by women in the 1970s-1990s, for instance Chantal Akerman's *News From Home* (1977), Su Friedrich's *The Ties That Bind* (1984), Camille Billops's *Finding Christa* (1991), and Rea Tajiri's *History and Memory* (1991). Like Varda's film, these texts are highly personal—making a feminist intervention into the male-dominated, aloof, documentary form. As works made by younger artists, they concentrate on their own generational issues: especially the mother/daughter relationship, a highly charged topic for second-wave feminists. *The Gleaners* also shares with these works a use of female voice-over that some critics have seen as a stylistic trope of women's counter-cinema (Silverman 1988, 141). Significantly, Varda has employed this technique in other films. In *Vagabond,* which begins as a conventional drama told from the perspective of an omniscient camera, her narration abruptly and erratically intrudes itself. After being introduced to the character of Mona (Sandrine Bonnaire), Varda's off-screen voice suddenly informs us that various people who remember Mona will help her "reconstruct the last weeks of the vagrant's life." Varda is the film's screenwriter and seems to address us vocally in a quite unexpected manner from behind the camera, though her persona as author will have no place within the film's diegesis. Similarly, in *Jacquot de Nantes* (a tribute to her deceased husband Jacques Demy), there are times when an unidentified female narrator speaks, telling us things about Demy (like the fact that the kitchen was the center of his family's life, or that events of his childhood inspired his films). Again, we assume the voice to be that of Varda—the film's author and the subject's wife—someone who has privileged knowledge of Demy's biography. But she is not identified as such, there is no particular pattern to the voice's emergence, and her words mix indiscriminately with those of other narrators (most especially Demy himself). Her use of voice-over in *The Gleaners,* however, is quite different from these dis-embodied precedents. Here, it is clearly marked as her own since she is frequently depicted within the image and we learn to match her voice with her person.

But having surfaced the subjective nature of Varda's documentary, we might ask: What is the relation between her personal deliberation on aging and the rest of film, which is cast in a more traditionally detached tone? In its classic sense, gleaning involves collecting the residue of the harvest, after the prime vegetation has been reaped. Put less generously, one gleans a crop's discards, its refuse, its detritus—products deemed less desirable than what is first accumulated. Some-times, what is gleaned has even begun to disintegrate (as we see when Varda shows us a potato that is decomposing and sprouting tubers). It is not a stretch, then, to imagine that Varda (at her grimmer moments) sees herself—an elderly woman—as somewhat akin to these vegetative "rejects," at least as seen by a youth-obsessed and patriarchal society. French feminist Simone de Beauvoir theorized this condition. In *The Second Sex* she notes: "Long before the eventual mutilation, woman is haunted by the horror of growing old" as she "looks on at the degeneration of this fleshly object which she identifies with herself." Further-more, woman experiences a kind of dissociation: "'This cannot be I' [she thinks], 'this old woman reflected in the mirror!' The woman who 'never felt so young in her life' and who has never seen herself so old does not succeed in reconciling these two aspects of herself" (1961, 645). Clearly, Varda rejects this duality—forc-ing herself to accept the mirror's image through the camera's lens. Even objects gleaned in an urban setting can be "past their prime." When Varda rummages through street trash one night with her friend François, she finds a transparent, handless clock that she later, defiantly, installs on her mantel—a fetish to ward off temporal progression. As she notes: "You don't see time passing."

Circulating in this discourse on maturation, rot, and debris, are questions of the abject—the miserable or wretched. For Julia Kristeva, in *Powers of Horror,* we experience it as a "threat" that we attempt to negate by summoning up a "dark revolt." As she notes: "It lies there, quite close, but it cannot be assimilated. It beseeches, it worries, and *fascinates* desire, which nevertheless, does not let itself be seduced" (1982, 1, my emphasis). For Kristeva, abjection "is experienced at the peak of its strength" when directed at the self (5). Clearly, Varda explores the dynamic of abjection: moving from the decay of external objects to the ravages of her own flesh. Kristeva also finds that abjection selectively attaches to the female—especially as she ages. She quotes Céline in this regard, who writes: "Women, you know, they wane by candle-light, they spoil, melt, twist and ooze! . . . The end of tapers is a horrible sight, the end of ladies too" (Quoted in Kristeva, 169).

But it seems significant that Kristeva also uses the word "fascinate" to characterize our reaction to the abject, implying that our response can be a love-hate affair. It is this urge to engage (as well as distance) the abject that characterizes *The Gleaners*. As Varda comments: "I like filming . . . waste, mold and trash." Sometimes the abject also involves deformity. One farmer picks up a fallen apple and states misogynistically: "It's like an ugly and stupid woman." In another sequence, a man shows Varda a heart-shaped potato and she begins to collect others with great affection. While rebuffed by growers, for her, they are valued artifacts—bizarre, melancholy, and evocative. In her love of the discarded, the anomalous, and the malformed, Varda also veers away from traditional associations of woman with the beautiful.

The reference to Rembrandt in the film also alerts us to the fact that, while, on the surface, *The Gleaners* is a social polemic about rural and urban collectors, it is also a reflection on creative production that borrows from the art documentary—a quite different mode. At one moment, linking painting and putrefaction, she points to mold on her ceiling, which she then frames like a series of canvases by Tapies, Borderie, and Quo-Qiang. Obviously, the film's title also invokes the visual arts in its reference to a famous painting of 1857 by Jean-François Millet, which Varda displays in the film. But other creative works also have a role. In the course of her travels, she passes an antique shop and fortuitously discovers within it an anonymous painting of gleaners that she purchases to exhibit in her home. As Varda opines: "It had beckoned us because it belongs in this film."

Over the course of the film, she visits numerous artists whose work is constructed of recycled scrap. One is an old folk craftsman (and former bricklayer), Bodan Litnanski, who makes totem towers from material found in dumps: plant pots, doll parts, hoses, wicker baskets, and pottery. His wife dismissively calls him an "amateur," but Varda admires how he "accommodates chance" (as does she, in her unexpected acquisition of the antique canvas). So, too, she calls upon renowned assemblage artist Louis Pons, who claims that the objects used in his constructions are his "dictionary" from which he makes "sentences." As he asserts: "People think it's a cluster of junk. I see it as a cluster of possibilities." Another artist Varda encounters deems himself "a painter and a retriever" who loves "anything that's been . . . discarded by society." For him, such objects "have a past," have "already had a life," which he supplements with "a second chance." She also visits an environmental center (which sports a banner reading "Trash Is Beautiful") where kids make sculptures out of refuse. Later, she stops to see some artists who use abandoned refrigerators as containers for surreal constructions (filling them with books, toy action figures, faucets, timepieces, etc.). At the end of the film Varda convinces a museum in Villefranche to remove from storage a painting by Pierre-Edmond-Alexandre Hédouin (1820–89) entitled *The Gleaners Fleeing the Storm*. She is ecstatic when the staff brings it into a courtyard where it is flooded by daylight and buffeted by the wind—the very environment in which its fictional rural subjects toil.

But Varda is interested in more than the history of the established plastic arts. She is concerned with photography and cinema (her own media), which catapults her documentary into Nichols's reflexive mode. At one point, she visits a museum in Arras and looks at a painting by Jules Breton (1827–1906) of a woman gleaning. She then mimics the painting's subject—eventually discarding a bundle of wheat and replacing it with her camera. Here, she cleverly fashions herself as both object (gleaner) and author (filmmaker) of the work of art—a pose that doubles her role in *The Gleaners*. Later, she visits some vineyards that were once owned by Étienne Jules Marey, the inventor of chronophotography, a precursor to cinema. Marey's status as the past owner of agricultural land conveniently links the topics of filmmaking and gleaning. On his property, we see a mini-museum honoring him as well as the tower from which he photographed animals and birds in motion. As we watch animated footage of Marey's work, the current vineyard owner deems it "experimental" and a "pure visual delight." As Varda notes, touting her vocational legacy, Marey "is the ancestor of all movie makers and we're proud to be family." Finally, at another moment, Varda sutures into her film a turn-of-the-twentieth-century actualité of gleaners working in a field, the film equivalent of Millet's painting. Significantly, the voice-over accompanying it is that of a contemporary female gleaner.

While on one level, Varda's depiction of farming and art is achieved through quasi-objective shooting (factual images of fields, reapers, paintings, sculptures, and the like), the topic has subjective meaning in its ties to her own creative endeavors. At one moment (following a discourse on laws against gleaning), she muses: "On . . . [the] gleaning, of images, [and] impressions, there is no legislation." At another point, she ruminates: "for forgetful me, it's what I have gleaned that tells where I've been." These two statements make us aware both of her pictorial craft and her fears of memory loss (and of the relation between the two). In another sequence (shot from a moving automobile), she puts one hand in front of the lens (while holding her camera with the other) and makes a circular matte with her fingers, using them to frame and isolate certain vehicles. In a self-conscious gesture, she encircles the image of an eye painted on the back of a passing truck. While she asserts that she likes to "capture" such fleeting views, she claims that it is not to "retain" but to "play" with them. Nonetheless, in her act of grabbing images, she seems to summon cinema's indexical status—its ability to seize and preserve traces of the mutable world (in a way that her failing memory cannot). André Bazin, for instance, talks of film as enacting a "preservation of life by a representation of life" (2004, 166). Furthermore, he notes: "Film is no longer content to preserve the object, enshrouded as it were in an instant. . . . Now, for the first time, the image of things is likewise the image of their duration, change mummified as it were" (169).

In an interview, Varda talks of how certain scenes in *The Gleaners* were only possible by using portable digital equipment that allowed her a certain intimacy and privacy in shooting: "I would have never asked my [Director of Photography] to film my hair or my hands," she says. "But by doing it myself, I felt it was natural. It was a cinematic act and not [one of self-] pity . . . I don't care if I'm aging. What can you do with your life? Create the cinematic act" (Hardy 2001). In the film itself, (moving further away from the objective potential of the camera), she applauds the transformative possibilities of digital imaging by playing with the camera's innovative techniques (its stroboscopic and cubistic possibilities), while simultaneously questioning its pull toward narcissism. Here, she affirms the cinema's experimental thrust by turning a mirror on herself but filling its frame with an abstract painting of a female face, while ironically intoning the word "hyperrealistic." Finally, we might imagine that there are aspects of digital (vs. photographic) imaging that especially appeal to Varda because her film is a meditation on aging and bodily decline. As Charles Swartz has noted, "In the digital domain, we can copy without deterioration, because every copy is a perfect clone of the original"; digital presentation is also "never dirty or scratched" (2005, 1–2).

The final artwork circulating in *The Gleaners* is *The Last Judgment* by fifteenth-century painter Rogier van der Weyden. In her voice-over, Varda acts as an art critic and directs our attention to those figures on the canvas who will be resurrected and those whose fate is Hell. While the picture seems to have no apparent link to gleaning, further thought reveals that it does. For gleaning is, on one level a feat of *salvage*—or an act of recovering "discarded or damaged material for further use" (*American Heritage Dictionary*). Put another way, such materials are *saved*—a word rife with spiritual overtones involving redemption (as at the Last Judgment).

But, aside from bearing an etymological trace, how does the link between salvage and salvation illuminate Varda's film? Here we must return to Millet's *The Gleaners* and the social implications of its iconography. When it premiered in the Paris Salon of 1857, it was considered a radical work. Its depiction of three stooped female gleaners in the foreground (scrounging for food) versus vital farmhands in the far background (presumably working for wages and amassing the fruits of the landlord's acreage) was seen to signify a strong contrast between the haves and have-nots. As art historian Robert Herbert remarks:

> Instead of sharing directly in the harvest, whose richness is evident in the great piles of grain, the gleaners are only allowed to gather leftover grain. Furthermore, we, the observers, are forced to be out here in the plain, close to them, taking as subject their labor and their poverty, rather than the fruitful work in the background. (1978, 18)

Some critics of the period were outraged by *The Gleaners,* calling its female subjects "scarecrows in rags" or the "Three Fates of Pauperism" (quoted in Herbert,
18). Others saw it as harking back to revolutionary times. The critic for *Le Figaro*
sensed behind it "the pikes of popular riots and the executioner's scaffoldings"
(quoted in Herbert, 18). One reviewer, Castagnary, however, was highly supportive
of Millet's project and wrote:

> Three peasants bent over, gleaning in the harvested field, while on the horizon,
> the master's wagons groan under the weight of the grain, wring[ing] the heart
> more painfully than seeing all the instruments of torture visited upon a mar-
> tyr. This canvas, which recalls frightful misery is not . . . a political harangue
> nor a social thesis: It is a very beautiful and very simple work of art, free of all
> declaiming. The motif is poignant . . . but treated as frankness itself, it is raised
> above partisan passions and removed from lies and exaggeration, reproducing
> one of the true great texts from nature. (Castagnary 1858, 35–37)

Ironically, Millet's canvas (initially seen as full of pity and moral outrage) would
later be viewed as a nostalgic treatise on the unity of Humanity and Nature—its
social critique long neutralized. In highlighting the painting once more, Varda
reinjects politics into the subject of gleaning—this time that of contemporary
ecologists who oppose the waste and pollution of consumer culture. These individuals also aspire to a form of self-sufficiency—much as Varda states that she
seeks to "film one hand with the other."

While the New Testament teaches us that "you reap whatever you sow," trying to assure us that there is an ethical order to the universe (Galatians 6:7), we
suspect there is not. As poet Madison Julius Cawein once stated: "Some shall reap
that never sow; And some shall toil and not attain" (quoted in Bartlett 1919, entry
8,192). From this perspective, Varda's film concerns the down and out—those
who are destitute and condemned to a bleak life outside the bourgeois safety
net. As Varda states in an online interview: "We try to illuminate the Fourth
World—the world of ghosts, the forgotten, the poor—but not the classic poor,
not the official poor. It's the poor nobody speaks of. They don't go to the Red
Cross. . . . They just pick things up that people have thrown away" (Hardy 2001).
Most poignant, in this regard, is Varda's portrait of a man she meets on the road
living with gypsies. He is a former truck driver who lost his job, his family, and
his home due to chronic alcoholism and has drifted ever since, obtaining food
and lodging wherever he may. Though he is a master of salvage, he is, clearly, not
saved—either in a spiritual or a material sense.

It is on this level (that of social exposé) that *The Gleaners* comes closest to
Vagabond, which might be seen as its dramatic counterpart—an indication that
beyond intermixing various documentary subgenres, Varda passes fluidly between fiction and nonfiction modes, representing her continuing interests in both.
It seems significant that *Vagabond* features a *female* vagrant, since early on in *The*

Gleaners Varda remarks that, originally, such foragers were women (as they are in Millet's painting—the so-called Three Fates of Pauperism). Thus, she reminds us that females are often twice damned—part of both an economic and a gendered underclass. Interestingly, in Greek mythology the Three Fates were portrayed as repellent old hags whose role was to determine human destiny, especially one's allotment of misery and suffering. This focus on the female subject is not new to Varda's work. As Alison Smith notes: "Throughout her career Varda's interest in a specifically feminine cinema has been constant. She is one of the very few French [filmmakers] who have been strongly involved in the women's movement: she has declared this involvement and explored it in her films" (1998, 92). We can see her brand of woman-centered cinema in *Cleo from 5 to 7,* which concentrates on two hours in the life of a female singer as she tensely awaits the results of a biopsy. *One Sings, the Other Doesn't* (*L'une chante, l'autre pas,* 1977) charts the fate of two female friends as they mature in post-1968 France and are affected by the women's movement. In *Jane B. by Agnès V* (*Jane B. par Agnès V,* 1988), Varda crafts an affectionate portrait of a close friend, the actress Jane Birkin.

Like these films, V*agabond* takes a woman as its prime subject. Set largely in the countryside (the traditional scene of gleaning), it follows Mona as she wanders through a mostly agricultural domain. The opening shot depicts a plowed but arid field in wintertime. It is by this meadow (where her narrative ends) that Mona dies and is discovered as a corpse in a ditch. When the drama circles back to its start at the close of the story, Mona squats in her final, but inadequate, shelter: a plastic-covered greenhouse, where radish cuttings are rooted. Signs warn against stealing them. Frequently in the film, Varda's camera rests upon dormant tractors or reapers, left in some pasture or parked by the road. At one point, Mona stays with a young, counter-culture sheep-herding family who offer her land on which to farm and residence in a trailer. Rather than exploit the opportunity, however, she slothfully languishes around and, eventually, they throw her out. At another point, Mona stumbles upon a Tunisian man who is pruning bushes; he gives her some water and asks his foreman if she can sleep in the laborers' quarters overnight (since his Moroccan co-workers are home in North Africa). The next day, she assists him pruning the vineyards and he promises to let her stay when his colleagues return. When they do, however, and object to her presence, he reneges on his vow and sends her packing. Later, she tells someone that she has also picked strawberries and grapes.

Throughout the narrative she encounters other members of the underclass, be they foreign workers or French youth on the skids (as when she hooks up with some drunken, drug-addicted drifters in a train station). A guy whom she temporarily befriends plans to put her in porno movies. In an innovative move, Varda has Mona's acquaintances speak of her while looking directly at the camera, as though interviewed by the nameless author of the text whose voice we hear but whom we never see. Some of these monologues precede the individual's encounter with Mona, and some follow—keeping the viewer continually off-balance on a temporal level.

People have wildly varying reactions to Mona. One woman discovers Mona and a male drifter in bed together in a vacant estate building, and imagines they are deeply in love (a fantasy of her own making). A female agronomy professor, who gives Mona a ride and becomes attached to her, talks of how filthy and malodorous she is, stating that she was horrified that she eventually became accustomed to the stench. The foreman of the vineyard where Mona briefly works sighs: "Poor girl. Where is she now?" His wife opines, less compassionately, that "Vine cutting isn't a woman's job." For his "interview," Mona's Tunisian friend simply stares sadly at the camera unable to say anything. The only one who remotely understands Mona is the hippie shepherd who was once a drifter himself. He admits that he has subsequently chosen a "middle path" between isolation and community because "wandering is withering." Thus, Varda lets Mona remain inexplicable to us and others. At times, she is also very unsympathetic: when people stop to give her a ride or offer her food, lodging, or a job, she is never grateful and is frequently sullen or obnoxious in return. Thus, if we are to wish for her salvation, we must do so without finding her vagrancy justified or her redemption earned.

In this perspective, Varda not only records various acts of salvage but practices an "*art of salvage.*" On the one hand, the artistic implications of salvage lead us to the familiar notion of the "found object"—as in the work of Surrealists Marcel Duchamp or Joseph Cornell. Here, Andy Warhol is also a force to be reckoned with. As he once stated: "I always like to work on leftovers, doing the leftover things. Things that were discarded, that everybody knew were no good. . . . [In so doing] you're recycling work" (1975, 93). Of course, in *The Gleaners* it is not only the protagonists who find things, but Varda—as the cast of eccentric characters she locates must be chosen and assembled from the pro-filmic universe. Furthermore, as the film proceeds she becomes a collector of objects, acquiring such items as heart-shaped potatoes, postcards, paintings, and eviscerated clocks.

But other aspects of Varda's career bespeak an ability to "salvage." When pregnant with her second child and wishing to refrain from travel, Varda "salvaged" her art (and professional status) by shooting a documentary on the street where she lived, using the trades people of the Rue Daguerre as "found characters." In *Jacquot de Nantes* (1991) and *The World of Jacques Demy* (1995)—which Varda calls a "diptych" (1996)—she salvaged the past in commemoration of her deceased and beloved mate, creating collages of restaged remembrances, documentary interviews, and cinematic excerpts. She also salvaged her grief: "I could say it was a cinematic mourning act. Can I say that? Does it make sense? I could be weeping and wearing black veils. And I did cry, I did mourn. My family was broken. It was painful. Ten years after and I still feel the pain. But I'm not just a widow. I'm a filmmaker. So, the widow business became my business to be a witness of what one can do with [the] ferocity of pain" (Hardy 2001). More recently, it became her "business" again in a video installation she presented in Europe entitled *L'île et elle* (*The Island and She* [2006]), a pun on the words *Il* and *Elle*: He and She. Here, she returns to the island of Noirmoutier (which she first visited with Jacques Demy and which was the site of their marriage) and interviews fourteen black-clad widows (represented by the same number of empty chairs) as the women speak about their experience of solitude (including herself as one of them). In another section of the installation, she mimics the way that cabins on Noirmoutier are often made of salvaged materials by constructing a miniature shack out of the celluloid remains of one of her films *Les Créatures* (1966). It is entitled *My Cabin of Failure,* since the film was a commercial flop.

But this miniature is not the only way that Varda salvages film (though it is the most material and literal example). To understand how she does this, we might draw upon Jim Collins's notion of "genericity." For him, modern film exists within a vast universe of imagery from both the present and the past—material that is now available through DVD, videotape, computer, and television. As he notes: "That a seemingly endless number of texts are subject to virtually immediate random access inevitably alters the relationship between classic and contemporary when both circulate alongside one another simultaneously" (2002, 279). Drawing upon the writings of Umberto Eco, he observes how now (because of the surfeit of historical imagery), the "already-said" is often the "still-being-said" with the "old" no longer automatically replaced by the "new" (279–80). Thus, rather than constitute "the mere detritus of exhausted cultures past," older cinematic "icons, scenarios, [and] visual conventions continue to carry with them a sort of cultural 'charge' or resonance that must be reworked according to the exigencies of the present" (286).

It is precisely this "rearticulation" of filmic and generic artifacts that we find in the complex discourse of *The Gleaners.* We might, for instance, imagine Varda as salvaging lessons of the French New Wave (of which she is often said to be the "grandmother") in her attempt to bridge the gap between experimental and conventional approaches. As she notes: "If you call yourself an independent filmmaker, you . . . do cinema out of the mainstream" (Hardy 2001). Thus, her innovative documentary work could be placed alongside that of the *Nouvelle Vague's* Chris Marker or Alain Resnais.

Moreover, in *The Gleaners* we might see Varda as "salvaging" other aspects of the documentary genre by acting upon a claim made long ago by Siegfried Kracauer that a "natural" subject of that mode is "refuse." As he once commented:

> Many objects remain unnoticed simply because it never occurs to us to look their way. Most people turn their backs on garbage cans, the dirt underfoot, the waste they leave behind. Films have no such inhibitions; on the contrary, what we ordinarily prefer to ignore proves attractive to them precisely because of this common neglect. (2004, 310)

Varda's choice to confront the "unnoticed," to overcome pictorial "inhibition," has ideological implications as well.

In *One Hundred and One Nights of Simon Cinema* (1995), a whimsical film that skirts the generic borders of farce, circus, camp, and parody, Varda seeks to salvage cinema itself in the one hundredth year of its existence—just as pundits have declared it dead and consigned it to the scrap heap of history. In fact, the film's premise is that M. Cinéma suffers from Alzheimer's disease and can't remember the celluloid past. Thus, he must be prodded into recollection by viewing movie clips and receiving visits from screen stars of yesteryear (creating the kind of temporal simultaneity of imagery of which Collins speaks). Thus, to make the film, Varda taps the dumpster of cinema—its archives—reviving arcane and forgotten footage. In so doing, she reminds us of the assemblage artist she visits in *The Gleaners* who speaks of junk as "having already had a life," to which he adds a "second chance." It is this wish to grant things "a second chance" (be the objects sublime or abject) that informs Varda's work. Though in her seventies, she has no intention of ending her days like M. Cinéma—forgetful of film history. We know this from her inclusion in *The Gleaners* of a turn-of-the-century actualité.

While Andy Warhol may have praised working with "leftovers," he feared becoming one. As he once said, "At the end of my time, when I die I don't want to leave any leftovers. And I don't want to be a leftover" (1975, 112). For Varda, however, leftovers are never loathsome "remains of the day." Rather they are sacred relics—poignant and precious remnants of sentient and insentient worlds.

PART THREE

GENDER AESTHETICS IN "MALE" GENRES

CHAPTER 9

IT'S A MANN'S WORLD?

ADAM SEGAL

The director Michael Mann generally works within the genre of the crime film. Within this genre, there is typically a focus placed on the relations among men, with very little emphasis on female characters. Susan White (2001), referring to a 1947 Anthony Mann police procedural, *T-Men,* writes that "with few exceptions, women cannot and must not traverse the boundary surrounding the criminal milieu the agents are investigating, for their investigation into the underworld is emphatically . . . an exploration of what it means to be a man among men" (98). Michael Mann's *Heat* (1995) explores this same kind of terrain.

Discussion of *Heat* has generally revolved around its generic status as a crime film, yet it also makes room for a female perspective in the story. Assuming female empathy with female characters and conventionally feminine concerns, the girlfriends and spouses of the film's main characters provide an entry point for female viewers. However, there are also moments in the film that invite female viewer engagement with the male characters. Thus the film's domestic scenes arguably construct a space for a "female" or feminized spectator, while opening up a realm of textual negotiation for cross-gender viewing. As Pam Cook points out in this volume (31), critical approaches to classical film genres have generally assumed a gender-specific address. This essay aims to show how there can be no easily assumed relationship between genres and gendered audiences, for as socially circulating gender assumptions change, they bring with them consequent shifts in audience address.

My argument concerns changes in Hollywood masculinity in the early to mid-1990s and how this is reflected in one particular film, *Heat*. Susan Jeffords (1993, 196) records that during the 1980s a men's movement emerged in the United States, focused on reevaluating the traditional roles and expectations of men's behavior in U.S. society. This movement produced discussion groups, therapy sessions, men's studies courses, and magazines that examined the question of men's changing roles in U.S. society. Jeffords notes that in mainstream Hollywood films, the hard-fighting, gun-wielding, muscular, and heroic men of the eighties gave way to the more sensitive and loving family men of the 1990s (197). The tension that the male protagonists face in many of these "sensitive man" narratives is whether excelling at one's job has to come at the expense of one's personal and family life (200).

Heat is a unique entry in the police procedural/crime genre in that it attempts to illuminate for its viewers the emotional toll that crime work takes on the police and thieves while also revealing the toll it takes on the spouses and loved ones who are left at home to wonder when the men will be coming home. Jackie Byars (1987) suggests that "if we can allow ourselves to recognize shifts between masculine and feminine modes of perception and to see differences between discursive practices rather than seeing just an overwhelming sameness that obscures discourses of women, we can—perhaps—make cultural interventions in reading and theory and in production as well" (302).

Heat focuses on the efforts of a driven police lieutenant, Vincent Hanna (Al Pacino) to bring down a crew of thieves led by the resourceful Neal McCauley (Robert De Niro). Over the course of this sprawling three-hour crime epic, much is made of the male characters' lack of time for emotional attachment to the women in their lives (Lindstrom 2000, 22). Lindstrom points out that "the criminals and the police value their personal relationships but ultimately sacrifice them" (23). Lindstrom also observes that all of the domestic scenes in the film "constantly insist that work consumes the time and energy that might otherwise go to personal relationships" (25). In *Heat,* domestic relationships are anything but invisible. Home life is no longer, as in traditional crime films, a retreat/respite for the hero of the narrative but instead a place where the domestic scenes consist of "emotional contestation" (25). The female characters do not dominate the narrative yet they inflect *Heat*'s film noir/gangster/police procedural narrative with a touch of contemporary feminist discourse. The major female characters in the film employ the kind of talk that might be heard in a marital counseling session or glanced at in self-help books.

If the presence of female talk in *Heat* exemplifies how "aesthetic and fictional practices . . . meet and negotiate with extra-textual social practices " (Gledhill 1988, 75), Frank Krutnik (1991) suggests that inclusion of heterosexual attachment, home, and family in the police procedural tends to be "highly 'tokenistic' and conventionalized," deflecting from "the drama's principal interest in the 'male couple'" (204). In *Heat,* the investigator (Vincent Hanna) and the criminal (Neal McCauley) essentially form the "male couple" of the crime film in that they are more devoted to their cat-and-mouse game than they are to their respective female lovers. Hanna is solely defined by his job as a detective, and this poses a problem since he has no identity apart from his job and whomever he is pursuing (205). The question remains as to how the text seeks to address a female viewer in a genre perceived to be aligned with a male audience.

Christine Gledhill (1988) argues that the inextricable intertwining of melodramatic and realist modes allows "a text to work both on a symbolic, 'imaginary' level, internal to fictional production and on a 'realist' level, referring to the socio-historical world outside the text" (75). The melodramatic conflicts internal to the text rely for their power "on the premise of a recognizable, socially constructed world" (76). The modern popular drama is a kind of negotiation between melo-drama's Manichaean moral frameworks (good vs. evil) and those contemporary discourses that provide the drama with a recognizable verisimilitude (76). In this respect, we need to take account of the distinction between what women recognize as "real life" and how films construct gender representation and address. As John Fiske (1987) points out, "the relationship between the social and the textual is never clear or singular and is certainly oversimplified to the point of distortion by the belief that the generic conventions by which gender is represented textually do nothing more than reproduce the social" (222).

In *Heat,* the viewer is presented with a generic construct that on its surface is about a police officer's quest to hunt down a criminal. Folded within the main story is a tale of fractured relationships between men and women. The film at-tempts to incorporate contemporary discourse relating to couples therapy, set against the backdrop of a crime and detective story. A culturally assigned women's discourse about relationships slowly begins to emerge in the film, as if to recog-nize that there is a female audience for this story. Gledhill (1988) has observed that "during a period of active feminism, of social legislation for greater sexual equality and corresponding shifts in gender roles, gender and sexual definitions themselves become the focus of intense cultural negotiation" (76). A film like *Heat* exists in the shadow cast by feminism, and as a result it chooses not to portray the women as mere tokens to the men.

Heat contains two female characters who do more than just function as an oasis of normalcy and calm. As Lindstrom (2000) points out, in the gangster films of the 1930s the domestic scenes showed gang members living middle-class lives where they have homes to maintain and children and wives who depend on them, all of which illustrated the notion that "criminal behavior is a means to entirely 'normal' ends" (25). However, the characters of Justine (Diane Ve-nora) and Charlene (Ashley Judd) constantly challenge their spouses at home. They are not mere appendages to their husbands. For example, Charlene, who is married to the criminal Chris Shiherlis (Val Kilmer) does not blindly accept whatever he tells her about how a heist job went. Upon returning home after the film's initial heist, Chris is questioned by his wife as to where his money from the job went. He tells her that he had to pay off some gambling debts. Charlene takes this moment to lecture Chris on how he should do his job: "It ain't worth the risks for $8000. It's about risk-reward baby. It means we're not making real forward progress like real adults living their lives because I'm married to a gambling junkie who won't listen!" Here, the home is a place for "emotional contestation" instead of a sanctuary for the gangster (Lindstrom 2000, 25). Charlene's behavior in this scene opens up a site of gendered discourse for the female viewer. This kind of marital discourse, familiar from its circulation in the popular press and television fictions and chat shows, provides a "recognizable verisimilitude" (Gledhill 1988, 76), derived from genres found (or thought) to be particularly appealing to female audiences. What is going on here is a kind of modification of law enforcement discourse associated with the gangster film and more masculinist discourses.

Justine is the film's central female character and receives the most screen time afforded to a woman. Married to Lieutenant Vincent Hanna, she is not shy about expressing her opinions to him. She does not fit the mold of the devoted cop's wife. In a film like *T-Men,* the wife is left unaware of the fact that her husband, Tony Gennaro, has gone undercover for the treasury department. At the Los Angeles Farmer's Market, Tony's wife and a friend are shopping and run into him while he is undercover. His wife's friend calls the agent by his real name. Tony's wife realizes that her husband must be undercover and tries to cover this up by telling her friend that she has mistaken this man for her husband. As Tony walks away, there is a cut to a close-up of his wife with a sorrowful look on her face. This is the one scene in the film where the audience actually sees Tony's wife; the rest of the film ignores the fact that he has a home life. It is the law enforcement job that is all consuming. In *Heat,* it is the opposite. Here, the character Justine wants to share in the details of her husband's job.

One evening, Vincent has to leave a dinner party to take a call on a homicide. When he returns, hours later, everyone has left except Justine. Instead of being a conventional supportive wife, Justine demands to be let in on some of the details of Vincent's work:

> Justine: You never told me I'd be excluded.
> Vincent: I told you when we hooked up baby that you were going to have to share me with all the bad people and all the ugly events on this planet.
> Justine: And I bought into that *sharing* because I love you. I love you fat, bald, young, old, money, no money, driving a bus—I don't care, but you have got to be present like a normal guy some of the time. That's sharing. This is leftovers.

Justine's assertiveness complicates her generic function as supportive wife to the film's detective hero. Here the scene morphs into something akin to "couples therapy," engaging with the kind of relationship discourse that is common on female-oriented talk shows like *The Oprah Winfrey Show* and in soap operas. In another scene, Vincent Hanna arrives home late from work after investigating a crime scene. As soon as Hanna walks in the door, Justine asks him if he's all right and then inquires where he has been. Hanna curtly answers "Work." Justine complains that she had made dinner for them over four hours ago and that "Every time I try to maintain a *consistent mood* between us, you withdraw." Nick James (2002) has complained that phrases such as "maintain a consistent mood" seem lifted out of self-help books, thereby making these sequences feel like "a therapeutic ghetto of sensitivity" (51). However, these domestic scenes make sense within the film's attempts to incorporate a female audience.

In this respect, a film like *Heat*, with its mixing of masculine and feminine narrative forms, is following in the footsteps of police series from the 1980s and 1990s like *NYPD Blue* (1993–2005), *Hill Street Blues* (1981–87), and *Cagney and Lacey* (1982–88). As John Fiske (1987, 220) has pointed out, soap operas take place in the realm of the home, while in masculine narratives like cop shows the action is public and not domestic and deals with public issues like murder, power, and money. A show like *Hill Street Blues* featured scenes where the cops took their work home with them, often in conversations in bed with their significant others, thus mixing the public and domestic. Such shows also tended to stage washroom chats between men more often associated with female soap opera characters. In these scenes, the male police officers would often take the opportunity to be more emotionally frank with each other.

These police series would constantly veer between the strict professionalism of police work and the messy entanglements of relationships and home life. The proximity of different generic formula in the "flow" of television encourages the creative bleeding of one genre into another, especially in a marketplace where there is much pressure to appeal to a mixed gendered audience so as to maximize potential profit. By showing what happens outside the male realm of criminal work and police work when these men have to come home to their families, the show is drawing on discursive constructions of gender to reinflect the genre in such a way that the hypothetical female viewer is given a chance to feel a part of this world. By including scenes of these women asserting themselves, the police series challenges the crime film's generic assumption that the spouse or girlfriend is only a token presence (see Krutnik 1991, 204).

In contrast to standard arguments about the male gaze in mainstream cinema, *Heat* addresses the female viewer through a male gaze primarily directed at other males and not at females. This characteristic of *Heat* is similar to Michael Mann's work on the television series *Miami Vice* (1984–90), in which the police detectives Sonny Crockett and Ricardo Tubbs directed their investigative gaze at the criminal suspects they put under surveillance (Jeremy Butler 1985, 132). In *Heat*, there is a tension in its mix of police procedural and feminized soap opera discourse. The marital relations discourse threatens to wipe out the generic pleasures of the police procedural and gangster film, which would include the homosocial bonding between men. The film creates a visual scheme in which the males' investment in gazing at each other functions as a kind of resistance to the female discourse that permeates the story. Jeremy Butler's discussion of *Miami Vice* points out that while the act of looking is a key component, the woman is not the object of the gaze. "The gratifiers of Crockett and Tubbs's visual pleasure are *men* involved with narcotics, prostitution or other criminal activities. Rather than the women of *film noir*, these men constitute the 'trouble' that inaugurates the plot" (133). In

Heat, the generic pleasures of the police procedural found in the bond between hunter (Vincent Hanna) and hunted (Neal McCauley) operates as counterpoint to the feminist discourse that is aired throughout the film. This bond is satisfying at the generic level yet also provokes anxiety because of its homosexual subtext. In *Heat,* Lieutenant Vincent Hanna's gaze is primarily directed toward Neal Mc-Cauley. In a sequence involving police surveillance of McCauley's gang at work on a heist job, the viewer is shown Hanna's intense gaze at a computer monitor containing an infrared image of McCauley in the dark. During the sequence, one of the police officers makes a sound that compromises the surveillance. Mann utilizes a series of cuts between close-ups of McCauley in the dark and McCauley as infrared image, and close-ups of Hanna looking with rapt attention at the infrared image. Like the detectives in *Miami Vice* survey criminals, Detective Hanna is gazing at a male who is almost a mirror image of himself (Jeremy Butler 1985, 133). In this orchestration of looks, McCauley's infrared outline attracts Hanna's sustained gaze far more than his flesh and blood wife Justine (132).

In writing about the masculine pleasures of Anthony Mann's violent police films and westerns, Paul Willemen (1981) argues that "the viewer's experience is predicated on the pleasure of seeing the male exist (that is walk, talk, ride, fight) in or through cityscapes, landscapes or, more abstractly, history. And on the unquiet pleasure of seeing the male mutilated and restored through violent brutality" (16). Willemen's insight here is that ultimately in male-oriented genre films (westerns, police procedurals), the look at the male figure in his "native" environment will predominate. Michael Mann ultimately tilts the balance in favor of the world of police work and crime over feminine discourse. This is aptly illustrated in a very telling sequence. After a day of trying to hunt down McCauley, Vincent comes home to find his wife getting dressed to go out without him. Justine is wearing an attractive and fancy black cocktail dress. Hanna inquires as to where she is going and Justine curtly responds that she is going out. Hanna barely notices his wife and instead chooses to go out once again to try and find McCauley. The film eagerly leaves this hot zone of marital discord. Hanna soon finds himself in a police helicopter navigating the Los Angeles skyline as he looks for McCauley's car on the freeway. Hanna is literally in his element. The helicopter lands and Hanna gets into a waiting squad car. He is soon following McCauley's car on the freeway. Mann orchestrates point-of-view driver shots and pulsating techno mood music to illustrate the rapid movement of the chase and Hanna's thrill in tracking down McCauley as opposed to the mess he has left at home.

At the same time, the film also has to grapple with the inhibitions of heterosexual society that work against the male body figured as the erotic object of another male look. It's not that the male body *cannot* be so marked, but that to do so involves certain difficulties and requires specific strategies; the look has to be motivated in some other way so as to disavow any erotic components (Neale 1983, 8). At the end of the film, McCauley and Hanna are engaged in a shoot-out at the Los Angeles International Airport in which McCauley is mortally wounded. Mann creates a zone for the two men to gaze at each other in which Hanna's cradling of McCauley is explained by his shooting of this master criminal. The anxiety provoked by the entry of female-oriented personal relations discourse into the film ends by amplifying the bond between these two men.

How might a female viewer find herself positioned in the filmic world of *Heat,* in which the men (Hanna and McCauley) are primarily consumed by their jobs and their surveillance of other men who are like themselves? Christine Gledhill (1995) has speculated about ways in which female audience recognition might be invited to a primarily male moment in a film. For Gledhill, "all recognition is based on a mixture of familiarity and difference in what is essentially a process of re-*cognition.* We need to see the familiar differently in order to see it at all" (79). Female recognition of the familiar is invited in an exchange between Hanna and McCauley discussing in a coffee shop how they view their lives, their work, and their relationships with women. What opens the scene to recognition is the subject of the discussion. This is the one moment in the film when the two men open themselves up for the viewer—in a manner reminiscent of the washroom scenes between male police officers in *Hill Street Blues,* offering "women a 'fly on the wall' spectatorial pleasure thereby enabling us, in Joseph Bristow's phrase, 'to occupy another's gender'" (79).

The coffee shop encounter between Vincent Hanna and Neal McCauley catches these two characters in a moment of candor. The moment is not so much a show-down as it is a moment for reflection on the part of these two men as to where their lives have gone:

> McCauley: I do what I do best. I take scores. You do what you do best: trying to stop guys like me.
> Hanna: You never wanted a regular type life?
> McCauley: What the fuck is that? Barbecues and ballgames?
> Hanna: Yeah
> McCauley: This regular-type life. That your life?
> Hanna: No. My life is a disaster zone. I got a step-daughter who's fucked up because her real father's this large type asshole. My wife and I are passing each other on the downslope of our marriage, my third, 'cause every moment I got I spend chasing guys like you around the block.
> McCauley: A guy told me one time, don't let yourself get attached to anything you're not willing to walk out on, if you feel the heat coming round the corner, in 30 seconds flat. So if you are on me and you gotta move when I move, how do you expect to keep a marriage?

There is a kind of intimacy between these two men who perfectly understand each other. Their intimacy, however, is not presented as akin to that of women. The sequence is restricted to a shot-reverse shot exchange, with both men staying on their opposite sides of the table. Mann chooses not to place these characters together in a two shot (James 2002, 63), yet the utilization of the shot-reverse shot structure actually promotes a heightened sense of connectedness between them. Initially, the shot-reverse shot structure keeps the two men at a distance in medium shots, yet gradually Mann shifts the framing into tight medium close-ups of both men that allow the viewer to observe the way they stare straight into one another's eyes. McCauley and Hanna are still keeping their guards up, yet glimmers of self-exposure peak through what Gledhill (1995) would term "the armour of masculinity" (80). The female viewer is able to eavesdrop on a form of masculinity that values work over domestic life, as when they both agree that a regular type of life is not the life for either of them. At one point, the two men both agree that they don't know how to do anything else and don't really want to either. Nick James (2002) points out that "McCauley and Hanna are explaining the psychology of the film to each other, making sure we know that there is more to these guys than the desire to do battle" (63). James, however, misreads the scene in suggesting that there is "something more" to these two men. In their exchange, Hanna and McCauley are merely using the intimacy of conventionally assigned female discourse to confirm the old (conventionally assigned) masculine values. There is no real sense that these two men plan to turn a new leaf and live more progressive lives. The scene also serves as a retranslation of the tradition of the bond between the hunter and the hunted but imbues it with the contemporary air of relations discourse. Like Ethan and Scar in *The Searchers* (1956), Hanna and McCauley share a common aversion to the domesticated life. In addition, it is this vocalizing of their outlooks on life, career, and commitment that also opens up a space for the female viewer to better recognize and see through the masculinity that is on display in the film. Even beyond the surface level of the dialogue where the two men both agree that they don't know how to do anything else and don't really want to either, it is what is unspoken in this exchange that reveals the deepest meaning for female as well as male viewers. There is a pause in the dialogue and as Mann cuts back and forth between Hanna and McCauley the viewer catches a faint glimmer of a smile between them that perhaps indicates a kind of complicity, as if they know their women might be eavesdropping on this conversation. The female is able to see the familiar male tropes of toughness but in a different way, via a semi-relaxed conversation over coffee, which offers a kind of "re-*cognition*" for the female viewer (Gledhill 1995, 79).

At first glance, Vincent Hanna is not a character appealing to the female viewer, since he embodies a very masculinist ethos, what Gledhill (1995) would refer to as the Crusading Hero (82). However, "because of their separateness from the heroine," such figures "dramatise the attractions" as well as the "repulsions of masculinity. . . . In particular, they represent lessons in the forms and exercise of power—physical, material, psychic or moral, and often violent" (82). From this perspective, the kind of appeal the female audience might find in Vincent Hanna is the possibility, even acceptability, of privileging work over domestic life and relationships that is difficult for women to attain in real life. Hanna is a type of male who excels at his job and who makes time for nothing else in his life. A colleague of McCauley's refers to Hanna as a "hot dog" cop who is "one of those guys out there, prowling all night, dedicated." Throughout, the film exemplifies the way in which he wields his professional power as a top-flight detective. Near the beginning of the film, Hanna and his subordinate detectives are investigating the crime scene of the heist pulled off by McCauley's crew of thieves. After one of Hanna's junior detectives evaluates the crime scene, Hanna takes over and dazzles his fellow detectives with his reconstruction of how the crime was committed. Hanna can walk into a club in order to question a confidential informant and act like he's the most important man there. Hanna's power is displayed plainly and clearly for the viewer and is probably especially validating for the male viewer. There are, however, moments in the film that pierce through the armor of this Crusading Hero to reveal a glimpse of some uncertainty that might be particularly appealing to the female audience, while opening up new perspectives for the male.

Near the middle of the film, Hanna is called away from a dinner party to a homicide crime scene. Before he is called away, Hanna and Justine are dancing to the strains of B.B. King's "The Thrill Is Gone," suggesting that their marriage is already on the rocks. Hanna has to break away from Justine when his beeper reads 911. As Hanna arrives on the crime scene, Mann utilizes a lot of high angles and melodramatic music to call attention to the pathos of this crime. He frames the crime scene in wide angle shots that emphasize its grand scale through careful placement of details such as the yellow police tape in the foreground, a medical examiner hovering over the body, and a helicopter hovering loudly in the background of the frame shining a spotlight on the proceedings below. Mann heightens the emotional atmosphere by steadily building the volume of the foreboding music to crest at the exact moment when the victim's mother arrives on the scene screaming "Where is my baby?" A hooker has been brutally murdered by a serial killer and her body left in a garbage can. As Hanna is hovering over the body, the mother of the victim arrives at the scene. She comes running toward her daughter's body and Hanna stops her from approaching it. The mother falls into Hanna's arms while a series of cuts framed in medium shot from various angles show a very uneasy Hanna, who cannot figure out a way to comfort this grieving woman. The combination of the camera tracking turbulently around Hanna and the mother, and the abrupt cuts that break up the sequence suggest an uneasy dance in which Hanna is doing his best to avoid any emotional attachment. This sequence actually repeats the uneasy dance between Justine and Hanna at the party. This visual link between the two sequences highlights the emotional detachment that Hanna brings to all facets of his life. Prior to the woman coming on the scene, Hanna was firmly in control, yet when confronted with the emotional consequences of this crime, Hanna cannot function. He internalizes his emotions and is not able to fully reach out to this mother. Here, there is a break in the masculine armor and an opening is offered to a female reading of Hanna. Later on, his wife serves as a surrogate for the female viewer when she comments that "you live with the remains of dead people. You sift through the detritus; you read the terrain; you search for signs of passing, for the scent of your prey, and then you hunt them down. That's the only thing you're committed to." Justine's feminist analysis of Hanna confirms what has already become obvious: Hanna only lives for the job and is not sure how to deal with emotions.

Heat on its surface may appear to be nothing more than a crime genre film in which feminine representation is kept to a minimum. By engaging with the text, one can see that the film takes account of contemporary feminist discourse in its depiction of its various couples. The film consciously tries to engage a feminist perspective on the male characters' devotion to their work. Yet at the same time it also raises the question as to what impact the female discourse might have for the male textual spectator. The male gaze is directed at the male protagonists, yet the ways in which the female characters in the film harangue the males thwart any attempt to objectify the women. The male viewer is presented with scenes articulating female discourse but the film also carves out a zone that allows a resistance to this discourse. For example, the coffee shop encounter between Hanna and McCauley is not just there to give female viewers insight into male behavior. The scene also functions as an address to male viewers, offering them support and justification for privileging male bonding and work over traditionally heterosexually engaged identities. The glimmer of a smile that passes between the two men as they realize that they're best suited for the work that they do also serves as a kind of conspiratorial "wink" to the male viewer.

This case study has demonstrated that male and female spectator relations in regard to traditionally masculine film genres cannot be viewed in essentialist terms. As Pam Cook in this volume points out, "the invitation to the cinema is based on the promise that spectators may experience the thrill of reinventing themselves rather than simply having their social identities or positions bolstered" (33). *Heat* exemplifies the ways in which conventional gender roles in masculine genres can be detached from traditional representations as socially circulating gender assumptions change.

CHAPTER 10

UP CLOSE AND PERSONAL:

FACES AND NAMES IN *CASUALTIES OF WAR*

DEBORAH THOMAS

"It was that shame we knew so well, the shame . . . that the just man experiences at another man's crime; the feeling of guilt that such a crime should exist, that it should have been introduced irrevocably into the world of things that exist, and that his will for good should have proved too weak or null, and should not have availed in defence."
—Primo Levi (1987, 188)

For obvious reasons, war films—especially those centered on the battlefield—are likely to be unbalanced in terms of their treatments of gender. The absence of a significant female presence in American films about wars fought overseas is due in part to the fact that their far-flung battlefields and home front are geographically split apart to a much greater extent than in certain British examples, say, where a female presence may be more strongly foregrounded in male characters' more frequent movements between battlefield and home, and where home itself comes under fire. However, rather than this implying that American war films comprise a masculinist genre of tough action at the expense of the tender feelings that women would provide, it could be argued that the frequent scenes of men dying in each other's arms allow male emotion considerable display. Indeed, men's feelings may actually be freed up by the absence of women who might otherwise "do the feeling" for them.

American films of the home-front variety—e.g., *Since You Went Away* (1944) or *Gardens of Stone* (1987)—reverse the tendency of American combat films and typically keep the *battlefield* almost wholly offscreen, with a consequently greater emphasis on women, even if some have argued that they therefore barely qualify as

war films at all. Thus, in Steve Neale's description of the war film, "scenes of combat are a requisite ingredient" (2000, 125). American war films of the type Neale
allows may open with pre-war scenes of "normal" life or of departures overseas,
and they may end with returns to wife and family, but once we are in the midst
of battle, we tend to stay there (or nearby) for most of the film. Any remaining
women are represented largely as foreign victims of the war, or perhaps as nurses
or other ancillary personnel. They may provide romantic interest, but most often
they inhabit the screen only briefly and exhibit little decisive narrative agency.

   Casualties of War (1989) is a partial exception: even if its most important female
character has a typically brief onscreen presence and is a passive victim to whose
subjectivity we have little access, she is crucial to our emotional involvement with
the film. What interests me is that her appearances are both compelling and a
linchpin to the film's effects, and yet difficult to characterize in terms of identification, regardless of how we understand this term. I intend to explore this while
drawing on my own reactions, though, since they respond to a number of the
film's strategies, it is likely they are shared. Why do we care about this character
so deeply when any sense of her interiority is so steadfastly withheld? Why is her
treatment at the hands of the American GIs so gut-wrenching when we know
so little about her? If identification is not the source of our emotional involvement with her, then what *is?* Finally, is there anything about the war film and its
concerns that shapes our responses in generically specific ways?

   Brian De Palma's Vietnam film of 1989 concerns a patrol of GIs who, during a
reconnaissance mission, kidnap, rape, and murder an innocent Vietnamese girl,
a story that is embedded in another story about how one of them, Private Eriksson (Michael J. Fox), who tried unsuccessfully to prevent these events, eventually
brings the others to justice. This second narrative is in turn embedded in the
film's brief framing scenes of Eriksson back home after the war, thus providing
us with a double look backward, from the postwar framing scenes to the earlier
court martial, and from the court martial back to the events for which the men
are on trial. One might even describe this as a triple look backward, since the
film itself was made years after the setting of its most recent scene. However, our
sense of the director looking back at the film's events from this later vantage point
is relatively underplayed. Stephen H. Burum's camerawork and other stylistic
strategies—for example, Ennio Morricone's score—tend to intensify the effects
upon us of the film's narrative events, rather than giving voice to an independent
perspective from 1989. Nevertheless, a critical moral position is implied by the
way such events are represented, despite a lack of acknowledgment of the time
the film was made.

   For example, our sense of Eriksson's growing isolation from the other men on
the reconnaissance mission is reinforced by frequent shots of him alone in the
frame, intercut with reverse angle shots of others sharing the screen. He briefly
shares a shot with Private Diaz (John Leguizamo) when they agree to back each

other up in refusing to rape the girl, but, when Diaz is put to the test, the cuts from Eriksson alone to Diaz side by side with the other men make Diaz's decision clear before he speaks. Similarly, back at the base camp, when Eriksson reports the girl's rape and murder to Captain Hill (Dale Dye) and is met by anger and verbal abuse, the skewed camera angles in many of the shots reinforce the sense of Hill's skewed values, which is simultaneously provoked in us by his response. The darkness at the heart of *Casualties of War* pulls us into itself, encouraging a visceral response to the film's key events, rather than the film's strategies conspiring to distance us from the narrative world in order that we make our judgments more consistently from its outer rim. Alongside our emotional involvement, however, the intensity of this response is moral as well. Primo Levi's words, with which I began this essay, capture some of this sense of moral implication in the events we witness: a sense not just of horror, but of *shame*.

De Palma's rhetoric is important in shaping our response. Indeed, any film's particular tone, point of view, visual and aural strategies, and so on, at any given moment, are not only crucial to our experience but complicate any notion of straightforward identification with a film's characters, unaware as they are of the choices informing the film's style. My present concern is to analyze some specific moments of emotional and moral intensity, without necessarily deciding whether or not to label them as instances of identification, mainly because, as I have admitted elsewhere (Thomas 2005), I often find it difficult to decide whether I am identifying with a character or not: how would I know? I am not suggesting that I have no access to my emotions nor any means of analyzing them in detail. Rather, I find myself unable to *name* my response as one of identification in the absence of any collectively agreed understanding of what this term involves.

A brief look at how identification has been understood suggests its inadequacy for explaining our intense involvement in *Casualties of War,* and may uncover the role played by genre expectations—and their undermining—in De Palma's film. For example, Laura Mulvey (1975) famously—and influentially—speaks in psychoanalytic terms about how male stars in active roles may represent what Freud describes as the ego ideal, which Freud argues "is the precipitate of the old picture of the parents" (1973, 96), thus linking it to the perceived perfection of *both* parents. Mulvey, in contrast, suggests that female viewers, through their likeness in gender, may identify with the less idealized, more passive female figures available to them in most mainstream narrative films (though she later refines this view and allows for identification across gender boundaries too). Her further point, that audiences see female characters through an alignment with the gaze of the (generally male) main character, will be strikingly undercut by Eriksson's look away offscreen as we witness the stabbing of the Vietnamese girl behind him.

Robin Wood (2002) also maintains that we are more likely to identify with a character whose point of view is affiliated with that of the culturally dominant male gaze, but he suggests other factors that tend towards identification as well. All else being equal, we are more likely to identify with a character played by a star, or with characters who are threatened or victimized, or with those for whom we feel sympathy or with whom we share a consciousness, or, finally, with those whose point of view is marked or privileged by the specific strategies of a given film. Like Wood, Murray Smith breaks down identification into its components. For example, what he calls *alignment* filters our access to the narrative world through the knowledge and emotions of particular characters so that we are "provided with visual and aural information more or less congruent with that available to characters" (1995, 75), whereas *allegiance* entails our sympathetic involvement with particular characters on the basis of how we evaluate them morally.

Both Wood and Smith avoid giving relative weightings to the various components of identification they describe, and this is a problem when some of these components are present and others missing. As a result, identification fragments into a set of disparate tendencies that may well pull us in different directions to varying degrees, with no means to arbitrate amongst them. While this complexity of response does seem true to our experience of narrative films, it may be more productive simply to describe the relative presence or absence of such multiple affiliations rather than to muddy the waters by labeling them all with the same term. With so many factors in play, it is unclear how many need to be present to produce a consensus that "identification" can usefully describe the multitude of things that are going on. Murray Smith seems aware of such difficulties when he speaks of character engagement rather than identification, allowing for more forms and degrees of involvement than the latter term would seem to allow. Thus, the central female character in *Casualties of War* is certainly a *victim* (one of Wood's criteria), but it is equally clear that Murray Smith's criterion of *alignment* is strikingly absent. Similarly, although the film encourages us to share Eriksson's decent and compassionate values (Murray Smith's criterion of *allegiance*), and Eriksson is played by a familiar and sympathetic star, there is no getting away from the fact that, at the moment of the girl's stabbing, Eriksson is oblivious to what is going on, so he is no surrogate for our own response, at least not at this point.

My purpose is not to resolve—or even significantly address—these issues, though the diversity of opinion on what constitutes identification certainly counsels caution. Rather, I will focus on what we seem invited to feel at specific highly charged moments, and why this might be so, while recognizing that such emotional experiences lack many of the conventional markers of identification. I am merely making explicit here what is implied in much film criticism, especially of the "close reading" variety: that our involvement in a film depends on the complex interactions of a large number of textual and textural details. It is clear that some types of audience engagement are not adequately covered by available accounts of identification. Further, some deeply felt audience reactions are not even engagements with characters at all, but with other aspects of the film (e.g., its moral values, which may be heavily critical of *all* the characters). Douglas Pye

(2007) gives much more prominence to *tone* as an anchor for viewer response, and this seems a useful corrective to an overemphasis on identification with characters, whatever that may be taken to imply.

If my own first viewing of the film is anything to go by, the emotional power of the scenes of rape and murder colors not only our experience of the remainder of the film while we watch it, but our *memory* of the film as well. This is all the more remarkable because, in a film of something like two hours, the rapes take up less than a minute of screen time and the murder (from the first stabbing until the girl is finally shot dead) around six or seven minutes, including intercut shots of the men in battle with the enemy when the girl herself is offscreen, though it could be argued that we anticipate, and then continue to imagine, what she's experiencing even when she's not visible. Although genre expectations kick in as soon as we become aware of the kidnap plan, so that the subsequent rape and murder are no surprise, the power of our response may still be unexpected and generically unusual.

The war film, perhaps more than any other genre, requires significant numbers of anonymous characters—both civilians and combatants, both "us" and "them"—in order to convey convincingly the scope of the battlefield and the magnitude of war. Even a small-scale war film like Nicholas Ray's *Bitter Victory* (1957) acknowledges this aspect through the words of its main character, Captain Leith (Richard Burton): "So the fine line between war and murder is distance. Anybody can kill at a distance with the same sort of courage that a man shoots rabbits." In other words, it is far easier to kill anonymous figures from afar than individuals up close. Clint Eastwood's *Letters from Iwo Jima* (2006) is a distinguished and exceptional example of an American war film exclusively from the enemy's point of view, producing a jolt to our generic expectations that forces us to reconsider our positioning—and the typical anonymity of the enemy—in other films of the genre.

Francis Ford Coppola's *Gardens of Stone* is a further example of a film that openly addresses and redresses the genre's use of anonymous combatants. The military cemetery referred to ironically in the film's title is in the business of burying soldiers returning from Vietnam in body bags, their interchangeability emphasized by the identical headstones we see and the obvious boredom of a young member of the honor guard at one such funeral, which both opens and ends the film. Rote responses to the young widow, referring to her "loved one" in an all-purpose condolence, reveal the film's acute awareness of the dehumanizing sameness of wartime deaths. Initially, we too may see the dead soldier as just one of many, until we begin to recognize familiar actors throughout the scene, signaling the importance of this particular death. The film's demand that viewers see the individuality of an anonymous dead soldier, Jackie Willow (D. B. Sweeney), through flashbacks is paralleled by the developing relationship between his former mentor, Sergeant Clell (James Caan) and anti-war journalist

Sam (Anjelica Huston), as they come to see and respect each other behind their superficially conflicting roles. At the end of the film, Clell's short speech about Jackie concludes: "I know him. I won't forget."

Gardens of Stone uses anonymity as a central motif, but much less typical is its deliberate and explicit reclaiming of the individuality of one such dead veteran (and, by implication, all of them). More commonly, anonymity is ubiquitous but unexamined. Nevertheless, at least some of the soldiers on "our" side of the war are inevitably made recognizable and memorable in order to sustain our interest in and understanding of events. The opposition between small groups of selectively individualized characters and widespread anonymity—between those who matter to the narrative and those who provide background spectacle—is a generic given. However, the explicit undermining of this opposition, which is central to Eastwood's, Coppola's, and De Palma's projects—where the person-hood of anonymous characters is reclaimed—is much more unusual, especially with respect to the enemy. Typically, the enemy's racial "otherness" may further contribute to the sense that they represent an undifferentiated threat. Enemy victims, in particular, are likely to lack individualizing stories or a sustained and recognizable visual presence. A number of aspects of the girl's presentation in *Casualties of War* would seem to reinforce this.

First, we know almost nothing about her as an individual: she speaks no English and her words are never translated either through subtitles or through bilin-gual characters offering explanations for the benefit of other characters, or even through the convention of having Vietnamese characters "speak Vietnamese" in English amongst themselves (as might have happened, for example, in the kidnap scene). She is given no background, no history, to help us understand her: we merely see her dragged kicking from what we assume to be her family, though their relationships to her are never clarified (at least not until the final credits, where they are listed as her mother and sister).

Second—and largely as a result of her presentation as an anonymous figure whose "otherness" is consistently stressed—unusually few clear indications are given of what she might be feeling as she is kidnapped, raped, and later killed: fear and panic, certainly, and physical pain, but what else? Does she understand what's in store for her at every stage? Does she feel ashamed? Angry? Disillu-sioned? Had she welcomed the American presence in her country, and is she now feeling betrayed? It is impossible to say. Her apparent bewilderment as she runs *towards* her killers, after the initial stabbing, only confirms the differences between her and us, since *we* see clearly that she is running to her death. Ironi-cally, it may well be the otherness of the GIs from *her* perspective that makes her unable to understand fully what they intend, though her actions further mystify *her,* rather than them.

Third, the camerawork does little to privilege her perspective. Not only is there an absence of point-of-view shots from her eyeline, but the rape takes place in the background of the shot with her face obscured, and the stabbing occurs in the background behind an extreme close-up of Eriksson aiming his machine gun offscreen in the right foreground of the frame, unaware of what is going on behind him. Thus, the placement of the stabbing in the background of the shot contributes to the difficulties in empathizing with the girl, even though the unfolding events both bind our eyes to her and—excruciatingly, even sickeningly—arouse our sympathies. However, as was mentioned earlier, the composition of the shot also puts insurmountable obstacles in the way of any alignment with the oblivious Eriksson. At this moment, what we are asked to feel and see is simply not what he feels and sees. In fact, precisely as we are forced to watch the Vietnamese girl being stabbed behind him, Eriksson is taking aim at other Vietnamese in a boat on the river down below him. The killing of Vietnamese enemies by the group of soldiers on the ridge above continues throughout the scene, though only the killing of the girl is riveting and emotionally laden. So, if the girl is presented as, in some respects, anonymous (with no personal history, no audience access to her consciousness, no developed point of view), it is different from the more generically typical anonymity of the other Vietnamese down below, whose suffering is not emotionally alive for us. The reason for this discrepancy may be simple: unlike them, she has a face.

In this way, we are presented with an intense sense of her *particular* humanness, as her suffering is seen to play across her features in heartbreaking close-up, giving us *this* mouth, *these* eyes, and so on. However, we are simultaneously pulled in another direction by the generalizing effect of all the strategies just discussed. Her combined presentation as anonymous Vietnamese girl plucked from nowhere in particular, and *this specific one* before us, makes it tempting to take her as an embodied representation of a more abstract idea: the rape and destruction of Vietnam more generally, her suffering bearing a heavy symbolic burden. Her femaleness may further contribute to the temptation to read her in more general terms as an emotive representation—with generic roots in melodrama—of innocence and virtue. Seeing her in any of these ways would be to collude in the process of removing her from history—from *her* history—which is the bedrock of the soldiers' treatment of her. Though viewers are never led to share the soldiers' sense that her suffering doesn't matter—even if we accept rather too easily the deaths of all the other Vietnamese in the film—we may still take for granted that, if Eriksson were to let the matter drop, it would be as if she had never existed, as though her life had no connection to anyone else: in Eriksson's words, "If I do nothing, she'd just vanish." Yet this is to see the girl from a position outside her culture. As Simone de Beauvoir (1961) argues, places like Africa and Asia are imagined from Western points of view as mysterious lands of darkness and impenetrability where it is easy to get lost and disappear. However, even if the girl's personhood is not in Eriksson's gift to bestow, but is rooted in her history and embedded in her culture, his insistence that her fate be told goes at least some way towards challenging the soldiers' view of her as anonymous "Other," which is so intrinsic to Western ways of thinking, as well as to the genre of the war film.

These matters come home to us very forcefully, I think, when, in the course of the trial in the later stages of the film, the prosecutor refers to the girl, for the first time in the film, by name: Tran Thi Oahn (Thuy Thu Le). This moment emphatically answers an earlier one, when the men marched her through a desolate burnt-out landscape after the abduction and Corporal Clark (Don Harvey) mockingly sang from a song by The Doors: "Hello, I love you, won't you tell me your name?" At the court martial, we *are* given her name, and her past is suddenly evoked, as we realize with a start that she has been traced and reclaimed—identified by those whose lives were interwoven with hers—and thereby reinserted in the history of her village and her family. This moment is crucial in providing a counterweight to the temptation to take Oahn as a representation of the suffering of Vietnam during her earlier ordeal.

Roger Ebert (1989), reviewing the film, found everything outside of the harrowing central events unnecessary. Yet loss of the present-day framing of the central action would have robbed the film of much of its complexity. Not only would we have missed the posthumous affirmation of Oahn's identity—an affirmation that underlines our own possible collusion in having reduced her to an abstraction (a "message," in Ebert's approving words, "that in combat human values are lost and animal instincts are reinforced")—but we would also have missed the present-day framing scenes of Eriksson back in the states following the withdrawal of U.S. personnel from Vietnam. This "narrative sandwich," as Ebert calls it, is significant to how we experience the film.

A suggestive parallel emerges between the way Oahn's past is suppressed and then publicly proclaimed, and the way Eriksson's life back home is taken from him, as we dissolve into flashback, and then returned in the final scene. However, when we see him in the states, he appears aimless and disconnected from any meaningful life, as though the war has deprived him of his place to such an extent that its restoration is no longer possible, thus further strengthening the links with Oahn: for both of them any genuine continuity with their past lives at the end of the film is only nominal (she's dead, he's traumatized). The postwar context of the framing story, and the cynicism of its repeated reference to Nixon's resignation, guide our reading of the flashback sequences during the war, emphasizing in particular the war's futility and the corruption of the government that waged it.

The framing scene that opens the film is set in the United States inside a crowded tram. The whooshing rush of airbrakes is audible before the shot begins, and it continues over the shot as the tram comes to a stop and a young Asian woman in modern American dress gets on, presumably a student, as her arms are full of books. The camera moves down the central aisle, then left onto Eriksson (until then a small, barely noticeable background figure), his head leaning against the window with eyes closed. As the tram sets off again, he opens his eyes with a start. A cut to a shot of the woman from Eriksson's point of view is accompanied by the sound of oriental pan pipes (their fluty breathiness recalling the earlier sound of airbrakes). We then cut to Eriksson's drained and listless face and again back to the woman, the camera moving in on her as it had previously moved in on him. Behind her, a headline ("Nixon Resigning") can be seen on a wide-open newspaper in another passenger's hands. Further cuts to Eriksson, to the young woman, and back to him complete the short opening scene as Eriksson turns back towards the blackness of the window next to him, his eyes closing again, and his brow furrowed, as we dissolve to Vietnam.

These few minutes link Eriksson and the woman, while contrasting her brisk purposefulness with the sense of lasting trauma conveyed by his listlessness and closed eyes at the start and end of the scene, as well as by the darkness of the window he turns towards before the final dissolve. The links between pan pipes and airbrakes make clear the way his Vietnam experiences continue to overlay his present experiences and block a full return to civilian life. Significantly, Eriksson's wife and young daughter are never seen—never recovered by him in a convincing way—so all we get is an impression of an aimlessly wandering ghost, rather than a man with any imminent prospect of settling down to his pre-war life.

By the end of the film, right after the other men in Eriksson's patrol are sentenced for their crimes and Sergeant Meserve (Sean Penn) has whispered what we take to be threats in Eriksson's ear as Meserve is led past him out of the courtroom, we return to the tram, and the opening scene is then completed. Eriksson follows the woman out of the tram to return a scarf she'd left behind. Ebert writes in his review that their subsequent conversation "is so forced and unnatural and tries so hard to cobble an upbeat ending onto a tragic story, that it seems to belong in another movie" (1989). But isn't this unconvincingness—the cobbled-together feel—of the film's resolution precisely the point? The music is particularly excessive and has the effect, whether intended or not, of beggaring belief in any immediate prospect of redemption and recovery. When the young woman responds to a couple of (presumably) Vietnamese words that Eriksson speaks to her as she walks off, it's as if she's heard it all before: "Do I remind you of someone?" She speaks sympathetically (the voice is Amy Irving's, though the onscreen actress is Thuy Thu Le, who plays Oahn as well), but impatiently dismisses his attempt to connect with her and project his guilt her way, as if needing her forgiveness for his failure to help Oahn. "You had a bad dream, didn't you?" "Yes." "It's over now, I think," she replies, saying goodbye and walking away without a backward glance. By refusing to relinquish her individuality (however Americanized) and become another representation of "Vietnam," the woman—nameless to Eriksson and us, but with a clear personal life of her own as she hurries off, arms full of books and looseleafs—escapes the allegorical burden Oahn was in danger of having to bear. It is a burden that Eriksson himself, to a lesser extent, seems now to be at risk of shouldering as an unmoored ghost: to stand in for the countless other "casualties of war" whose fates echo their own.

As Eriksson returns the woman's scarf, we may be reminded of the scarf Oahn's mother held out to her as she was kidnapped, and which Corporal Clark grabbed and used as a gag stuffed in Oahn's mouth. The mother's odd gesture in offering the scarf contributes to our impression of Vietnamese "unknowability," which pervades the scenes with Oahn: why is she holding out the scarf at the moment of separation from her daughter? To keep her warm? As a reminder of home, of who she is? As all she can think to do in her helplessness, when doing nothing is unthinkable? It is a poignant yet unreadable moment whose significance seems weighty and impenetrable at the same time (though a deleted scene included on the DVD of the film suggests the scarf is a particular treasure of Oahn's). In contrast, the scarf Eriksson returns to the woman on the tram is simply a scarf. I see no "upbeat ending" here, though camera and music may attempt to instill some hope as Eriksson glances up at a sunny California sky. However, any implied optimism will take time to bear fruit. The young woman seems to be advising Eriksson, politely but firmly, to get on with his life when he has no life to get on with. Meserve's threat from the end of the courtroom scene continues to hang over him. And the insistent visual reference to Nixon's resignation paints a picture of a country divided against itself, and equally unable to get over its traumas in a hurry.

So Eriksson's experiences are part of a larger context. He is linked to other new recruits, throughout his onscreen time in Vietnam, by the nickname "Cherry," whose connotations of female sexuality once again connect him to Oahn: the nickname sets him up as another innocent who will be violated and changed forever as a consequence of the war. This connection is made more blatant when Eriksson is trying to make sense of the kidnapping and protests to Meserve that "she's just a farm girl," with Meserve replying calmly, "Eriksson, look, you're the cherry here, right? So lighten up." After the rapes, another link between Eriksson and Oahn is made when Meserve warns Eriksson that he could easily get killed "by accident" by one of the men: "I mean, a body bag's a body bag, right? Who's countin'? Your mama's cryin' and your daddy pissin' and moanin.'" At this point, Eriksson interrupts: "He's dead." "*What?*" "He's dead. My father's dead." Clark, the most sadistic of the men, then intervenes: "Who cares, man? Nobody cares about your goddamn family history, pal." The GIs themselves are not only expendable—indistinguishable from one another in their body bags—but also disconnected from any personal history before the war. More specifically, the nickname links Eriksson with the other "Cherry," the inept young conscript who is killed by a booby-trap when Eriksson and the rest of the patrol return to the base camp after Oahn's death.

However, the two deaths—of Oahn and the hapless Cherry—are far from the same in their emotional effects, despite the shared innocence and bewilderment both victims display and the similar shots of them lying on their backs, as Eriksson and others stare down at their horrifically damaged corpses on the ground.

Where Oahn's ordeal is heartrending, Cherry's is not. The reason for this may be partly due to the fact that Oahn's goes on for so much longer, and her bewilderment is so much more complete. If she has been wrenched from her history, the time she spends with Meserve and his men gives her a new history—a sustained stretch of narrative—that arouses our desires for a particular sort of story: that she somehow be saved. Although the film is based on true events, I don't think this fact is a prerequisite to our intense involvement. It is enough to be compelled to hold these things in mind—to commit ourselves to the narrative, to the genre, and to Morricone's score—for the effects to follow, though I guess we need to live in a world where such things are at least plausible in order for the film to hit us so hard. The escalating of the violence against Oahn, and Eriksson's inability to help her, no doubt contribute further to the emotional intensity of our reaction to her death. But there is a more important difference from our reactions to pain and suffering elsewhere in the film, for example, our horror at hearing a soldier screaming in agony and seeing that he doesn't have any legs, or the mild regret we feel at the unlucky Cherry's death, or our surprise at the sudden gunning down of Brown (Erik King)—part of the original patrol—much earlier. Oahn's suffering is deeply *shaming* to have to witness (thus, the aptness of Primo Levi's words about the Holocaust and the shame of the surviving witnesses, a shame that may seem misplaced when shouldered by those who were blameless victims themselves, but that was nonetheless both debilitating and apparently widespread).

What we are forced to contemplate is a world in which injustice exists, and where a group of men fail to recognize the humanness of a face in pain. We don't need to identify with Oahn (or Eriksson) to experience a sickening feeling of moral revulsion at this prospect, though some minimal sense of our shared humanity coupled with a refusal to reduce her to a symbol of "Vietnam" (or, indeed, of human suffering more generally) is required. I assume that the majority of male viewers will experience this revulsion too, though rape-and-murder scenarios will inevitably have different meanings and emotional shadings for women and men.

Oahn's femaleness, like her humanness, helps us to recognize broad areas of similarity between her and (some of) us, but the film holds us back from more intimate access to her consciousness and more specific affinities with her situation. Our emotional involvement in her fate rests on a recognition that she is a person like us—in spite of her presentation as largely inaccessible and in spite of vast cultural differences—but equally that she is separate from us, as *this particular face* before us. Recognizing her inviolable personhood is to accept the outrageous immorality of treating her in lesser terms. Even Sergeant Meserve, when asked by one of the other men when he had last had a "real" woman, replies of Oahn, "She was real. I think she was real." His uncharacteristic remark suggests that the acts of violence and violation he has orchestrated against Oahn, though thoroughly condemned by the film, are Meserve's attempts to counter his own perceived loss of personhood—of humanness—in Vietnam. If Oahn is real, as Meserve suspects, then he must be too.

CHAPTER 11

GENDER HYPERBOLE AND THE
UNCANNY IN THE HORROR FILM:

THE SHINING

KATIE MODEL

At its simplest, genre is a play of the familiar and the different. Gender poses similarities and differences between men and women. The uncanny, in all its renditions, flickers between familiarity and strangeness. Gender, genre, and the uncanny in various ways all engage, resist, and toy with similarity and difference. The horror film is an ideal site to explore the interrelations of gender, genre, and the uncanny, and their chiasmic exchange. Horror's grappling with gender and the uncanny has been extensively discussed (see Wood 1978). The pioneering work of Linda Williams and Carol Clover has identified gender slippage as a defining trait of the horror genre. As Clover (1992) notes, ambiguity, instability, or slippage of gender often gives rise to the uncanny by triggering "intellectual uncertainty," in this instance over sexual identity.

While the literature on the horror film has explored in depth the issue of gender slippage, it has devoted little attention to the inverse—gender hyperbole. If gender slippage or ambiguity activates the uncanny by drawing on intellectual uncertainty, gender hyperbole draws on another source of the uncanny—doubling. A hyperbolic performance is in continual play with its referent, or double, the actual or "normal" other, which it exaggerates. When hyperbole takes on gender, the negotiation between the hyperbolized creation and its familiar "normal" referent becomes especially tricky. Since gender, to draw on the work of Judith Butler (1993 and 1999), is itself a performance, we often find that the familiar referent, which shadows the hyperbolic male or female spectacle, seems at times strange. Likewise, the hyperbolic construct at times appears uneasily familiar. The uncanny insinuates itself into the interplay between these two images. Called forth by gender hyperbole in the horror film, the uncanny can contaminate a film's overall cinematic mimesis, drawing our attention to the uncanny status of all film images. Instances of gender hyperbole in the horror film hence awaken in us a sense of cinema's particular strangeness as a mimetic medium dealing in shadows or doubles of the beings and things around us in the world.

I have selected Stanley Kubrick's 1980 film, *The Shining*, based on Stephen King's eponymous novel (1977), as a particularly striking example of the intertwining of gender hyperbole, genre, and the uncanny. While participating in horror's generic codes, *The Shining,* like most of Kubrick's works, also exceeds its genre. It is, in Frederic Jameson's description, "metageneric" (1992, 4). By featuring Jack Nicholson—whose acting style, as Dennis Bingham (1994) has argued, makes a performance of masculinity—the film immediately raises the issue of gender extremes. *The Shining* also links directly to Freud's 1919 essay, "The Uncanny." As many critics have noted, Kubrick and co-screenwriter Diane Johnson studied Freud's essay while writing the script for *The Shining.* The essay leaves its imprint on the film through visual and verbal references. More elusively, the film's treatment of the uncanny structurally echoes Freud's essay.

Sites of the uncanny tend to hold us in their thrall, leading us to return to them again and again. It is therefore not surprising that *The Shining,* Freud's essay "The Uncanny," and a text on which Freud's essay turns—E.T.A. Hoffmann's tale "The Sand-Man" (1967)—have all unleashed a plethora of critical literature. As the uncanny by nature eludes our grasp and is a tensile term, it both invites multiple readings and simultaneously frustrates any reading. The circulating familiar-but-different renditions of uncanny texts, in a way, enact the uncanny itself. *The Shining,* in the hands of numerous critics and scholars, takes on slightly different shapes, and these disseminated variants double back on our understanding of the film. If horror films, as Clover articulates, function like folktales or oral narratives, which have "no original" but "only variants" (1992, 11), then the many essays on *The Shining* add another cluster of iterations to a story with no single origin. So I turn to *The Shining* and the works embedded in its nucleus—"The Sand-Man" and "The Uncanny"—indebted to the scholarship on the film and to invaluable past work on gender, genre, and the uncanny.

From Freud onward, the uncanny has been linked to castration anxiety, a repressed fear that, in Freud's view, returns in strangely familiar guises to haunt us. For Freud, who associates castration with blindness or assault on the eyes, the Sand-Man—a horrifying character in Hoffmann's tale, who grabs sleepless children's eyes and feeds them to his monstrous offspring—becomes an emblematic figure for the uncanny. If we read "The Sand-Man" through the customary lens of castration anxiety, we are likely to associate the uncanny with sexual difference rather than with gender. However, if we allow ourselves a broader perspective, we may find an additional source of the tale's uncanniness: gender hyperbole. Furthermore, if we unyoke blindness and ocular metaphors from the idea of castration, we bring into view another element of the story: Hoffmann's trenchant critique of the Enlightenment's ocularcentrism. Repeated remarks by Hoffmann's ironic narrator such as "it is clear," "it is patent," "it is true"—in a tale that continually undermines vision, clarity, and truth—satirize the Enlightenment's obsession with transparency. Hoffmann's story, alongside other Romantic works, calls for a new kind of visuality. *The Shining* too, through interweaving the uncanny with gender hyperbole, calls for alternate ways of seeing.

The protagonist of the "The Sand-Man," Nathaniel, is given a magic spyglass that brings his neighbor, the beautiful young woman Olimpia into pellucid focus. He is transfixed. Seeking out her company, Nathaniel discovers to his delight that Olimpia's disposition is as peerless as her beauty. He finds he can easily talk to her for hours as she wordlessly conveys a deep understanding and empathy. However, Nathaniel will discover to his horror that the spyglass is not a clarifier but an obfuscator, a false animator of things inanimate: Olimpia is a *man*made automaton. She is also a comically hyperbolic figure of the "ideal" woman (and Hoffmann's humorous treatment of the spyglass is a remarkably prescient commentary on apparatus theory's study of voyeurism and fetishism in cinema). Hoffmann's linking of the uncanny to gender (a societal creation) rather than sexual difference (a biological determination) allows for the tale's witheringly ironic view of social conventions. The tale also maps the uncanny's spreading force, its refusal to be contained within a single locus. Hoffmann teases the reader with obvious sites of the uncanny—Olimpia and the Sand-Man—while infusing all ontological levels of the tale with the uncanny. Olimpia is an exaggerated double of a particular "real" woman, Nathaniel's fiancée, Clara. The revelation that Olimpia is an automaton ripples back in the text, imbuing Clara's feminine traits with an automaton-like quality. Moreover, the uncanny, not content to stay within the diegesis, moves into mimesis itself. Hoffmann's narrator, a friend of Nathaniel's, introduces the reader to the story's protagonist as a "likeness" to the "real" Nathaniel, a likeness he hopes will have something in common with the original. Throughout the tale we are brought close to the protagonist and simultaneously estranged through the reminders that our encounter is with a double, or "likeness." Lastly, the uncanny reaches across that final border between text and reader and touches us. We come away from the tale with an unsettling sense of the strangeness inherent in everyday life, what Stanley Cavell (1988) calls "the uncanniness of the ordinary."

This quotidian strangeness is as central a concern in *The Shining* as it is in "The Sand-Man." Kubrick, like Hoffmann, masterfully deceives us with conspicuous sites of the uncanny only to arouse the uncanny *feeling* more powerfully through different, and more elusive, means. *The Shining* realizes visually many of the uncanny-inducing examples that Freud "musters" in "The Uncanny": telepathy (or "shining"), doublings, doppelgangers, ghosts, corpses, and mirrors. However, the mere presence of materializations of the uncanny does not necessarily elicit an uncanny sensation. As Freud reminds us, the uncanny is, above all, a feeling, one that Freud himself needed to summon at the beginning of his essay. *The Shining's* searing analysis of gender and the horror genre exploits the distinctly embodied sensation of the uncanny. The film most often elicits the uncanny feeling through images of mundane middle-class family activities, textured by Nicholson's star persona. These scenes evoke in us an uncanny familiar-but-different sensation as they draw attention to gendered power relations embedded in white middle-class "norms." The supernatural, on the other hand, when it appears in *The Shining,* serves less to summon the uncanny than to articulate a difference between the uncanny as material source and the uncanny as *feeling.* As Samuel Weber points out in his essay, "The Sideshow, or: Remarks on a Canny Moment" (1973), the fact that the uncanny cannot be "mustered" is essential to its workings. Indeed, the tension in Freud's essay between numerous examples of the uncanny and an overriding slipperiness of definition has prompted Hélène Cixous (1976) to argue that "The Uncanny" is itself an uncanny text. Freud, as Weber remarks, cannot look the uncanny "straight in the eyes" (1973, 1114). For Weber, this is precisely because the uncanny cannot be fixed or stared down. It moves from an oblique angle, from the *side.*

The power of *The Shining* derives, in part, from the film's incorporation of the uncanny's sensory qualities and its sideways or oblique movement. Near the beginning of the film, there is a superficially mundane but critical scene, in which all ontological levels are imbued with the uncanny. The scene cues the spectator to our position in relation to the subsequent eruption of gender hyperbole. The Torrance family is driving to the Overlook Hotel to begin their winter-long stay. In a long-take shot in medium close-up, we watch the protagonists—the nuclear family, appearing together for the first time in the film—as they interact in the claustrophobic space of their Volkswagen. Jack (Jack Nicholson) is in the driver's seat; Wendy (Shelley Duvall) is in the passenger seat; and their son Danny (Danny Lloyd) is in the back, but leans forward to insert himself between his parents. The immobile camera is locked in place just outside the car on *Jack's side*, and the driver's window is rendered invisible, eradicating the glass barrier between Jack and us. The fixed camera holds the family in its view, keeping them a unit, refusing to cut between them as they speak. The following conversation ensues:

Wendy: Boy, we must really be high up; the air feels so different.
Jack: (with obvious boredom): Mhmmm.
Danny: Dad.
Jack: (after a slight pause) Yes.
Danny: I'm hungry.
Jack: (after a moment): Well, you should have eaten your breakfast.
Wendy: We'll get you something as soon as we get to the hotel, OK?
Danny: OK, Mom.

Wendy: Hey, wasn't it around here that the Donner party got snowbound?

Jack: (after pausing and glancing in the rearview mirror): I think it was farther
west in the Sierras.

Danny: (turning to Jack): What was the Donner party?

Jack: (beginning to smile after pausing as if to recall): They were a party of settlers
in covered-wagon times. They got snowbound one winter in the mountains
and had to resort to cannibalism in order to stay alive.

Danny: You mean they ate each other up?

Jack: (with a smile of delight): They had to, in order to survive.

Wendy: Jack!

Danny: Don't worry Mom, I know all about cannibalism. I saw it on TV.

Jack: (smiling ironically and raising his eyebrows): See, it's OK. He saw it on
the television.

Through visual, verbal, gestural, and acoustic registers, this brief scene instantiates what will be enacted metaphorically throughout the film. Countering the
horror genre's characteristic gender instability, the camera rigidly *fixes* white
middle-class gender positions through the devices of the car and the long take.
Throughout the entire scene, male and female roles are held in place: Jack as
driver; Wendy in the passenger seat. Jack presents mastery over information,
answering questions, while Wendy is relegated to the domestic sphere, tending
to her son's needs. Yet, like the high-altitude air, which surrounds the family
and feels "different," the uncanny envelops these gender norms. Each time Jack
speaks, his voice emerges as if from elsewhere and is infused with either mocking
sarcasm or menacing authoritarianism. Although driving gives Jack a narrative
justification for distraction, the exaggerated pauses that precede his responses
and his excessively deliberate way of speaking infect the conversation with an
eerie strangeness. Camera and music assist in conjuring the uncanny: the long
take keeps the family in its sight for an unnervingly long time while the score
that opened the film (itself a play on the familiar and different as it is a *variation*
on the classic *Dies Irae*) now unsettlingly holds one note.[1]

Perhaps the most discomfiting aspect of the scene is the overriding impression that communication between members of the nuclear triad is exceedingly
amiss. There is a sense that something is out of sync, that Jack's words to his
wife and son are not directed to them alone. Jack's pauses, his sarcasm, and the
crescendo of raised eyebrows, smirking face and mocking tone, which close the
scene, all gesture outwards, beyond the contained space of the car, towards us.
And positioned as we are just outside the driver's window, we are ideally situated
to receive his sideward address.[2]

Significantly it is here, at the window—a standard divider between inside and
outside—that we especially strongly experience Jack Nicholson's star presence. The
marker of a signature Nicholson performance is an ironic, winking, self-conscious
delivery, one that continually throws *sideward* glances at the spectator. And, as

Dennis Bingham has persuasively argued, the Nicholson performance entails a deconstruction of masculinity by making a spectacle of machismo, swagger, and bravado. In the car scene, Jack Torrance/Nicholson educes the uncanny by blending gender hyperbole and star presence. While Nicholson's exaggerated masculine performance rouses the double it hyperbolizes, the actor's play with the line between character and star pulls us into a liminal space between film and viewer. The elimination of the driver-side window concretizes the way that Jack acts like a portal between the audience and the projected world, drawing us into and pulling us out of the film, conjuring the porosity of the membrane dividing audience from screen. For not only are we on Jack's side, but it seems that we are touching Jack, that he is touching us. This perception of haptic contact is furthered by the bodily response that Nicholson's performance frequently elicits in the viewer—laughter.

As we go forth into the scenes that follow, our alignment with Jack, literalized in the car scene, continues metaphorically. The complicity between viewer and Jack becomes increasingly unnerving as Jack's monstrosity fully emerges. Once the Torrance family is ensconced in the Overlook, Jack's growing insanity, or possession, is accentuated by his exchanges with Wendy. These moments function in the text as a barometer of Jack's madness/possession, moving along a continuum from condescending sarcasm and semi-lucidity to full-fledged misogyny and raging insanity. Two crucial scenes between husband and wife bracket the film's terrifying moment of discovery: the revelation that Jack's all-important writing project consists of the repetition, page upon page, of one phrase: "All work and no play makes Jack a dull boy"—a phrase, Brigitte Peucker notes, "not even of his own devising" (2001, 668).

In the first of these scenes, Wendy, wearing a bathrobe, rolls an enormous room-service cart down the long hotel corridor to serve her husband breakfast in bed. Upon entering the bedroom, she cheerfully announces: "I made [your eggs] just the way you like them, sunny-side up!" Before a bedside mirror, the couple carry on a clichéd conversation in which Jack complains about his "work" and responds to his wife's perky support with snide retorts.

The breakfast scene enacts the way in which gender hyperbole, having evoked the uncanny, estranges the cinematic medium itself. The image of Wendy pushing the hotel-sized serving cart is a parody of subservient femininity. Her double, the "real" woman, who in a less exaggerated way partakes of feminine dutifulness, is automatically implied. As Wendy enters the bedroom, the doubling continues when the camera cuts to Jack's reflected image in the bedside mirror. We now see Wendy standing in the bedroom and her reflection in the mirror. Hence the doubling implied through her hyperbolic portrait becomes a tripling as we see onscreen two Wendys: the filmic "real" protagonist and her reflected image. As the conversation continues, the camera moves in towards the mirror so that the couple's reflected image takes over the entire frame, replacing the "real" one. There is only one eerie reminder that we are watching a mirror image: the inverted lettering on Jack's T-shirt. The uncanny feeling, already evoked by the multiple images is compounded when Jack describes the sensation the hotel stirred in him, using words that refer directly to Freud's 1919 essay, "It was as though I'd been here before."

The scene that closes the bracket around the horrifying exposure of Jack's "manuscript" is the last interaction that we see between the couple before a raging Jack chases his wife and son throughout the hotel with an axe. Jack enters the vast space he has taken as his study and demands that Wendy tell him what she thinks should be "done" with Danny. Backing up the stairs, defending herself with a baseball bat, Wendy responds, "I think, maybe, he should be taken to the doctor." Mockingly reuttering his wife's words, exaggerating their timidity and "feminine" intonation, Jack responds, "You *think, maybe,* he should be taken to the doctor?!" Jack's imitation of Wendy's stereotypical female tentativeness—his performance of clichéd "femininity"—holds up a metaphoric mirror to Wendy. We behold a terrifying reflection of passive femininity. *The Shining* gives us an opportunity to recognize ourselves in Wendy's meekness or in Jack's sneering condescension. The scene plays out the uncanny's oscillation between, or blending of, recognition and fear.

Mirrors and mirroring pervade *The Shining.* They appear literally, as in the haunting breakfast scene, just discussed, and metaphorically, as we witness in Jack's scathing mimicry of Wendy. They seem to translate crucial things for us, as in the notorious revelation in the mirror that REDRUM spells MURDER backwards; or they reveal the back or underside of things, as when a delusional Jack, in another scene, reaches for a beautiful naked woman but to his horror discovers through her reflection in a bathroom mirror that her backside is an abject rotting corpse. Mirrors tempt us to find meanings in things through their inversion. And *The Shining,* by stretching male and female gender farther out on their opposing poles, appears to invert the gender indeterminacy associated with a number of its horror forebears, contemporaries, and successors. However, as might be expected in the province of the uncanny (and in a Kubrick film), *The Shining's* treatment of gender hyperbole is not a simple inversion of the horror genre's gender slippage. Like the trace that past events leave on the Overlook, which those with "the shine" can see, *The Shining* complicates inversions even as it puts them forward.

In discussing Villiers de l'Isle-Adam's *Claire Lenoir* (1887), a tale with numerous references to, and shared concerns with, Hoffmann's "The Sand-Man," Weber draws out the significance of the story's conclusion, when the titular character dies before the eyes of the hero, Tribulat Bonhomet, a professor of physiognomy. The professor seizes the moment to test whether an assertion about animals—that the final image they see before death imprints itself in their eyes—holds true for humans. Taking out his ophthalmoscope to examine Claire's glassy eyes,

Bonhomet "remembers that this is impractical if not impossible. For if he looks directly into those eyes, the image will be inverted." Bonhomet considers hanging the dead woman upside down but rejects this idea as indecent, deciding instead, in order to "get a right-side-up image" to "lay the body *sideways* on the bed . . . so that the head will hang down over the bedside" (S. Weber 1973, 1130). For Weber, the spectacular concluding moment in Villier's uncanny tale literalizes the way in which the uncanny can neither be looked "straight in the eyes" nor simply inverted, but must be viewed from the side, "offside," "sideways," in an *"oblique direction"* (1122).

The implications for *The Shining* of the uncanny's sideward movement are numerous, pulling in gender, genre, stardom, and visuality. Without the uncanny's disruptive, oblique presence, realized most forcefully through the viewer's complex relation to Jack, the film would appear to uphold the very gender binaries it also simultaneously complicates. *The Shining* undermines Jack's hyperbolic masculinity by linking it directly to his professional failure: Jack's eruption into a full-blown patriarchal monster, wielding language as his weapon against Wendy, follows the shattering of his identity as an important writer. However, Jack's label as a failure depends on intact gender binaries. When *The Shining* slides into the generic realm of the occult, however, the film takes gender binaries and generic horror tropes in an uncanny direction. Male possession, as Cyndy Hendershot points out, "poses a problem for Western culture because . . . [while the] possessed woman merely underscores cultural stereotypes about the female subject position . . . the possessed male body potentially undermines stereotypes" (1998, 43). Male possession in *The Shining* presents a paradox: Jack's possessors are hyper-masculine, misogynist, and racist evil spirits who emasculate their "medium." The more Jack violently asserts his power over Wendy, drowning out her voice, the more he is simultaneously overtaken by others' voices. When Jack's attempt to control his family turns murderous, he is merely following the orders of his possessor.

Yet even as Jack Torrance's masculinity is undermined by his fecklessness and possession, Jack Nicholson's star aura continues. The uncanny force of Jack's sidelong glances to the viewer disturbs and supersedes the gender binaries. Nicholson's charisma is accentuated further by Kubrick's choice to deprive the viewer of a female fetish object—Wendy, the only significant female character, is divested of any sex appeal. The uncomfortable mixture of laughter, horror, and uncanny sensations, which Jack and the film evoke, reaches an apex in the later parts of the film when Jack more fully identifies with his possessors. If occult films involve "a crossing over," a breakdown of the boundary between the world of spirits and that of mortals, then *The Shining* extends this permeability to include the border between film and viewer. Indeed, as Jack descends more deeply into madness/possession, the uncanny sense that he gestures and performs for another interlocutor, the audience, increases. And this crossing over becomes a chiasmic exchange between Jack and us.

Interesting things happen at borders, as Christine Gledhill (2000) has asserted in relation to genre. And, in *The Shining*—a film that insistently draws our attention to borders and their dissolubility, whether through the crossing of generic boundaries; the film's use of chapter headings that blur months, days, and hours; or through unnerving cuts from exteriors to interiors—a particularly rich and porous border proves to be the one between perceiver and perceived. We continuously and vertiginously shift and reshift our position in relation to the protagonist. In the most horrifying scenes, we are likely to find ourselves laughing with Jack because Nicholson's performance is brilliant and hilarious. But even as we experience a connection and closeness, even as we join Jack and the camera in ridiculing Wendy, a feeling of distance creeps in—a discomfort about our complicity with the monster.[3] If this discomfort drives us away from Jack Torrance, paradoxically it may simultaneously draw us closer to Jack Nicholson as we try to buffer ourselves against the primal fear of a murderous father and husband that the film evokes. Yet the connection with the star is further complicated by the now widely known extra-textual information about Kubrick's mistreatment of Duvall and overt admiration for Nicholson, which Vivian Kubrick documents in *The Making of The Shining*.[4] Whether or not merely a ploy to draw out their respective performances (and Kubrick's comments in interviews suggest there was more to it than that), the director's differential treatment of the two actors results in a highly complex negotiation of power dynamics.[5] While the film goads us to participate in untoward gender relations, the extra-textual information doubles back on the viewing experience, adding another layer of discomfort to our connection with Jack.

In the process of summoning the uncanny, exploring the limits of genre, and arousing uneasiness around gender, *The Shining* also unsettles traditional representational mimesis through the viewer's complex relationship with Jack. However, another form of mimesis opens up. In the analyses of Michael Taussig and Laura U. Marks, both drawing on the work of Walter Benjamin, mimesis involves contact. For Taussig, there is in mimesis both a copying or imitation and "a palpable, sensuous connection between the very body of the perceiver and the perceived" (1993, 21). For Marks, "mimesis is a form of representation based on contact, getting close enough to the other thing to become it" (2004). To make contact with something, to sensuously connect with it, to get close enough to it to become it . . . what does this mean when the object that touches us is monstrous as well as mesmerizing? And when it is male? *The Shining* powerfully poses these questions.

The play of closeness and distance, familiarity and difference, that Jack/Nicholson provokes in the viewer troubles the gendered troping of proximity (feminine) and distance (male) elaborated by psychoanalytic theories of the gaze. Feminist theorists such as Luce Irigaray have sought to form a subversive antiocularcentric form of mimesis prizing closeness and the sensual. While Irigaray (1985) hoped to free vision from masculine transcendentalism, her gendered conceptions, as Martin Jay (1994) discusses, have been attacked for essentialism. Paradoxically, *The Shining* displays gender hyperbole at the diegetic level, but complicates the gendering of vision through our uncomfortable closeness with Jack.[6]

Our contact with Jack exemplifies the way that stars, as Gledhill has noted, "reach us through bodies" (1991, 210). Ironically, though we may describe Jack's contact with the viewer in ocular terms—he winks or glances at us—the uncanny *feeling* his presence evokes circumvents the scopic regime that Clover and other scholars have argued governs the horror genre. Clover contends that in horror two gazes reign: assaultive and reactive. Scholars of the horror genre, Clover stresses, have long overemphasized the sadistic, assaultive gaze, whereas it is the reactive, masochistic, "feminine" gaze, Clover maintains, that predominates in the genre (1992, 205). However, the uncanny's oblique movement disrupts and supersedes the binary that is established by the assaultive/reactive gaze paradigm. Furthermore, since the uncanny, a sensation not associated with a particular gender, is identified through feeling (traditionally a feminine sphere), not through scientific rational investigation (traditionally the province of men), it "infects" putatively gendered forms of knowledge and vision.

The Shining, like Hoffmann's "The Sand-Man," reminds us of an alternate way of seeing, one we might call an uncanny visuality. This visuality not only takes us outside of gendered vision but also blurs the boundaries between closeness and distance. We are both touched by the images and estranged from them when the uncanny is present. In an emblematic scene, Jack stands menacingly over a model of the hotel's topiary maze, peering down from above at two figures below. A dissolve takes us down to ground level, inside the maze, where the camera ominously follows Danny and Wendy feeling their way through the winding passageways. The scene both visualizes two types of seeing that Marks discusses, optic (distant and mastering) and haptic (on the ground, contact-based), and simultaneously blurs the distinction because of the uncanny's presence. When the uncanny is stirred, *The Shining* seems to suggest, a way of seeing arises that can encompass both optic and haptic visualities, or reside somewhere in between.[7]

An uncanny visuality insists on an embodied knowledge, countering the Enlightenment's transcendentalism parodied in Hoffmann's "The Sand-Man." *The Shining* deftly plays with the distinction between speaking to the head and to the body in its handling of race and gender. In a vivid description of ventriloquism, Danny tells his doctor that his imaginary friend Tony lives in his mouth but hides in his stomach. Like Tony, the uncanny speaks to us from and through the body. In *The Shining,* spoken racism or misogyny does not elicit the uncanny. However, there is something uncomfortably familiar in the way that the film toys with gender, race, and generic conventions. A feeling that we've "been here before," familiar from other films, is here played differently. Kubrick foregrounds two common racist generic tropes, the "Magical Negro" and the horror film's "Dispensable Black Man," by collapsing them in the sole African American character, Dick Hallorann (Scatman Crothers). Hallorann is the only other figure apart from the Torrance's son with "the shine," and he is killed when he attempts to rescue Danny and Wendy from Jack's assault. Hallorann's character elicits a complex response in most viewers—Crothers's superb performance connects us to him, yet the roles his character is relegated to uneasily recall racist filmic patterns. The film's juxtaposition of explicit spoken racism and misogyny with a more complex "familiar but different" treatment of gender and race suggests that there is a way of knowing that needs to pass through the uncanny.

In *The Shining*'s famous concluding scene, Danny eludes his father in the Overlook's labyrinth by retracing his footsteps in the snow and jumping to the side to hide in the hedges. Jack, unable to find his son, collapses. The camera cuts from the image of Jack, frozen to death in the labyrinth with open stony eyes, to a slow zoom into an old photograph of a group of people. On the lower part of the frame are the words, "The Overlook Hotel, 1922." As the zoom closes in, it centers on a familiar but unexpected sight: the smirking face of Jack! In this final frame, Kubrick encapsulates the uncanny visuality—that play of closeness and distance, familiarity and strangeness, haptic and optic—that pervades the entire film. The zoom, which brings the photograph into view, also shrouds the image in opacity. The photograph even upends indexicality by Kubrick's choice to superimpose Jack's face onto an actual archival photograph. Like the uncanny itself, the image of Jack cannot be contained by the frame, or by temporality, or indexicality. Instead, it eerily jumps out to make contact with us one last time, bearing out Kubrick's hope that when we leave the theater we will "retain some sense" of the film.[8] Perhaps we will even view the world from a slightly different angle.

Notes

Greatest thanks to Christine Gledhill, Pamela Grace, and Vito Mennella.

1. Invoking the Donner party both adumbrates the violence that will befall the snowbound Torrance family and also foretells the slipperiness of boundaries that will pervade the film. Foiled in their Manifest Destiny driven attempt to "civilize" through conquest of Native American land, the stranded Donner party becomes the "barbarian." According to Fredric Jameson, *The Shining* cannibalizes various horror subgenres, including the "evil child" film and the possession film, before settling on the ghost story (1992, 89).

2. In Stephen King's novel, the following passage suggests that things from henceforth can only function from the side: "Half an hour ago they had passed another sign that Daddy had said was very important. This sign said ENTERING SIDEWINDER PASS, and Daddy said that sign was as far as the snowplows went in the wintertime. . . . In the winter the road was closed from the little town of Sidewinder" (1977, 62).

3. For a detailed discussion of Jack Nicholson's and Shelley Duvall's different acting styles in *The Shining*, see Sharon Marie Carnicke, 2006.

4. Included in the supplementary material of the Warner Home Video DVD.

5. On Nicholson, Kubrick commented: "I believe that Jack is one of the best actors in Hollywood. . . . His work is always interesting . . . and has the X-factor, *magic*. . . . He is an intelligent and literate man, and these are qualities almost impossible to act." On Duvall: "I think she brought an instantly believable characterization to her part. The novel pictures her as a much more self-reliant and attractive woman, but these qualities make you wonder why she has put up with Jack for so long. Shelley seemed to be exactly the kind of woman that would marry Jack and be stuck with him" (Ciment 2001, 187–89).

6. Our connection with Jack adds a complicated gloss to Marks's notion of yielding to the haptic image: "I found that haptic visuality invites a kind of identification in which there is a mutual dissolving of viewer and viewed, subject and object; where looking is not about power but about yielding; or even that the object takes on more power than the subject" (2004, 2). Marks later stresses the importance of recognizing exactly what we are yielding *to* in haptic visuality. Kubrick's film also seems to urge us to consider this.

7. That the uncanny resists localization is wonderfully illustrated in Kubrick's revision to the injury Jack inflicts on Danny when he returns home drunk to find Danny has scattered his papers on the floor. In the novel Jack breaks Danny's arm. In the film, Jack *dislocates* Danny's collarbone.

8. Ciment asks Kubrick, "And when the film is finished, what then?" Kubrick responds "I hope the audience has had a good fright, has believed the film while they were watching it, and retains some sense of it. The ballroom photograph at the very end suggests the reincarnation of Jack" (2001, 194).

PART FOUR

GENRE AND GENDER TRANSNATIONAL

CHAPTER 12

EMOTION, SUBJECTIVITY, AND THE LIMITS OF DESIRE:

MELODRAMA AND MODERNITY IN BOMBAY CINEMA,
1940s–'50s

IRA BHASKAR

Let us begin with three scenarios of extremity, depictions of limit situations that concern ultimate questions of life, love, death, and meaning:

> A woman is seated on the floor, with her head on her arm on the bed against which she leans, staring out into space, while a blind singer outside sings of separation and deep anguish, ironically evoking *rāga malhār*—the *rāga* of union and joy.

> In deep space composition, in the foreground, a woman in black lies on a bed on a terrace under a flowering tree, and in profile looks off and away at the festive terrace opposite where wedding celebrations take place while her life ebbs away.

> A young man lies dying, unable to speak, under a tree outside the palatial house of the woman whom he loved, whom he could not accept, and for whom he destroyed himself, while she is unable to emerge and take leave of him.

These sequences, taken from Mahesh Kaul's *Gopinath* (1948), Kamal Amrohi's *Daera* (1953), and Bimal Roy's *Devdas* (1955), represent the tragic denouement of their protagonists, bringing into sharp relief a particular melodramatic embodiment of gender and identity in Bombay cinema of the 1940s and 1950s. What are the issues at stake? What is the historical conjuncture that pressures gender and genre to take such forms? What significances does the aesthetic mode employed here press forth from the situations that the films outline? What specific contours does the Indian melodramatic form take to signify its historical meanings? These are the questions I will address in this chapter.

Shifting the ground from discussions of melodrama as genre, recent work on melodrama has focused on the workings of the melodramatic mode, demonstrating how it constitutes cinema itself (Gledhill 1987, 2000; L. Williams 1998, 2001). As one of the most popular and enduring cultural forms through which contemporary social and political crises are cinematically represented and negoti- ated, melodrama's "capacity to respond to the questions of modernity" (Gledhill 2000, 232) accounts for its pervasive influence in different cinemas of the world. Theorized as an aesthetic form that emerges in transitional periods, melodrama is seen as negotiating the dislocating traumas of class and gender struggle, answer- ing the doubts and aporias consequent on secularization and the breakdown of the "traditional sacred" understood as constituting the modern.[1] Locating myself within this force field, and using concepts of gender, identity, and subjectivity, I respond to questions of melodrama and modernity in the context of Bombay cinema. I focus particularly on certain films from the first decade after Indepen- dence in order to explore whether the postcolonial moment in its first flush did indeed generate a euphoric sense of liberation as a transformative experience of the self; or whether the intense pressure that modernity placed upon traditional conceptions of self and community, gender and identity, released desires that the historical moment could not fulfill. Crumbling yet deeply entrenched social mores, contradictory desires, and dissonant experiences that characterized the transitional moment of the Indian modern in the 1940s also inspired narratives that articulated a tragic sense of desolation, incomprehension about rapid social changes, and their confounding experiences that were narrated in forms that are readily identifiable as melodramatic.[2] As a form characterized by its generation of "sympathy for the virtues of beset victims," for "protagonists beset by forces more powerful than they" (L. Williams 1998, 42), melodrama is clearly relevant in contexts other than Euro-American ones.

Across different cultures, then, melodrama is found as a form capable of nar- rating intense experiences of crises in particular historical moments. One such moment is the transition to modernity. The dislocations, ruptures, and aporias so central to modernity in different contexts get expressed in distinctive melo- dramatic forms that are socially and culturally charged. This is not surprising, since as a global form from its very inception, cinema and its generic forms have circulated worldwide and been reinvented and inflected differently in their interaction with local social, cultural, and performative traditions. Though the historicization of Indian melodrama[3] is not the task of this chapter, I will indicate several features that contextualize the form on which I focus.

Two key ideas in melodrama debates are central here in terms of their sig- nificance for the Indian context: melodrama as a form of "high emotionalism" (Brooks 1984, 12), and one that deploys nonpsychologized, monopathic characters (Heilman, cited in Brooks 1984, 12). Most theorists who identify melodrama with emotion also point out that since emotion is gendered feminine, melodrama has been understood as addressed to women. It is this gendering of melodrama—its association with women and feminized men—that I address via the example of Bombay cinema. I will also extend Gledhill's emphasis on "personality" and the "person" as the source of "desire" and "motivation," "morality and ethics," preparing the way for "the psychologization of character and performance of twentieth-century popular culture" (1991, 209). Thus I suggest that the expression of intense emotion communicates a charge of subjectivity arising from the externalization of the interior self that is normally unexpressed. I want to argue via my exemplary films that emotion is key to subjectivity, and in the expressionist foregrounding of emotion, melodrama also enacts subjectivization, not as the realization of gender, but rather as the embodiment of the individual's most intense condition of felt selfhood. This is because at the root of melodrama as expressive form is the emotional self, the self that in its expression takes different cultural forms.

Recent work on emotion has not only reaffirmed Raymond Williams's intervention underlining the centrality of feeling to everyday experience, but has also demonstrated that an analysis of emotions will reveal "a great deal about how emotions might operate in the reproduction of subjectivity, culture and power relations" (Harding and Pribram 2004, 864). Clearly this is not to divorce emotion from thought or affect from cognition; rather this body of work argues that "emotional experience can be seen as a creative and insightful route to knowledge" (865). Interestingly, Linda Williams has also pointed out, albeit briefly, that the reception and understanding of melodrama has been "impeded by the failure to acknowledge the complex tensions between different emotions as well as the relation of thought to emotion" (1998, 49). It is this line that I pursue here, drawing also on Harding and Pribram (2004), who use Alison Jagger to say that "emotions are pivotal in identity formations" and that affect is "integral to the notion of individuality" and plays a "formative role in subjectivity" (875). Using this perspective, I argue that melodrama is a form that instantiates the centrality of affect for the embodiment of subjectivity.

Furthermore, I argue that Indian cinemas developed not only a distinctly expressive melodramatic language of affect to articulate specific cultural and social experiences, but also, and obviously, that this language drew upon indigenous cultural, expressive, and performative forms that give Indian melodrama a different experiential texture and feel. The privileging, amplification, and orchestration of desire, the structuring of the narrative drive along an emotional line, and the expressive realization of subjective emotion is one cluster of features that I discuss. Reading the "melos" of melodrama literally and metaphorically, I foreground another typical feature of this form: the centrality of the song as the language of the ineffable and the manner in which the expression of individual desire is central to the process of individuation. My third focus is the idiom and significance of the sacred in Indian melodrama, and what this idiom enables, as well as the charge that it creates in the narrative. Crucial, then, to my analysis of the Indian melodramatic as a distinctive mode of cinema are the particular cinematic effects that generate the melodramatic affect of these films. But in order to identify and understand the aesthetic, moral, and social significances that these melodramas articulate, I start by outlining certain critical historical and cultural constellations that give them meaning.

While made in the first decade after Independence, *Gopinath, Daera*, and *Devdas* do not respond to the postcolonial Nehruvian imaginary found in other films from the 1950s.[4] It is with a more general experience of modernity that these films engage in different ways: a modernity that challenges and brings into critical focus relations of caste, class, and gender and their constitutive and determining impact on individual subjectivity. At the same time, in their dark and tragic evocation of melodramatic pathos, they differ from other films and genres (action, stunt, crime, and even the social melodramas) that responded to the dynamism, frenzy, and thrills of the urban experience of the modern.[5] The city in *Gopinath, Daera*, and *Devdas*, inasmuch as they deal with it, has dark connotations and represents not an enabling matrix of self-development and growth, but rather the inescapable, dangerous, and destructive potential of the modern. While in *Devdas*, the modern is constituted as a horizon challenging a feudal worldview, in *Gopinath*, modernity is embodied as the allure of cinema that represents a space of enchantment, mobility, the possibility of self-transformation, and yet is also complicit in the destruction of other, deeper forms of being. In *Daera*, the modern is once again an enticing frame of reference, of potential self-fulfillment that is aborted before it can even be articulated. All three films deal with the betrayal and failure of women by men, but also with the inability of men either to effectively face their own desires, confront their own unresolved schisms, or take affirmative action against the force of circumstances. An incipient transformative modernity releases desires that exceed the abilities of individuals for realization. The melodramatic mode underlines the pathos of an unsuccessful human struggle against an existential condition within which are inscribed an authoritative patriarchal law, entrenched social codes, and the magnified, destructive consequences of impulsive actions.

Twinned with the experience of colonialism,[6] modernity in India generated among the nineteenth-century elite a critical look at tradition, and later in the century a nascent nationalist urge for self-reliance, both of which resulted in different reform movements. Obscurantist religious practices, education, and especially the position of women in society were central to the controversies over social reform, inspired by Enlightenment ideals and liberal ideas from Europe. The "women's question" was a central issue here, but historians wonder at its sudden disappearance from public debate towards the end of the century. The politics of nationalism seemed to have overtaken gender issues. Partha Chatterjee's seminal formulation of the nationalist resolution of the "women's question" explicates how and why issues related to women and modern society were relocated within the nationalist ideological realm, specifically, "in an inner domain of sovereignty, far removed from the arena of political contest with the colonial state" (1993, 117). This move placed educated and modern women at the center of the nationalist project, but also placed upon them the burden of preserving the true spiritual and cultural identity of the nation, crucial to an essential and inner sovereignty as a bulwark against the experience of subjection to the colonial state. And it is from this inner and sovereign domain of spiritual essence, embodied in the home with the woman as its "representation" (120), that the battle for sovereignty in the external material world of politics and economics—a world taken to be the world of men—would also be launched. If social roles were thus clearly identified by gender in a patriarchal, nationalist ideology, this did not represent, as Chatterjee points out, the "dismissal of modernity" but was in fact "an attempt to make modernity consistent with the nationalist project" (121). The desire for the modern was the obverse face of the desire for the nation.

If education was central to the project of women's emancipation, it also meant the development by the educated woman of key feminine virtues of "chastity, self-sacrifice, submission, devotion, kindness, patience and the labors of love," as well as the inculcation of "the typically bourgeois virtues characteristic of the new social forms of 'disciplining'" (Chatterjee 1993, 129). Historians like Chatterjee, Chakrabarty (1994), and Sarkar (2001) have demonstrated how women subscribed to this hegemonic construct of the "new woman," producing themselves in accordance with the nationalist project of creating the modern nation. Women's writing from the nineteenth and early twentieth centuries is a testimony to the coalescence of their sense of emancipation via education with the ideological burden of embodying a reformed, classicized, and disciplined tradition.[7] At the same time, the narratives of struggle for education and self-emancipation are shot through with other desires that do not quite square with the disciplinary regimes and ideals of modern selfhood that nationalist ideology gifted women. It is these contradictions and ambivalences constitutive of gender identities and of a modernity that was "itself not one" (Chakrabarty 1994, 87) that makes for a "drama of inertia and entropy" (Rodowick 1987, 275) as characteristic of the particular form of the melodramatic in the films I am discussing.

The impact of the contradictory project of cultural reform that nationalist ideology had placed on the agenda in the latter half of the nineteenth century continued into the next century as well, as decadent feudal aristocracies and entrenched class structures experienced the disintegrating forces of the modern. The popularity of Bimal Roy's *Devdas*, a remake of P. C. Barua's film from 1935, indicates something of the significance of its appeal. The filmic narrative follows Saratchandra's novel about Devdas, the scion of a rich feudal aristocratic family who is in love with his neighbor and childhood sweetheart, Parvati (Paro), whom he cannot marry because his father forbids an alliance with a family that, though also Brahmin, is of a lower Brahmin caste as well as of inferior social status. Perhaps the film, like the novel, spoke to the hegemonic power of social codes and structures, offering gender roles and images that expressed the poignancy of a moment when individuals were unable to go against determining and constricting structures of caste, class, and family to seize and mould their lives in accordance with individual desire. In its portrayal of the suffering male protagonist, the tragic tale of Devdas, drinking himself to death at the loss of his beloved Paro, unable to accept the courtesan Chandramukhi's devotion and love, is a destabilization of gender roles that inverts the active male figure of nationalist ideology. Having failed in his attempt to challenge family and patriarchal strictures against dishonorable association with a family of a caste and class position inferior to his own, Devdas's only form of protest is perhaps an effete one—to reject the norms and standards of a world with which he is at odds. Self-destruction then marks the entropic failure and collapse of the attempt to reconcile patriarchal law and individual desire. While the narrative of *Devdas* clearly marks the melodramatic crisis of an individual identity "out of sync with the relations of authority which are required to legitimate it" (Rodowick 1987, 271), resulting in angst, internalized self-violence, and psychic disorders, cinematically, the experience of the film communicates by privileging a performance of suffering and an intensification of emotion via music and mise-en-scène.

This brings me to crucial features of the Indian melodramatic form indicated earlier—the privileging and amplification of emotion, and the centrality of music and the song as the vehicle for this expression, as well as the development of the song as the language of the ineffable. While many theorists of melodrama identify emotion and expressive performativity as its key constitutive features, not only does the Indian melodramatic form manifest these elements in a hyperbolic manner, their orchestration, usually via the song, foregrounds emotion as the key to subjectivity in a manner that is distinctive. In climactic moments in *Devdas,* it is the song that expresses the central meaning of the sequence—meanings that have to do with emotional intelligibility and the exteriorizing of inner subjective states. The lyrics, music, and the performance of the *mitwā* song that Devdas in desperation sings to mark his loneliness and his helplessness are a case in point:

Mitwā, mitwā	O beloved, dear beloved
Lāgi re yeh kaisi unbujh aag	What kind of inextinguishable fire am I consumed by?
Mitwā, mitwā	O dear darling beloved
Mitwa nahin aaye	My beloved hasn't come

The music has a slow tempo as Talat Mahmood sings in a slow, saddened emotion-laden voice to Dilip Kumar's restrained and quiet performance of a deeply wounded, suffering man whose every fiber of being calls out to the beloved he has lost, while the camera slowly pans over the empty landscape, marking the absence of the one he quests for. Here we have an image of the suffering lover whose deep passion and desire for the beloved, a desire that defines his very being, resonates with echoes of valued cultural figures. These range from classical Sanskrit drama's King Dushyant in Kālidāsas's *Abhijnāna Shākuntalam,*[8] suffering from the loss of his beloved Shakuntalā through the curse of amnesia, to Majnun, the iconic lover in the Arabian legend of Laila-Majnun, wandering the desert obsessed with the image of his unattainable beloved. First versified by the eleventh-century Persian Nizami, this romance circulated in India through its thirteenth-century version by the poet Amīr Khusrau, also celebrated for sacred-erotic songs desiring union with the beloved. The nineteenth-century *ghazals* of Mirza Ghalib express a similar subjectivity, while Krishnā, the divine Lover in Jayadevā's *Gīta Govinda* (twelfth century) also undergoes the fires of separation and yearning.[9] What these references foreground is the cultural value of desire—of the immersion of the self in a passion that ultimately goes beyond the self—and its heightened emotional expression that has deep roots in different traditions of devotion and the sacred. At the innermost core of the self, then, is a being that goes beyond gender, and the expressive tradition that I am indicating here recognizes and reinscribes this.

Devdas exemplifies this point further in the devotion of the two women, Paro and Chandramukhi, for both of whom deep love for Devdas remained uncon-

Fig. 12.1 The performance of suffering: Devdas in *Devdas* (1955)

summated, and yet transformed their lives. Paro could not imagine a husband other than Devdas, and her suffering both as a child separated from her playmate and as a woman destined to marry another is communicated through two songs sung by *Vaishnav* mendicants[10] that both exteriorize and ironically comment on her emotional condition (see figs. 12.2 and 12.3). In each song, the Rādhā-Krishnā relationship is evoked, and it is Rādhā's suffering at the separation from Krishnā (a separation that will be life-long) that is indicative of both Paro's subjectivity and her devotion.

Similarly the *Jise tu kabūl kar le*[11] song that Chandramukhi sings, like the songs picturized on Paro,[12] exteriorizes and amplifies the interiority of her character, making intelligible the emotion that the world outside would rather ignore or repress. Paradoxically, the "text of muteness" (Brooks 1984, 56–80) takes a very particular form in Indian cinema. If conventional language is inadequate to express the stress of emotion, the language of poetry, music, and gesture enables a spontaneous and immediate contact with "the occult realm of true feeling and value" (Brooks 1984, 75). The song used in this way is not, then, a disaggregated "para-narrative" element, added for spectacular effect, during the performance of which narrative suspension takes place (see Vasudevan 1989).[13] Rather, the song is central to the Indian melodramatic narrational form, an element that, when used creatively and intelligently, is not only crucial to the

Fig. 12.2 Paro and the Vaishnav singers in *Devdas* (1955)

Fig. 12.3 The performance of suffering: Paro in *Devdas* (1955)

focus and development of the narrative, but is expressive, as I have been arguing, of the subjectivity of the characters. In addition, of course, it provides the
characteristic pleasure that this narrational form affords.

　If the amplification and exteriorizing of emotion is manifested usually via the
song in Indian cinemas, these cinemas share with other traditions of cinematic
melodrama the intensification of emotion and interiority articulated through
an expressive and dynamic mise-en-scène. This includes "studied composition,"
tableaus, and an "expressive play of mourning and pathos" (Petro 1989, 32, xxiii).
And yet here too, the dual fluid movement from image to sound produces an
intense emotional texture that is distinctive. Kamal Amrohi's *Daera* illustrates
this point. The film narrates the desire of a young man, Sharan, for his neighbor Sheetal, a dying consumptive married to an old man from whom she has
contracted the disease. He has only sighted her from afar, and yet is captivated
by the sight of her lying on a bed under a flowering tree on the terrace opposite
(fig. 12.4). While the film makes an explicit commitment to discourses of reform,
especially to the unfairness of the practice of marrying young girls to old men
and to the issue of widow remarriage, the form of the film is an extended tableau
with a hyperbolization of desire via mise-en-scène. Following his first vision
of Sheetal, Sharan is fixated on the image and articulates his desire directly in
his first song:

| Aa bhi ja merī duniyā mein koī nahīn | Come to me, there is no one in my world |
| Bin tere kab talak yūn hi ghabrāye dil | Without you, how long must my heart be anxious |

Complex crane and tracking movements connect the two terraces, enabling the flow of desire across from one side to the other, while the lyrics put into words the connections that the camera is making. All the while, in mid-space between the terraces, two carpenters on a raised platform saw a huge plank of wood that finally falls apart at the end of the film (figs. 12.4 and 12.5). While Sharan's passion is exteriorized via mise-en-scène, Sheetal, the dying woman on the terrace responds with a seeming indifference to his passion, of which she is aware, remaining committed all the while to her dharma (duty/ honor) to her husband. The ideology of feminine devotion is undermined, however, by Meena Kumari's tragic performance, as well as by one song picturized on her that works metaphorically to destabilize her assumed role, and indicates an internal turmoil that she cannot express or even fully acknowledge:

Deep ke sang jalūn mein, aag mein jaise jale baati	I burn with the lamp, as the wick burns in the flame
Jaise jale baati, vaise jale jiyā mor	As burns the wick, so burns my heart
Hai rām, vaise jale jiyā mor.	O Lord, so burns my heart.

While these two songs express Sharan's and Sheetal's internal state separately, focusing on the articulation of desire and conflict, these emotions come together for the two in another song sung by Sharan when he has realized that Sheetal is unattainable:

| Aansū toh nahin hai aankhon mein | While there are no tears in my eyes |
| Pehlū mein magar dil jaltā hai | My heart burns in the emptiness of the absent embrace |

While Sharan is visible through the windows, pacing in his room and singing behind closed doors, the camera, placed outside on the terrace, begins to crane out slowly, moving back and away from his door, over the terrace, past the temple spire and further back to the other side of Sheetal seated in a chair on her terrace. All the while the lyrics of the song articulate "the blood of desire on the lips" as "the heart is being rent in two." The remaining two stanzas are played in a long-take medium shot of the seated Sheetal in profile, visibly ill and deeply distraught, while Sharan's voice continues to sing how every heartbeat, every breath is a wounding, how the pain is unbearable when the moth burns as the tears of the flame fall.[14] The lyrics and the camera movement bring the intensely desiring pair together even as they are hopelessly sundered—their desirous connection completely impossible. Thus, the mise-en-scène, soaked with desire, figures forth a "hysterical" text while its unrepresentable and unspeakable material has been

Fig. 12.4 The captivating vision: *Daera* (1953)

Fig. 12.5 Sharan's heart being rent in two: *Gopinath* (1948)

siphoned off into the mise-en-scène (Nowell-Smith 1987, 73). While Sharan's desire may be legitimately expressed, Sheetal's incipient desire for him, trammeled as it is in the web of *dharma* and tradition, collapses inward—an entropic collapse that consumes her both literally and metaphorically. Too often has gender been conceptualized as feminine identity rather than as roles that men and women both enact, internalize, and are trapped within, clearly demonstrated here in both characters. Meanwhile, the stylized, saturated mise-en-scène is intensely expressive of unrealizable desire for both male and female protagonists: a desire that needs to be aborted, for the historical moment of its birth is not yet here.

The struggle for subjective individuation, for an articulation of acceptable individual desire, and the ultimate failure of its realization that all these examples express, including the one that I am now going to use from Mahesh Kaul's *Gopinath,* are deeply connected to the project of the modern, to its desires, its ambivalences, and the excesses that spill over and cannot be contained within its disciplinary regimes. Paradoxically, the language of the spillover, the excess in these films, is the language of *Vaishnav bhakti,* a traditional devotional idiom that on the face of it seems to run counter to the melodramatic modern. This raises my third point concerning the distinctiveness of the Indian melodramatic form, which does not seem to occupy the postsacred, desacralized secular world identified by melodrama theorists as its "public space of social imaginings" (Gledhill 2000, 232). According to Brooks, melodrama uncovers "the moral occult" in lieu of the destroyed "traditional sacred" in an urge towards "resacralization" (1984, 16), and as a means of "investing individual everyday lives with significance and justification" (Gledhill 1987, 29). Given that the "traditional sacred" is very much intact in Indian melodrama, how appropriate is the notion of "resacralization" to the expressive work of the Indian melodramatic form? For it functions neither as an alternative to, nor a replacement for a lost sacred. Arguably the deployment of the *Vaishnav bhakti* idiom evokes the continuum of the sacred in the everyday, a ritual affirmation of faith in the spiritual that is integrally connected to the significant place of tradition in the nationalist ideology of the modern, rooted not in an identification with, but a difference from, "the perceived forms of cultural modernity in the West" (Chatterjee 1993, 117). A reformed "tradition," with spirituality as its core, was crucial to the inner domain of national culture that marked the distinctiveness of the Indian modern.

However, the work that this idiom of the sacred does in these films is a little more specific than would seem from the above account. Mahesh Kaul's *Gopinath* illustrates this point. The film is a narrative about a young man's, Mohan's, simultaneous attraction for two women: Neela, a film actress who takes a fancy to his innocence and naïveté, qualities that are rare in the world of cinema, and his childhood sweetheart Gopi, who continues to passionately adore him. Gopi is also Mohan's mother's choice for him, a choice that Mohan resists only because he would like to be more modern in the procedures of choosing a wife. Love as it is articulated in cinema is his model, and he wants to experience such magic for himself. Gopi's desire is expressed in a displaced form via the sacred erotic songs of Meerā and Sūrdas,[15] a tradition of *Vaishnav bhaktī* in which the sacred and the profane are intertwined realms, imbuing each other, and in which human desire has a spiritual aspiration and resonance. Neela's power play finally destroys Gopi. Madness overtakes her as the outcome of the irresolvable contradiction between her love and Mohan's aspiration for a form of subjectivity promised by cinema's allure, at the very moment when Mohan awakens to Neela's perfidy and insincerity. By then Gopi is lost to the world, lost in an interior world where nothing exists but Mohan, and where she sees Mohan everywhere and in everyone (fig. 12.6). Of course, Gopi's love for Mohan is resonant with Meerā's for Krishnā. What the sacred idiom is doing here, as in the other two examples cited earlier, is dual. On the one hand, it intensifies human experience in the light of the sacred, or rather establishes a continuum between the human and the divine, thereby giving hyperbolic expression to human desire. Devotion is not just the trope of the erotic; it sacralizes the human erotic and uncovers the spiritual at the core of erotic experience. On the other hand, the idiom of *Vaishnav bhaktī* also underscores the circumscribed, even tragic nature of human possibilities. At this point, the realm of the sacred provides a horizon of transcendence achieved via renunciation or immersion in the divine. While the idiom of *Vaishnav bhaktī* is an older

Fig. 12.6 Gopi lost in an interior world: *Gopinath* (1948)

cultural idiom, and is not necessarily modern, it inflects the cinematic modern at a crucial point in its history, giving voice to the ambivalences, the failures of the modern, and embodying the excess that the modern cannot contain.

While the allure and the fear of the modern is symbolically figured in *Gopinath* as the cinema, the tragic consequences of desire in all these films that I have mentioned underscore the failure to realize subjective individuation for both men and women at this moment of incipient modernity. While human desire is articulated, the possibilities of its full-bodied realization and consummation are denied. The instabilities of cultural and historical transition that led to a questioning of class, caste, and gender roles have not caused a breaking away from the constructions of the past, nor congealed into newer forms. At this point, not only do we see a full melodramatic embodiment of the shattering impact of modernity, but it is melodrama that provides the modalities by which the problems of subjectivity and gender identities are articulated within specific historical and social matrices. However, as I have argued, one cannot assume an unproblematic identification of gender and melodrama. Individual subjectivization, rather than gender concerns, may actually more accurately typify the melodramatic drive. Using the examples of a particular kind of cinematic formation in Bombay cinema of the 1940s and 1950s, I have attempted to demonstrate that emotion, subjectivity, and individuation are key to the melodramatic form. At the same time, the intersections of gender with class, caste, and a particular social and cultural history constitute both gender and genre in particular ways, even while an expressive modality like melodrama may function as an Ur-form. If conditions of impossibility circumscribe especially female, but also male desire in these films, the pressure of a melodramatic modern articulates this failure cinematically, encapsulating and expressing the contradictions of modernity.

Notes

I would like to thank Christine Gledhill and Richard Allen for comments on an earlier version of this chapter, given at the annual Society for Cinema and Media Studies (SCMS) Conference, Chicago, March 2007. Thanks also to Mr. Shashidharan, former director of the National Film Archive of India, and others at the National Film Archive for access to the films and material: Mr. Dhiwar, Chief Preservation Officer; Mrs. Urmila Joshi, Librarian; Lakshmi and Arti of the Documentation Section; and Salaam and Manohar.

Transliteration and diacritics have been used only for songs, unfamiliar words, and titles of well-known literary works. Names of films and characters are used without diacritics—in the form that they have circulated in the public domain.

1. The phrase is Peter Brooks's (1984, 5). Most writers on melodrama associate its emergence with transitional periods (Brooks 1984; Elsaesser 1987 [1973]; Gledhill 1987; L. Williams 1998; Singer 2001; Kaplan 2001).

2. While the Indian melodramatic form is distinctive, it shares certain fundamental features with the melodramatic mode as it has been theorized and debated in film studies.

I therefore draw on key writings from the field, in particular, evocative formulations suggesting what is fundamental about the form, even as it is culturally distinctively expressed.

3. I am using examples from Bombay cinema, though the features of the melodramatic form I discuss are also applicable in other language cinemas of India.

4. The liberal, secular, democratic, modern, and cosmopolitan imaginary, justifiably associated with Nehru, came to have widespread currency in the years of his leadership. The different language cinemas of India responded in various ways to the euphoria of the early years of Independence, to the modernizing impulse that provided the ideological impetus of these years, as well as to the complex negotiations of region, community, and nation during a critical period of the nation's history. Films that responded to this Nehruvian imaginary include Raj Kapoor's *Awaara* (1951) and *Shri 420* (1955); B. R. Chopra's *Naya Daur* (1957); Mehboob's *Mother India* (1957); and Guru Dutt's *Aar Paar* (1954), *Mr. & Mrs. 55* (1955), and *Pyaasa* (1957).

5. Such genre films from the sound period onwards include Wadia Movietone's stunt and action films (1935–45), especially those featuring their lead star, Fearless Nadia; 1940s crime films like Filmistan's *Kismet* (1943); and reformist social melodramas like V. Shantaram's *Kunku* (1937) and *Manoos/Aadmi* (1939). See Rosie Thomas's work on Nadia (2005), Ravi Vasudevan's on *Kismet* (1995); Kaushik Bhaumik on reform socials of the silent period (2001); and Anupama Kapse's dissertation on these genres from the silent period to 1939 (2009).

6. There is a wider argument to be made about the relationship between colonialism, modernity, and Indian melodrama that I cannot cover here.

7. For examples of this work see Susie Tharu and K. Lalitha (1991).

8. Dates for Kālidāsa range from first century BC to fifth century AD. For Kālidāsa's selected works, including *Abhijnāna Shākuntalam,* see Chandra Rajan's translation (1989).

9. For a brief introduction to Khusrau, see Sunil Sharma (2006); for an introduction to Ghālib, see Ralph Russell (1997); for Jayadevā, see Barbara Stoler Miller's translation of his *Gīta Govinda* (1977).

10. Vaishnavism, a movement of Krishnā *bhaktī* (devotion), extremely popular in North India, took intense form through several sixteenth-century saint-poets and singers. Also popularized by Chaitanya Mahāprabhu, a sixteenth-century scholar and reformer, Vaishnavism is rooted in the *bhaktī* of Krishnā and Rādhā. The songs of this tradition are located in the imaginative landscape of Braj where Krishnā was raised and where his union with Rādhā took place, immortalized in Jayadevā's *Gīta Govinda*. It is this tradition that inspired several saint-poets and provided the emotional and imagistic reservoir for the poetic efflorescence associated with the vernacular literatures of Krishnā devotion.

11. Jise tu kabūl kar le woh adā kahān   From where do I bring the grace
    se layūn,   that you will accept
Tere dil ko jo lubhā le, who sadā   How do I find the voice that will
    kahān se layūn   charm you

12. "Picturized on" is a term used by the Indian film industries to signify the "realization" of the song on screen using playback, with the characters lip-synching the songs.

13. Ravi Vasudevan sees the song and dance and comic sequences as "not merely part of a narrative continuum," suggesting that these "para-narrative" elements insert "the film and the spectator into a larger field of coherence, one that stretches beyond the immediate experience of viewing films" (1989, 45, 46). I argue for a conception of narrational form in which the song has crucial functions central to the narrative.

14. I am paraphrasing the lyrics of the last two stanzas.

15. Meerā, a sixteenth-century saint figure from an aristocratic Rajpūt family from Rajasthan, gave up married life and her palace to wander the villages of North India, composing and singing of her passionate love for the Lord Krishnā. Her poems are still sung and have been used in several films as well as in *Gopīnāth*. Meerā's passion for Krishnā echoes that of his consort Rādhā, who too, after their intense consummation, was separated from him for life. Rādhā, as the *Virahīnī* (the separated lover) becomes metaphoric of the separation of the human soul from the divine. Sūrdas was another well-known Bhakti poet of the sixteenth century from the Mathura region, also a devotee of Lord Krishnā, whose well-known poems in praise of Krishnā are collected in his *Sursāgār*.

CHAPTER 13

WOMAN, GENERIC AESTHETICS, AND THE VERNACULAR:

HUANGMEI OPERA FILMS FROM CHINA TO HONG KONG

XIANGYANG CHEN

In 1963, an article entitled "The Wondrous Tale of *The Love Eterne* & the Miracle of a Film Industry" in *Southern Screen,* the trade journal of Hong Kong-based Shaw Brothers, captured the phenomenal reception of the studio's Huangmei opera film, *The Love Eterne.* Published in both Chinese and English, the English version runs like this:

> Throughout May and June the hottest thing in Taiwan was not the weather, but Shaw brothers costume musical "*Love Eterne*" [*sic*]. Never in China's history has a picture—Chinese or foreign been welcomed with such fervor and adoration. Everyone, native born or mainlander, has seen the historical love movie. The street loudspeakers fill up the air with its songs. People smile broadly whenever the name Betty Loh Tih or Ivy Ling Po is mentioned. An anxious wife reported to police her husband, after having taken money from the bank early in the morning, had been missing. He was finally located in the theatre watching "*The Love Eterne.*" He had been there all day. All box office records were shattered. After 47 days of showing in Taipei alone, "*The Love Eterne*" grossed NT$8,383,077.40, far more than the previous record of NT$5,060,000 made by "*Ben Hur.*" And the number of Taipeilanders who had seen the movie was 717,833, nearly two thirds of the capital city's population. (*Southern Screen* 65, 1963: 51)

The Chinese version provided further details, for instance audience statistics—one lady was reported to have seen the film seventeen times—and commented on the film's significance to Chinese cinema (50). The film's popularity led to subsequent Hong Kong and Taiwanese film and TV productions and the consolidation of a genre, supported by related products—song recordings, advertisements cleverly using the film's dialogue and star fandom. Scholarly discussion of this "cultural fever" focuses on cultural nationalism in Chinese communities divided by geopolitical borders and the Cold War (Liao et al. 2003). This essay, however, explores the significance of gender in the translation of a genre—the Huangmei opera film—between nationalist mainland China and diasporic Chinese filmmakers based in Hong Kong. In particular it examines the impact of China's investment in film genres based on national traditions—specifically, cultural practices involving opera, music, and choral chant—on the representation of woman, exploring the way femininity intertwines with the genre's negotiations between opera form, national discourse, and commercial demands. My focus is on three films, *The Fairy Couple* (1955), produced in mainland China, and *Diau Charn* (1958) and *The Love Eterne* (1963), both made in Hong Kong by Shaw Brothers, a transnational company that virtually monopolized the city's film industry from the mid-1960s to the early 1970s.

More commonly referred to as Huangmei opera film, the appellation "costume musical" used by *Southern Screen* indicates the film's production context. According to Li Hanxiang, the genre's progenitor and most prominent practitioner, his goal was to produce nationally authentic costume dramas that would also satisfy Shaw Brothers' need for marketable films (1987, 408–9). Inspired by spontaneous audience sing-alongs accompanying Hong Kong screenings of *The Fairy Couple,* and the popularity of local Cantonese operatic films, Li's first film, *Diau Charn,* emulated the form of Huangmei opera. Its success, winning four awards at the Fifth Asian Film festival, emboldened the director and his studio to follow up with a string of similar productions, climaxing in *The Love Eterne.* Between 1958 and 1969, more than forty Huangmei opera films were made, the majority under the aegis of Shaw Brothers (Chen 2005, 203–14). By the 1970s, the film genre had largely disappeared, with only one produced, *The Dream of Red Mansion* (1977). However, opera filmmaking continued tenuously in Taiwan into the 1980s, and Huangmei opera on stage is still performed by professional opera troupes in contemporary China and Taiwan.

The Fairy Couple emerged in the 1950s from the regional Huangmei opera from Anhui province in southeast China. Originally performed by part-time farmer-performers to a rural population, the opera entered a metropolitan setting by the 1920s, undergoing gradual professionalization, audience expansion, and repertoire enlargement. By the 1950s, with the promulgation of socialist China's policy to excavate the country's cultural traditions and popularize national art through film, the Huangmei opera film spills over the national border to Hong Kong, Singapore, and Malaysia, providing audiences that the Hong Kong brand sought to pool in a combined address.

The convergence of Chinese regional rather than national opera forms with film in Hong Kong cinema—first Cantonese then Huangmei opera, to name two of the most popular types—hinges on certain qualities of regional opera. One such quality, as Run Run Shaw, the founder of Shaw Brothers, has put it, "has to do with the vernacular speech used" (quoted in Zhang Che 2002, 112). However,

Hong Kong productions replaced the dialect of Huangmei opera with Mandarin so as to net the widest audience. Nevertheless, compared with (the national) Beijing opera's highly schematic role typology and its composite performance conventions—which (unlike Western opera) encompassed singing, speaking, gesture, movement, and martial arts/acrobatics—Huangmei opera is characterized by more flexible role types and a primary emphasis on music and singing, and remained vernacular in practice. These qualities enabled it to meld more easily with other, transnational, mass-media forms such as cinema.

THE VERNACULAR, HUANGMEI OPERA, AND WOMAN

The Fairy Couple initiated a turn to vernacular arts to craft a cinematic idiom. Vernacular here opposes the scholarly/official orthodoxy that constitutes written history. It is a "low" form, authorless, circulating among the people by word of mouth or in popular forms such as opera, fiction, or sung narrative. In both subject matter and address, the vernacular differs from orthodox culture, dealing not with stories of royalty or affairs of state, but the heroes and stories of the folk, addressing the people. But neither vernacular nor orthodox literature is ever entirely self-sufficient, with the latter often absorbed into the vernacular, and the orthodox constantly drawing from the vernacular.

In relation to cinema, my use of the vernacular is inspired by Miriam Bratu Hansen's "vernacular modernism," defined as a "modernist aesthetics . . . encompass[ing] cultural practices that both articulated and mediated the experience of modernity" (2000, 333). Central to Miriam Hansen's argument is the encounter with modernity, in which cinema is not only symptom, but also its articulation, providing the space in which the experience of modernity is reflected and negotiated. My reading of the relation between the vernacular, the woman-centered Huangmei opera, and modernity is indebted to this conceptualization, while at the same time I focus on the fate of traditional vernacular forms in Chinese modernization, and the negotiations of a cinema looking to go global. This includes the crafting of a distinct film genre through melding opera with the cinematic, its popular status, and the genre's orchestration of affect. The rush to vernacular forms in the era of mass production and mass consumption represents a kind of cultural raiding for speedy production of new works. Equally, it taps into their pervasiveness. However, a tension emerges between film as an industry and its cultural ambition as high or national art. Indeed, it is built into the fabric of *opera film,* which straddles two modes of representation signifying uneven temporalities and different audiences. In this context, I am interested in uncovering how gender is enlisted in the formal rejuvenation of traditional vernacular forms, and in particular how gender and the national intersect in Huangmei opera film.

As a translation of an opera performance to screen, *The Fairy Couple* re-presents the regional opera. A singing-dominated form characterized by its largely female cast and their genre-defining performance, Huangmei opera finds its gender distinctiveness translated into a cinematic genre, characterized by the woman's voice and female viewpoint. The film features the love story of a fairy (Yan Fengying), the seventh daughter of the heavenly king, and a human, a young man sold to a landlord as an indentured slave in return for money to bury his deceased father. It begins with a panoramic shot of a cloud-tumbling place soon revealed to be the heavenly kingdom. A disembodied female voice singing the loneliness of days in heaven wafts from within, permeating the landscape. The tracking camera unveils its owner, the seventh fairy, who finds life in heaven boring and life on earth full of promises. The establishment of the woman's perspective through her singing is soon followed by shots that identify her with the look, a desiring look as she surveys humankind below, enabling her to cross the gap separating look and spectacle. Through such framing, the woman takes up the role of a spectator, an initiator of action, and even of the cinematic apparatus itself, making the film an articulation of her story.

Similarly, the woman's voice is crucial in *Diau Charn,* structuring the narrative, orchestrating its rhythm, and setting its tone. The film opens with a picture of social and political turbulence triggered by war. After a brief prologue, a choral voiceover, becoming female-dominated over its course, is employed for a number of functions: to propel the narrative, relate the back-story, link scenes, comment on a character's state of mind, externalize Diau Charn's interior monologues by relaying her asides, and provide a concluding coda. The choral voiceover punctuates the rise and fall of the drama, forging an alliance between the diegetic and nondiegetic, aural and visual, interiority and exteriority, while acting as a bridge between the film and its spectator. The enveloping nature of sound thus saturates the film in the feminine. A female structuring voiceover is common to most films of the genre produced in Hong Kong: *Madam White Snake* (1962), *The Love Eterne* (1963), *Beyond the Great Wall* (1964), *The Story of Sue San* (1964), and *The Mermaid* (1965), to name a few.

This feminine emphasis is traceable to the stage opera, in which female characters often take the titular role or outnumber male ones—e.g., *The Fairy Couple, The Cowherd and the Weaving Maid, Female Princess,* and *Meng Jiangnu.* Moreover, the opera's traditional repertoire includes a considerable number of lament-based plays, staging exclusively female roles; for instance, *A Girl's Lament, The Lament of Yingtai, The Lament of Zhao Wunian,* or *The Lament of a Suffering Daughter-in-Law.* As a result, female performers and their characters—for instance, Yan Fengying, leading actress in the films *The Fairy Couple, Female Princess* (1959), and *The Cowherd and the Weaving Maid* (1963)—have become defining icons of the opera and its counterpart film genre. Femininity can also be traced to the opera's origin in folksongs sung by women during tealeaf-picking in the township of Huangmei, Hubei province. Following a huge flood at the end of the eighteenth-century, the songs migrated to Anhui province as a tool of survival for migrants on the road. They later synergized with other arts—sung narrative, local folk music—eventually evolving into stage form, first documented in 1896 (Anhui Arts Institute 2000, 15). According to Shi Bailin, an expert on Huangmei opera music, women's tealeaf-picking folksongs, strictly defined, no longer exist in the repertoire, but some operatic tunes show affinity with their tonal system, use of musical accompaniment, and insertion of lyrical words for balance or euphony (1993, 20–6). Moreover, as Liu Jing'an indicates in a study devoted to women and folksongs, one fourth of the songs collected are related to women and their problems (1971, 224–25). He suggests that patriarchal oppression in the strictly hierarchical Chinese extended family makes women resort to song (4–5). The sequences featuring female vocals singing desire, suffering, or other feelings in *The Fairy Couple, Diau Charn,* and most other Hong Kong films bear the unmistakable imprint of the opera's lament series (see fig.13.1). The pathos of these laments is comparable to that of the folksongs; the mode of address directly solicits spectator empathy and active response.

Fig. 13.1   Diau Charn sings her conflicting thoughts in *Diau Charn* (1958)

THE FEMALE LOOK AND PERFORMATIVITY

In this context, woman's relation to the look demands more exploration. Framed by a thinly disguised patriarchal structure, with the father eventually sending heavenly soldiers to enforce her punctual return from earth, *The Fairy Couple*'s main story enacts a woman's search for conjugal bliss. Her desire to bridge the opposite worlds of fairy and human drives the narrative. When the fairies look at the human world, they are found admiring, respectively, a fisherman, woodcutter, farmer, and a student at work. But this scene also reflects film watching, since both the distance separating the fairies from human and the height from which they look echo the omniscient distance from which spectators watch a film. Only here, the look has been invested with layered complexity. The fairies look at and mimic the human world; the spectators, while looking at them admiring, look at the human world from their perspective; and all these acts of looking emerge from the act of watching a film entitled *The Fairy Couple*. Such organization raises three issues: 1) self-reflexive spectatorship, 2) slippage from spectating to entering the spectacle, and 3) imbrication of the female look with the spectacle.

The fairy's ensuing plucky adventure launches the narrative on *her* quest for love generated by *her* look. She initiates a romantic liaison with a stranger, while her negotiation with the local landlord, coupled with successfully weaving ten silk brocades within one night, demonstrates her quick wit. In the courtship sequence, Yan Fengying, as the fairy, consciously performs dual roles, that is, performing the country girl to seduce the man *and* performing the fairy as the country girl for the spectator who is privy to the previous goings-on in the fairy world (see fig. 13.2). Here performance is an element of narrative and spectacle constructed for the spectator, but also a subjective component of the woman's attempt to reach her object of desire. Woman as performer is not extraneous to her performance, but is imbricated in the process, that is, her performance is performative.[1] Indeed, she renders such a good performance of an earthly being that she forgets entirely her fairy identity until rudely awakened. If she is forced to depart the human world, her leaving disturbs the preceding equilibrium of conjugal bliss, hence suggesting the fragility of the myth of romance.

As initiator of action and a smart person utilizing her backup resources, the seventh fairy echoes her stage counterparts. Featuring the labor and love life of farm girls, Huangmei stage opera is no stranger to girls with bold emotions, often intense and unrestrained, who initiate romantic unions, illicit rendezvous, and promiscuous sexual relations, earning for the opera the nickname, "promiscuous theater of flower drum song," which resulted in frequent banning for its subversive qualities (Anhui Arts Institute 2000, 25–26). According to the film's director, both he and its star were initially doubtful about representing the fairy as a country girl boldly courting a stranger but went ahead to preserve the operatic protagonist (Shi Hui 1982, 246).

The female look and performance of desire is also central to *Diau Charn,* the

Fig. 13.2 Yan Fengying as the fairy consciously performs performing in
The Fairy Couple (1955)

Hong Kong film made in emulation of *The Fairy Couple*. It is based on a female character in the fiction, *The Tales of the Three Kingdoms* (hereafter *Three Kingdoms*). Occupying only a few pages, Diau Charn is nonetheless legendary, one of four classic beauties in ancient China causing the downfall of power-greedy men. In *Three Kingdoms,* Han minister Wang Yun uses her as pawn against Dong Zhuo and Lu Bu, a father and his adopted son threatening the ruling Han emperor and his kingdom. Taking advantage of their lasciviousness, Wang has Diau Charn alienate father from son. Succeeding, she becomes thereafter a *femme fatale,* and her story a cautionary tale about female beauty and sexuality. Although *Three Kingdoms* leaves her final whereabouts a mystery, speculation crops up later in folklore and oral narratives. Retaining the basic plot, the film details the process by which Diau Charn (Lin Dai) pits father against son. Crucially, what enables the fairy to get into the spectacle in *The Fairy Couple*—the look—is also what effects Diau Charn's entanglement in the scenario of seduction. Her desire for Lu Bu (Zhao Lei), triggered by a secret look from behind a screen, constantly delays her, generating repeated asides questioning the task entrusted. These asides represent a thinking Diau Charn. The key question is how she will outwit both father and son. Like the fairy in *The Fairy Couple,* she resorts to performance, though in her case aiming to keep Dong and Lu alternatively at bay/on hook *and* to elicit the complicity of an omniscient audience already privy to her plans. While she produces performances to convince both Dong and Lu, she is also convincing the spectator of her performance powers through showing her detachment from the job—i.e., she performs "performing." Here a female point of view frames the film as a woman's pursuit of romance intimated by the look and reinforced by verbal asides. The feisty characterization of Diau Charn, drawing on the stardom of Lin Dai, fostered by Shaw Brothers as a marketing device, exceeds the totemic literary figure.

If Diau Charn is the prototypical female spy of traditional Chinese literature (Hong 2004, 31), the film's story of how two lovers from opposite camps come together against all odds displaces political intrigue and military combat. Lu Bu, though attired in military outfit, appears the love-smitten heartthrob of the latter-day youth film rather than a mighty warrior and lascivious schemer. Indeed, the use of the youthful stars, Lin Dai and Zhao Lei, is aimed at the city's young demographics. As the 1961 census reported, youths under the age of fifteen accounted for 40 percent of Hong Kong's population (Law 1996, 10).

HONG KONG'S "CHINA FOR EXPORT,"
THE VERNACULAR, AND WOMAN

As the first film of its kind in Hong Kong, *Diau Charn* appears as a "bad" copy of *The Fairy Couple*. Its actors lacked years of operatic training and indulged in showy performances, its décor is florid, character relations are convoluted, and its representations of decadence appear alien to an opera form emphasizing rustic simplicity and sincere expression. As the director, commenting on its kitschy feel twenty-six years later, says, it is a "hybrid. A bastard not resembling opera or film" (Li 1987, 276). The songs are delivered by pop singers, a result both of the scarcity of opera personnel and the need to recontextualize a regional opera.[2] The melding of opera tunes with strains of westernized popular music increasingly sung in the city's bars, nightclubs, streets, and homes aims at modernizing Huangmei opera for an urbanizing population. Thus, though the Hong Kong brand is referred to as Huangmei opera film, it differs from the mainland versions in its delivery of singing, musical accompaniment, performance, and speech.

Central to this amalgamation of traditional and modern vernaculars is a group of displaced mainland Chinese filmmakers producing films aimed at world distribution. For the relocated filmmakers, Hong Kong provides a needed milieu of artistic freedom and social stability. But it is not home in the true sense, particularly since "the 'exotic' local dialect and customs, as well as what they considered its (Hong Kong) 'slavish' mentality—simultaneously colonial, feudal, provincial and backward"—alienates them (Fu 2003, 51). This awkward cultural division epitomizes *Diau Charn*: an emulation of a Chinese opera turned awry. In this sense, its kitschy feel does not imply a bad imitation of the original, or a trite product reeking of bad taste, but an awkward hybrid, not only in terms of representation but also as a product of filmmakers undergoing temporal and spatial translation.

In this context, the director's intention to create a marketable costume drama is central. As the critic Sek Kei asserts: "the cinematic dream created by the Shaw Movie Town was primarily a China dream. Its permanent street sets comprised mostly exquisite bridges, rivers, city walls, palaces, pavilions, and shops gracing the landscape of ancient China" (2003, 37–38). *Diau Charn* and its companion pieces are the expression of a dream China boasting classic gardens, strumming zithers and flutes, and peopled with scholars, generals, and courtesans (see fig. 13.3). Sek's assertion is also true of the genre's ideological sentiments, aesthetics, and industrial conditions. The genre canvasses, like its progenitor, *The Fairy Couple,* critical issues haunting Chinese filmmakers: filmizing national arts to create a national cinema. Aesthetically it searches for, as Zhang Che, one of the pioneers of the Hong Kong martial arts film, later put it, a "uniquely" Chinese genre (1989, 93). Commercially, Shaw Brothers sought to open up and expand a global market, undergirded by the extensive distribution and exhibition network it had built across Southeast Asia. By 1958, the company already possessed over one hundred theaters across Malaysia, Singapore, North Borneo, Vietnam, and other countries. To these theaters and those in Europe and North America, its studios aimed to supply signature Mandarin film (*Southern Screen* 2, January 1958: 2). They were, as the company announced, "all united in one effort—the

Fig. 13.3 The cinematic re-creation of ancient China in *Diau Charn* (1958)

production of Hong Kong films that can hold their own in the world market" (*Southern Screen* 47, January 1962: 29).

Thus the nexus of the Hong Kong Huangmei opera film with Chinese national arts signifies cultural raiding and reconstruction by a dislocated community in order to go global in a rapidly urbanizing city on the boundary between East and West. For example, a waning cultural practice, the choral chant, is a sung narrative performed not only on stage, but also in teahouses and other entertainment venues. The first traceable use of the chant as sung female voiceover on screen is the Yue opera film *Liang Shanbo and Zhu Yingtai* (1954), an earlier version of *The Love Eterne*.[3] The female chant was then picked up and built into the structure of most Hong Kong–made Huangmei opera films. It can also be traced biographically to *Diau Charn*'s director, who grew up in Beijing, where he immersed himself in folk arts and popular entertainments (Pu 2007, 36–40, 42–47). Given that the choral chant hooks into the oral storytelling tradition familiar to most Chinese before the advent of film, radio, and later TV, the film genre captures the dwindling role of an oral representation. But equally significant is the larger context of the Cold War, which strictly policed films distributed outside China. Opera film, its focus on traditional Chinese culture avoiding blatant propaganda, is often considered "apolitical," allowing the genre to bypass censorship in countries vigilant against Communism (Xu 2005, 38). According to Xu Dunle, general manager of China's Hong Kong film distribution company from 1965 to the mid-1980s, fifty-nine films were submitted to the British colonial government for inspection. Only seventeen films, comprising five features, six opera films—including *Liang Shanbo and Zhu Yingtai* and *The Fairy Couple*—and six documentaries passed inspection (33). Crucially, this turn to the "apolitical" for "political correctness" coincides with China's utilization of nationally popular forms to create a socialist art, facilitating the synergy between Huangmei opera and a female-dominated oral mode.

The success of both *The Fairy Couple* and *Diau Charn* has been rightly attributed to the performance skills of Yan Fengying and the rising star power of Lin Dai.[4] But the historical relation of women's visibility on screen to self-expression merits further examination in order to account for the genre's gender prominence. If Chinese women had traditionally been confined to the home, at the beginning of the twentieth century theater and cinema provided public forums where they began to be heard and seen (Zhang Zhen 2001, xxv). The opening of *The Fairy Couple* intimates the role of theater and film as a means for women to enter the public sphere and as a platform for articulation. Here the camera searching for the owner of the voice comments on the means, both theatrical and filmic, with which the woman, hidden in an inner recess, gains public visibility and articulation symbolized by operatic singing as spontaneous self-expression. If *The Fairy Couple* hints at meta-commentary, *Diau Charn* and its Hong Kong successors provide amplification. Thus the intention to re-create an ancient China cinematically, which entails constructing a historically verisimilar world, inadvertently enables the genre to capture a historically gendered moment. The place from which the woman sings, whether a boudoir in a remote part of the household or a long, winding path to the outer reaches of a garden, requires a camera-tracking, scroll-like movement that follows the set's architectural layout in order to capture the singing woman, while unveiling different views of the household/garden—a visual aesthetics governing garden architecture in ancient China.[5] Scenes showing Diau Charn singing alone, and other such moments in, for example, *The Adultery* (1963) and *Beyond and Great Wall* (1964), are realized in this manner. That is to say, gender is encoded, if unwittingly, into the aesthetics of the genre.

AFFECT, CROSS-DRESSING, AND *THE LOVE ETERNE*

Apart from female encoding of the voice—especially through the choral voiceover—the look, and the image of a woman singing in the deep recesses of Shaw's dream China, a feminine sensibility genders the genre through the orchestration of emotion and affect. Like many spectators deeply touched by the tragic tale of the lovers fated by bad timing, class, and arranged marriage, Ang Lee was deeply swayed by *The Love Eterne*. "Every time I see this movie, I cry. It's a little embarrassing. From when I was a little boy until now, I always cry" (Lyman 2001). The story of the doomed romance between cross-dressing school friends, Liang Shanbo (Ivy Ling Po) and Zhu Yingtai (Betty Loh Tih), *The Love Eterne* consists of two halves distinguished by tone, mood and the lovers' separation. While the first half is bolstered with humor, playfulness, and youthful vitality, the second is filled with tears, crying, blood, and finally death. Here female cross-dressing is adopted not only by Ivy Ling Po as the hero, but, to evade the prohibition on girls attending school, by Zhu in the film's first half (see fig. 13.4). The rapid downward spiral of tone and mood between the two halves, from levity to ponderous tragedy, underscored by profuse tears, death, and mourning, skillfully steers the emotional register.

Unlike *Diau Charn*, *The Love Eterne* does not emulate Chinese operatic performance conventions nor Chinese opera films. Rather it seeks fluid coordination of singing and performance, establishing an internal rhythm in accordance with mood, character psychology, and unfolding drama aided by sinuous editing. "Costume musical" aptly captures its generic identity, which shares only a tenuous relation with Huangmei stage opera, primarily through its tunes. The film is lauded for its realization of Chinese aesthetics, particularly the 18-*li* escort scene in which the camera follows the meandering of the two protagonists as they walk along a mountain trail with each twist or wind revealing differing views.[6] *The Love Eterne* does not, however, deploy the abstract stylization of Chinese opera. Here, plain speech replaces stylized narration, spontaneous acting replaces the carefully patterned and rehearsed opera performance, and, in place of minimalist staging, profuse sets dot the lane of the lovers' farewell walk. Moreover, rather than

Fig. 13.4 Affect and cross-dressing in *The Love Eterne* (1963)

disposing elements in a relationship of equality aiming at a "unified" aesthetic impression—as Eisenstein described Japanese Kabuki and Chinese theatrical style (1977, 20)—*The Love Eterne* centers on a few dominant elements, those evoking emotion, tears, and crying, to which others are subordinated in order to achieve amplified affect. Signs of the drastic swing to tragic mood first appear with the helplessness of the lovers to un-cast the die, a state reinforced by the constraint of timing: Liang does not arrive at Zhu's home in time to propose and she has already been promised to the dissipated son of the local governor, despite her pledge of undying love for Liang. He is fatally lovesick, with no hope of winning her hand. Romance ends in his tragic death, orchestrating pathos to even greater intensity. For after coughing up profuse blood, he dies at the moment of her wedding, amongst adverse elemental forces, fiercely blowing wind, and falling leaves. His last cry is followed by the sound of the *suona,* a brass instrument blowing out happy music for the festive wedding procession. But the pathos does not stop there: his bloodied handkerchief is presented as a token of remembrance in exchange for her lock of hair. Her father is brutally nonchalant. She insists on saying farewell at his grave on her way to the groom's house, crying heartbrokenly. However, the union of the lovers on his grave and their transformation into butterflies brings the film to a quick conclusion. Thus narrative rhythm is synchronized with emotion and reinforced by music and visual details, to create amplified affect. The film abandons the restraint on tears that, in the Yue opera version, Zhu's father warns defies "protocol." The film's commercial success in Hong Kong and Taiwan shows how such female-orientated representation strikes chords with spectators and demonstrates the emotional power of cinema aiming at the mass, popular market. "How a scene was shot, that is minor to me," Ang Lee said of the film. "It is more the juice, the core emotion, how it moves us. It is whether the whole film works at a deep level. You know, that primo feeling. There is no word for it. But that is what this movie did to me, and ever since, I am always trying to recapture it" (Lyman 2001).

Following the phenomenal success in Hong Kong, Taiwan, and Southeast Asian countries of *The Love Eterne,* female cross-dressing became recurrent, particularly in films starring Ling Po. For Peggy Chiao and her contemporaries, its significance resided in the symbolic sexual outlet it promised.

> Falling for a surrogate male figure (Ling Po's cross-dressing role), who represents no "gender" or "gender difference" is . . . the closest to a safe extramarital affair. This is a spiritual derailment prior to the era of the sexual revolution, a spiritual exit of repression called for by a whole generation of women. (2003, 84)

Cross-dressing has precedent on the traditional Chinese stage, while the androgynous female knight in early Chinese martial arts films suggests the gender performativity of sartorial codes. However, Chiao's take on the significance of cross-dressing, like Ang Lee's response to its affectivity, underscores the mediating role of performance in the encounter between film and spectator. In this respect, the Ling Po character's gender is far from hidden: if the facial features and demeanor are not enough to render her feminine, her voice and singing make her unmistakably female. Arguably the significance of cross-dressing lies in performativity, as in *The Fairy Couple* or *Diau Charn.* But here performance as performing is bolstered by a touch of playfulness. If costume is the sign that ensures Ling Po's maleness throughout, and Zhu's for the first half of the film, its primary function is to establish a contract with the spectator who sees cues betraying the cross-dresser—primarily her female voice—but nonetheless disavows them: I know this is cross-dressing, but I am willing to go along with it. Where cross-dressing on the traditional Chinese stage aims for authenticity, here incongruities are ignored. What sustains the spectator's disavowal is not theatrical illusion but the rules of play, girded by a touch of levity permeating the first half. Cross-dressing is a representational device enlisting spectator participation in a performance of role-playing. The film's second half, different in tone and mood, detailing character psychology and a tragic ending, reinforces this. The tragic outcome may be attributed to the director's goal of faithful adaptation, or to thematic defiance against arranged marriage. More likely it is a cautionary statement of the ultimate need to observe prescribed gender roles rather than follow the alternative possibilities playfully chronicled in the first half. However, the potential of this *imagined* alternative for women is enormous.

Zhang Che frequently cites the Huangmei opera film as instigating the reactive rise of the martial arts genre and the "staunch masculinity" of his own films (1989, 38–39). His gender-biased comment nonetheless highlights how gender intersects with the genre. In the only Huangmei opera film he directed, *The Butterfly Chalice* (1965), Zhang scripts mostly male characters, casts male actors in male roles, and incorporates martial arts combat to "masculinize" the genre. However, they appear square pegs in round holes. Zhang justifies his casting by the gender of his characters. But generic practices that I have analyzed, especially the use of the female voice, look, image, and affective registers, play as big a role in feminizing the Huangmei opera film.

Notes

1. This understanding of the performative is indebted to Judith Butler (1999, 172–73), who argues that gender identity is a discursive and disciplinary signification. I argue here that performance is a woman's subjective intention to take on alternative demeanor and postures, and in practice she is taken for that identity, making performance performative in nature.

2. Li Hanxiang recalls that he initially hired an actor trained in Huangmei opera to sing the role of Lu Bu, but he turned out to be so incompatible that it provoked laughter in the test run. So he employed a pop singer instead (1984, 269–70).

3. Yue opera is another female-centered regional opera that originated from a storytelling form in the mid-nineteenth century. Similar Yue opera films had also been produced in Hong Kong, but they are not comparable with the Huangmei opera film in quantity, audience reach, or popularity. The more refined role typology, stricter performance code, and language might account for the failure to capture audiences.

4. The leading role in *Diau Charn* won Lin Dai an award for best actress, one of four such awards she has won at the Asian Film Festival.

5. In Chinese garden architecture, the layout is designed to enable a different view with each turn of the lane or each wind in the corridor. This aesthetics also governs Chinese scroll painting.

6. *Li* is a measurement of distance in China. One *li* is half a kilometer.

CHAPTER 14

HOMOEROTICISM CONTAINED:

GENDER AND SEXUAL TRANSLATION
IN JOHN WOO'S MIGRATION TO HOLLYWOOD

VICENTE RODRIGUEZ ORTEGA

This essay compares John Woo's Hong Kong and Hollywood outputs in order
to scrutinize the differing representations of gender they offer in relation to the
different generic configurations at work in each production context. I aim to
pinpoint which aspects of these representations have passed the test of cultural
translatability and which have not. More specifically, given the diverse roles of
several "generic contact zones"—action and melodrama, melodrama and comedy,
comedy and action—in each of these two different cinematic traditions, I explore
how the dynamic between genre and gender varies between Woo's Hong Kong
and Hollywood films. I examine how Woo's generation of a series of action and
pathos driven films negotiates generically gendered bodies and how these undergo
a radical shift within his Hollywood output. I ask what were the perceived assets
of Woo's *crossover* appeal for Western audiences that led Universal to make him
the first ever Chinese director in charge of a multimillion dollar motion picture
and what were the seemingly *dangerous* aspects of his representational templates
that had to be "translated" to the social, sexual, and cultural codes of Western
popular culture, whether in the view of Woo himself, his artistic partners, and/
or the Studio executives in charge of financing and approving his projects. In
particular I explore the shift from male-to-male narratives and subordinated femininity to the heterosexual romance that dominates most of his American films.

Consequently, this project is less concerned with determining how Chinese
and Western spectators actually read Woo's gender representations than with
establishing the kind of spectator that Woo's Hong Kong and Hollywood films
construct as the result of this complex network of industrial, social, cultural, and
aesthetic factors. Taking account of the ways in which the contemporary action

film constructs gender categories, I analyze how the shift of gender roles between Woo's Hong Kong and American films reveals the presence of different cultural dominants. First though, we need to understand the full impact of Woo's triad films in the Hong Kong and the global film market in the late 1980s and early 1990s. This requires elucidating the generic fabric of his films and exploring how gender comes into play in negotiating the dynamic cross-fertilization between action and melodramatic pathos.

CONTEXTUALIZING JOHN WOO'S "HERO FILMS"

In the 1980s, the Hollywood action film produced a string of global smash hits. Films such as the first two installments of the *Lethal Weapon* franchise (1987 and 1989), *Die Hard* (1988), and Schwarzenegger's and Stallone's macho, bullet-driven vehicles had positioned action as a globally operative form of address that has become commercially central in world film markets, providing cultural pointers for audiences from Los Angeles to Singapore and Spain. Non-American film industries then attempted to capitalize on the privileged status of the action film, both to conquer a share of their domestic markets and succeed internationally. These *indigenous* rewritings of the successful formulae of the American action-oriented generic powerhouse produced the rise of directors such as John Woo in Hong Kong. In fact, the cross-fertilization of action with generic categories clearly *recognizable* in terms of industrial production and spectatorship—e.g., *The Terminator* (1984) or *Total Recall* (1990), combining action and sci-fi; *Back to the Future* (1985), comedy and action; *Raiders of the Lost Ark* (1981), adventure and action; *Desperado* (1995), action and western—allows us to rethink the action film at this historical juncture not as a genre per se but as a global transgeneric mode attached to a variety of visual and aural conventions drawn from other genres, which relies heavily on the spectacularization of onscreen violence-driven action, anchoring its sensational appeal to spectators through the recurrent enactment of highly aestheticized set pieces.

While mobilizing a variety of generic fabrics from different origins and time periods, John Woo explores the dimensions of the action mode, starting with defining markers from the cinematic history and contemporary social field of his native country.[1] His first triad film, *A Better Tomorrow* (1986), was a Hong Kong box-office hit and subsequently a national media event, catapulting Woo and Chow Yun-Fats's shaky film careers into immediate stardom (Fang 2004).[2] Chow, a former TV romantic lead, known in film circles as "box-office poison," became an immediate national icon whose look, demeanor, and black trench coat became commonplace in the Hong Kong sociocultural landscape. The "yingxiong pian" or "hero film," the label local Hong Kong critics coined to identify *A Better Tomorrow* and most of Woo's late 1980s and early 1990s work, became the formula to imitate—one producing "highly stylized and dynamic action/crime films which feature glamorized protagonists motivated and challenged by such traditional chivalric concerns as love, honor and vengeance" (Fang 2004, 50).[3] With a single stroke, Woo had delivered the first installment of a widely successful cycle of generic films that dominated Hong Kong film production for almost a decade, and became its most coveted star-director.

A Better Tomorrow is, in fact, a remake of Patrick Lung Kong's *Story of a Discharged Prisoner* (1967), which Woo adapted into the Hong Kong triad milieu while wrapping it within the highly iconic traits of his own pantheon of auteurs—Sergio Leone, Jean-Pierre Melville, Samuel Peckinpah, and Hong Kong's martial arts director, Chang Cheh. In this sense, the mixed transcultural stylistic and narrative fabric points to the rise of a generic subset of films that are both culturally and aesthetically Chinese (via the weaponry of the martial arts film) and western (via noir, revisionist westerns such as Peckinpah's, and the work of New Hollywood mavericks like Martin Scorsese).[4] Woo's works are thus a typical product of the Hong Kong industry—a type of cinematic product that is remarkably open to aesthetic borrowing from other modes of address, and, especially, Hollywood.

While, prior to his migration to Hollywood, Woo had a cult status amongst film buffs in the West, in Hong Kong he was a commercial, mainstream director, after *A Better Tomorrow,* repeatedly topping Hong Kong's star director charts. If he had a cult following in the West, it is precisely because, as Jinsoo An points out, he offered "a particular viewing pleasure not available in American films" (2001, 96). As Hong Kong critic, Li Cheuk-to comments: "a lot of times we cannot take the passionate action films of John Woo, but Western genre film fans love them precisely because such uninhibited wildness is almost impossible to find in Western genre films" (quoted in Ciecko 1997, 231). It was the generation of this *other, unavailable pleasure*—namely, an idiosyncratic combination of action and melodrama via the translation of the acrobatics of martial arts choreography into a contemporary triad milieu—that gave Woo cult status for Western audiences within the video rental circuit and elevated him to the shrine of auteurism. This was reinforced after Criterion edited a laser disc of *The Killer* (1989) and *Hardboiled* (1992), while both Hollywood veterans such as Martin Scorsese and young guns such as Quentin Tarantino explicitly acknowledged Woo's vital influence in reinventing the action film in the late 1980s and early 1990s.

Whether Woo is a mass-market auteur, as David Bordwell (2000) claims,[5] or a typical product of the always-recycling Hong Kong film industry (Aufderheide 1998, 191–99), his rise unequivocally signals the increasing growth of the action film as a global phenomenon for audiences around the world. This raises the question of how its generic fabric interacts with the diverse modes of production and social fields it engages. In addition, Woo's appropriation of the action mode works within what Christine Gledhill (2000) and Linda Williams (1998) have each theorized as the "melodramatic mode," allowing Woo to traverse a series of generic worlds, bringing them into a series of contact zones within the bullet-driven milieu of contemporary Hong Kong cinema. This involves affect and action in ways arguably "new" yet recognizable to the Western spectator. How do affect and action and their differently gendered dimensions combine in Woo's films? What was so *new* about this combination for Western spectators and how did that newness translate into his Hollywood motion pictures?

ACTION AND AFFECT: CREATING THE MALE DUO IN HONG KONG

The shift in male and female roles from Woo's Hong Kong to his Hollywood action films poses a central question about the role of gender in negotiating two dominant intertwined modes of address—namely, visceral action and melodramatic pathos. Furthermore, given its role within the American action film, we need to ask how the comedic interweaves with both these modes.

Woo's Hong Kong film, *The Killer* (1989), begins as Jeffrey, a contracted assassin, enters a bar where Jenny is singing. A series of repeated dissolves connect the two characters visually, establishing an affective link between male and female. While accomplishing his deadly task, Jeffrey accidentally shoots Jenny, making her blind. From this point, Jeffrey's only obsession is to gather enough money to pay for the cornea transplant she needs to recover her sight and then retire with her from the criminal world. She becomes romantically involved with him; Jeffrey becomes a fatherly, caretaker figure towards her. She embodies an innocence he does not appear to covet sexually; rather, he must protect and heal its wounds. This affective attachment is triggered by Jeffrey's need to uphold his chivalric identity—a Confucian-based code of honor he maintains despite his violent day-to-day occupation.[6] *The Killer* thus reworks the textual fabric of the Hollywood action film within the Hong Kong triad underworld to showcase a story of male sacrifice dedicated to saving innocence. This ultimately involves male bonding between Jeffrey and his initial nemesis, Inspector Lee, later to become his "brother in arms." Heterosexual romance functions merely as an intermediary step towards the display of unambiguous male-to-male friendship between Jeffrey and Lee through "weaponized action."

Halfway through the film, Lee, now obsessed with Jeffrey, sits mindfully in a chair in the middle of the room where the killer had perpetrated his last bloody act. The stereo blasts a romantic ballad sung by Jenny, a song the killer himself had played while waiting in that very same chair before the latest gunfight. As Lee stares blankly, searching for clues to lead him into the assassin's mindset, Woo cross-dissolves between the two men, linking them visually. Even if they are on opposite sides of the law, they are not that far apart from each other. Soon thereafter it becomes clear that they represent two sides of the same coin; they both live through an unbreakable code of honor that invests their "in-the-making" friendship with high, emotional, moral value. Woo expresses this fact through their matching positions in the chair, their complementary impeccable white and black outfits and a match-on-action cut that shows the assassin dispatching a gunman in an earlier scene and then Lee imitating the killer's action as he shoots his partner's would be assailant. Lee is now able to *read* Jeffrey's mind. From this point, the film's narrative links them further through a series of editing devices and graphic matches, elaborating the theme of the double that recurrently structures Woo's triad action films. Here this doubling underscores a growing friendship, cemented by two goals: saving Jenny—"virtue embodied"—from death and eliminating the ruthless villain that threatens their lives. In other words, the newborn male-to-male bond between Lee and Jeffrey will ultimately guarantee justice, preserving Jenny's untarnished innocence—if not her life—in the process. In addition, Jenny's romantic ballad adds a layer of affect, intensifying the tone of unambiguous emotion that structures the film. *The Killer* is in the end nothing but the story of Jeffrey's redemption in sacrificing his life for the sake of morally righteous values and individuals.

The Killer offers a series of clues to the structural principles of Woo's triad action films. First, it capitalizes on the realization of male-to-male bonding via mutual compliance with an unbreakable code of honor as a key narrative thread. Second, it utilizes ambiguous affect to showcase the central themes of redemption, innocence, and the ultimate accomplishment of justice. Third, it is remarkably explicit in depicting onscreen violence and, at the same time, extremely chic and glossy. Finally, melodrama's goal of full moral legibility poses the two virtuous components of the male double against a ruthless gang lord whose actions denote capitalist greed and disrespect for human life and any moral code, whether the triad's or Christian. While showcasing some of the same motifs, Woo's Hollywood films break the affective bonding of the male duo that in his Hong films ultimately unites law enforcer and lawbreaker against the irredeemable villain. Instead the opposition between law enforcers and villains is centralized and the heterosexual family becomes a dominant organizing construct within the action film's generic field. In other words, if Woo's Hong Kong films can arguably be defined as male-centered, action-packed, and highly melodramatic gangster films, the bulk of his Hollywood output displays a significant reorganization of gender roles so as to establish the narrative centrality of the heterosexual couple while stylistically rearticulating both Woo's bullet-showered fests and unambiguous displays of affect.

RECODING THE MALE DUO IN USA: *FACE/OFF*

This reorganization is most starkly apparent in *Face/Off* (1997), scripted by an American and the Chinese director's first Hollywood global hit. Here *The Killer*'s bonding of pursuer and pursued is reworked as opposition between ruthless terrorist Castor Troy and U.S. agent Sean Archer, whose son Troy has previously killed. These roles are initially played by Nicholas Cage and John Travolta, who then, as their characters swap faces, swap roles. In order to discover the location of a bomb that Troy had placed in downtown Los Angeles before a police shoot-out left him in a coma, Archer literally adopts Troy's face. Through this deception he hopes to dupe Troy's brother—now imprisoned—into telling him where the bomb is hidden. In a weird reversal of fate, Troy recovers from his coma, forces the surgeon to change Archer's preserved face for his own, and kills everyone with knowledge of the swaps. Locked in a high-security prison in the middle of the ocean, Archer's future is now grim: Troy will continue impersonating Archer indefinitely, leaving him to rot in prison for the rest of his life. After Troy-as-Archer's visit to the prison, the narrative contrasts the fate of the two men in order to establish their radically opposed psychological states. Archer-as-Troy is in solitary confinement, looking at himself in the mirror in absolute despair since he is now condemned forever to stare at the face of the man who killed his son years ago—whose eyes, the audience soon knows, are at this moment devouring his teenage daughter's buttocks. Thus the threat of incest is activated. In contrast, Troy-as-Archer *goes home* after becoming a national hero by deactivating the bomb at the LA convention center. There he sets up a romantic candlelit dinner with Archer's wife. He will sleep with her.

The juxtaposition of these two sequences does not attempt to establish any kind of spiritual link between the two men. Instead, the parallelism is used to emphasize Archer's pathetic helplessness in contrast to Troy's perverted joy. The different fates of the two men cue the spectator to embrace Archer's desperation and identify Troy as the villain. What is at stake is Archer's very masculinity and his family's well being. From here on, *Face/Off*'s high-octane action ride will be mostly concerned with restoring the familial order under jeopardy. In this respect, the film suggests Archer's initial fault is neglecting his family and his wife's desires in his obsessive pursuit of Troy. He consequently needs to regain his masculine identity by reinstating his family position. Far from emotionally, intellectually, or spiritually matching Archer and Troy's personae, the film's field of morality clearly separates them. Nicholas Cage's Archer, entrapped as Troy, is redeemed by virtuous suffering, while Travolta's Troy-as-Archer incarnates iconoclastic evil as arch seducer. Troy's performative hypersexuality poses the ultimate threat Archer must contain inasmuch as it exposes Archer's dissolution as both a father and a husband—a dissolution set up from the very beginning of the film through the highly stylized black-and-white scene in which Troy kills Archer's only son. The void left by the death of Archer's male child is closed at the film's end when Archer—finally restored to his own identity—and his wife adopt Troy's child. The kid himself embodies a space of unambiguous innocence in a scene where he peacefully listens to "Over the Rainbow" as he strolls through the corridors of his house, unaware of police and terrorists engaged in a gunfighting and explosion-filled shooting marathon. Once Archer eventually kills Troy, the specter of evil that Troy had conjured in assassinating Archer's son is canceled out and the family restored as a self-sufficient unit.

While Woo's U.S. films preserve a number of the stylistic trademarks that made him a name worldwide, Woo's Hong Kong quasi all-male universes turn into familial/heterosexual love narratives, sometimes featuring strong female characters who fight alongside the males. Closure typically renders the reunion of the heterosexual couple denied in his Hong Kong films. Despite the fact that he continues to use the famous "Woo shots" that grounded his reputation for innovation in violence, the degree of bloodletting—body count and explicitness— has significantly diminished. In addition, the nuanced set of visual rhymes and narrative twists Woo utilizes in his Hong Kong films to play out the ambiguity of doubling between criminal and policeman is rearticulated. The paired duo is realigned in opposition in order to redefine the good and evil sides of masculinity and so heal the cracks within the heterosexual couple and nuclear family, affirm- ing them as an ideal social construction.

However, what remains fundamentally the same is Woo's reliance on an exces- sive affective discourse that runs in parallel to his aestheticized representation of violence and that, in combination with his action spectacles, constitutes the ideological, narrative, and stylistic core of his works. While many critics of Woo's Hong Kong works have emphasized the spectacular power of the "ballet of the bul- let" (Stokes and Hoover 1999; Heard 2000) and the presence of the melodramatic channeled through the importance of the concept of *yi qi* (self-righteousness), they often neglect the importance of this affect as a dominant mode of address. This is crucial for understanding the ways in which Woo's violent marathons oper- ate in both aesthetic and ideological terms.[7] If Woo's use of slow motion is hailed as a radically different way to shoot gangster/noir gunfights, this same technique functions also, as David Bordwell argues, to magnify the dramatic impact of his characters' expressions of emotions in close-ups (2000, 105). The inseparability and stylistic consistency of these two modes—action and affect—working within a dynamic of unambiguous excess constitutes the most significant aspect of Woo's oeuvre, particularly, as I shall argue below, in relation to the transmutation of gender roles in the shift from Hong Kong to Hollywood.

BROTHERHOOD, HOMOEROTICISM, AND THE ACTION FILM

In Woo's Hong Kong hero films, hyperbolic emotion not only works narratively as an ethical justification for excessive displays of violence but is integrated into scenes of spectacular bloodletting. If typically these sequences offer kinetic spectacles, masterfully articulated through the interplay of different film speeds and painstakingly planned choreographies of male bodies carrying heavy-duty weaponry, they generally come to a halt midway. It is then that Woo turns to his actors' faces through a series of close-ups, accompanied by pathos-laden music, highlighting the dramatic disadvantage in which the heroes are placed once Evil—the triad gang typically—has managed to corral them. It is a moment in which characters speak their mind and emphatically declare their commitment to their bloodline despite their past quarrels (Leslie Cheung and Ti Lung in *A Better Tomorrow*) or to the eternal value of friendship (Chow Yun-Fat, Ti Lung, and Dean Shek in *A Better Tomorrow II* [1987]); close the gap that prevented them from having full mutual understanding (Chow Yun-Fat and Tony Leung in *Hardboiled*); or reinforce the ties of their newly established friendship (Chow Yun-Fat and Danny Lee in *The Killer*). Then they continue carrying out what seemed to be their hopeless crusade against the gang lord. It is a momentary pause in the audience-gratifying rain of bullets by which Woo's heroes dispose bodies with suspect complacency, a pause supplied to reiterate that behind the carnage there is a higher moral ground that elevates their actions: male-to-male friendship and the defense and preservation of innocence. Even when the theme of redemption expressed as heterosexual romance is incorporated into the action, as in *The Killer,* this male-female relationship gets overwritten through the emphatic articulation of the male double and the elevation of gangster–police officer bonding to a higher status through the display of Christian imagery.[8]

These humanizing gestures in the midst of havoc mobilize unambiguous sentiment to engender full moral legibility, mostly eschewing character complexity but establishing the typification that runs across Woo's Hong Kong works and into Hollywood. Via exaggerated affect, all psychological gray zones fade away as Woo's characters resort to the repeated firing of a .45 to achieve the narrative goal that their defense of moral righteousness permits. It is a combination of overwhelming sentiment and high-octane action that reiterates a fixed set of friendship (Hong Kong films) and familial values (Hollywood) as the lofty ideals his characters aspire to but achieve only by the violence that concludes their redemptive pilgrimage. It is a release of violent action that traditionally only male bodies can perform. Thus the male protagonist accesses both masculine and feminine modes of expression—through violent action and affective bonding with their male double, respectively. Moreover, in Woo's Hong Kong films, once the ballet of the bullet kicks off, women are either excluded or become weak others to be protected—the helpless woman required for male heroism. Via the high value accorded to hyperbolic male-to-male bonding, blood-spattered action becomes the means to render moral closure as loyalty to a male fraternity. Such action nevertheless fails to protect the innocent. It is precisely through this failure that the pathos of masculinity comes to the fore.

This characteristic interplay of pathos and action made Woo a perfect fit for the talent-hungry Hollywood industry since this very combination, as Linda Williams (2001) argues, constitutes the fundamental form of address through which popular U.S. moving pictures narrativize the complexity of the social. In

Williams's analyses, D. W. Griffith, the Rambo series, *Titanic* (1997), the coverage of U.S. athletic performances in the Olympics, and the O.J. Simpson trial become components of a cultural continuum that constitutes the core of popular U.S. culture. The melodramatic mode, then, is not an excess that threatens the self-effacing cause-effect paradigm that Bordwell, Staiger, and Thompson (1985) label classical Hollywood cinema. It is rather a complementary, transgeneric form of address that structures popular modes of storytelling, facilitating their combination of realism, sentiment, spectacle, and action in the production of moral legibility, and construction of American society as a "locus of innocence and virtue" (Williams 2001, 17). In understanding the melodramatic mode as the basic vernacular of American moving pictures, Williams not only emphasizes what Altman calls the "interfertile" character of genre films but also the functioning of filmmaking across the wider social and cultural panorama (1998, 70).

If we look at Woo's Hollywood films through the lens of Williams's perspective and in the context of American cinema's prevailing constructions of gender and sexuality—privileging heterosexuality and marginalizing, ignoring, or punishing homosexuality—then the shift from male-to-male bonding to heterosexuality refocalizes the space of primary innocence, shifting its moral guarantee from the Confucian chivalry of brotherhood to the nuclear family. This in turn requires the polarization of Woo's Hong Kong male duo into the foregrounded opposition between heroes and villains. These shifts represent a process of cultural translation designed to contain the threat of homosexuality potentially suggested by Woo's Hong Kong films to the diverse players involved in the making of his American films—from studio executives to censorship boards. For the series of bodily contacts and highly sentimental verbal exchanges by which Woo's male characters relate to each other in his Hong Kong films are beyond Hollywood's norm. Untrained in the particularities of Chinese modes of address in relation to same-sex friendship, Western spectators could typically interpret such gestures as projecting "homoerotic overtones." This is not to reduce the Western spectator to a singular identity but to read the textual transmutation of gender representations of Woo's Hollywood films as a direct consequence of the prevailing representational templates and industrial conditions wrapped around their production. Nor am I claiming that certain sectors of the Hong Kong audience did not respond to the potential subversiveness of homoerotic visibility that Woo's extremely affect-laden male-to-male relationships open up. At a historical time—late 1980s and beginning of the 1990s—when gay sexuality was growing more visible in the Hong Kong social field, this other form of film viewing pleasure did indeed exist. However, Hong Kong Chinese culture provides codes of male interpersonal address that accommodate such gestures. Therefore, given that Woo was hired to make mainstream action films in the U.S. market, the potential contamination of homoeroticism in the film-to-spectator relationship threatened Hollywood's norms, as a matter of transcultural misrecognition. In addition, the potential danger of the implicit homosexual undercurrent in Woo's Hong Kong films was a risk the Hollywood studios and stars of the caliber of Tom Cruise (*Mission Impossible II*, 2000), Nicholas Cage, and John Travolta could not afford to take. In *Face/Off*, for example, the structure of the double is transformed into a playground for Travolta and Cage to copy each other's acting routines and show off their versatility. In other words, the characteristic freeze-frames, cross-dissolves, and graphic matches that psychologically link the two characters in Woo's Hong Kong films are subordinated to showcasing Travolta and Cages' acting skills.

These distinctions become clearer if we examine the key role in contemporary American action films of the comedic as a means of containing the threat of homosexuality. Scrutiny of two of the most successful action franchises of the mid-1980s and early 1990s—*Lethal Weapon* and *Die Hard*—suggests that the action film often mobilizes the discursive power of comedy to contain the threat of homosexual desire inherent in male-centered genres. In her analysis of these two franchises, Sharon Willis suggests that the comedic register—specifically in the form of diverting punch lines—functions to "diffuse and contain the overtly homoerotic charge" that characterizes the buddy formula within the action genre and consequently to "offer and then withdraw the lure of homoeroticism" (Willis 1997, 28–29). Comedy, in fact, seems to be everywhere in the contemporary action field, acting as a counterpoint to the ubiquity of violence across multiple narrative strands while signaling a postmodern ironic drive that self-consciously exposes the film's deployment of generic conventions. Arnold Schwarzenegger's films, for example, need their punctuating comic punch lines to fully deliver their high testosterone spectacles of violence while bracketing the heights to which his revengeful, body-as-spectacle delivering narratives aspire. Thus Williams's understanding of the melodramatic mode as a combination of alternating pathos and action must be qualified by highlighting the recurrent utilization of the comedic register in direct contact with these two registers.

The presence of the comedic in Woo's Hollywood films throws into relief the structuring "otherness" of his Hong Kong productions—their threat of sexual deviance, which comedy serves to contain. For, even though Woo's Hong Kong films typically contain brief episodes of comedic relief, male-to-male bonding overrides this. The potential homoeroticism of this commitment to the male couple, which opens an entry point for the male spectator into homosexual identification, could not be transferred into Hollywood's action-comedy safe-box. A necessary translation had to be performed to make Woo's universe conform to Hollywood's representation of sexual identity. Thus Woo's nonchalant knight was turned into a family man, and male partners converted into wives and sons or daughters. However, in a shared melodramatic pattern, innocence and virtue remain the ultimate goal characters fight, shoot, and kill for. While in his Hong Kong films victimized innocence acts as a pretext to facilitate the narrativization of male chivalry and honor, in his Hollywood films it is the hero's very masculinity, as the central asset binding the family together, that becomes the principal preoccupation. Thus, given the family's dominant role in Hollywood productions, we confront a process of "automated adjustment" to achieve cultural legibility. If the effects of the role reversal on the representation of Archer's family expose a more ironic and less idealistic take on its status as a space of innocence and virtue, *Face/Off* also eliminates any trace of homoerotism.

In this respect, whereas the use of Christian imagery in Woo's Hong Kong films reinforces the moral identity of a chivalric hero, its use in the conclusion of *Face/Off* is rearticulated as the means by which the family man recovers his masculinity within the realm of the heterosexual couple and a productive family scenario. In *The Killer,* the church represents a space of tranquility where Jeffrey (even though a declared unbeliever) can shelter from the evils of the world and encounter his own self. The destruction of the Virgin Mary's statue in the last shoot-out metaphorically signals the start of the battle Jeffrey and Lee must face against the gang lord's powerful henchmen. In *Face/Off,* the church setting of the final shootout is used to re-emphasize Troy's evil—for example, his mocking crucifixion pose as he enters the church, echoing his depraved ruthlessness and iconoclastic irreverence established at the start, when, clad in a black priest outfit, he placed the bomb in the Los Angeles Convention Center. In contrast, Archer-as-Troy walks into the church, lights a votive candle, looks at a photograph of his son, and crosses himself, before confronting Troy and his gang. As the confrontation ensues, Woo deploys his arsenal of camera movements, film speeds, and quick-paced cuts, in combination with recurrent shots of flying doves, a wooden Christ, and Virgin Mary, who act as silent witnesses (and moral supporters) of Archer's endeavor. However, whereas in his Hong Kong films the female characters representing innocence appear only to showcase the skill by which the gun-armed hero saves them, here both Archer's wife and daughter are a constant presence, becoming integral to his success by getting involved in the weaponized exchange. In other words, *Face/Off* not only equates Archer's virtue with Christianity but also situates the family as a central component of the moral righteousness that Christian faith seems to guarantee.

CONCLUSION

Woo's symphonies of bloody gunfighting and affect-driven spectacles proved particularly exportable because, despite his substantial stylistic idiosyncrasies and his emphasis on male-to-male, larger-than-life relationships, they present two fundamental features central to mainstream American motion pictures. First, Woo's narratives revolve around a series of variations on a confrontation between good versus evil in a violence-mediated environment in which good ultimately prevails and justice finds its way in defense of virtue and innocence. Second, Woo's audiovisual craftsmanship organizes these narratives through an alternating dynamic between sensorial and affective spectacles within the rules of a contemporary transgeneric powerhouse—the action film. If Woo's Hong Kong films were already transnational products, functioning in the margins of the world film market and in the mainstream of Hong Kong's and parts of East Asia's cinematic and cultural life, his Hollywood films are designed to deliver *everywhere*. While Woo's partially successful stint in Hollywood proves the transnational malleability of the action-affect modality that organizes his works, the disparate roles of male and female characters between his Hong Kong and Hollywood films points to the necessary process of translation between different national film industries and cultures. Given the privileged status of the heterosexual match as a Hollywood problematic, the shift from all male to male-female coupling represents an instance of cinematic translation between two cultures and modes of production that share a flexible action generic register but ultimately rely on different strongholds of sexed character types. In this sense, Woo's Hong Kong homoeroticism has been contained and locked inside a high-security vault where the heterosexual match occupies an uncontested position that Hollywood studios do not typically challenge.

Notes

1. John Woo was born in China but migrated to Hong Kong when a child.
2. Karen Fang reports that the film made $4.5 million (U.S.) on tickets and played for two months in the movie theaters—triple the average. It was the highest-grossing film in the Hong Kong industry when it was released, recognized by critics and industry. It was nominated in eight categories for the 1987 Hong Kong Film Awards and Chow Yun-Fat won the prize for best actor.
3. The Chinese title, *The Essence of Heroes,* emphasizes honor and friendship and points to the combination of high-octane action and affect that constitutes the consistent core of Woo's works.
4. *A Bullet in the Head* (1990) is clearly influenced by Scorsese's *Mean Streets* (1973) in its use of music and choreographed action scenes. Wong Kar-Wai's first feature, *As Tears Go By* (1988), is a loose remake of Scorsese's film and one of the many triad films the Hong Kong film industry produced riding the wave of *A Better Tomorrow.*
5. Bordwell identifies the mass-market auteur filmmaker, beyond the auteur's art-house niche. He places John Woo in a commercial auteurist tradition that links him with Orson Welles and Alfred Hitchcock.
6. For the influence of Confucian thinking on Woo's films, see Magnan-Park 2007, 37–46.
7. In contrast to the Hong Kong term "hero film," Western critics and fans initially labeled Woo's films as "heroic bloodshed," once again emphasizing violence. The sentimental core of Woo's films becomes encapsulated in "heroic," normally associated with a very different spectrum of cultural codes.
8. The final shootout in *The Killer* is set in the church where the film opens. Dozens of doves, the Holy Spirit indeed, fly around peacefully until the violent confrontation between Jeff and Lee and the gangsters ensues.

PART FIVE

GENERIC "TRANS-INGS":

BETWEEN GENRES, GENDERS, AND SEXUALITIES

CHAPTER 15

TRASH COMES HOME:

GENDER/GENRE SUBVERSION IN THE FILMS OF JOHN WATERS

DEREK KANE-MEDDOCK

"The only gross [movies] people try to make now are in Hollywood.
The golden age of trash is over."
—John Waters, 2001

John Waters's career trajectory is commonly described as a process of assimilation. His early films earned him prominence as a nonconformist, and he seemed
to revel in being perceived as a social misfit. When the controversial director
published two books in the early 1980s, *Shock Value* and *Crackpot,* their titles
drew on the image of Waters as outsider that he had cultivated from the beginning of his career. Yet, for many critics, Waters's transgressive reputation has been
undermined by his transformation into an eccentric but essentially mainstream
filmmaker in the 1980s. The seemingly obvious differences between Waters's first
few movies, fantastically perverse works shot on 16mm film with initial funding
supplied by parental loan, and his later films, produced with studio money and tar-
geting a wider audience, have encouraged this fragmented approach to his career.
Indeed, even Waters himself has explained the changes in his filmmaking style in
terms of appropriation: "First I made underground movies, and then there were
no underground movies. Then it was midnight movies, and they disappeared.
Then independent movies, but they were co-opted by Hollywood. Now it's all the
same. So I make Hollywood movies" (quoted in Pela 2002, 147). This comment
suggests an enduring tendency to organize films generically, but it simultaneously
reveals an underlying volatility in the meaning and viability of these cultural
categories. Judith Butler, in *Gender Trouble,* sees gender as a similarly persistent
phenomenon that is nevertheless fraught with concealed ambiguities. Butler

insists that sex and gender are neither natural nor universal, instead offering a performative theory that emphasizes the constructed and conditional nature of gender. In a brief discussion of Waters in the introduction to her landmark work, Butler notes the subversive potential of the director's cross-dressing star, Divine: "Her/his performance destabilizes the very distinctions between the natural and the artificial, depth and surface, inner and outer through which discourse about genders almost always operates" (1999 [1990], viii). It is this tension between recycling familiar representational tropes and ironically deconstructing their social power that animates Waters's work. Although his subversive parodies of gender and genre share an emphasis on performativity, they have been mistakenly perceived as the products of two self-contained and diametrically opposed filmmaking spaces, underground cinema and Hollywood, neither of which are as consistent or as isolated as is frequently implied.

The propensity to brand Waters as a provocateur who lost his edge in Hollywood belies the fact that his films have always acknowledged a wide variety of influences, from Herschell Gordon Lewis and Andy Warhol to William Castle and Douglas Sirk. With the residue of "trash" cinema finding its way into mainstream Hollywood, Waters's industry films have often been characterized as tepid, unable to effectively recapture the rebellious spirit of the 1970s. This familiar refrain, used to account for the demise of many alternative modes of filmmaking in 1980s American cinema, is exemplified by Jonathan Rosenbaum in the 1991 addendum to *Midnight Movies*: "You can say that midnight movies succeeded rather than failed, in the sense that the major figures in this movement . . . have all made it into the mainstream. But it's a kind of success that resembles failure on certain fronts" (Hoberman and Rosenbaum 1991, 322). What this popular conception of Waters has overlooked is a significant affinity between the two periods of the director's career. This affinity, derived from his ambivalence about all forms of social categorization, is manifested on screen in the form of a performative excess that foregrounds artifice and denaturalizes the familiar.[1] Whereas Waters's early works overtly flaunt their contempt for traditional gender roles, most visibly through the ambiguity of Divine, his later films show a similar disregard for generic integrity. Both gender conventions and genres are parodied and combined in atypical ways, recycled in order to cast a critical eye on that evocative symbol of normalcy and repository of morality, the family.

In order to demonstrate the structural link between gender and genre in Waters's work, I will examine three of the director's films: *Pink Flamingos* (1972), representing his early career, *Polyester* (1981), which marks his transition to Hollywood, and *Serial Mom* (1994), a movie from what has been called Waters's "safe and formulaic" period (Hoberman and Rosenbaum 1991, 322). Despite their stylistic and thematic differences, these three movies each expose the inconsistencies inherent in gendered and generic representation.

Originally exhibited as midnight movies for an audience seeking an experience that pushed the limits of conventional narrative cinema, Waters's early films
tend to emphasize performance over plot, creating an absurd space in which the
perverse and the mundane switch roles. The director's breakthrough hit, *Pink
Flamingos,* is a celebration of social outsiders without an obvious generic ante-
cedent in the cinema. As the authors of *Midnight Movies* write, "*Pink Flamingos*
is less a narrative than a vaudevillian string of prize gross-outs" (Hoberman
and Rosenbaum 1991, 152). At the center of the film is Divine, Waters's muse
and biggest star. Born Harris Glenn Milstead, Divine used elaborate costuming
and makeup to transform himself for movie roles. This, in conjunction with his
growing celebrity, made artifice and performance key subtexts for the audience,
as sometimes happens with Hollywood stars who have grown too famous to
completely inhabit a character. In *Pink Flamingos,* Divine encourages the viewer
to take pleasure in the "filthiness" of nontraditional gender roles and family
structures, but New Line's trailer uses no actual footage from the film. Instead,
the preview foregrounds the importance of the collective moviegoing experience,
showing the shock and astonishment of a group of spectators who have just seen
Pink Flamingos and concluding with a still photograph of Divine accompanied
by the tagline, "An Exercise in Bad Taste." In this context, Hollywood genres are
overwhelmed by the aesthetics of trash.[2] As Babs Johnson, the unforgettable
protagonist of *Pink Flamingos,* proclaims, "Filth are my politics. Filth is my life."

Polyester, Waters's first 35mm film, signals an important thematic shift in his
work. Interrogating normative family values in an imagined suburban community that merges a standard depiction of domesticity with Waters's more unusual
childhood experiences in suburbia, the movie recycles the generic conventions
of family melodrama in order to challenge the trope of domestic bliss.[3] Walter
Metz, stressing the importance of the 1960s radical avant-garde as an influence
on Waters's work, sees *Polyester* as a response to changing economic conditions
in the film industry. Metz observes, "Waters found a way to make avant-garde
melodramas within the Hollywood cinema at precisely the time . . . the avant-
garde cinema's parodies of Hollywood were losing their currency" (Metz 2003,
162). However, despite careful attention to the variety of genres that underpin
Waters's work, Metz tends to read such generic ambiguity within a coherent version of underground cinema. For example, he sees Divine's shoplifting scene in
Pink Flamingos as an allusion to Kenneth Anger's ironic use of popular music in
Scorpio Rising (1964), neglecting the mainstream cinematic intertext, the Jayne
Mansfield vehicle *The Girl Can't Help It* (1956), which introduced Little Richard's
song of the same name. In *Polyester,* Divine plays Francine Fishpaw as a woman
who represses her desires, suffering for the good of her deviant family. Francine,
unlike the heroine of *Pink Flamingos,* seeks to contain the smut that threatens her
vision of idyllic home life. The narrative structure seems to comment on Waters's

own career path; Divine's excesses are tempered so that she can inhabit the world of the family melodrama. Yet, in Waters's version, the traditional family becomes the very site of perversity; father is a porn king, daughter an exhibitionist, and son a foot fetishist. In this case, filth surrounds the maternal figure instead of deriving from it as in *Pink Flamingos*. At the film's conclusion, the reconstitution of the family is incomplete and the patriarch is violently removed from the narrative.

Serial Mom has a similar disdain for dominant social and narrative structures but, unlike *Polyester*, it foregrounds a multiplicity of generic influences. In creating a world of generic hybridity, Waters references the family melodrama, the horror film, and the courtroom drama. Partially displacing the gender confusion of a cross-dressing protagonist, *Serial Mom*'s Beverly Sutphin is played by Kathleen Turner instead of Divine, who died in 1988.[4] Combining the unconventional maternal figure of *Pink Flamingos* with the suburban family dynamics of *Polyester*, Waters contaminates the imaginary purity of domestic space. By citing a variety of generic referents, many of which reinforce popular gender stereotypes, *Serial Mom* confronts oversimplified assumptions about the intersection of genre and gender. Any film with a protagonist who is both a loving mother and a serial killer is clearly a cultural aberration, the consequence of Waters's engagement with the restrictions inherent in normative Hollywood representation.

In considering Waters's evolution as a filmmaker, the theory of disidentifica-tion offers an explanatory link between the director's resistance to the rules of both gender and genre. José Esteban Muñoz, building on the work of French linguist Michel Pêcheux, frames disidentification as a response to the failure of dominant forms of representation to include unconventional perspectives. For Muñoz, "Disidentification is meant to be descriptive of the survival strategies the minority subject practices in order to negotiate a phobic majoritarian public sphere that continuously elides or punishes the existence of subjects who do not conform to the phantasm of normative citizenship" (1999, 4). Waters has consistently been suspicious of the ordinary, and his characters are frequently celebrated for their ability to transcend the limitations of normalcy. As Muñoz describes it, "Instead of buckling under the pressures of dominant ideology (identification, assimilation) or attempting to break free of its inescapable sphere (counteridentification, utopianism), this 'working on and against' is a strategy that tries to transform a cultural logic from within" (11). As Waters has become identified as a mainstream director, his means of "working on and against" tra-ditional representational strategies has changed. By engaging with the limita-tions of mainstream media, the director has expanded his focus from ridiculing gender norms to parodying the conventions of Hollywood storytelling. In the process, he has paradoxically been disparaged for his refusal to conform to the established rules for underground filmmakers.

POSING, PASSING, GENRE, AND GENDERED PERFORMANCE

"All camp objects, and persons, contain a large element of artifice" argues Susan Sontag (2001, 279). In this section I explore the ramifications of this contention.

Discussing performativity in James Whale's *Show Boat* (1936), Linda Williams makes a distinction between white *posing* and black *passing* in order to account for how social power influences the ways in which racial categories can be transgressed. As Williams argues, "Where whites who pose as black intentionally exhibit all the artifice of their performance—exaggerated gestures, blackface make-up—blacks who pass as white suppress the more obvious artifice of performance. Passing is a performance whose success depends on not overacting" (2001, 176). Using this formula, cultural verisimilitude is crucial to an audience's investment in the passing narrative but runs counter to the excess that empowers posing. In considering Divine's contravention of gender boundaries in *Pink Flamingos* and *Polyester,* we can see that Waters emphasizes the artifice of Divine's performance of femininity to varying degrees. The extravagance of Babs Johnson in *Pink Flamingos* foregrounds the posed nature of the performance, while a more subtle portrayal of Francine Fishpaw in *Polyester* overtly recalls the passing narrative. By *Serial Mom,* Kathleen Turner had replaced Divine, muting the theme of gendered passing. However, as gender became a more subtle influence on Waters's work, the exaggeration of generic conventions took on added importance. *Polyester* marks the transition in each case.

Closer examination of the films reveals how Waters's use of excess to challenge gender stereotypes presages his treatment of genre. Gender is made visible in *Pink Flamingos* and *Polyester* through the appropriation of highly gendered conventions for fashion and beauty.[5] Visually, the two films use Divine to achieve different effects. Although both Babs Johnson and Francine Fishpaw can be considered excessive representations of femininity, the two characters are positioned quite differently in relation to the normative ideal, which is briefly manifested in the form of *Serial Mom*'s Beverly (before it is undermined by her characterization as a generically ambiguous killer).

Clearly, Divine's performance in *Pink Flamingos* is not meant to allow him to pass in plain sight. In a radio interview, Waters reveals just how far his star deviates from the norm: "I actually was with Divine . . . when Divine was walking down the street and caused a car accident from people gawking and [they] smashed right into another car" (Gross 2004). *Pink Flamingos* explicitly mobilizes the stunned reaction of passersby within the text. As Babs Johnson struts down a city street, Waters's hidden camera follows her from a passing car. The crowds gathered on the sidewalk, unable to situate Divine within the context of a movie production, are visibly shocked and turn to stare as she passes.[6] Within this framework, Divine's construction of femininity takes on the nature of posing—marked by an exaggeration and overstatement that fit within the tradition of camp.[7] Partially bald (her hair line shaved back to allow for more eye makeup) with ornate two-toned hair, dramatically painted-on triangular eyebrows, and glittery earrings, Babs is an unbelievable woman, an absurd, embellished version of femininity (fig. 15.1). A series of brightly colored, revealing outfits draw attention to and display her body. In this case, Divine's appearance complements a flamboyant personality.

In *Polyester,* Divine's character enacts the passing scenario amidst the restrictive suburban setting of the film. The opening scene introduces Francine in her bedroom, seated before a large mirror. Dressed in white underclothes, she primps. In one of the film's winking references to gender confusion, Francine trims her nose hair and shaves her armpits before completing her ablutions and slipping into a white dress. Weighing more than 300 pounds and described by her husband

Fig. 15.1 Postcard: Babs the unbelievable woman in *Pink Flamingos* (1972)

Fig. 15.2   Postcard: Francine, normal woman, in family melodrama: *Polyester* (1981)

as "the hairiest women I have ever laid eyes on," Francine is only distantly related to Babs. Instead of reveling in eccentricity, Francine seeks to fit in, to contain her undesirable characteristics in order to pass as a normal woman within the generic context of the family melodrama (fig. 15.2). Her hair is conventionally styled and her dress is respectable, concealing instead of emphasizing Divine's massive body after the opening scene.

It is worth noting that neither *Pink Flamingos* nor *Polyester* explicitly reveals Divine's biological maleness *within the text*. Yet we can assume that the vast majority of spectators were aware of the cross-dressing subtext. As Jack Stevenson has noted, "[Waters's] favourite approach to portraying sexuality . . . was to have straights playing gays and gays playing straights so that all roles ended up ridiculously over-played" (Stevenson 1996, 12). Certainly, part of the pleasure of watching Divine is in viewing his performance as a deconstruction of normative gender and sexuality. Unlike the typical passing narrative, there is no moment of revelation in *Polyester* that allows for the recuperation of the dominant social structure. It is difficult to imagine exactly what would be revealed, since Waters's films facilitate the audience's identification with Divine's transgression of norms of gender and sexuality. In this context, attempts at passing accentuate (instead of suppress) the characteristics that society has deemed abnormal or inferior.

Although *Polyester* puts Divine through a series of indignities, it seems tame by the standards of *Pink Flamingos*. However, this distinction between the films should not be overstated. Ultimately, the relationship between public flamboyance and control of the narrative is more crucial to understanding how the films use humiliation. The narrator in *Pink Flamingos* (Waters himself with an exaggerated Baltimore accent) asks a question that is central to all of the director's films: "Is there no shame?" Ideally, the films seem to answer, no. In *Pink Flamingos,* Waters shows Divine in the act of public defecation, eating dog shit, and engaging in (mock) cannibalism. Through their contempt for typical standards of decency, the films highlight the perversity of shame itself. This theme is manifested in the narrative arc of *Polyester*'s main character. Whereas Babs is celebrated for her refusal to adhere to the conventions of "normal" society, Francine's desire for social acceptance is a constant source of pain. While Francine clings to a conventional notion of propriety, she suffers a comic array of personal traumas: divorce, the institutionalization of her son, her teenage daughter's pregnancy, alcoholism, and so on. Ultimately, Francine's angst can only be alleviated by the dissolution of the existing patriarchal family structure and its reconstitution in a nontraditional form, challenging the conventions of the family melodrama.

As John Waters's *Serial Mom* begins, the camera sweeps down upon the sub-urban home of the Sutphin family. The shot closely parallels the opening of *Polyester* and, at this point, a viewer might expect the director to maintain that film's attention to the generic conventions of the family melodrama. In the distance, a passing garbage truck foreshadows the impending trashing of generic integrity. While mother Beverly serves breakfast to husband Eugene and children Chip and Misty, the exchanges between the family members evoke the scenes of impossible domestic bliss that *Polyester*'s Francine desired so intently. However, a persistent fly draws Beverly's attention and is swatted with malicious intensity before two detectives disturb breakfast to inquire about a threatening note that reads, "I'll Get You Pussy Face." Waters takes great pride in staging creative and bizarre disruptions; *Serial Mom* uses obscene phone calls, a series of violent murders, and an elaborate courtroom scene to playfully acknowledge the excesses of family melodrama. A collage of generic references to horror films, legal thrillers, and family comedies, each taken to ludicrous extremes, recalls the mischievous use of Divine's indefi-nite gender. Though the pre-credit titles insist, "This is a true story," the claim is undermined in short order by a sweetly chirping bird that fits uncomfortably in the crime genre. A few scenes later, Waters cuts from Beverly eagerly watching the gory *Blood Feast* (1963) with her son to the glistening red meatloaf of a family dinner. The juxtaposition of these incongruous generic elements highlights their artifice and raises conflicting generic expectations.

If the early films of John Waters undermine the social endorsement of het-erosexuality and stable gender identification, offering an alternative to norma-tive gender roles, they likewise bear little relation to the normal depiction of suburban America. Nearly a decade later, *Polyester* moves inside the American family, deconstructing the family melodrama in order to confront the mythical resolutions that are common in mainstream cinema. Finally, *Serial Mom* brings

Waters's earlier rejection of gendered conventions to genre, critiquing the social and generic structures that appropriate transgression.

HOME VIDEO CULTURE AND GENERICITY

"Without video, my early filthy films could never have infected such a motley group of young malcontents. A few kids in the sticks still remember me as their first bad influence, and I can only thank the video business," reminisces John Waters (2003, 192). Here I consider the impact of changes in postmodern technology and culture that have led some scholars to conclude that the prevailing model of film genres is overly static. The explosion of the home video market in the 1980s and the further expansion of that market with the availability of DVD have impacted not only the circulation of films but also the very function of genre. As Jim Collins notes, "That a seemingly endless number of texts are subject to virtually immediate random access inevitably alters the relationship between classic and contemporary when both circulate alongside one another simultaneously. This simultaneity does not diminish the cultural 'status' of the former so much as it changes its possible functions" (1993, 246). Waters's films bear the trace of these developments in genericity, engaging with the shifting role of media in the generic process.

Waters's work consistently acknowledges the importance of film and television in shaping public opinion, even as it ridicules the limitations of conventional media structures.[8] In *Pink Flamingos,* the media takes the form of newspaper reporters who bear witness to Babs's filthiness. The reporters bring a certain kind of legitimacy to the perversity even as they condemn it in print. Similarly, both *Polyester* and *Serial Mom* include scenes in which genres are publicly decried even as they reach a new level of cultural visibility within the film. In *Polyester,* Francine's husband, Elmer, owns a pornographic theater that their neighbors denounce during elaborate "down with smut" protests that are designed for the local television media. To emphasize the hypocrisy of the community's outrage, Elmer's ironically named Charles Art Theatre is contrasted to the "very highbrow" drive-in theater owned by a rival exhibitor. On the marquee at the upscale venue: a Marguerite Duras triple bill. Responding to the increasingly central role of the home video market, *Serial Mom* explicitly posits the video store as the site of Beverly's son Chip's obsession with graphic horror films. At the same time, the video store, like the movie theater, is a semi-public space in which characters can express suspicion of low-cultural forms. In *Serial Mom,* the middle-aged patron who rents *Annie* (1982, a mainstream film from the more highly esteemed musical genre) dismisses Chip's interest in the horror genre as vulgar. In the same vein, Chip's math teacher warns Beverly about her son's "unhealthy obsession with sick horror films," an interest that Beverly not only shares but will soon enact by crushing the teacher with her station wagon.

All three films exhibit a fascination with media and notoriety, but use the theme quite differently within the structure of the narrative. The loose plot of *Pink Flamingos* is largely based on Babs's desire to protect her title, "The Filthiest Person Alive," which has been bestowed by a local newspaper. The title captures Babs's abnormality and the open recognition (or even admiration) of that abnormality. Her fame is based on her deviance, embodied in her willingness to *publicly* perform acts that others eschew. Babs's ability to effectively manage the media is foregrounded in the murder scene near the end of the film. She sells three newspapermen on her prepackaged story with pictures and clever quotes. *Polyester* positions Divine very differently in relation to the media. Francine is appalled by the unwanted attention given to her. Although her husband skillfully uses the local news to attract patrons to his porn theater, the critical gaze of her neighbors horrifies Francine. She falls over in front of the news cameras, a mishap that is exacerbated by its broadcast recurrence on the local news. Unable to embrace deviance in order to satisfy her desires, Francine is a prisoner of public perception. *Serial Mom* also suggests the social power of disorder by allowing Beverly to profit from it. While her trial is ongoing, Beverly becomes a major media figure, immortalized on t-shirts and targeted for movie deals. Misbehave, Waters seems to say, and Hollywood is sure to appropriate your image.

Writing in the late 1980s, Andrew Ross noted that bad taste was finding a new level of commercial viability. In the film industry, Ross argued, "the popular market in hard-core porn, horror, gore, and splatter movies has entered a boom period in the last fifteen years as censorship laws have eased off" (1989, 155). In the 1990s, other genres similarly pushed the boundaries of good taste. Gross-out comedies like *There's Something About Mary* (1998) and the *American Pie* trilogy borrowed liberally from the trash aesthetic. As Waters notes, "Today mainstream movies like *There's Something About Mary* have close-ups of come and testicles caught in zippers. I think that's great . . . I like to think I've had a little bit of influence in making that possible" (quoted in Pela 2002, 148). *American Wedding* (2003), the third film in the *American Pie* series, even restages the infamous shit-eating sequence from *Pink Flamingos*.

The growing importance of genre in Waters's films raises questions about how his use of multiple generic referents differs from single genre parody. For example, Julianne Pidduck views *Serial Mom* as part of an individual cycle derived from film noir, alongside thrillers like *Fatal Attraction* (1987) and *Basic Instinct* (1992). In this generic context, Pidduck argues, "Explicit moments of self-parody in a film like *Serial Mom* function partly to comment on the thematically-connected films of the fatal femme cycle generally, creating patterns of ironic overlay—a certain critical distance from which to interrogate strikingly resilient, idealized fifties models of happy families" (1995, 67). Yet, as I have suggested, the movie emphasizes the hybridity of its generic influences; the serial killer film lurks just beneath the surface of the family comedy (fig. 15.3). This hybridity, like the gender confusion that surrounds Divine in *Pink Flamingos* and *Polyester*, reveals

Fig. 15.3 Publicity still: serial killer lurking beneath the surface of family comedy in *Serial Mom* (1994)

the power of social taxonomy. In a way, generic multiplicity allows Waters to mock not just the conventions of the fatal femme cycle but also the limitations of predictable Hollywood storytelling.

While providing a viewing space that celebrates social disorder, Waters's films explicitly satirize the presumed inviolability of generic and gendered categories in Hollywood films. Uncertainty about the gendered body endangers the reproduction of the social hierarchy. In *Pink Flamingos* and *Polyester,* procreative sex is considered abnormal. Despite a multitude of couplings, neither film offers the viewer a traditional example of a male and a female producing healthy children. The reasons—birth control, menopause, bestiality, miscarriage, and fetishism—are worth listing, as they suggest the lengths Waters will go to in order to avoid this combination. This is carried into *Serial Mom,* which prefaces its scene of heterosexual sex with Beverly's first murder, the violent act arousing her passion in a reversal of a narrative trope that has been prevalent since Alfred Hitchcock's *Psycho* (1960). Waters subjects all his characters to parody, regardless of gender or sexuality. The director admits, "I don't think any sexual preference is better or worse than any other" (quoted in Stevenson 1996, 24).

In his work on the evolution of genre in the 1990s, Jim Collins uses the phrase "eclectic irony" to describe one cinematic response to the media-saturated environment of the 1980s and 1990s. Eclectic irony emphasizes generic hybridity and an appropriation of generic signs that can redefine conventions, both of which are visible in *Serial Mom*. For Collins, this group of texts assumes that past "icons, scenarios, visual conventions continue to carry with them some sort of cultural 'charge' or resonance that must be reworked according to the exigencies of the present" (1993, 256). As Hollywood has appropriated the symbols of Waters's trash aesthetic (for example, reshaping them as teen gross-out comedies), the director has replied by mocking the rigidity of generic conventions. If, as Waters implies in the epigraph, Hollywood is responsible for ending the golden age of trash, his recent films have increasingly mined the conventional structures of mainstream filmmaking to continue challenging the desirability of normative social relations, celebrating the pleasure of a generic deviance that recalls his earlier treatment of gender.

PERFORMING JOHN WATERS

John Waters remembers "sitting at the top of the steps as a child, eavesdropping on my parents' conversation and hearing my mother confide to my father: 'I don't know what to do. He's just an odd duck.' Thrilled that they could see the future, I plotted how to further my 'odd-duckism'" (1995, 231). This chapter concludes by considering the relation implied here between nonconformity and performance.

Jeffrey Sconce and Susan Sontag both suggest explanations for the widespread rejection of Waters's adventures in Hollywood. Using the concept of paracinema as a reading practice that celebrates and legitimates "trash" cinema, Jeffrey Sconce argues that paracinematic excess is often registered "in a film's failure to conform to historically delimited codes of verisimilitude" (1995, 387). Similarly, Susan Sontag's writing on camp implies that camp spectatorship provides a space for reveling in difference. For Sontag, "the essence of Camp is its love of the unnatural: of artifice and exaggeration. And Camp is esoteric—something of a private code, a badge of identity even, among small urban cliques" (2001, 275). Waters's early work provided an alternative cinematic space that promoted a flexible understanding of gender and sexuality by effectively denaturalizing it. As we might expect, Waters describes his audience in terms that problematize essential categorizations. Despite consistently being referred to as a gay filmmaker, Waters insists, "My audience . . . was never gay or straight; it was gay people that didn't like other gay people. It was hippies that didn't like hippies. It was always the outsider of another outsider group. That's what my audience began with" (Gross 2004). As a result, Waters's early films celebrate a gendered deviance that is grounded in Sontag's "artifice and exaggeration." But when the director uses cinematic excess to similarly undermine genre, critics have largely failed to make the connection because Hollywood genres do not have the same marginal status.

As Sconce notes, "paracinematic culture celebrates the systematic 'failure' or 'distortion' of conventional cinematic style by 'auteurs' who are valued more as 'eccentrics' than as artists, who work within the impoverished and clandestine production conditions typical of exploitation cinema. These films deviate from Hollywood classicism not necessarily by artistic intentionality, but by the effects of material poverty and technical ineptitude" (1995, 385). In a sense, Waters's films became too expensive and technically accomplished to fit within the paradigm of trash established for understanding his work. Although Waters's earliest projects were influenced by both Hollywood and underground cinematic traditions, their production values and exhibition strategies situated these movies as an alternative to the commercialism of mainstream cinema. Waters has embraced his image as the "Pope of Trash" for promotional purposes, but he has also demonstrated a flexible approach to production that has allowed him to continue making movies despite changing industrial conditions.

Viewed in this way, Waters's career is best understood not as a process of assimilation but as a direct engagement with the limitations of gender and genre. As the mainstream has absorbed certain aspects of a previously marginalized approach to cinema, Waters has increasingly subjected it to his perverse mode of filmmaking. *Hairspray,* Waters's 1988 film about racial segregation as a failed means of social categorization, achieved enough popularity in its reincarnation as a Broadway musical to be remade by New Line Cinema, the company that released *Pink Flamingos* twenty-five years earlier. Since distributing Waters's first hit, New Line had grown from a small independent company specializing in midnight movies, exploitation cinema, and horror films into the powerful studio behind the *Lord of the Rings* trilogy.[9] With John Travolta in the Divine role, the new version of *Hairspray* grossed over $100 million in U.S. box office in 2007. Although some might view it as merely the latest confirmation that Waters has sold out, we should wonder about precisely what Hollywood has agreed to buy.

Writing about the subversive potential of drag, Judith Butler insists that these gendered performances can expose the illusory nature of stable gender identity, writing emphatically, "*In imitating gender, drag implicitly reveals the imitative structure of gender itself—as well as its contingency*" (1990, 137). The films of John Waters, whether they are subverting the notion of stable gender identity or parodying the integrity of Hollywood genres, ridicule and expose those cultural values that are so pervasive that they have rarely been subjected to such scrutiny.

Notes

1. Consider a scene from *Mondo Trasho* (1969), Waters's first feature film, in which two women eager to categorize the female protagonist subject her to an absurdly lengthy litany of social labels. She is erroneously identified as "a drug dealer, a communist, a lesbian, a beatnik, a junkie, a shit kicker, a Pollack, a warmonger, a dingleberry, a yippie, and a jetsetter" (quoted in Metz 2003, 168).

2. "Trash" cinema can certainly be explored as a genre but, as with art films, the tendency to focus on directors in celebrating trash often leads away from a consideration of genre.

3. Waters has written about his parents' mixed reaction to his childhood obsessions with car accidents, horror films, rock and roll, and hurricanes. See Waters 1995, 24–31.

4. Divine died from a heart attack. Kathleen Turner's deep voice and penchant for portraying active women makes her a compelling choice for the maternal role that had previously been played by Divine.

5. The perversity inherent in the beauty industry has been a key theme from the beginning of Waters's career. His first 16mm film, *Eat Your Makeup* (1968), is about a pair of lunatics who kidnap fashion models and force their victims to model themselves to death.

6. Waters's recollection of his father's reaction to seeing Divine suggests an early inspiration for this scene: "Each morning, as my father drove me and my brothers and sisters to school, we'd pass Divine waiting on the corner for the bus to whisk him away to beauty school. Divine, at the time, was a living Clairol color chart, and I could see my father looking at him and shivering" (Waters 1995, 234).

7. Play with gender and sexuality continues in Waters's other films. For example, in *Female Trouble* (1974) Divine plays both rebellious schoolgirl Dawn Davenport and her onetime lover Earl Peterson. Unpacking the complex gender signification in the film becomes even more difficult when Earl impregnates Dawn on a dirty mattress before telling her, "Go fuck yourself." Divine also muddied the waters concerning his personal life by responding playfully to questions about his presumed homosexuality: "Gay? Are you kidding? I've got a wife and two kids back in Omaha" (Waters 1995, 145).

8. This is not surprising given Waters's childhood fascination with entertainment media. As he recounts, "I started getting *Variety* in my early teens . . . I'd pore over the local entertainment pages, clipping and collecting the most violent movie ads. I'd pretend I owned a movie theater and book the most notorious films, redesigning their ad campaigns in a much more sensational manner and imagining the outrage it would cause in the religious community. At last I had a goal in life—I wanted to make the trashiest motion pictures in cinema history" (Waters 1995, 34).

9. For more on the history of New Line, see Justin Wyatt 1998, 74–90.

CHAPTER 16

FEMME FATALE OR LESBIAN FEMME:

BOUND IN SEXUAL *DIFFÉRANCE*

CHRIS STRAAYER

In its black-and-white opening title sequence with stark lights and deep shadows, foreboding music, and a moving camera that waves from extreme close-up obscurity to distanced readability (of the title), *Bound* (Wachowski Brothers, 1996) immediately stirs memories and expectations of film noir. The film's first scene, however, poses a neo-noir twist. Trapped inside a clothes closet, the camera slowly descends from the ceiling, pointing downwards, alongside what appears to be the ceiling light's fixture, enlarging and distorting it to vulgar proportions and thus creating for the viewer a bulbous projection that suggests a sex toy as much as a ceiling light. Continuing downwards, the camera surveys a variety of hat boxes, evening dresses, and high heels and then careens the length of a woman's body lying on the floor: from her heavy boots and ankles tied with rope; past work pants, ribbed undershirt, and biceps displaying a labrys tattoo;[1] to her face slashed alongside one eye and her mouth gagged. In voice-over, two females amplify the intrigue with remarks about sex and sexual merging, plans and choices, the "business" and wanting out of it. In the following scene, presumably a flashback, the previously bound woman enters an elevator followed by a hetero-coded couple. The man stands up front, facing the door, while the two women exchange seductive glances behind his back. Both women wear black leather jackets despite their butch-femme contrast. Suddenly an overhead shot graphically articulates sexual triangulation. The man leaves the elevator, followed by the femme, whose legs are shot in classic film noir style except, in this instance, from the point of view of a (butchy) woman. As the man unlocks one door in the hallway, never acknowledging the femme who accompanies him, implications of prostitution arise. As the butchy woman enters the next-door apartment with a bucket of tools, it becomes clear that she is a handyman.

Bound revisits and revises film noir. The protagonist, here a dyke rather than the conventional male, is an ex-con who gets talked into a *femme fatale*'s proposition to steal from the mob. The film's flashback structure, which originates from midway in the story, is supplemented by a flash forward that liberates the narrative's conclusion from film noir destiny. Camera angles, plot twists, character types, and other motifs enlist film noir conventions for neo-noir purposes. This essay first locates the *femme fatale* figure in films noirs and neo-noirs as a site of gender and genre turbulence and then, more particularly, analyzes the sexual *différance,* to invoke a Derridean concept, instigated by a lesbian butch-femme couple in *Bound.* I use the term *genre* because I am concerned with how film noir functions *now* as a remembered fictional world with characteristic conventions. Film noir's conspicuous lack of solidity and its tendency towards genre mixing can only serve my purpose here by suggesting a predisposition to the contemporary scatterings and fusions of neo-noir. My interest lies not in defining film noir but in its discursive valence. My description, at times necessarily generalizing, will conjure associations of "classic film noir." The majority of neo-noirs employ parody and pastiche in relation to film noir, although some attempt a continuation of the genre while others strive for a metaposition. Many elements, stylistic and thematic, that are associated with film noir now signal the genre even when embedded in other environments. I am particularly concerned in this respect with the *femme fatale,* whom film noir was unable to contain even in the 1940s and '50s.[2] I argue that today her presence has the ability to contribute a noirish quality to any genre. Moreover, film noir's femme (sexualized woman) today always connotes deadliness until proven otherwise. Such is the lasting strength and timeliness of the *femme fatale.*[3]

The *femme fatale* of contemporary film operates as an independent agent, always signaling but no longer contained by film noir. Today we watch women *from* film noir as often as *in* film noir. Perhaps the *femme fatale* always did transcend the film text if we recollect Janey Place's argument that viewers' memories privilege the *femme fatale*'s dangerously exciting incarnations over the defeats that most often awaited her in film noir conclusions (1998). Now the *femme fatale* is a metonym that travels among a variety of genres, summoning film noirness for atmospheric or hermeneutic effect.[4]

Ever since film noir's heyday in the 1940s and '50s, high femme characters not only carry the mark of sexuality but also stand charged with deceit and potential violence.[5] And yet the *femme fatale* has multiplied in meanings and possibilities, not only as a result of sociohistorical factors (for example, Alfred Kinsey's *Sexual Behavior in the Human Female* [1953]; the second-wave feminist movement) but also due to an increase of explicit, on-screen sexual imagery[6] and proliferating media representations of fictional and nonfictional female killers. In the days of classic film noir, the depiction of women as killers was unusual compared with the more recent prevalence of violent women, whether crazed or justified, in horror movies, cop shows, gangster films, thrillers, action adventures, and reality television. *Femmes fatales* now circulate in a cultural milieu that has been sexually aroused by *Goldfinger* (1964) and sensitized to domestic violence by *The Burning Bed* (1984). Even the male buddy film has been invaded by *Thelma and Louise* (1991), which extends rape-revenge fight-back to other pervasive acts of sexism.

The problematic of classic film noir included economic hardship as a (re-membered, existing, or possible) social condition. One logical response to class inequality and material desires is theft. Certainly the male protagonist's suscep-tibility to stealing schemes, fueled not only by the humdrum nature of his job, if he had one, but also by his otherwise unsuitability as the *femme fatale*'s mate, was sympathetically rendered, despite (and via) his fearful hesitations, practical concerns, and ethical anguish (Krutnik 1991). The sex-based underclass status of women, however, received little generic sympathy. That men remained women's primary conduit to economic status was overshadowed by the *femme fatale*'s criminal dealings; she answered sex-based inequity with sexual manipulation. In other words, the *femme fatale*'s greediness occasioned the (newly romantic) tough guy's responsibility, and his superego buckled under her clear thinking. Despite a façade of deference, the *femme fatale*'s take-charge decisiveness mobilized the narrative. Despite his masterminding attempts, the male protagonist was led to his destiny by the *femme fatale*. Ultimately, his psychological dimensionality yielded to her sexual dimension(s).

The radical intervention achieved by the original edition of *Women in Film Noir* (1978) three decades ago was its celebration of this male-imagined genre as a rare acknowledgement of female sexuality and power, i.e., of the *femme fatale* as an agent within the popular sexual economy. It is important to note, however, that the classic *femme fatale*'s lust was overwhelmingly for money rather than sexual pleasure.[7] Despite her sexualized image, economic ambition supplanted her libido and violence displaced sexual pleasure. The classic *femme fatale* was known for her trigger-happy killings, not her orgasms. Her sexuality *per se* was passive, limited to its allure. Although narratively she maneuvered the male protagonist with her sexuality, the sexual desire and pleasure it served belonged to the male.[8]

By contrast, the neo-noir *femme fatale* wants sexual pleasure as well as economic power. In *The Postman Always Rings Twice* (1946), platinum blond Cora (Lana Turner) trades in her older husband for the younger and more erotically appealing Frank (John Garfield), but in the film's remake (1981, with Jessica Lange) Cora not only gets off on rough sex but arouses herself manually while Frank (Jack Nicholson) is still getting into position—thus making her sexual goal explicit (to us as well as him). In *Double Indemnity* (1944), Phyllis (Barbara Stanwyck) teases Walter (Fred MacMurray) with double entendres, but in *Body Heat* (1981), black widow Matty (Kathleen Turner) entreats her lover-attorney Ned (William Hurt)—who thinks it was his idea to break through her door and have sex on the floor—"Yes, yes, yes. Please do it." The orgasmic *femme fatale* has become a staple of neo-noirs such as *Black Widow* (1986), *Fatal Attraction* (1987), *After Dark, My Sweet* (1990), *Basic Instinct* (1992), *Body of Evidence* (1992), *Romeo Is Bleeding* (1994), *The Last Seduction* (1994), *Diabolique* (1996), and *Lost Highway* (1997).[9]

In classic film noir, the *femme fatale* propelled the action, but her narrative options were numbered: she died, reformed, or turned out not to be a *femme fatale* after all.[10] Most adamantly, the *femme fatale* was denied romantic coupling. The implied author of film noir was morally superior to, yet sexually empathetic with, the male protagonist—an ambivalence that licensed the protagonist's confessional voice-over. The words of the unrepentant *femme fatale*, however, should not have been trusted in the first place. It is her duplicity that precludes romantic coupling in these films. Typically, after sharing in murder, the female-male partners-in-crime are destroyed by mutual, although dissimilar, distrust and disgust.[11] While the femme is clearly put off by the male protagonist's wimpishness more than the murder, it remains unclear whether his guilty conscience or his realization of her seductive deception (of him) is what turns him off. It appears likely that romantic union was impossible even before the unbearable (to him) crime occurred. In other words, the couple's downfall seems located in their individual characters rather than merely in their joint action. In classic film noir, the sexes do not complement and complete each other; instead, sexual attraction ignites a destructive combustion.

In fact, the male protagonist's desire for romantic coupling usually exceeded the *femme fatale*'s, who only deployed (false) promises of romantic permanence to secure his commitment to her crime. Although the male protagonist was often portrayed initially as a loner, his generic goals included coupling. Often, one of his primary dilemmas was whether to settle with the good woman or to follow the *femme fatale*.[12] The *femme fatale*'s coupling remained more problematic, presumably because she loved only herself. Perhaps it is our own commitment to romantic formulas that produces such speculations in the first place. But undoubtedly, the *femme fatale* intended to elude fulfillment in the American dream of home, family, and "security" (Harvey 1998). Within 1950s U.S. culture (not to mention Hollywood's long-standing obsession with romance), the fact that the femme really never wanted to couple, by itself, warranted her a narrative disadvantage.

The implied author of neo-noirs of the 1980s and '90s has tempered his self-righteousness and now, on occasion, seems capable of switching sexual affiliation. With this new flexibility in governing attitude, it becomes possible for shared crime to strengthen the bond between partners and fuel their sexuality. Of course, a male's attraction to a *femme fatale* still threatens his demise, as *Fatal Attraction* frantically emphasized. And, still, a male's nerve rarely matches that of the *femme fatale*: the willing vulnerability of Dan (Michael Douglas) during the final sex scene of *Basic Instinct* is a rare, and probably foolish, instance.

The reflexive remake *Gun Crazy* (1992) dares to postulate that impotence underlies the cowardliness of many film noir male protagonists and, further, that such impotence might respond favorably to a concentrated dose of middle-class fantasy. Prior sexual abuse by her surrogate father and high school boyfriends makes Anita (Drew Barrymore) amenable to the sexual impotence of her ex-con boyfriend, Howard (James LeGros). A rampage of violence stands in as surrogate consummation of their marriage (until the film's ending, when intercourse prepares the male protagonist for death). In other words, the displacement of sexuality onto violence, once primarily associated with the *femme fatale,* here accomplishes a phallic performance for the impotent male protagonist. Film noir's slippery signification between violence and sexuality extends its purview to the male protagonist, whose criminal involvement (or reservations) reads as compensatory for (or demonstrative of) sexual inadequacy. *Gun Crazy* further suggests that, just as the dream of upward mobility propels the *femme fatale's* violence, so might it animate the male protagonist's sexuality. When Anita and Howard hide out in a middle-class home, dressing up in the owners' clothing to watch vacation slides of the "legitimate" inhabitants, they at last succeed in having sex. The fantasy of class privilege makes them sexually functional. Immediately afterwards, however, the male protagonist offers his body for repetitive penetration by police bullets so that his now properly (de)sexualized wife might immortalize their short-lived romance via a (possible) teenage pregnancy.[13]

The most remarkable elaboration of the neo-noir *femme fatale* occurs in *The Last Seduction.* Bridgette (Linda Fiorentino), a hard-driving sales manager, has ambitions beyond corporate promotions. After getting her petty criminal husband to pull off a drug deal, she steals the payoff. Hiding out in a small town, she uses a good-looking country guy for sexual pleasure and exploits his romanticism to trick him into killing her husband. Naturally, the plan backfires because, when the two men realize who connects them, they can only commiserate. As a result, Bridgette has to kill the husband herself and frame her country stud for the murder. By taunting him with ill-gained knowledge of his sexual naïveté (during an earlier try at city living, he unwittingly married a transvestite), she makes him so angry that he rapes her. At the same time, she methodically arranges the phone so that the rape as well as a macho but untrue murder confession are overheard by an emergency telephone operator. *The Last Seduction* offers a prime example of neo-noir's implied author switching his sympathy from the male protagonist to the *femme fatale,* or, to put it another way, allowing his superego to lighten up. With resolute style, *The Last Seduction's femme fatale* rejects romance, claims abundant sexual satisfaction, and walks away free with the money.

The gun that the classic *femme fatale* carried coded her as phallic, but her masculinity was also demonstrated by a ball-busting dominance over her male lover. This gender reversal at the level of the couple (the combined result of each character's individual gender inversion) deconstructed yet maintained difference-based coupling. This couple was heterosexual and hetero-gender, but its gender difference did not align conventionally with its heterosexuality; rather, as a result

of each partner's flipping gender, the conventionally heterosexual couple supported an unconventional hetero-gender. In other words, this couple matched a
feminine man (challenged masculinity) with a masculine woman (*femme fatale*).
Now, decades later, this configuration facilitates a displacement/queering of binary
sex by binary gender in certain neo-noir (same-sex, hetero-gender) couplings.
Such coupling will inform my reading of *Bound*.

Classic film noir offered a variety of couples in addition to the emasculated
protagonist and phallic *femme fatale*. The coupling of a macho private eye and his
secretary (for example, in *Kiss Me Deadly*, 1955) relied on more traditional gender
roles. Unlike those that deployed gender reversal, this stereotypically gendered
couple upheld gender difference as well as sexual difference. Other noir couples
undermined gender difference via a certain equality that existed between partners. In the mutually attracted Humphrey Bogart and Lauren Bacall characters
of *Dark Passage* and *The Big Sleep*, an overlapping gender coupling (masculine
man and sexual femme) advocates a pleasant sexiness in sexual equality. In *Gilda*
(1946), Johnny (Glen Ford) and Gilda (Rita Hayworth) form an overlapping
gender couple (feminine man and sexual femme) that attributes a hateful sexiness to sexual equality (until the film's ending). Because a sexually inclined but
nonviolent femme does not fit exactly into either masculinity or femininity, she
makes a good match for a male protagonist who also steps out of gender. The
Bogart characters mentioned above were actively flirtatious and sexy in their
willingness to be caught, and Ford's Johnny was an erotic object himself. Rather
than simply being entrapped by her otherness, these male protagonists shared
some of the femme's qualities. Although the same-genders of these couplings
differ (the first pair being more masculine than the second), both challenge the
gender binary, for the better. The femme, as opposed to the phallic femme or the
feminine woman, can be read, albeit inadequately, with or against either gender.

The ability of gender to turn cartwheels on both male and female characters
within a system of sexual difference suggests that the notion of binary sex in the
broader culture (which does assume parallel sex and gender binaries) depends
on a tripartite structure obtained by doubling woman into whore and virgin,
masculine and feminine. Only via contrast with the feminine good girl, however
much she is relegated to the diegetic background, can film noir's male protagonist
maintain his claim to masculine gender next to the *femme fatale*. Although permanent romantic coupling is forbidden to the gender-inverted couple of classic
film noir (and often is problematized in the other configurations), all of the various gender couplings outlined above remain heterosexual. In this way, film noir
maintained difference-based coupling while deconstructing gender-sex alignment
and allowing for gender inversion, gender trading, and same-gender coupling.
Classic film noir established a scene of gender fluidity that now facilitates queer
readings of and representations in neo-noir.[14]

Fig. 16.1 Gender turns cartwheels on binary sex: Violet and Corky in a publicity still for *Bound* (1996)

Other scholars have deliberated on the same-sex configuration and its lesbian connotations in the neo-noir *Black Widow*, in which a data analyzer turned investigator (Debra Winger) is read as masculine in her hypo-feminine plainness next to the high femme spectacle of a black widow (Theresa Russell).[15] Because a (masculinized) woman holds the position of film noir's generic male protagonist in *Black Widow*, the film provides another instance of the phallic femme's gender versatility via a nonfeminine contrast with masculinity.[16] Here the *femme fatale* reads as the opposite of the masculine (woman) protagonist, although this opposition does not produce femininity per se in the *femme fatale*. While *Black Widow* might seem the obvious precursor to *Bound*, the vigorous femme and humbled male in *A Rage in Harlem* (1991) also warrant mention.[17]

A Rage in Harlem's clean-cut male protagonist Jackson (Forest Whitaker) is drawn into a dangerous criminal world by the seductive Imabelle (Robin Givens). From the beginning, Jackson is feminized in ways that support the film's comic aspects without reinstating traditional (white) gender roles.[18] He is infantilized not only by his short pants and by a picture of his mama hanging over his bed, but also by his religious sincerity and sexual naïveté. Although the other characters (as well as film viewers) question Jackson's dedication to Imabelle, it is unfaltering. Despite being ill-equipped for the mission of saving Imabelle from her threatening mobster man, Jackson doesn't abandon her, he doesn't give up on her, and he doesn't read her as duplicitous. He is steadfast in being her partner. His vulnerability, in fact, favorably competes with the macho maleness around them. Although Imabelle has the sexual experience and initiates sex with Jackson, and although this sex is followed (generically) by danger and criminal involvement, her affection for him and presumably her sexual satisfaction are eventually confirmed by the narrative. In what seems the ultimate move away from mainstream masculine representation, the sex scene displays his face in orgasmic abandon rather than hers. Yet, in no way does this display of vulnerability imply sexual impotence on his part or sexual dissatisfaction on hers.

A neo-noir built on the romance and gangster genres, *Bound* pushes gender revisions still further. Femme and butch lesbians Violet and Corky (Jennifer Tilly and Gina Gershon) meet in an elevator at the film's beginning, and drive away together in a new red truck at its end. Between these romantic bookends, they steal $2,000,000 that Violet's mobster boyfriend Ceasar (Joe Pantoliano) is laundering (figuratively and literally) for the mafia. They expect Ceasar to run when the evidence points towards him, thus freeing Violet from her position as a *kept* woman. Instead, Ceasar decides to fight it out in what he thinks is a duel of wits with the boss's son Johnnie.

Whether gangster or film noir protagonist, Ceasar is a parody of masculinity. He is absurdly gutsy, yet out of control. When he opens his briefcase and finds newspapers instead of the two million, the room spins around him. He talks frantically to himself while wrecking Johnnie's apartment in a vain search for the missing money. Later, after killing him, he shouts triumphantly into Johnnie's motionless face. Multiple plot twists tear Ceasar apart, yet he refuses to give up. Finally he discovers that Violet has crossed him, which leads to Corky's entrapment in the closet. He makes a final mistake, however, when he misjudges Violet. He refuses to believe that she is a *femme fatale.*

The primary enigma of *Bound* is its femme character. This is consistent with many films noirs and neo-noirs. From the point of view of Corky, who is both suspicious of and attracted to Violet, the crucial question is whether Violet is a *femme fatale* or a lesbian femme. Violet certainly comes on to Corky with a sex kitten voice, but, if she's a *femme fatale,* she might seduce Corky into crime and then double-cross her. This is why Corky declares that, although having sex with a stranger is fine, to steal with someone requires considerably more knowledge. That said, Corky joins Violet in crime shortly after sleeping with her. By stating the risk and then taking it, Corky enlists viewers in a familiar film noir hermeneutic. In an important shift, however, Corky faces the enigma not by scrutinizing Violet's criminality but rather by doubting her lesbian status.

In the femme-butch pairing of Violet and Corky, *Bound* puts pro-sex lesbian discourse and lesbian feminism into dialogue. The fact that Violet sleeps with men puts her lesbianism into question for Corky. Violet defines sex with men as work, but Corky sees duplicity. Violet claims to be a lesbian, but Corky can see only their difference. The implication is that, fatal or not, this femme is not trustworthy. Corky's lesbian feminism translates into a macho inclination to judge and delimit Violet's sexuality, until Violet proves that lesbian femmes are real lesbians too. She certifies this by shooting Ceasar.

Earlier I argued that classic film noir covered over women's sex-related economic disadvantage by portraying the *femme fatale* as greedy and crazy, as unexplainable. And yet there was in the femme's iconography the trace of a sex-specific economics. Because a sexualized woman, within a virgin-whore dichotomy, always hints at prostitution, the *femme fatale* contains an association with sex work. In *Bound* the connection between the *femme fatale* and sex work becomes tangible and, just as sex work can be made criminal, it can also motivate crime.

Corky and Violet are testing one another. Like Cora putting her life in Frank's hands by swimming as far as she can into the ocean with him in *The Postman Always Rings Twice,* Violet and Corky take part in a joint scheme that leaves each vulnerable to the other. Only at the end do they know for sure that they can trust each other. This knowledge is acquired through shared criminality but has larger implications. Violet is revealed to be both *femme fatale* and lesbian femme, duplicitous with men but not with Corky. And, in comparison with film noir's usual male protagonist, Corky offers a masculinity much more attractive to a femme. When Ceasar asks Violet, "What'd she do to you?" Violet answers, "Everything you couldn't."

Swaggering with a difference, Corky is a masculine partner worthy of romantic coupling. Her plan is not perfect and she wrongly predicts Ceasar's reaction to the set-up, but she is calm-headed and steady in her support of Violet. Although Violet does the killing, Corky doesn't get squeamish on her. She is not fearful, naïve, or moralistic about crime. She accepts and shares Violet's need and desire for money. Most importantly, Corky finally admits that she and Violet are alike, something Violet has been telling her all along. In contrast to film noir's male protagonist, who is sucked in by female sexuality, Corky knows Violet's desire. Unlike the classic *femme fatale,* Violet is knowable after all.[19] And, all along she was knowing.

Corky is engulfed by Violet's world. As Corky renovates the apartment next door, she hears Violet having sex with Ceasar and, later, another man. Violet says that the thin wall makes it like they are in the same room, suggesting voyeurism on Corky's part. Violet's neighborly displays of femininity—she brings coffee to Corky and requires her help after losing an earring down the sink—are transparent, flagrant flirtations. Corky is wise to them but nevertheless willing, ready with her own double entendres. When retrieving Violet's earring, Corky is framed in medium close-up with Violet's legs behind her. Then in extreme close-up, we see water slowly seep from the pipe she is twisting. In no time at all Corky's hand is up Violet's dress. That Violet put it there is no small detail, nor is her sexual responsiveness. She's been thinking of Corky all day, she says, and her wetness confirms it.

In what seems a parodic homage to the wet streets of film noir, fluidity inundates *Bound*. The lesbian bar that Corky visits in a failed attempt to get laid is named "The Watering Hole." When Violet first visits her, Corky is snaking out a bathtub drain. The sounds of a vicious beating move with agonizing clarity from Ceasar's toilet to Corky's. Sex and crime travel the same raunchy metaphor. In *Bound*, where there is no proper symbolic, action is restricted to a claustrophobic intersection of lesbian and mafia underworlds—just enough room for homosexuality to ruin a "family."[20]

One could build on psychoanalytic readings of film noir (Johnston 1998 and Doane 1991b) by interpreting the sex that Corky overhears as a primal scene and her replacement of Ceasar as Violet's lover as an oedipal overthrow. However, what I think is more important to understanding the *différance* of *Bound* is its impropriety, the anti-symbolic quality of its entire world. Corky's masculinity benefits from the lack of a symbolic father, and, most notably, appeals to femme sexuality. In addition to numerous tomboy poses, complete with baggy pants and dirty face, Corky's body is repeatedly put on erotic display, for example, in an overhead shot of her lying on her bed in jockey shorts and a side view of her modeled statuesquely while painting the ceiling. Like Johnny in *Gilda*, the camera finds Corky beautiful.[21]

Gilda and *The Big Sleep* can be seen as forerunners for the neo-noir coupling in *Bound*. These films combine difference and sameness to spark sexual attraction and secure romantic coupling. Equality between partners eventually enhances rather than destroys sexuality. *Bound* also blends difference and sameness. While Violet and Corky's femme-butch iconography destines them for an attraction of opposites,[22] their shared voice-over foreshadows compatibility. In contrast to the most cynical films noirs, such as *Double Indemnity* and *D.O.A.* (1950), in which dying men narrate bad-luck stories in flashback, Violet and Corky author a series of flash-forwards that puts a success story into motion.

Violet and Corky's criminal and romantic accomplishments derive from the exploitation of, rather than investment in, traditional sex roles. Even as she worries about Violet's trustworthiness, Corky urges her to manipulate Ceasar by crying and threatening to leave. Although Violet makes the threat and slaps Ceasar when he insinuates that Johnnie has bought her for two million dollars, she does not cry. Furthermore, Violet does not play housewife to Ceasar, nor does she help him wash and iron the bloodied money or clean up the living room after he slaughters Johnnie and his father. But she does stall the police, trick Ceasar, and sweet talk other mobsters to her advantage.

Bound combines the classic *femme fatale*'s predilection for gender disobedience with neo-noir's orgasmic female sexuality and then locates an equally evolved masculinity in the lesbian butch. During Violet and Corky's first conversation, Violet twice says, "my pleasure." For her, serving coffee is an aggressive move towards sexual pleasure. Although she does recruit Corky for a criminal partnership, she also wants to seduce her. Interestingly, despite Violet's short skirts and low-cut necklines, the breasts we finally see are Corky's. And, like Jackson's in *A Rage in Harlem*, Corky's openly displayed orgasm augments rather than disturbs a nouveau masculinity.

Bound deconstructs the sexual binary, not just through its queer coupling, but also through its complex rendering of feminist and lesbian discourse. Sexual difference theory, which many feminists and lesbians uphold, sees women and men as naturally different. As a consequence of this, an essential sameness is posited among women and another sameness among men. *Bound* ends on a statement that would support such an ideology. Butch Corky asks femme Violet, "Do you know what the difference is between you and me?" Violet answers, "No," to which Corky adds, "Me neither." The sameness embraced here celebrates their proven trust in one another. Through its narrative, *Bound* suggests that, in contrast to the heterosexual failings of classic film noir, women can trust one another. Because they are same sexed, lesbians make better partners in crime than heterosexual pairings. Moreover, this mutual trust allows for romantic coupling. But what prevents this sameness from desexualixing into sisterhood?

At the same time that *Bound* reproduces a lesbian feminist discourse, it counters it with femme-butch difference alongside female violence. Corky's masculinity suggests a difference from other women. But Violet, too, is unfeminine. A popular tenet in the sexual difference school is that men are inherently violent and women nonviolent. Violet's killing, then, fundamentally separates her from other women. Like *femmes fatales* before her, Violet is phallic. *Bound* complicates the binary of sameness versus difference, wrapping them around each other until there is only constantly varying relation. Violet and Corky's attraction rests on femme-butch difference; yet their sameness as women supports mutual trust. And, through this play of *différance* the film accomplishes a noir romance. In generic overkill, Violet plugs Ceasar with six bullets and leaves for a new world with Corky. Violet is both a *femme fatale* and a lesbian femme.

The classic *femme fatale* was a significant building block for the contemporary attack on binaries. This force should not be attributed solely to her phallic gun. Although her active sexuality was displaced onto violence, the *femme fatale*'s status

as femme paved the way for neo-noir's orgasmic femme through its difference
from and deferral of *both* femininity and masculinity. But *différance* doesn't produce freedom, just play. Similarly, genre relies simultaneously on both variation
and repetition. So, *Bound* ends on a joke. No sooner are we freed by Violet and
Corky's gender insurrection than stereotypes spring back into play with Tom
Jones singing "She's a Lady" over the ending credits. "I can leave her on her own,
knowing she's OK alone, and there's no messin.'" "Will they never learn?" the film
seems to ask with this ironic reminder of masculine ego. "She knows what I'm
about; She can take what I dish out, and that's not easy." But miscalculations can
be fatal. "Talkin' about the little lady."

Notes

1. A double-edged axe used by pre-patriarchal Amazon women, adopted as an identity
symbol by lesbian feminists in the 1970s.

2. *The Paradine Case* (1948) exemplifies the black widow in a courtroom drama.

3. On neo-noir, see Erikson 1996, Grist 1995, and Palmer 1994.

4. *The Crying Game* (1992) offers an unfortunate example: the murder of Jude (Miranda
Richardson) is naturalized by her coding as a film noir spider woman. See Kotsopoulos
and Mills 1994.

5. These associations are narratively powerful whether true or false. In *Body of Evidence*
(1992), Madonna's casting as an S/M dominatrix caricatures her presumed identity as a
black widow who killed her older love with a sexual overdose. In *Blood Simple* (1984),
Ray (John Getz) automatically assumes that his lover Abby (Frances McDormand) is a
killer because her husband (Dan Hedaya) earlier described her as duplicitous, whereas,
far from fatal, she experiences the film's diegesis as gothic.

6. Although classic film noir was praised for its erotic daring, Marc Vernet argues that
it was at most a return to pre-Code standards. This is succinctly demonstrated by a photo
from the 1931 version of *The Maltese Falcon*, which he captions, "The *femme fatale*, as she
will never be shown in the 1940s and 1950s: in the detective's bed" (1993, 13).

7. Only a portion of film noir's femmes were *femmes fatales*. See Walker (1995, 12) and
Martin (1998). At the same time, the sexuality of femmes separated them from the genre's
domestic good girls. Within a virgin-whore dichotomy, *femmes fatales* and femmes (sexual
women) occupy the same endpoint. That we remember the *femme fatale* as a dominant
generic character speaks to the believed danger of female sexuality. Thus, even when she
is not murderous, the noir femme triggers suspicion and fear.

8. A half-hearted twist to this paradigm occurs in *Detour* (1945), with Vera (Ann Sav-
age) blackmailing Al (Tom Neil) rather than controlling him sexually. In one scene she
acts disgruntled when he refuses to accompany her into the bedroom, but not nearly so
disappointed as when she is unable to buy a fur.

9. Many neo-noir *femmes fatales* retain a traditional use of sex primarily to manipulate
men, for example, in *Final Analysis* (1992). Arguably, although such films update the genre
in other respects, their *femmes fatales* are more classic than neo. Conversely, many neo-
noir femmes who use their sexuality to manipulate men also actively gratify themselves
in the process, for example, in *Red Rock West* (1992) and *Body Heat*.

10. In such films as *The Big Sleep* (1946) and *Dark Passage* (1947), the *femme fatale* im-

plications of Lauren Bacall's characters were crucial to the audaciously sexy Bogart-Bacall star couple, yet eventually required denial to secure romantic coupling at the narrative's conclusions.

11. In *Red Rock West,* such a partnership precedes the film's beginning. Once viewers realize why a husband and wife want to knock each other off—for the money they earlier stole together—the generic partners-in-crime plot with all its sexual promise and final bitterness flashes into relevance. Because the original partnership and crime predates the film's beginning, *Red Rock West* reads like a sequel. This shorthand referencing, which immediately fleshes out the characters' motivations and frees the film's main protagonist from conventional plot obligations, provides another instance of metonymic play in neo-noir.

12. *Out of the Past* (1947) provides the ultimate example via the starkly contrasting *femme fatale* Kathie (Jane Greer) and the hometown girl and confidante Ann (Virginia Huston). In the film's pastoral beginning, Jeff (Robert Mitchum) is courting Ann; then his past reclaims him for *amour fou* with Kathy. *Raw Deal* (1948) foregrounds the element of choice but bends the formula. Joe (Dennis O'Keefe) is sprung from jail by his girlfriend Pat (Claire Trevor) but then falls for the good girl Ann (Marsha Hunt). Joe eventually dies in Ann's arms after turning her into a killer.

13. This contrasts with an equally ironic twist in *Fargo* (1996), a neo-noirish mid-western in which a small-town woman police officer kills nonchalantly as part of the job, all the while obviously pregnant.

14. Queer readings have also been performed on classic film noir. See Dyer 1998a; Dyer 1998b; Johnston 1998; Buchsbaum 1995; and Corber 1997.

15. See Holmlund 1993 and de Lauretis 1990. *Jagged Edge* (1995) offers a further role reversal: the woman lawyer (Glenn Close), with a past and lustful for sex, is attracted to male black widower (Jeff Bridges). In both *Black Widow* and *Jagged Edge* the conventionally male investigator's role is held by a woman whose sexual desire challenges her progress.

16. Again, femme is distinguished from feminine. Whereas the femme is defined as sexual, femininity requires its domestication. Elsewhere, I argue for an understanding of the femme (the actively sexual woman, whether straight or lesbian) that differs significantly from the theorization of femininity as masquerade, for example, by Mary Ann Doane (1991a, 17–32), following Joan Riviere (1966, 213). See chapter 5 of my book, *Deviant Eyes, Deviant Bodies: Sexual Re-Orientations in Film and Video* (1996).

17. For a discussion of *A Rage in Harlem* (film and book) in relation to the differing functions of blackness, see Diawara 1993.

18. Chester Himes's novel, on which the film is based, contained a more elaborate complication of gender, but the film does retain some serious gender disordering. Although often slapstick, the film's comic aspects—which exceed gender issues—are not self-derogatory. The film seems to celebrate a history of black comic performance without totally converting film noir into comedy.

19. On the (un)knowability of the woman in *Gilda,* which I posit as a precursor to *Bound,* see Doane (1991b) and Dyer (1998a). For Doane, Gilda demonstrates "the difficulty posed by the woman as a threat to (phallocentric) epistemological systems" (118). Doane compares the narrative's revelation of Gilda as a good girl after all to the striptease, which ultimately reveals the naturalness of women's nakedness; and yet, Doane argues that this quest for knowledge fails because the film's ending lacks credibility and because Gilda is inseparable from her appearance/act (106–8). Also noting the phallocentric character of cultural knowledge, Dyer states: "Any film that allows us to 'know' the *femme fatale,* not

in the way the hero comes to know her (i.e., by having knowledge of her, finally controlling her), but in the way we 'know' all major characters in novelistic fiction, is making
trouble for itself. Once the woman is not the eternal unknowable, the hitherto concealed
inadequacy of the hero is liable to become evident. This is what happens in *Gilda*" (116).
In *Bound*, Ceasar's death is the exact point between his misjudging and knowing Violet.
It is also the point at which Corky (along with the viewer) knows Violet as a *femme fatale*.
This knowledge, however, does not impinge on Corky's adequacy as criminal or romantic
partner, nor on Violet's qualification as a lesbian femme (if the stereotype of lesbians as
man-haters still holds any valence).

20. See Harvey (1998) for a discussion of film noir's attack on "dominant social values
normally expressed through the representation of the family" (36). And "family," of course,
carries mafia connotations.

21. See Dyer (1998a) for a discussion of the feminization of Johnny in *Gilda*.

22. Providing an in-joke for many lesbians in the audience, Susie Bright, a high femme
icon in her own right, is listed in the credits as technical adviser. This raises the issue of
authorship. Just as it was ironic that the collected authors of the first edition of *Women
in Film Noir* discovered an image of powerful, sexual women in the male-imagined genre
of film noir, my identification of lesbian discourse in male-directed neo-noir is ironic.
Rather than ask if or how men might produce such a discourse, I take as my starting point
a recognition that contemporary lesbian discourse has now entered the mainstream to the
extent that it not only can serve as subject matter but also can contribute to a theatrical
film's intertextual make-up.

CHAPTER 17

"THE GAY COWBOY MOVIE":

QUEER MASCULINITY ON BROKEBACK MOUNTAIN

STEVEN COHAN

Before *Brokeback Mountain* opened theatrically in December 2005, commercial prospects were uncertain for "this ostensible gay Western," as Todd McCarthy (2005) called it when reviewing the film at the Telluride film festival for *Daily Variety*. The gay male demographic was assured, of course, but the film's potential to attract a crossover audience remained an open question. "With critical support," McCarthy observed, "Focus [Films] should have little trouble stirring interest among older, sophisticated viewers in urban markets, but trying to cross this risky venture over into wider release reps a marketing challenge for the ages; paradoxically, young women may well constitute the group that will like the film best."

Following its premiere in several of those urban markets, reviews of *Brokeback Mountain* appreciated its groundbreaking gay story as far as Hollywood was concerned, but, in describing the film's achievement, these reviews treated it as a contemporary equivalent of a 1940s social problem film, with homophobia succeeding the postwar era's anti-Semitism or racism as the pressing issue. This framework resulted from the circumstantial timing of the film's release upon the heels of the gay marriage debate as well as the coincidental resemblance of the *Brokeback* narrative—in the Wyoming setting, the death of Jack Twist—to the brutal hate-crime killing of Matthew Shepard. The *New York Times*'s Stephen Holden (2005) concluded his favorable review by reminding his readers: "'Brokeback Mountain' is not quite the period piece that some would like to imagine. America's squeaky closet doors may have swung open far enough for a gay rodeo circuit to flourish. But let's not kid ourselves. In large segments of American society, especially in sports and the military, those doors remain sealed. The murder of Matthew Shepard, after all, took place in 'Brokeback' territory."

A few weeks later, as *Brokeback Mountain* successfully broadened out across the country, the mainstream press and Internet news sites tried to account for the unexpected popularity beyond urban markets of what had by this point become widely known as "the gay cowboy movie." By now, however, its social currency as a period study of internalized homophobia with contemporary significance had pretty much disappeared from the national coverage, which seemed to condense into the "gay cowboy movie" tag all reference to the same-sex desire driving the central relationship of Ennis Del Mar (Heath Ledger) and Jack Twist (Jake Gyllenhaal). The consensus among commentators, as McCarthy had predicted, was that straight women, packing the multiplexes in all locations, whether attending alone, with friends, or with begrudging husbands and dates, readily "got" the film, whereas straight men did not—or they were afraid to.

In confirmation of the heterosexual panic that this film could instill in straight men, the gay cowboy jokes began as soon as *Brokeback Mountain* opened at year's end, too. The jokes provided fodder for TV comics and cartoonists, while expressing indignation at this film's apparent sullying of both a cherished icon of masculinity and the myth of the American West as celebrated by the movies.

From this twinned perspective of *Brokeback Mountain*'s seemingly axiomatic appeal to women on the one hand and the homophobic disavowal of that appeal through the gay cowboy jokes on the other, the public discourse recounting audience responses to the film heterosexualized its affect according to gender. Regardless of their sex, engaged viewers were feminized through their emotional reaction to the film, while alienated viewers, including those who refused to buy a ticket, were masculinized. Both gendered responses, moreover, were positioned at a distance from the homoerotic intensity driving the narrative of *Brokeback Mountain*: if the masculinized audience simply could not get past the tent on the mountain and made fun of the movie's cowboys for acting upon their homosexual desire, the feminized audience looked beyond the cowboys' homosexual desire to appreciate the love story's universality. Singly and in conjunction, these two configurations of the audience articulated the impact of *Brokeback Mountain* as a cultural event in terms of what it signified for heterosexuals, respecting the hegemony of a straight mainstream marketplace.

In what follows I examine how the "gay cowboy movie" tag condensed the slippages in thinking required to sustain this dualism, which structured accounts of the film's reception. Because the tag's indelible attachment to *Brokeback Mountain* carried with it implications of mockery and scorn, the tag became the banner cry of those most offended by the film's supposed repudiation of John Wayne and the Marlboro Man. Likewise, the tag was indirectly referenced by assertions from the other side of the gender divide that, as a universal love story, *Brokeback Mountain* was much more than a gay movie. Nevertheless, the tag's omnipresence in the public discourse about *Brokeback* also interrupted this dominant account of its reception by refocusing attention on the film's homoerotic specificity, which is, after all, what audiences *were* responding to in one way or another, whether crying at, not being moved by, or mocking the central love story, and however differently they articulated their responses. It is in this context, I argue, that *Brokeback Mountain* worked most effectively as a "gay cowboy movie."

According to author Annie Proulx, the "gay cowboy" tag began with her story's publication, and it disregards the careful attention she pays to the destructive impact, viewed internally and socially, of the closet. From her perspective, the "gay cowboy" tag misidentifies the two main characters just as it obscures her intention. When writing about the transformation of her short story into a film, Proulx emphasizes that her two leading characters cannot be considered bona fide cowboys:

> Both wanted to be cowboys, be part of the Great Western Myth, but it didn't work out that way; Ennis never got to be more than a rough-cut ranch hand and Jack Twist chose rodeo as an expression of cowboy. Neither of them was ever a top hand, and they met herding sheep, animals most real cowpokes despise. Although they were not really cowboys (the word 'cowboy' is often used derisively in the west by those who do ranch work), the urban critics dubbed it a tale of two gay cowboys. No, it is a story of destructive rural homophobia. (2005, 130)

Proulx's dismissal of the "gay cowboy" tag applies equally well to the film version. Although set in the West, it is generically not a western, and although Ennis and Jack exist on the fringes of cowboy life as traditionally represented on film—ranches and rodeos—they are not working as cowboys the summer they fall in love on Brokeback Mountain. When accepting the BAFTA award for best film, *Brokeback Mountain* coproducer and Focus Films head James Schamus felt obliged to reject what he called "this terrible epithet of the gay cowboy movie," replacing it with another joke: "It truly is a universal story of two gay shepherds. It's a gay shepherd movie" (Dawtrey 2006). But neither are Ennis and Jack *gay* cowboys—or *gay* shepherds, for that matter—at least not in the sense that the term "gay" has come to mean having an acknowledged, active, and eroticized if not politicized homosexual identity.

Responding to the negative implications of the "gay cowboy" tag, Schamus's "gay shepherds" joke at the BAFTA ceremony typifies how, in managing the film's nationwide release, the marketing by Focus ended up overlaying *Brokeback Mountain* with contradictory impressions. The marketing discretely acknowledged the film's homoerotic subject matter but emphasized, along with the critical praise and accumulation of awards leading up to the Oscars, the film's universal appeal. In this regard, its inclusion in the lineups at the Telluride, Venice, and Toronto festivals several months before the U.S. release was crucial for Focus's initial marketing. "Before Venice," Schamus remembered, "'Brokeback Mountain' was more or less a late night TV joke—by the end of the festival, its reception in Venice had given it invaluable credibility" (Saperstein 2006). To achieve credibility as a film that could then cross over from Landmark cinemas to AMC and Regal megaplexes, however, meant shifting its generic categorization from art film, which could accommodate its gay subject matter, to romance, which could not do so as easily.

Here, numerous comparisons of *Brokeback Mountain* to *Titanic* (1997), both in statements made by people at Focus and journalists, helped to direct the progress of that crossover and to manage further the terms by which the film appeared more heterocentric as a story of doomed romance. "From early on," one writer for MSNBC.com noted, "Focus said the film was aiming for the same female fans with upscale tastes who loved 'Titanic'" (Schrobsdorff 2006). In fact, it was not too long before Internet bloggers began to point out the striking, and it appears from interviews, intentional resemblance between the poster art for the two films. "The people who marketed *Titanic* didn't call it 'the greatest straight love story ever made,' so why should we call this 'a great gay love story,'" Schamus stated during one of his many interviews, "especially since anyone who sees the trailer knows exactly what it is? We're very straightforward about everything in the film. We don't shade anything" (quoted in Sterritt 2006).

At the same time, Schamus admitted he agreed in part with Daniel Mendelsohn (2006), whose piece in the *New York Review of Books* shortly before the Oscar ceremony critiqued the film's marketing and reception for evading its poignant study of homophobia. "It tells a distinctively gay story that happens to be so well told that any feeling person can be moved by it," Mendelsohn wrote. "If you insist, as so many have, that the story of Jack and Ennis is OK to watch and sympathize with because they're not really homosexual—that they're more like the heart of America than like 'gay people'—you're pushing them back into the closet." Replying to this critique, Schamus acknowledged, "In many responses to the movie . . . a 'logic of displacement' has been at work. People say it's not [really] a gay movie; it's a romance. But it's not a question of one or the other—the movie is both" (quoted in Sterritt 2006, original brackets).

Schamus said much the same in a letter published in the *New York Review of Books* that addressed Mendelsohn's criticism point by point. While recognizing the "telling and disturbing logic that underlies and legitimizes a great deal of the public discourse surrounding the film," Schamus reasoned that Mendelsohn's piece betrayed his nervousness "about what happens when a gay text is so widely and enthusiastically embraced by mainstream hetero-dominated culture." The producer then clarified how he understood the purpose of the marketing: "we solicit every audience member's *identification with* the film's central gay characters; the film succeeds if it, albeit initially within the realm of the aesthetic, *queers* its audience. But in so doing, it paradoxically figures its gayness not just as a concretely situated identity, but also as a profound and emotionally expansive experience, understandable by all" (Schamus et al. 2006, original emphasis). This claim, however, returns Schamus to the contradictory impression of the film solicited by the marketing—the "paradoxical" figuration of gayness as both specific and universal. Furthermore, Schamus's claim sidesteps how, in mediating the film's reception, the public discourse surrounding *Brokeback Mountain* also scripted the terms by which such identification with Ennis and Jack was often articulated (by audiences and for audiences) and did so in order to disavow the queer desire with which audiences were identifying.

The "logic of displacement" to which Schamus alludes produces heterosexual-ized depictions of the film's powerful affect by making the male couple's sexual desire for each other fade into the background as a mere circumstantial detail. When George W. Bush admitted to a college student that he had not seen *Brokeback Mountain* but would be happy to talk about ranching, Oscar blogger and freelance writer Sasha Stone (2006) wrote an open letter to him in the *Santa Monica Mirror*:

> Mr. President, [Ang Lee] did not make a movie about gay cowboys; he made a movie about loneliness, isolation, and not living in a world that accepts you as you are. . . . You won't find a better acted, emotionally moving, universal love story than this one. After about fifteen minutes you aren't watching two men together so much as you're watching how living a life that is a lie can destroy everyone around you. . . . It is my hope, Mr. President, that you will take the time to open your heart and mind to Brokeback Mountain. You will be the better for it—a better husband, a better father, a better man.

As Stone's testimony indicates, writers for the mainstream press as well as Internet news sites explained why, with its emphasis on male emotions and relationships as well as male vulnerability and suffering, *Brokeback Mountain* had immediate appeal for women because it stirred recognizable emotions yet could, at the same time and as part of that appeal, be instructive for men.

The campaign to draw women to the film's romantic melodrama succeeded, as Choire Sicha (2005) in the *New York Observer* predicted it would do shortly before the first limited runs began. After all, she wrote, "it's men being victimized by society . . . which superimposes an erotic of powerlessness on the chiseled rodeo riders. It's the horse opera become pomo soap opera." And she was right. Once *Brokeback Mountain* was in wide release, a Gannet syndicated article reported on the "Brokeaholics" phenomenon, noting that women as well as gay men were "deeply affected" by the film. One woman wrote to the reporter in an email: "It's like experiencing a color I'd never seen before . . . I am in a quandary as to why I feel elation, a certain weightiness in the chest and tightening at the throat and euphoria over this picture. I guess—to quote director Ang Lee—it is the 'unique and universal love story' aspect that touches my heart" (Baxter, 2006). That very kind of language prompted a nurse to write a clever etiology of "Brokeback Fever" on ADVANCE for Nurses Online, the Web site of a journal for the nursing pro-fession. "Symptoms include obsessive thinking about the award-winning motion picture, disturbed sleep patterns, weeping, sobbing, and a need to discuss the movie endlessly with family, friends, and coworkers" (Nicoll 2006).

The film's reported appeal as a "chick flick" because of its two doomed same-sex lovers likewise determined why straight males were then believed to perceive *Brokeback Mountain* as some sort of threat due to its obvious "ick factor" (Pitts 2006). As Ruby Rich notes, "the 'chick flick' accusation . . . allowed pundits to dismiss the film without charges of homophobia," despite the way, in its masculinist dismissal of the chick-flick genre (the granddaughter of the woman's film), the label "conflated homophobia with misogyny" (Rich 2007, 46).[1] Alternatively, as if in repudiation of that illiberal response, more "sensitive" and younger men were discovered to openly embrace *Brokeback* as "a test of [their] hipness," since attending the film enabled them to show off their ability to talk about "vulnerability" with their dates afterward; and some of these men even entertained "nonsexual crushes" on Heath Ledger, who, as one young straight man gushed to *USA Today,* "makes being a cowboy look awesome again" (della Cava 2006).

Echoing Stone and reading the film in terms of the contemporary era of metrosexuality, male writers chimed in to point out that *Brokeback* could teach all men something valuable about their masculinity. "It's not the sex but the emotion" that made men fearful of watching the film, wrote one commentator in the *Salt Lake City Tribune* (Pitts 2006). Another explained in the *Chicago Tribune* that *Brokeback Mountain* shows "the bravery of submitting to the heart," which he stated is "troubling to the guys" because they think that "the people who are seeing [the film] will expect" that same bravery from "their husbands, boyfriends, brothers, and sons. . . . It is wonderfully deft that a film about the archetypal male—the cowboy—exposes the central weakness of masculinity. When it comes to connection, men are the weaker sex" (Tapley 2006). Yet put quite another way, as co-screenwriter Larry McMurtry (2006) declared on the *CBS News Sunday Morning* show shortly before the Oscars, the film's meaning for men could be summarized in a simple statement: "Life is not for sissies."[2]

McMurtry's reduction of the film's meaning to that message seems especially charged to me in its ambiguity. On the surface and reiterating the story's universality, he appears to be stating the truism that life—or even love, as he went on to modify the message—is hard for men who lack the proper manly virtues of strength, fortitude, and stoicism. Does he therefore mean that Ennis survives whereas Jack dies because Ennis is not a sissy? Or that Ennis suffers because he is the sissy? Or, given how the word "sissy" still conflates gender and sexuality to equate effeminate men with being gay, that it's really tough being a homo on the range? The "gay cowboy movie" tag packs together all these possibilities insofar as the tag highlights how *Brokeback*'s depiction of queer male desire—at once open (on the mountain and its surrogate locations) and closeted (in town and with family)—draws its powerful affect from the instability of masculinity in the twenty-two-year span of the narrative as embodied in the figure of the movie cowboy.

Writing in *Daily Variety,* Henry Sheehan (2006), a TV-radio film critic and president of the Los Angeles Film Critics Association, pointed out how *Brokeback Mountain* does indeed conform to the western genre at least in thematic and visual terms. With its "two cowboys . . . suffering a fate that's endemic to the modern Western," Sheehan observed, the film reflects the dissipation of "the regenerative power of the wide-open Western spaces," so it is "simply another step along this Western route" traced by earlier films set after the closing of the frontier, notably

Hud (1963), *The Ballad of Cable Hogue* (1970), and *Comes a Horseman* (1978). To make his case that "it's the freed-up ability of its characters to bond that informs the genre," Sheehan also effaces the gayness of these two cowboys even while recognizing the extent to which "the urban strictures are, this time, sexual rather than social or economic." His conclusion about *Brokeback*'s ultimate significance is that, as a western, a genre not traditionally showered with year-end awards and honors, its "uniqueness resides more in the number of its Oscar nominations than its themes or story."

Nonetheless, at least in terms of the time period of the *Brokeback* narrative, Sheehan makes a valid point about its relation to the modern-day western. Like the short story, *Brokeback Mountain* begins in 1963, which saw the release of *Hud,* based on a novel by McMurtry, its antiheroic cowboy starkly contrasting with the ideological nostalgia for the western frontier celebrated by a much bigger hit, *How the West Was Won* (1962); and *Brokeback* closes in 1984, the year after both *Terms of Endearment* (1983), yet another adaptation of a McMurtry novel, and *The Right Stuff* (1983) showed how the astronaut had displaced the cowboy in iconic value. Schamus's joke at BAFTA notwithstanding, the cowboy does serve, textually and extra-textually, to supply the socioeconomic as well as filmic referential backdrop for Ennis and Jack who both, as Proulx states, "wanted to be part of the Great Western Myth" even though "it didn't work out that way." And because they are failed cowboys in the landscape of the western genre, what remains all the more "awesome" about Ennis and Jake, to borrow the term from that guy with a nonsexual crush on Heath Ledger, is that their queer desire never emasculates or feminizes them. These men are not sissies.

Even so, McMurtry's comment about the film's "simple" meaning that "life is not for sissies" helps to contextualize the omnipresence of all those gay cowboy jokes, the point of which was in large part to show up the gay cowboy as a sissy and thus make fun of the homosexual desire of the two *Brokeback* cowboys; if that desire were made unmanly it could not imply anything about the manliness of "real" men. The jokes by Jay Leno, David Letterman, and the like, along with news articles reporting on them, effectively turned the gay cowboys of *Brokeback* into rhinestone cowboys on Rodeo Drive.[3]

In much the same spirit as the jokes, at this same time numerous mashups, combining *Brokeback* and iconic films from the past several decades, appeared on Internet sites such as YouTube. Numerous fan and blogging sites announced the mashups as soon as they were discovered and provided links, thereby increasing their visibility. By recutting footage from other male genre films to the music and advertising copy of the trailer for *Brokeback Mountain,* these mashups humorously "outed" such films as *Top Gun* (1986), and the *Back to the Future, Star Wars,* and *Lord of the Rings* trilogies.[4]

Offering another perspective on this type of humor, the Web site Low Culture (2006) paid satiric homage to the *Brokeback Mountain* gay cowboy jokes through a semi-fictitious excavation of their presence in history and politics as well as the movies throughout the twentieth century. Surveying a supposed hundred years of *Brokeback Mountain* jokes, this piece mixes prose with advertising imagery, magazine covers, cartoons, and TV frame captures (some obviously invented, some tweaked with Photoshop, some genuine and recognizable as the twentieth century reached its end and the next one began). In recognition of the jokes' omnipresence during the wide release of and coverage about *Brokeback,* Low Culture offers what amounts to a winking queer reading of the dominance of male bonding in U.S. culture, whether the pairings are Theodore Roosevelt and his vice president in a tent, Bob Hope and Bing Crosby in "Road to Brokeback Mountain," or Fozzy Bear and Rowlf in a "Furbank Mountain" segment of *The Muppet Show.* The satire similarly imagines Will Rogers returning from Brokeback Mountain to say he never met a man he didn't like, Orson Welles and Herman Mankiewicz working a *Brokeback Mountain* joke into *Citizen Kane* (1941, only to have RKO insist "that their reference to 'stemming the rose' be changed to 'rosebud'"), and speculates that the missing minutes on Richard Nixon's White House tapes were devoted to *Brokeback Mountain* jokes made by H. R. Haldeman. With the publication of Proulx's short story in 1997, the anonymous writers note, "Centuries of gay cowboy jokes finally make sense." If the gay cowboy jokes and mashups can then be said to have reached their crescendo, it was at the 2006 Academy Awards. In his opening monologue, which until 2007 had been posted on YouTube, host Jon Stewart sounded the same note as the mashups but made more pronounced his debunking of the notion that *Brokeback Mountain* purportedly "tarnishes the noble western tradition, rugged men who represent the heterosexual ideal." Before cuing to a montage of clips edited to prove otherwise about that "noble" tradition, Stewart insisted with his version of a straight face that there is "nothing remotely gay in the classic Hollywood westerns." After the montage he confessed that he didn't really know what his point was except that Charlton Heston was *really* cut when in his prime, wasn't he?

Rather like Low Culture's pseudo-historical survey of the gay cowboy jokes, the Oscar montage and mashups all appeared to recognize what academic critics, going back to Leslie Fiedler's influential reading of Huck Finn and Jim, have long claimed is the homoerotic current in buddy narratives, where the close bonding of men traveling in, working on, or escaping to the frontier, be it the West or in space, gives way to implied sexual expressions of that bond, crossing over into what culture still views as the final frontier. Yet unlike the Low Culture satire, the Oscar montage and mashups were more easily recuperable as innocent genre parodies insofar as they followed the same strategy of disavowal that characterized the omnipresent gay cowboy jokes: it's there all right, but if we twit it then it's not, not really, since now the joke's no longer on *us.*

Yet even with that apparent safety net, and as the Low Culture satire implied, the Oscar montage and mashups of *Brokeback Mountain* made more immediately visible what in fan fiction communities has long been the "slash" rewriting of buddy genres in film and on T.V.[5] In fact, the mashups were simply playing out in video form the same gay subtext that many female fan writers have long been exposing or teasing out of their favorite same-sex couples, first in fanzines and now on the Internet; their slash fiction offers an often astute perception of the homoerotic affection between two male characters. While this was not necessarily their intention, the mashups recognized how, as a gay cowboy movie, *Brokeback Mountain* may even make slash pairings obsolete—it's now there on the surface and not buried in subtext. That the film delivers the same fantasy of homoerotic affect that slash writers have found in buddy narratives and then expanded upon in their fan fiction may well have been a considerable factor behind the strong female interest in this "horse opera become pomo soap opera." Its imagery of two attractive young male stars coupling delivered what Choire Sicha (2005) also called "emotional porn, an array of hot, spread-eagled men with feelings." Female slash writers often render such a vivid impression of homoeroticized masculinity, of men whose intimacy—not necessarily "spread-eagled" but nonetheless narrativized in spatial terms, be it the close confinement of a space craft or a sleeping bag—gives rise to expression of their "feelings." That eruption of suppressed emotionality, the countercurrent of the "hard" masculinity of the buddy action film, is likewise what the mashups parody. For that matter, it is also what *Brokeback* itself displays selectively and in moments of solitude, as when Ennis leaves Jack after their summer together on the mountain.

In keeping national attention focused, even if not always directly, upon the homoerotic content of *Brokeback Mountain,* the "gay cowboy movie" tag reversed the "logic of displacement" otherwise governing the universalizing discourse constructing the public reception of *Brokeback Mountain.* The tag may misrepresent *Brokeback* in some respects, but it nonetheless registered the impact of homophobia as well as the power of homoerotic desire dramatized by the film's narrative, and it does so thrice over: as a mocking or disdainful epithet, as a prod to interrogate the precarious heteromasculinity enforcing that homophobia, and as a constant reminder of the homoerotic intensity driving the passion and suffering of the film's two central characters.

However much everyone involved in the making and promotion of *Brokeback Mountain* tried to quit themselves from the "gay cowboy movie" label, the tag was consequently a significant index of the film's impact as a cultural event. As the unavoidable sign of its resistance to being universalized, the tag epitomized how *Brokeback* never entirely relieved audiences of the burden of confronting the specificity with which its closeted lovers play out their love story in the landscape of the movie western. Ennis and Jack may be shepherds when *Brokeback* begins, but their marginalized socioeconomic position as wannabe cowboys bound to each other sexually and emotionally gives historical as well as ideological weight to their queer desire. This is the reason why their desire does not make them less

manly but instead challenges notions of masculinity, straight or queer, to mark
the fissures and contradictions within it; why their desire can only be imagined
as a utopian fantasy of erotic liberation on Brokeback Mountain; and why, with
the cowboy figure's cultural value diminished by the 1980s, the film instead offers
Ennis a token of redemption through fatherhood, in contrast with the short story,
which begins and ends with him awakening from a dream about Jack. As Ang
Lee said to a colleague after one of the first screenings, "this movie was special
. . . because this is really a cowboy film" (quoted in Sterritt 2006).

Notes

1. As Rich's title—"Brokering *Brokeback*: Jokes, Backlashes, and Other Anxieties"—suggests, her discussion overlaps mine insofar as we share a concern with showing how the
public discourse surrounding *Brokeback* mediated the film's reception, but Rich is interested in examining how that discourse "slotted" responses "into the relevant categories of
tolerance, antagonism, or ridicule," and not gender specifically (2007, 47).

2. McMurtry offered this summary to explain why he thought the controversy elicited
by the film "for its gay cowboy plot" was "off-base." "It doesn't present any kind of agenda,
any politics at all, one way or the other at all. It just says life is not for sissies." Elaborating,
he said, "You need strength; love is not easy. . . . It's not easy if you find (it), it's not easy
if you don't find it. It's not easy if you find it but it doesn't work out. It merely says the
strong survive, but not everybody is strong" (parenthesis in original).

3. See, for instance, "Ridin,' Ropin,' Redecoratin' and Jokin' on the Late Shows," and
Susan Wiuoszczyna, "Film Spurs Culture of Gay Cowboy Jokes," both in *USA Today*
January 25, 2006, at www.usatoday.com (accessed January 26, 2006); and "Did You Hear
the One About 'Brokeback'?" *Yahoo! Movies,* February 6, 2006, at www. movies.yahoo
.com (accessed February 7, 2006).

4. The mashups also were covered by the press: see Virginia Heffernan, "Brokeback
Spoofs: Tough Guys Unmasked," *New York Times* March 2, 2006, at www.nytimes.com
(accessed March 9, 2006).

5. "Slash" is the genre of fan fiction that, taking two male characters from a TV series
or film (most famously Kirk and Spock from *Star Trek*), explores or brings to the surface
what fans recognize or fantasize is the implied homoerotic undercurrent of the friendship,
the expression of which ranges from intense emotionality to graphic sexual action. The
term itself derives from the slash separating the names or initials of the two characters as a
means of identifying the story's protagonists. According to all accounts, both the audience
for slash and the writers of it are predominantly female, and the venues of distribution for
their fiction tend to be within a fan community dedicated to a particular TV show or film;
some gay men also read and write slash fan fiction, but they as often post their stories on
amateur erotic fiction sites or gay discussion boards. Increasingly, too, slash fiction has
come to be accepted as a major expression of fandom, and I have even seen actors refer
to the slash pairings of their characters in interviews. Henry Jenkins (1992) offered one
of the first thorough analyses of fan fiction (152–84) and slash (185–222). See also David
Plotz, "Luke Skywalker Is Gay? Fan Fiction Is America's Literature of Obsession," April
14, 2000, at www.slate.com (accessed June 27, 2006).

BIBLIOGRAPHY

Ahmed, Sara. 2004. *The Cultural Politics of Emotion.* New York: Routledge.

Ali, Lorraine. 2000. "Coming to a Gym Near You." *Newsweek,* December 11, 76.

Altman, Rick. 1999. *Film/Genre.* Bloomington: Indiana University Press.

American Heritage Dictionary of the English Language. 2000. 4th ed. Boston: Houghton Mifflin.

An, Jinsoo. 2001. "*The Killer:* Cult Film and Transcultural (Mis)Reading." In *At Full Speed: Hong Kong Cinema in a Borderless World.* Ed. Esther C. Yau. 95–115. Minneapolis: University of Minnesota Press.

Andrew, Dudley. 1993. "The Unauthorized Auteur Today." In *Film Theory Goes to the Movies.* Ed. Jim Collins, Hilary Radner, and Ava Preacher Collins. 77–85. New York: Routledge.

Anhui Arts Institute. 2000. *An Overview of Huangmei Opera.* Hefei, China: Anhui People's Press.

Aufderheide, Patricia. 1998. "Made in Hong Kong: Translation and Transmutation." In *Play It Again Sam: Retakes on Remakes.* Ed. Andrew Horton and Stuart Y McDougal. 191–99. Berkeley: University of California Press.

Baker, Aaron. 2000. "A New Combination: Women and the Boxing Film. An Interview with Karyn Kusama." *Cineaste* 25.4: 22–26.

———. 2003. *Contesting Identities: Sports in American Film.* Chicago: University of Illinois Press.

Bakhtin, M. M. 1986a. "Response to a Question from the *Novy Mir* Editorial Staff." In *Speech Genres and Other Late Essays.* Trans. Vern W. McGee. Ed. Caryl Emerson and Michael Holquist. 1–9. Austin: University of Texas Press.

———. 1986b. "The Problem of Speech Genres." In *Speech Genres and Other Late Essays.* Trans. Vern W. McGee. Ed. Caryl Emerson and Michael Holquist. 60–102. Austin: University of Texas Press.

Barefoot, Guy. 2001. *Gaslight Melodrama: From Victorian London to 1940s Hollywood.* New York: Continuum.

Bartlett, John (Ed.). 1919. *Familiar Quotations.* 10th ed. Boston: Little Brown. www.bartleby.com/100 (accessed May 18, 2011).

Baxter, Robert. 2006. "Moved By a 'Mountain': Love Story Captivates Wide Array of Movie Fans." http://www.wkyc.com/news/story.aspx?storyid=48638 (accessed May 18, 2011).

Bazin, André. 2004. "The Ontology of the Photographic Image." Trans. Hugh Grey. In *Film Theory and Criticism.* 6th ed. Ed. Leo Braudy and Marshall Cohen. 166–70. New York: Oxford University Press.

Beltrán, Mary C. 2002. "The Hollywood Latina Body as Site of Social Struggle: Media Constructions of Stardom and Jennifer Lopez's 'Cross-over Butt.'" *Quarterly Review of Film & Video* 19.1: 71–86.

————. 2004. "Mas Macha: The New Latina Action Hero." In *Action and Adventure Cinema*. Ed. Yvonne Tasker. 186–200. London: Routledge.

Berlant, Lauren. 2008. *The Female Complaint: The Unfinished Business of Sentimentality in American Culture*. Durham, N.C.: Duke University Press.

Bhaumik, Kaushik. 2001. *The Emergence of the Bombay Film Industry, 1913–1936*. Ph.D. diss., Oxford University.

Bingham, Dennis. 1994. *Acting Male: Masculinities in the Films of James Stewart, Jack Nicholson, and Clint Eastwood*. Piscataway, N.J.: Rutgers University Press.

Bordo, Susan. 1997. *Twilight Zones: The Hidden Life of Cultural Images from Plato to O.J.* Berkeley: University of California Press.

Bordwell, David, and Janet Staiger. 1985. "Since 1960: The Persistence of a Mode of Film Practice." In *The Classical Hollywood Cinema: Film Style and Mode of Production to 1960*. Ed. David Bordwell, Janet Staiger, and Kristin Thompson. 367–77. New York: Columbia University Press.

————. 2000. *Planet Hong Kong: Popular Cinema and the Art of Entertainment*. Cambridge, Mass: Harvard University Press.

Bordwell, David, Janet Staiger, and Kristin Thompson. (Eds.) 1985. *The Classical Hollywood Cinema: Film Style and Mode of Production to 1960*. New York: Columbia University Press.

Bordwell, David, and Kristin Thompson. 2004. *Film Art: An Introduction*. 7th ed. New York: McGraw Hill.

Breillat, Catherine. 2001. *A ma soeur (Fat Girl)*. DVD commentary. CB Films.

Brooks, Peter. 1984. *The Melodramatic Imagination: Balzac, Henry James, Melodrama, and the Mode of Excess*. New York: Columbia University Press.

Bruzzi, Stella. 1997. *Undressing Cinema: Clothing and Identity at the Movies*. London: Routledge.

Buchsbaum, Jonathan. 1995. "Tame Wolves and Phoney Claims: Paranoia and Film Noir." In *The Book of Film Noir*. Ed. Ian Cameron. 88–97. New York: Continuum.

Buscombe, Edward. 1993. *Stagecoach*. London: BFI.

Butler, Alison. 2008. "Feminist Perspectives in Film Studies." In *Handbook of Film Studies*. Ed. James Donald, Patrick Fuery, and Michael Renov. 391–407. London: Sage.

Butler, Jeremy G. 1985. "*Miami Vice*: The Legacy of Film Noir." *Journal of Popular Film and Television* 13.3: 127–38.

Butler, Judith. 1993. *Bodies That Matter: On the Discursive Limits of "Sex."* New York: Routledge.

————. 1999 [1990]. *Gender Trouble: Feminism and the Subversion of Identity*. New York: Routledge.

————. 2002 [1998]. "Gender Is Burning." In *The Visual Culture Reader*. 2nd ed. Ed. N. Mirzoeff. 448–63. London: Routledge.

Byars, Jackie. 1987. "Reading Feminine Discourse: Prime-Time Television in the U.S." *Communication* 9 (3–4): 289–304.

Canby, Vincent. 1969. "Film Fete: Viva, Ragni, and Rado in *Lion's Love*: Movie by Agnès Varda Is Set in Hollywood." *New York Times,* September 22.

Carnicke, Sharon Marie. 2006. "The Material Poetry of Acting: 'Objects of Attention,' Performance Style, and Gender in 'The Shining' and 'Eyes Wide Shut.'" *Journal of Film and Video* 58 (1–2, Spring/Summer): 21–30.

Carter, Helen. 2002. "Agnès Varda." *Senses of Cinema* 22 (September–October). http://www.sensesofcinema/2002/great-directors/varda/ (accessed May 18, 2011).

Castagnary, Jules-Antoine. 1858. *Philosophie du Salon de 1857*. Paris.

Cavell, Stanley. 1988. "The Uncanniness of the Ordinary." In *In Quest of the Ordinary: Lines of Skepticism and Romanticism*. 153–80. Chicago: University of Chicago Press.

Cawein, Madison Julius. 1919. "Success." In *Familiar Quotations*. 10th ed. Ed. John Bartlett. Entry 8,192. www.bartleby.com/100 (accessed May 18, 2011).

Chakrabarty, Dipesh. 1994. "The Difference-Deferral of a Colonial Modernity: Public Debates on Domesticity in British India." In *Subaltern Studies VIII: Essays in Honour of Ranajit Guha*. Ed. David Arnold and David Hardiman. 50–88. New Delhi: Oxford University Press.

Chatterjee, Partha. 1993. *The Nation and Its Fragments: Colonial and Postcolonial Histories*. Princeton, N.J.: Princeton University Press.

Chen, Weizhi. 2005. *I Love Huangmei Diao*. Taipei, Taiwan: Mucun Books.

Chiao, Peggy Hsiung-ping. 2003. "The Female Consciousness, the World of Signification, and Safe Extramarital Affairs: A 40th Year Tribute to *The Love Eterne*." In *The Shaw Screen: A Preliminary Study*. Ed. Wong Ain-ling. 75–85. Hong Kong: Hong Kong Film Archive.

Ciecko, Anne. 1997. "Transnational Action: John Woo, Hong Kong, Hollywood." In *Transnational Chinese Cinemas: Identity, Nationhood, Gender*. Ed. Sheldon Hsiao-peng Lu. 221–37. Honolulu: University of Hawaii Press.

Ciment, Michel. 2001. *Kubrick: The Definitive Edition*. Trans. Gilbert Adair and Robert Bonono. New York: Faber and Faber.

Cixous, Hélène. 1976. "Fiction and Its Phantoms: A Reading of Freud's *Das Unheimliche*." *New Literary History* 7.3 (Spring): 525–48.

Clover, Carol J. 1992. *Men, Women, and Chainsaws: Gender in the Modern Horror Film*. Princeton, N.J.: Princeton University Press.

Collins, Jim. 1993. "Genericity in the Nineties: Eclectic Irony and the New Sincerity." In *Film Theory Goes to the Movies*. Ed. Jim Collins, Hilary Radner, and Ava Preacher Collins. 242–63. London: Routledge.

———. 2002 [1993]. "Genericity in the Nineties: Eclectic Irony and the New Sincerity." In *The Film Cultures Reader*. Ed. Graeme Turner. 276–90. London: Routledge.

Comolli, Jean-Louis, and Jean Narboni. 1971. "Cinema/Ideology/Criticism." *Screen* 12.1: 131–44.

Connell, R. W. 2002. *Gender*. Cambridge: Polity Press.

Cook, Pam. 1983. "Melodrama and the Women's Picture." In *BFI Dossier 18: Gainsborough Melodrama*. Ed. Sue Aspinall and Robert Murphy. 14–28. London: BFI.

———. 1993. "*Cape Fear* and Femininity as Destructive Power." In *Women and Film: A Sight and Sound Reader*. Ed. Pam Cook and Philip Dodd. 132–37. London: Scarlet Press.

———. 1995. "Outrage." In *Queen of the 'B's: Ida Lupino Behind the Camera*. Ed. Annette Kuhn. 57–72. Westport, Conn.: Praeger.

———. 1996. *Fashioning the Nation: Costume and Identity in British Cinema*. London: BFI.

———. 1998. "No Fixed Address: The Women's Picture from *Outrage* to *Blue Steel*." In *Contemporary Hollywood Cinema*. Ed. Steve Neale and Murray Smith. 229–46. London: Routledge.

Corber, Robert J. 1997. *Homosexuality in Cold War America: Resistance and the Crisis of Masculinity*. Durham, N.C.: Duke University Press.

Corliss, Richard. 2000. "An Indie Knockout." *Time,* October 2. www.time.com/time/magazine/article/0,9171,998100,00.html (accessed March 11, 2011).

Corrigan, Timothy. 1991. *A Cinema Without Walls: Movies and Culture After Vietnam.* New York: Routledge.

Corrigan, Timothy, and Patricia White. 2004. *The Film Experience: An Introduction.* Boston: Bedford/St. Martin's Press.

Creed, Barbara. 1993. *The Monstrous Feminine: Film, Feminism, Psychoanalysis.* London: Routledge.

Dawtrey, Adam. 2006. "Brits Back 'Brokeback': Focus Gets Four Awards at BAFTA." *Variety,* February 19. www.variety.com.

de Beauvoir, Simone. 1961 [1949]. *The Second Sex.* Trans. H. M. Parshley. New York: Bantam Books.

de Lauretis, Teresa. 1986. "Feminist Studies/Critical Studies: Issues, Terms, and Contexts." In *Feminist Studies, Critical Studies.* Ed. Teresa de Lauretis. 1–30. Bloomington: Indiana University Press.

———. 1990. "Guerilla in the Midst: Women's Cinema in the 80s." *Screen* 31:1. (Spring): 6–25.

Deleuze, Gilles. 1994 [1968]. *Difference and Repetition.* Trans. Paul Patton. Reprint. New York: Columbia University Press.

della Cava, Marco R. 2006. "It's a Date: 'Brokeback' Romance Draws Couples." *USA Today,* January 9. http://www.usatoday.com/life/movies/news/2006–01–09-brokeback-date-movie-main_x.htm (accessed May 18, 2011).

Derrida, Jacques. 1980. "The Law of Genre." Trans. Avital Ronell. *Critical Inquiry* 7.1 (Autumn): 55–80.

Diawara, Manthia. 1993. "Noir by Noirs: Towards a New Realism in Black Cinema." In *Shades of Noir.* Ed. Joan Copjec. 261–78. New York: Verso.

Doane, Mary Ann. 1987. *The Desire to Desire: The Woman's Film of the 1940s.* Basingstoke, U.K.: Macmillan.

———. 1991a. "Film and the Masquerade: Theorising the Female Spectator." *Femmes Fatales: Feminism, Film Theory, Psychoanalysis.* New York: Routledge.

———. 1991b. "*Gilda*: Epistemology as Striptease." *Femmes Fatales: Feminism, Film Theory, Psychoanalysis.* New York: Routledge.

Dupré, Francis. 1984. *La 'solution' du passage à l'acte.* Toulouse: Erès.

Dyer, Richard. 1998a. "Resistance through Charisma: Rita Hayworth and *Gilda*." In *Women in Film Noir.* Rev. ed. Ed. E. Ann Kaplan. 115–22. London: BFI.

———. 1998b. "Postscript: Queers and Women in Film Noir." In *Women in Film Noir.* Rev. ed. Ed. E. Ann Kaplan. 123–29. London: BFI.

———. 2007. *Pastiche.* New York: Routledge.

Ebert, Roger. 1989. Review of *Casualties of War. Chicago Sun-Times,* August 18.

Edwards, Rachel, and Keith Edwards (Eds.). 2001. *The Papin Sisters.* Oxford: Oxford University Press.

Eisenstein, Sergei. 1977. *Film Form.* Ed. and trans. Jay Leyda. New York: Harcourt Brace & Company.

Ellis, Jack C., and Betsy McLane. 2005. *A New History of Documentary Film.* New York: Continuum.

Elsaesser, Thomas. 1987 [1973]. "Tales of Sound and Fury: Observations on the Family

Melodrama." In *Home Is Where the Heart Is: Studies in Melodrama and the Woman's Film.* Ed. Christine Gledhill. 43–69. London: BFI.

Erikson, Todd. 1996. "Kill Me Again: Movement becomes Genre." In *Film Noir Reader.* Ed. Alain Silver and James Ursini. 307–29. New York: Limelight Editions.

Errigo, Angie. 1991. "Cry Baby." *Empire* 30 (December 1): 70–74.

Fang, Karen. 2004. *John Woo's* A Better Tomorrow. Aberdeen, U.K.: Hong Kong University Press.

Felski, Rita. 2003. *Literature after Feminism.* Chicago: University of Chicago Press.

Fields, Sarah K. 2005. *Female Gladiators: Gender, Law, and Contact Sport in America.* Chicago: University of Illinois Press.

Filmsite Glossary. www.filmsite.org/filmterms7.html.

Fiske, John. 1987. *Television Culture.* London: Methuen.

Flitterman-Lewis, Sandy. 1993. "Magic and Wisdom in Two Portraits by Agnès Varda: *Kung-Fu Master* and *Jane B. by Agnès V.*" *Screen* 34.4 (Winter): 302–20.

———. 1996. *To Desire Differently: Feminism and French Cinema.* New York: Columbia University Press.

Flory, Dan. 2008. *Philosophy, Black Film, Film Noir.* College Park: Penn State University Press.

Forbes, Jill. 1993. *The Cinema in France after the New Wave.* Bloomington: Indiana University Press.

Fortin, Geneviève. 2000. *L'affaire Papin.* Lanham, Md.: University Press of America.

Francke, Lizzie. 1994. *Script Girls: Women Screenwriters in Hollywood.* London: BFI.

Freud, Sigmund. 1959 [1919]. "The Uncanny." In *Collected Papers,* Vol. 4. Ed. Ernest Jones, trans. Joan Riviere. 368–407. New York: Basic Books.

———. 1973 [1933]. *New Introductory Lectures on Psychoanalysis.* Harmondsworth: Penguin.

Frow, John. 2006. *Genre.* London: Routledge.

Fu, Poshek. 2003. *Between Shanghai and Hong Kong.* Stanford, Calif.: Stanford University Press.

Gaines, Jane. 2002. "Of Cabbages and Authorship." In *A Feminism and Early Film Reader.* Ed. Jennifer Bean and Diane Negra. 88–118. Durham, N.C.: Duke University Press.

———. 2004. "Film History and the Two Presents of Feminist Film Theory." *Cinema Journal* 44.1: 113–19.

Garber, Marjorie. 1992. *Vested Interests: Cross-Dressing and Cultural Anxiety.* New York: Routledge.

Gledhill, Christine. 1987. "Introduction" and "The Melodramatic Field: An Investigation." In *Home Is Where the Heart Is: Studies in Melodrama and the Woman's Film.* Ed. Christine Gledhill. 1–4; 5–39. London: BFI.

———. 1988. "Pleasurable Negotiations." In *Female Spectators: Looking at Film and Television.* Ed. E. Deidre Pribram. 64–89. London: Verso.

———. 1991. "Signs of Melodrama." In *Stardom: Industry of Desire.* Ed. Christine Gledhill. 207–29. London: Routledge.

———. 1995. "Women Reading Men." In *Me Jane: Masculinity, Movies, and Women.* Ed. Pat Kirkham and Janet Thumin. 73–93. New York: St. Martin's Press.

———. 2000. "Rethinking Genre." In *Reinventing Film Studies.* Ed. Christine Gledhill and Linda Williams. 221–43. London: Arnold.

Goodman, Dena (Ed.). 2003. *Writings on the Body of a Queen.* New York: Routledge.

Grant, Barry Keith. 2004. "Man's Favourite Sport? The Action Films of Kathryn Bigelow." In *Action and Adventure Cinema.* Ed. Yvonne Tasker. 331–84. London: Routledge.

Grimsted, David. 1968. *Melodrama Unveiled: American Theater and Culture, 1800–1850.* Chicago: University of Chicago Press.

Grist, Leighton. 1995. "Moving Targets and Black Widows: Film Noir in Modern Hollywood." In *The Book of Film Noir.* Ed. Ian Cameron. 267–85. New York: Continuum.

Gross, Terry. 2004. Interview with John Waters. On *Fresh Air.* National Public Radio, February 25.

Halberstam, Judith. 1998. *Female Masculinity.* Durham, N.C.: Duke University Press.

Hansen, Miriam. 1991. *Babel and Babylon: Spectatorship in American Silent Film.* Cambridge, Mass.: Harvard University Press.

Hansen, Miriam Bratu. 2000. "The Mass Production of the Senses: Classical Cinema as Vernacular Modernism." In *Reinventing Film Studies.* Ed. Christine Gledhill and Linda Williams. 332–50. London: Arnold.

Harding, Jennifer, and E. Deidre Pribram. 2004. "Losing Our Cool? Following Williams and Grossberg on Emotions." *Cultural Studies* 18.6 (November): 863–83.

Hardy, Ernest. 2001. "Trembling Like When You Are in Love: French Filmmaker Agnès Varda." *LA Weekly,* April 5.

Harper, Sue. 1994. *Picturing the Past: The Rise and Fall of the British Costume Film.* London: BFI.

Harvey, Sylvia. 1998. "Woman's Place: The Absent Family in Film Noir." In *Women in Film Noir.* Rev. ed. Ed. E. Ann Kaplan. 35–68. London: BFI.

Haskell, Molly. 1987. *From Reverence to Rape: The Treatment of Women in the Movies.* 2nd ed. New York: Holt, Rinehart & Winston.

Hayward, Susan. 2000. "Beyond the Gaze and Into Femme-Filmécriture: Agnès Varda's *Sans toit ni loi* (1985)." In *French Film: Texts and Contexts.* 2nd ed. Ed. Susan Hayward and Ginette Vincendeau. 285–95. London: Routledge.

Heard, Christopher. 2000. *Ten Thousand Bullets: The Cinematic Journey of John Woo.* Los Angeles: Lone Eagle.

Heath, Stephen. 1973. "Comment on 'The Idea of Authorship.'" *Screen* 14.3 (Autumn): 86–91.

Hendershot, Cyndy. 1998. *The Animal Within: Masculinity and the Gothic.* Ann Arbor: University of Michigan Press.

Herbert, Robert. 1978. *Millet's Gleaners.* Minneapolis: Minneapolis Institute of Art.

Heywood, Leslie, and Shari L. Dworkin. 2003. *Built to Win: The Female Athlete as Cultural Icon.* Minneapolis: University of Minnesota Press.

Hillier, Jim. 1993. *The New Hollywood.* London: Studio Vista.

Hoberman, J., and Jonathan Rosenbaum. 1991. *Midnight Movies.* New York: Da Capo Press.

Hoffmann, E. T. A. 1967. "The Sand-Man." In *The Best Tales of Hoffmann.* Ed. E. F. Bleiler. 183–214. New York: Dover Publications.

Holden, Stephen. 2005. Review of *Brokeback Mountain. New York Times,* December 9. www.nytimes.com.

Holmlund, Chris. 1993. "A Decade of Deadly Dolls: Hollywood and the Woman Killer." In *Moving Targets.* Ed. Helen Birch. 127–51. Berkeley: University of California Press.

———. 2005. "Postfeminism from A to G." *Cinema Journal* 44.2: 116–21.

Hong Shuling. 2004. *Woman in Traditional Literature.* Taipei, Taiwan: Li Ren Press.

Houdyer, Paulette. 1996. *L'affaire de soeurs Papin.* Paris: J'ai Lu.

Hutchings, Peter. 1995. "Genre Theory and Criticism." In *Approaches to Popular Film.* Ed. Joanne Hollows and Mark Jancovich. 60–77. Manchester: Manchester University Press.

Independent, The. 2006. "Sofia Coppola: Style Queen." October 15. http://www.independent .co.uk/news/people/profiles/sofia-coppola-style-queen-419802.html (accessed March 11, 2011).

Irigaray, Luce. 1985. *Speculum of the Other Woman.* Trans. Gillian G. Gill. Ithaca, N.Y.: Cornell University Press.

James, Nick. 2002. *Heat.* London: BFI.

Jameson, Fredric. 1991. "The Cultural Logic of Late Capitalism." In *Postmodernism, or, The Cultural Logic of Late Capitalism.* 1–54. London: Verso.

———. 1992. "Historicism in *The Shining.*" In *Signatures of the Visible.* 82–98. New York: Routledge.

Jay, Martin. 1994. *Downcast Eyes: The Denigration of Vision in Twentieth-Century French Thought.* Berkeley: University of California Press.

Jeffords, Susan. 1993. "The Big Switch: Hollywood Masculinity in the Nineties." In *Film Theory Goes to the Movies.* Ed. Jim Collins, Hillary Radner, and Ava Preacher Collins. 196–208. New York: Routledge.

Jenkins, Henry. 1992. *Textual Poachers: Television Fans and Participatory Culture.* New York: Routledge.

Johnston, Claire. 1973. "Women's Cinema as Counter-Cinema." In *Notes on Women's Cinema.* Ed. Claire Johnston. 24–31. London: Society for Education in Film and Television.

———. 1998. "*Double Indemnity.*" In *Women in Film Noir.* Rev. ed. Ed. E. Ann Kaplan. 89–98. London: BFI.

Kaplan, E. Ann (Ed.). 1978. *Women in Film Noir.* Rev. ed. 1998. London: BFI.

———. 1983. "Theories of Melodrama: A Feminist Perspective." In *Women & Performance: A Journal of Feminist Theory* 1:1 (March):40–48.

———. 1987. "Mothering, Feminism, and Representation: The Maternal in Melodrama and the Woman's Film from 1910 to 1940." In *Home Is Where the Heart Is.* Ed. Christine Gledhill. 113–37. London: BFI.

———. 1992. *Motherhood and Representation: The Mother in Popular Culture and Melodrama.* London: Routledge.

———. 2001. "Melodrama, Cinema and Trauma." *Screen* 42.2 (Summer): 201–5.

Kapse, Anupama. 2009. *The Moving Image: Melodrama and Early Indian Cinema, 1913–1939.* Ph.D. diss., University of California, Berkeley.

Karlyn, Kathleen Rowe. 1998. "Allison Anders's *Gas Food Lodging:* Independent Cinema and the New Romance." In *Terms of Endearment: Hollywood Romantic Comedy of the 1980s and 1990s.* Ed. Peter William Evans and Celestino Deleyto. 168–87. Edinburgh: Edinburgh University Press.

King, Stephen. 1977. *The Shining.* New York: Doubleday.

Klinger, Barbara. 1986. "'Cinema/Ideology/Criticism' Revisited: The Progressive Genre." In *Film Genre Reader.* Ed. Barry K. Grant. 74–90. Austin: University of Texas Press.

———. 1994. *Melodrama and Meaning: History, Culture, and the Films of Douglas Sirk.* Bloomington: Indiana University Press.

Kotsopoulos, Aspasia, and Josephine Mills. 1994. "*The Crying Game:* Genre and 'Postfeminism.'" *Jump Cut* 39 (June): 15–24.

Kozloff, Sarah. 2000. *Overhearing Film Dialogue.* Berkeley: University of California Press.

Kracauer, Siegfried. 2004. "The Establishment of Physical Existence." In *Film Theory and Criticism.* 6th ed. Ed. Leo Braudy and Marshall Cohen. 303–13. New York: Oxford University Press.

Krane, Vikki, Precilla Y. L. Choi, Shannon M. Baird, Christine M. Aimar, and Kerrie J. Kauer. 2004. "Living the Paradox: Female Athletes Negotiate Femininity and Muscularity." *Sex Roles* 50.5–6 (March): 315–29.

Kristeva, Julia. 1981. "Women's Time." Trans. Alice Jardine and Harry Blake. *Signs: A Journal of Women and Culture in Society* 7: 31–53.

———. 1982. *Powers of Horror: An Essay on Abjection.* Trans. Leon S. Roudiez. New York: Columbia University Press.

Krum, Sharon. 2006. "Leader of the Pack." *The Australian,* November 17.

Krutnik, Frank. 1991. *In a Lonely Street: Film Noir, Genre, Masculinity.* London: Routledge.

Kuhn, Annette (Ed.). 1995. *Queen of the 'B's: Ida Lupino Behind the Camera.* Westport, Conn: Greenwood Press.

———. 2006. "Woman's Pictures." In *Schirmer Encyclopedia of Film.* Vol. 4. Ed. Barry Keith Grant. 367–73. New York: Gale Cengage.

Lane, Christina. 1998. "From *The Loveless* to *Point Break:* Kathryn Bigelow's Trajectory in Action Cinema." *Cinema Journal* 37.4 (Summer): 59–81.

———. 2000. *Feminist Hollywood: From Born in Flames to Point Break.* Detroit: Wayne State University Press.

———. 2005. "Just Another Girl Outside the Neo-indie." In *Contemporary American Independent Film: From the Margins to the Mainstream.* Ed. Chris Holmlund and Justin Wyatt. 193–209. New York: Routledge.

Lant, Antonia. 2007. *Red Velvet Seat: Women's Writing on the First Fifty Years of Cinema.* London: Verso.

Law, Kar. 1996. "Introduction." In *The Restless Breed: Cantonese Stars of the Sixties.* Ed. Law Kar. 10. Hong Kong: The Urban Council.

Levi, Primo. 1987 [1963]. *If This Is a Man* and *The Truce.* Trans. Stuart Woolf. London: Abacus.

Li, Hanxiang. 1987. *A Life with the Silver Screen.* Beijing: Rural Village Books.

———. 1984. *Thirty Years in Retrospect II.* Hong Kong: Tiandi Books.

Liao, Jinfeng, Poshek Fu, Cheuk-pak Tong, and Sai-shing Yung (Eds.). 2003. *The Film and Movie Empire of Shaw Brothers: The Imaginary of Cultural China.* Taipei: Rye Field Press.

Lindstrom, J. A. 2000. "*Heat:* Work and Genre." *Jump Cut* 43: 21–43.

Liu, Jing-an. 1971. *Women in Folksongs.* Taipei: Eastern Cultures Press.

Lott, Eric. 1997. "The Whiteness of Film Noir." *American Literary History* 9.3: 542–67.

Low Culture. 2006. "Didja Hear the One About the Gay Cowboys? *Brokeback Mountain* Jokes, A Look Back . . . in Laughter." March 1. http://www.lowculture.com/archives/2006/03/brokeback.html (accessed May 18, 2011).

Lyman, Rick. 2001. "Watching Movies with Ang Lee." *New York Times,* March 9.

MacCabe, Colin. 2003. "The Revenge of the Author." In *Film and Authorship.* Ed. Virginia Wexman. 30–41. New Brunswick, N.J.: Rutgers University Press.

Magnan-Park, Aaron Han Joon. 2007. "The Heroic Flux in John Woo's Trans-Pacific Passage: From Confucian Brotherhood to American Selfhood." In *Hong Kong Film, Hollywood, and the New Global Cinema: No Film Is an Island.* Ed. Gina Marchetti and Tan See Kam. 35–49. London: Routledge.

Mahar, Karen Ward. 2006. *Women Filmmakers in Early Hollywood*. Baltimore: Johns Hopkins Press.

Margolis, Stacy. 2005. *The Public Life of Privacy in Nineteenth-Century American Literature*. Durham, N.C.: Duke University Press.

Marks, Laura U. 2004. "Haptic Visuality: Touching with the Eyes." *Framework: The Finnish Art Review*. http://www.frame-fund.fi/images/stories/pdf/Fw2004/fw-issue2-screen .pdf (accessed May 18, 2011).

Martin, Angela. 1998. "'Gilda Didn't Do Any of Those Things You've Been Losing Sleep Over!': The Central Women of 40s Film Noirs." In *Women in Film Noir*. Ed. E. Ann Kaplan. 200–228. London: BFI.

Mayne, Judith. 1990. *Women at the Keyhole: Feminism and Women's Cinema*. Bloomington: Indiana University Press.

———. 1993. *Cinema and Spectatorship*. New York: Routledge.

———. 2002. "Women in the Avant-Garde: Germaine Dulac, Maya Deren, Agnès Varda, Chantal Akerman, and Trinh T. Minh-ha." In *Experimental Cinema: The Film Reader*. Ed. Wheeler Winston Dixon and Gwendolyn Audrey Foster. 81–111. New York: Routledge.

McCarthy, Todd. 2005. Review of *Brokeback Mountain. Variety*, September 3. http://www .variety.com/review/VE1117928059/ (accessed May 18, 2011).

McMahan, Alison. 2002. *Alice Guy Blaché: Lost Visionary of Cinema*. New York: Continuum.

McMurtry, Larry. 2006. "'Brokeback' Writer Summarizes Film." *CBS News*, February 16.

McRobbie, Angela. 2008. *Displacement Feminism*. London: Sage.

Mendelsohn, Daniel. 2006. "An Affair to Remember." *New York Review of Books*, February 23. http://www.nybooks.com/articles/archives/2006/feb/23/an-affair-to-remember/ (accessed May 18, 2011).

Mercer, John, and Martin Shingler. 2004. *Melodrama: Genre, Style, Sensibility*. London: Wallflower.

Metz, Walter. 2003. "John Waters Goes to Hollywood: A Poststructural Authorship Study." In *Authorship and Film*. Ed. David A. Gerstner and Janet Staiger. 157–74. New York: Routledge.

Miller, Barbara Stoler (Ed. and Trans). 1977. *The Gitagovinda of Jayadeva: Love Song of the Dark Lord*. Delhi: Motilal Banarsidass.

Moretti, Franco. 1989. "The Genetics of Genres: An Interview with Franco Moretti." *Polygraph* 2–3: 158–65.

Mulvey, Laura. 1975. "Visual Pleasure and Narrative Cinema." *Screen* 16.3 (Autumn): 6–18.

———. 1987. "Notes on Sirk and Melodrama." In *Home Is Where the Heart Is: Studies in Melodrama and the Woman's Film*. Ed. Christine Gledhill. 75–79. London: BFI.

———. 1990. "'It Will Be a Magnificent Obsession': The Melodrama's Role in the Development of Contemporary Film Theory." In *Melodrama: Stage/Picture/Screen*. Ed. Jacky Bratton, Jim Cook, and Christine Gledhill. 121–33. London: BFI.

Muñoz, José Esteban. 1999. *Disidentifications: Queers of Color and the Performance of Politics*. Minneapolis: University of Minnesota Press.

Neale, Steve. 1980. *Genre*. London: BFI.

———. 1983. "Masculinity as Spectacle: Reflections on Men and Mainstream Cinema." *Screen* 24.6: 2–16.

———. 1993. "Melo Talk: On the Meaning and use of the Term 'Melodrama' in the American Trade Press." *The Velvet Light Trap* 32 (Fall): 66–89.

———. 1995. "Questions of Genre." In *Film Genre Reader II*. Ed. Barry Keith Grant. 160–84. Austin: University of Texas Press.

———. 2000. *Genre and Hollywood*. London: Routledge.

Nichols, Bill. 2001. *Introduction to Documentary*. Bloomington: Indiana University Press.

Nicoll (RN), Leslie H. 2006. "Brokeback Fever." Advance Online Editions for Nurses, February 16. http://nursing.advanceweb.com/Article/Brokeback-Fever.aspx (accessed May 18, 2011).

Nowell-Smith, Geoffrey. 1987. "Minnelli and Melodrama." In *Home Is Where the Heart Is: Studies in Melodrama and the Woman's Film*. Ed. Christine Gledhill. 70–74. London: BFI.

Oates, Joyce Carol. 1987. *On Boxing*. London: Bloomsbury.

Oliver, Kelly. 2004. *The Colonization of Psychic Space: A Psychoanalytic Social Theory of Oppression*. Minneapolis: University of Minnesota Press.

Palmer, R. Barton. 1994. "Conclusion." *Hollywood's Dark Cinema: The American Film Noir*. New York: Twayne.

Pela, Robrt L. 2002. *Filthy: The Weird World of John Waters*. New York: Alyson Books.

Petro, Patrice. 1989. *Joyless Streets: Women and Melodramatic Representation in Weimar Germany*. Princeton, N.J.: Princeton University Press.

Peucker, Brigitte. 2001. "Kubrick and Kafka: The Corporeal Uncanny." *Modernism/Modernity* 8: 663–74.

Pidduck, Julianne. 1995. "The 1990s Hollywood Fatal Femme: (Dis)Figuring Feminism, Family, Irony, Violence." *Cineaction* 38 (September): 64–72.

———. 2004. *Contemporary Costume Film: Space, Place, and the Past*. London: BFI.

Pitts, Leonard. 2006. "Why 'Brokeback Mountain' Is So Frightening." *Salt Lake City Tribune*, January 7. www.sltrib.com (accessed January 18, 2006).

Place, Janey. 1998. "Women in Film Noir." In *Women and Film Noir*. Rev. ed. Ed. E. Ann Kaplan. 47–68. London: BFI.

Proulx, Annie. 2005. "Getting Movied." In *Brokeback Mountain: Story to Screenplay*. Ed. Annie Proulx, Larry McMurtry, and Diana Ossana. 129–38. New York: Scribner.

Pu, Feng. 2007. "The Beijing Factor in Li Hanxiang's Films." In *Li Han-hsiang: Storyteller*. Ed. Wong Ain-ling. 42–47. Hong Kong: Hong Kong Film Archive.

Pye, Douglas. 2007. *Movies and Tone*. London: Wallflower.

Rajan, Chandra (Ed. and Trans). 1989. *Kālidāsa: The Loom of Time: A Selection of His Plays and Poems*. New Delhi: Penguin Books.

Ransley, Hannah. 2002. "Kathryn Bigelow." In *Contemporary North American Film Directors: A Wallflower Critical Guide*. Ed. Yoram Allon, Del Cullen, and Hannah Patterson. 50–51. London: Wallflower.

Redmond, Sean. 2003. "All That Is Male Melts into Air: Bigelow on the Edge of *Point Break*." In *The Cinema of Kathryn Bigelow: Hollywood Transgressor*. Ed. Deborah Jermyn and Sean Redmond. 106–24. London: Wallflower.

Reynaud, Berenice. 2000. "John Woo's Art Action Movie." In *Action/Spectacle Cinema*. Ed. José Arroyo. 61–65. London: BFI.

Ribiero, Aileen. 2002. "On Englishness in Dress." In *The Englishness of English Dress*. Ed. Christopher Breward, Becky Conekin, and Caroline Cox. 15–27. New York: Berg.

Rich, Ruby. 2007. "Brokering *Brokeback*: Jokes, Backlashes, and Other Anxieties." *Film Quarterly* 60.3: 44–48.

Rivette, Jacques. 1953. "Génie de Howard Hawks." *Cahiers du Cinéma* 23 (May): 16–24.

Riviere, Joan. 1966. "Womanliness as a Masquerade." In *Psychoanalysis and Female Sexuality*. Ed. Henderik M. Ruitenbeek. 209–20. New Haven, Conn.: College and University Press.

Robe, Chris. 2009. "Taking Hollywood Back: The Historical Costume Drama, the Biopic, and Popular Front US Film Criticism." *Cinema Journal* 48 (Winter): 71.

Rodowick, David N. 1987. "Madness, Authority, and Ideology: The Domestic Melodrama of the 1950s." In *Home Is Where the Heart Is: Studies in Melodrama and the Woman's Film*. Ed. Christine Gledhill. 268–80. London: BFI.

Rosen, Philip. 2001. *Change Mummified: Cinema, Historicity, Theory*. Minneapolis: University of Minnesota Press.

Ross Andrew. 1989. *No Respect: Intellectuals and Popular Culture*. New York: Routledge.

Rubin, Gayle. 1975. "The Traffic in Women: Notes on the 'Political Economy' of Sex." In *Toward an Anthropology of Women*. Ed. Rayna Reiter. 157–210. New York: Monthly Review Press.

Russell, Ralph (Ed.). 1997. *Ghalib: The Poet and His Age*. Delhi: Oxford University Press.

Ryall, Tom. 1975. "Teaching Through Genre." *Screen Education* 17 (Winter): 27–28.

Saperstein, Pat. 2006. "Hooked on a Biz-Friendly Mantra: Buying and Selling Movies Just Got Easier on the Lagoon." *Variety,* August 27. www.variety.com (accessed February 23, 2007).

Sarkar, Tanika. 2001. *Hindu Wife, Hindu Nation: Community, Religion, & Cultural Nationalism*. New Delhi: Permanent Black.

Schamus, James, et al. 2006. "'Brokeback Mountain': An Exchange." *New York Review of Books,* April 6. http://www.nybooks.com/articles/archives/2006/apr/06/brokeback-mountain-an-exchange/ (accessed May 18, 2011).

Schatz, Thomas. 1988. *The Genius of the System: Hollywood Filmmaking in the Studio Era*. New York: Pantheon.

Schrobsdorff, Susanna. 2006. "Chick-Flick Cowboys: 'Brokeback Mountain' Has Stolen the Hearts of Women in Middle America." *Newsweek,* January 20. www.msnbc.msn.com (accessed January 26, 2006).

Schwartzman, Jason. 2006. "Kirsten Dunst." *Interview* (September): 166–71

Sconce, Jeffrey. 1995. "'Trashing' the Academy: Taste, Excess, and an Emerging Politics of Cinematic Style." *Screen* 36.4 (Winter): 371–93.

Sek, Kei. 2003. "Shaw Movie Town's 'China Dream' and 'Hong Kong Sentiment.'" In *The Shaw Screen: A Preliminary Study*. Ed. Wong Ain-ling. 37–47. Hong Kong: Hong Kong Film Archive.

Sharma, Sunil. 2006. *Amir Khusraw: The Poet of Sultans and Sufis*. Oxford: Oneworld Publications.

Sheehan, Henry. 2006. "Cowpokes Outed as Archetypes: 'Brokeback's' Love Story Echoes and Deepens Themes of Classic Hollywood Westerns." *Variety,* February 21. www.variety.com (accessed February 24, 2006).

Shi, Bailin. 1993. *An Overview of Huangmei Opera Music*. Beijing: People's Music Press.

Shi, Hui. 1982. *Shihui on Art*. Ed. Shaochang Wei. Shanghai: Shanghai Arts Press.

Sicha, Choire. 2005. "Chokeback Mountain." *New York Observer,* November 21. www.observer.com (accessed January 5, 2006).

Silverman, Kaja. 1988. *The Acoustic Mirror: The Female Voice in Psychoanalysis and Cinema*. Bloomington: Indiana University Press.

Singer, Ben. 2001. *Melodrama and Modernity: Early Sensational Cinema and Its Contexts.* New York: Columbia University Press.

Smith, Alison. 1998. *Agnès Varda.* Manchester: Manchester University Press.

Smith, Murray. 1995. *Engaging Characters: Fiction, Emotion, and the Cinema.* Oxford: Clarendon Press.

Sontag, Susan. 2001 [1964]. "Notes on 'Camp.'" In *Against Interpretation and Other Essays.* 275–92. New York: Picador.

Southern Screen 2 (January), 1958.

Southern Screen 47 (January), 1962.

Southern Screen 65 (July), 1963.

Stacey, Jackie. 1994. *Star Gazing: Hollywood Cinema and Female Spectatorship.* London: Routledge.

Staiger, Janet. 1985. "The Hollywood Mode of Production to 1930." In *The Classical Hollywood Cinema: Film Style and Mode of Production to 1960.* Ed. David Bordwell, Janet Staiger, and Kristin Thompson. 85–154. New York: Columbia University Press.

Sterritt, David. 2006. "Beyond *Brokeback*: Has Gay Cinema Entered the Mainstream?" *MovieMaker* 62. www.moviemaker.com (accessed May 4, 2006).

Stevenson, Jack. 1996. *Desperate Visions: Camp America.* London: Creation Books.

St. John, Mia. 1999. *Playboy* (November): cover and 76.

Stokes, Lisa Odham, and Michael Hoover. 1999. *City on Fire: Hong Kong Cinema.* London: Verso.

Stone, Sasha. 2006. "At the Movies: When *Brokeback Mountain* Met America." In *Santa Monica Mirror Online,* January 26–February 2. www.smmirror.com (accessed February 3, 2006).

Straayer, Chris. 1996. *Deviant Eyes, Deviant Bodies: Sexual Re-Orientations in Film and Video.* New York: Columbia University Press.

Swartz, Charles. 2005. *Understanding Digital Cinema: A Professional Handbook.* Burlington, Mass.: Focal Press.

Tapley, Brendan. 2006. "Decoding 'Brokeback': Why Women Get It and Men Don't Go." *Chicago Tribune,* February 26. www.chicagotribune.com (accessed March 1, 2006).

Tasker, Yvonne. 1993. *Spectacular Bodies: Gender, Genre, and the Action Cinema.* London: Routledge.

———. 1999. "Bigger Than Life." *Sight and Sound* 9.5 (May): 12–15.

Tasker, Yvonne, and Diane Negra. 2007. *Interrogating Postfeminism.* Durham, N.C.: Duke University Press.

Taussig, Michael. 1993. *Mimesis and Alterity: A Particular History of the Senses.* New York: Routledge.

Tharu, Susie, and K. Lalitha (Eds.). 1991, 1993. *Women Writing in India.* Vols. 1 and 2. New Delhi: Oxford University Press.

Thomas, Deborah. 2005. "Knowing One's Place: Frame-breaking and Embarrassment in Claude Chabrol's *La Cérémonie.*" In *Style and Meaning: Studies in the Detailed Analysis of Film.* Ed. Douglas Pye and John Gibbs. 167–78. Manchester: Manchester University Press.

Thomas, Rosie. 2005. "Not Quite (Pearl) White: Fearless Nadia, Queen of the Stunts." In *Bollyworld: Popular Indian Cinema through a Transnational Lens.* Ed. Raminder Kaur and Ajay J. Sinha. 35–69. New Delhi: Sage.

Tudor, Andrew. 1973. *Theories of Film.* London: Secker and Warburg.

Varda, Agnès. 1996. "The Grandmother of the New Wave." Interview by Carol Allen. www
.talkingpix.co.uk/Interview_Agnes%20Varda.html (accessed March 14, 2011).

Vasudevan, Ravi. 1989. "The Melodramatic Mode and the Commercial Hindi Cinema:
Notes on Film History, Narrative, and Performance in the 1950s." *Screen* 30.3 (Summer): 29–50.

———. 1995. "Film Studies, New Cultural History, and Experience of Modernity." *Economic
and Political Weekly,* November 4: 2809–14.

Vernet, Marc. 1993. "Film Noir on the Edge of Doom." In *Shades of Noir.* Ed. Joan Copjec.
1–31. New York: Verso.

Vitali, Valentina. 2003. "Still Looking for Kathryn Bigelow." *Filmwaves* 21 (July): 24–26.

Walker, Michael. 1995. "Film Noir: Introduction." In *The Book of Film Noir.* Ed. Ian Cameron. 8–23. New York: Continuum.

Warhol, Andy. 1975. *The Philosophy of Andy Warhol: From A to B and Back Again.* New
York: Harcourt Brace Jovanovich.

Warshow, Robert. 1974. *The Immediate Experience.* New York: Atheneum.

Waters, John. 1995. *Shock Value.* New York: Thunder's Mouth Press.

———. 2001. "Filth 101: An Open Discussion with John Waters." The European Gradu-
ate School, August. www.egs.edu/faculty/waters/waters-filth-101–2001.html (accessed
March 16, 2011).

———. 2003. *Crackpot: The Obsessions of John Waters.* New York: Scribner.

Weber, Caroline. 2006. *Queen of Fashion: What Marie Antoinette Wore to the Revolution.*
New York: Picador Press,

Weber, Samuel. 1973. "The Sideshow, or: Remarks on a Canny Moment." *MLN Comparative Literature* 88.6 (December): 1102–33.

White, Susan. 2001. "T(he)-Men's Room: Masculinity and Space in Anthony Mann's
T-Men." In *Masculinity: Bodies, Movies, Culture.* Ed. Peter Lehman. 95–114. New York:
Routledge.

Willemen, Paul. 1981. "Anthony Mann: Looking at the Male." *Framework* 15/16/17: 16.

Williams, Linda. 1991. *Hard Core: Power, Pleasure, and the "Frenzy of the Visible."* London.
Pandora.

———. 1994. "Learning to Scream." *Sight and Sound* 4.12 (December): 14–17.

———. 1998. "Melodrama Revised." In *Refiguring American Film Genres: History and
Theory.* Ed. Nick Browne. 42–88. Berkeley: University of California Press.

———. 2000 [1991]. "Film Bodies: Gender, Genre, and Excess." In *Film and Theory: An
Anthology.* Ed. Robert Stam and Toby Miller. 207–21. Oxford: Blackwell.

———. 2001. *Playing the Race Card: Melodramas of Black and White from Uncle Tom to
O.J. Simpson.* Berkeley: University of California Press.

Williams, Raymond. 1977. *Marxism and Literature.* Oxford: Oxford University Press.

———. 2009. "On Structure of Feeling." In *Emotions: A Cultural Studies Reader.* Ed. J. Harding and E. D. Pribram. 35–49. London: Routledge.

Willis, Sharon. 1997. *High Contrast: Race and Gender in Contemporary Hollywood Film.*
Durham, N.C.: Duke University Press.

Wilson, Jake. 2002. "Trash and Treasure: *The Gleaners and I.*" *Senses of Cinema* 23 (November–December). http://www.sensesofcinema.com/2002/feature-articles/gleaners/
(accessed May 18, 2011).

Wollen, Peter. 1972. *Signs and Meanings in the Cinema.* Bloomington: Indiana University Press.

———. 2002. "Who the Hell Is Howard Hawks?" *Framework* 43.1 (Spring): 9–17.

Wood, Robin. 1978. "The Return of the Repressed." *Film Comment* 4 (July–August): 24–32.

———. 2002. "Star and Auteur: Hitchcock's Films with Bergman." In *Hitchcock's Films Re-visited*. Rev. ed. 303–35. London: Faber and Faber.

Wyatt, Justin. 1998. "The Formation of the 'Major Independent': Miramax, New Line, and the New Hollywood." In *Contemporary Hollywood Cinema*. Ed. Steve Neale and Murray Smith. 74–90. London: Routledge.

Xu, Dunle. 2005. *Scribing in Light and Shadows: 50 Years of Nanfang Distribution Company*. Hong Kong: MCCM Creations.

Zhang, Che. 1989. *Thirty Years of Hong Kong Cinema in Retrospect*. Hong Kong: Joint Publishing.

———. 2002. *Memoirs and Film Reviews*. Hong Kong: Hong Kong Film Archive.

Zhang, Zhen. 2001. *An Amorous History of the Silver Screen: Shanghai Cinema, 1896–1937*. Chicago: University of Chicago Press.

CONTRIBUTORS

IRA BHASKAR is associate professor, Cinema Studies, School of Arts & Aesthetics, Jawaharlal Nehru University. She co-authored *Islamicate Cultures of Bombay Cinema* (2009) and is currently editing *Ghatak's Partition Quartet,* working on a book on "Historical Trauma, Memory and Representation in Bombay Cinema," and co-editing *Bombay Cinema and Islamicate Cultures: A Reader.*

STEVEN COHAN is professor of English at Syracuse University. His books include *Masked Men: Masculinity and the Movies in the Fifties* (1997), *Incongruous Entertainment: Camp, Cultural Value, and the MGM Musical* (2005), and *CSI: Crime Scene Investigation* (2008). He is editor of the new collection *The Sound of Musicals: New Essays* (2010).

LUKE COLLINS is a practicing artist. He has exhibited nationally and internationally and completed residencies in Montreal, Cove Park (Scotland), and Belfast. He edits the magazine *Erotic Cakes.* His work is held in the collection of the Arts Council of England and select projects can be found at lukecollins.co.uk

PAM COOK is professor emerita in Film at the University of Southampton. She is the author of *Screening the Past: Memory and Nostalgia in Cinema* (2005) and editor of *The Cinema Book, Third Edition* (2007). Her latest book is *Baz Luhrmann* (2010), and she is currently working on a monograph about Nicole Kidman.

LUCY FISCHER is a distinguished professor of Film and English at the University of Pittsburgh and director of the Film Studies Program. Her works include: *Shot/Countershot: Film Tradition and Women's Cinema* (1989), *Cinematernity: Film, Motherhood, Genre* (1996), *Designing Women: Art Deco, Cinema, and the Female Form* (2003), *American Cinema of the 1920s* (2009), and *Teaching Film* (2011, with Patrice Petro).

JANE M. GAINES is professor of Film at Columbia University. She has published two award-winning books, *Contested Culture: The Image, the Voice, and the Law* (1991) and *Fire and Desire: Mixed Race Movies in the Silent Era* (2001), and is currently completing *Fictioning Histories: Women Film Pioneers.*

CHRISTINE GLEDHILL is visiting professor, Cinema Studies, University of Sunderland. She has written extensively on feminist film criticism, melodrama, and British cinema, including *Reframing British Cinema, 1918–1928: Between Restraint and Passion* (2003). She is currently coordinating an Arts and Humanities Research Council funded Women's Film History Network—UK/Ireland.

DEREK KANE-MEDDOCK is a Ph.D. candidate in Cinema Studies at New York University. His research focuses on the intersections between genre, race, and gender, and he is currently at work on a dissertation about the biracial buddy film.

E. ANN KAPLAN is distinguished professor, English and Comparative Literary and Cultural Studies, Stony Brook University, where she founded and directs The Humanities Institute. She is past president of SCMS. Recent publications include *Feminism and Film* (2000) and *Trauma Culture* (2005). Current projects are *Trauma Future-Tense: Futurist Dystopian Discourse in Media and Literature* and *The Unconscious of Age: Screening Older Women.*

SAMIHA MATIN completed her Ph.D. on the costume film and the aesthetics of femininity in the Steinhardt School of Education, New York University. An earlier version of her essay in this collection was presented at the 2008 SCMS conference. Previously she taught writing, visual communication, and media literacy as Russell Fellow, Writers House, Rutgers University.

KATIE MODEL is a Ph.D. candidate in Cinema Studies at New York University. She is writing her dissertation on "Denial in documentary interview films about the Holocaust, the Palestinian Nakba, and the Iraq War."

E. DEIDRE PRIBRAM is co-editor of *Emotions: A Cultural Studies Reader* (2009) and author of *Cinema and Culture: Independent Film in the United States* (2002). She is an associate professor in the Communications Arts and Sciences Department at Molloy College, Long Island, New York. She has recently published *Emotions, Genre, Justice in Film and Television: Detecting Feeling* (2001).

VICENTE RODRIGUEZ ORTEGA is a postdoctoral fellow, Universidad Carlos III (Madrid). He has essays in *Reverse Shot* and *Senses of Cinema* and contributions in *A Companion to Pedro Almodóvar's Cinema, Cinema, Globalização e Interculturalidade,* and *Companion to Spanish Cinema.* He co-edited *Contemporary Spanish Cinema and Genre* (2009). He recently finished his first feature-length documentary, *Freddy's.*

ADAM SEGAL has taught film and television courses at New York University, City University of New York, College of Staten Island, Fordham University, and Boston University. He is completing his Ph.D. on "Quality TV in a Multi-channel Universe" at New York University.

CHRIS STRAAYER is faculty in the Department of Cinema Studies at New York University and, in addition to numerous articles and chapters, author of *Deviant Eyes, Deviant Bodies: Sexual Re-Orientations in Film and Video* (1996).

YVONNE TASKER is professor of Film and Television Studies at the University of East Anglia. She has written and edited a number of books on gender and popular cinema. Her most recent book is *Soldiers' Stories: Military Women in Cinema and Television since World War II.*

DEBORAH THOMAS is the author of *Beyond Genre: Melodrama, Comedy, and Romance in Hollywood Films* (2000), *Reading Hollywood: Spaces and Meanings in American Film* (2001), a monograph on *Buffy the Vampire Slayer,* and numerous articles. Until her retirement in 2007, she was professor of Film Studies at the University of Sunderland.

XIANGYANG CHEN is completing her Ph.D. in Cinema Studies at New York University. She has published a number of essays on Chinese cinema and taught Film Studies at New York University and Guangdong University of Foreign Studies, Guangzhou, China. Her research interests include film history/historiography, cultural studies, Chinese and East Asian cinemas, and Asian American literature and films.

INDEX

abjection, 75, 114–15, 152

action: and emotion, 7, 42–43, 49–51, 195, 197, 202, 135, 241; and pathos, 8, 9, 10, 11, 191, 192, 194, 198, 200; as redemption, 43, 49–50

action movies, 3, 54–55, 58, 60, 62–63, 65, 66, 241; and adventure, 192; aesthetics of, 192, 197, 198, 202n4; and comedy, 191, 192, 194, 200; and family, 195–97, 199, 200–201; and gender, 3, 39, 46–47, 50–51, 191–92, 194, 195; for global markets, 39, 192, 193, 195, 202; as global transgeneric mode, 8, 9, 192, 202; as male melodrama, 19, 195; and sci-fi, 39, 192; and spectacle, 56, 58, 63, 192, 197, 201; and violence, 49, 58, 192, 195, 197, 198, 200, 201; violent women in, 221; and the western, 192; by women, 39, 54

Adultery, The (1963), 187

aesthetics, 1–2, 97; and affect, 2, 3, 6, 8, 11, 48–49, 63, 65, 99, 100, 105, 108, 136–37, 179, 187–88, 192, 197, 202, 234, 241; as displaced response to *Brokeback Mountain*, 236, 237; and femininity, 39, 97, 103, 104, 105, 107, 109, 110, 110n4; gendered, 2, 3, 6, 8, 9, 11, 187; history aesthetic, 99, 108–10

After Dark, My Sweet (1990), 222

Ahmed, Sara, 48–49, 51

Alien series (1979, 1986, 1992, 1997), 39

Altman, Rick, 3, 5, 20, 28, 71, 72–73, 199

American Pie trilogy (1999, 2001, 2003), 214

Amrohi, Kamal, 169

An, Jinsoo, 193

Andrew, Dudley, 28n1

anti-colonialism. *See* colonialism

Apocalypse Now (1979), 58

art cinema/television, 213; European, 5, 8, 74, 79; and gay subject matter, 236

Arzner, Dorothy, 16, 17; as auteur director, 22

As Tears Go By (1988), 202n4

audience(s), 4, 6, 11, 27, 54, 55, 57, 62–63, 66, 125, 178, 190n3, 207; address, 7, 22, 29–30, 31, 32–40, 73, 74, 79, 98, 125, 134, 153, 178, 189, 199, 227; cross-gender addressed, 35–36, 129; crossover straight, 233, 236; cult, 9, 191, 193, 199, 202n7; fans, 236, 239, 241, 242–43n5; female, 27, 29–30, 40, 40n1, 40n4, 98, 125, 127–28, 129, 131, 132, 233, 236, 237, 241, 242–43n5, 188; gendered, 6, 35, 37, 145, 153–55, 234; and genre, 19, 21, 29–31, 34–39, 43, 53, 55, 57–58, 63, 65, 66, 71, 83n4, 84, 85, 98, 125, 126, 128, 129, 178, 180, 190n3, 193–94, 207, 239–41; global, 39, 179, 192, 193; historiographic approach to, 31, 34–35; Internet and blogging, 236, 237, 241; intersubjective, 6, 8, 11; involvement/response, 7, 38, 136, 137–39, 140–41, 145, 151, 153, 187, 199, 209, 227, 234–35; for John Waters's films, 216; lesbian, 232n22; male, 133, 134; and mashups, 239–41; masquerading, 37–38; memory, 19, 139, 220; (mis)recognition by, 7, 131, 199, 209; neglected by auteurism, 15; queered, 236; sing-along, 178; for slash fiction, 21, 242–43n5; star contact, 7, 30, 40n1, 150–51, 153, 155, 156; Western, 191, 199. *See also* audience demographics; *Brokeback Mountain*; marketing; markets

audience demographics: gay male, 233; Hong Kong youth, 184; of taste, 55

auteur/authorship, 2, 4, 17, 54, 54n1, 57, 64, 67n7, 232n22; and apparatus theory, 21, 26; auteur theory, 15–16, 21–22, 28n1, 57; and authorial self, 5–6, 113, 114, 116; as bricolage/recycling, 6, 112, 114–16, 118, 120, 122, 207; female/feminist, 2, 3, 5–6, 17, 22–23, 25–26, 39, 113; genius of, questioned, 16, 17, 26; and genre, 16–18, 19–23, 26, 34–35, 56–58; and the individual, 17, 26, 64; John Waters as genrified auteur, 10, 205, 216, 217; John Woo as mass-market auteur, 193, 202n5; as marketing instrument, 4, 57, 67n7; and psychoanalysis, 21, 26; versus collaborative film industry, 17, 54–55, 64. *See also* Waters, John; Woo, John

avant-garde cinema, 111, 207

Index

265

femme, 10, 224, 231n16; as feminization, 6, 144; historical, 99, 100; iconography of, 99, 103; as identity style, 97, 101; in Indian culture, 164–65, 170; parodied, 210; passive/subservient, 151, 152; and power, 102–3; and privacy/interiority, 5, 96–97, 98, 99, 100, 103, 105, 110; and publicness, 97, 98, 99, 101–3, 104–5; and time, 74–75, 76, 77, 82, 97, 100, 101, 106–8, 114

feminism/feminist, 4, 5–6, 38, 86, 88, 100, 107, 127; American domestic feminism, 22; appropriated, 37; discourse, 7, 126, 130, 134, 229; imaginary, 6, 79, 187; impact on representation, 36, 37, 39, 90, 98, 127; lesbian feminism, 227, 230n1; politics, 22, 37, 54, 98, 99; second-wave, 5, 6, 18, 74, 103, 113, 220; and sexual violence, 36, 39

feminist film history/historiography, 17, 23, 28n4, 39, 40, 40n4; and women's contribution to silent cinema, 23

feminist film theory/criticism, 2–3, 5, 6, 9, 11, 17, 22–25, 28, 29–30, 57, 71, 72, 75, 92, 154; and auteur theory, 16; on feminist cinema, 4, 75, 76, 77, 79, 82, 84, 93, 113, 119; and film noir, 16; as a genre, 27–28; inventing the woman's film, 5, 28, 72–73, 75, 77, 80, 82, 83n4; and male directors, 22; and melodrama, 2, 3, 16, 17–19, 21–22, 24–28, 29, 34–35, 42–43, 53, 72–73, 126–27; and men in movies, 6, 34, 38; and recuperation, 24; and resistance, 22, 23, 33, 73, 77; and spectorship, 21, 26, 29, 32–34; and subversion, 22–25; and *Women in Film Noir* (1978), 17, 221. *See also* psychoanalytic film theory; spectatorship/spectator

Fiedler, Leslie, 240

Fields, Sarah K., 85, 90

Fight Club (1999), 58

Filmmakers, The (company), 36

film noir/neo-noir, 5, 73, 74, 79, 80, 81, 82, 129, 214, 219; black widow, 221–22, 225, 230n2, 230n5, 231n15; black widower, 231n15; and class, 221, 222–23; classic conventions of, 220–25; *différance* in, 219, 220, 223, 228; difference-based coupling in, 223–24; family in, 222, 228, 232n20; in feminist film theory, 17, 221; femme in, 221, 225, 226, 229; *femme fatale*, 220–24, 225, 227, 229, 230nn5–6, 230n9, 231n12, 231n19; femme fatale in neo-noir, 221–22, 223, 225–27, 229–30, 231–32n19; female sexuality acknowledged in, 221; female sexuality as danger in, 220–21, 230n7; female violence in, 221, 231n13; as filmnoirness, 220; flashbacks in,

219, 220, 228; gender binaries undermined by, 223–24; gender/genre turbulence in, 220; as genre, 220; good girl in, 222, 224, 231n19; heterosexuality deconstructed by, 223; implied author of, 222, 223; male impotence in, 222–23; male protagonist in, 221, 222–23, 224, 226; neo-noir conventions, 10, 19, 220–25, 230n3; parody and pastiche in neo-noir, 220, 226, 228; phallic woman, 223, 224, 225, 229; play with sexual/gender sameness and difference, 10, 223, 224, 225–26, 227–28, 230–31n10, 231n15; realignment of heterosexual and hetero-gender systems, 223–26; romantic coupling destroyed in, 222, 224, 231n11; sexuality and violence in, 223; spider woman, 230n4; voice-over in, 219, 222, 228; women in, 17, 220–22, 230n7. *See also Bound*

film studies/film theory, 1, 8, 31, 43, 75; changes in, 34; comparative, 8; emotion in, 43; historiographic, 31, 34–35, 40; on melodrama theory for Indian cinema, 161–69; on vernacular modernism in Chinese cinema, 179

Final Analysis (1992), 230n9

Finding Christa (1991), 113

Fischer, Lucy, 5, 111–22

Fiske, John, 127, 129

flashbacks, 136, 139, 142, 219, 220, 228

Flitterman-Lewis, Sandy, 17, 111

Focus Films (company), 233, 235, 236

Ford, John, 31

Fox, Michael J., 136

Franke, Lizzie, 40n4

Frenzy (1972), 36

Freud, Sigmund, 147, 148–49; and "The Uncanny," 147, 148–49, 152

Frow, John, 20, 28n6

Gaines, Jane, 2–3, 4, 15–28

Garber, Marjorie, 103

Gardens of Stone (1987), 135, 139–40

Gas, Food, Lodging (1992), 84

gender/gendered, 6, 11, 101, 146; address, 22, 31, 73–74, 76, 77, 79, 80, 98, 125, 126, 127, 162, 194; aesthetics, 2, 3, 6, 8, 9, 11, 187; ambiguity/fluidity/slippage, 40, 87, 146, 210; androgyny, 55, 62, 189; binaries, 153, 209, 223–26, 229, 230n7; as constructed roles, 72, 76, 104, 172, 205–6, 207, 208; conventions/norms, 2, 7, 24, 25, 28n6, 48, 58, 73, 75, 76, 78, 91, 92, 150, 156, 206, 208, 209, 211, 212, 213, 215; and critical value, 54, 56; and cross-dressing, 189, 206, 207, 210–11;

The University of Illinois Press
is a founding member of the
Association of American University Presses.

———————————————————————

Designed by Matthew Smith
Composed in 10.5/13 Adobe Minion Pro
with Vectora display
by Jim Proefrock
at the University of Illinois Press
Manufactured by Thomson-Shore, Inc.

University of Illinois Press
1325 South Oak Street
Champaign, IL 61820-6903
www.press.uillinois.edu